D0446548

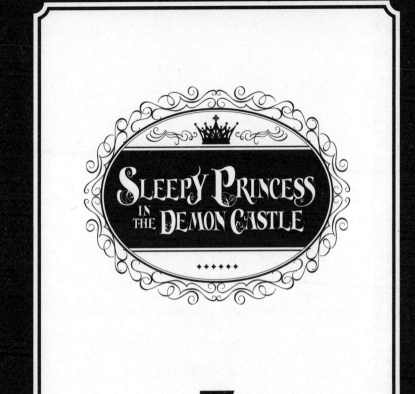

SLEEPY PRINCESS IN THE DEMON CASTLE

5

STORY & ART BY
KAGIJI KUMANOMATA

NIGHTS

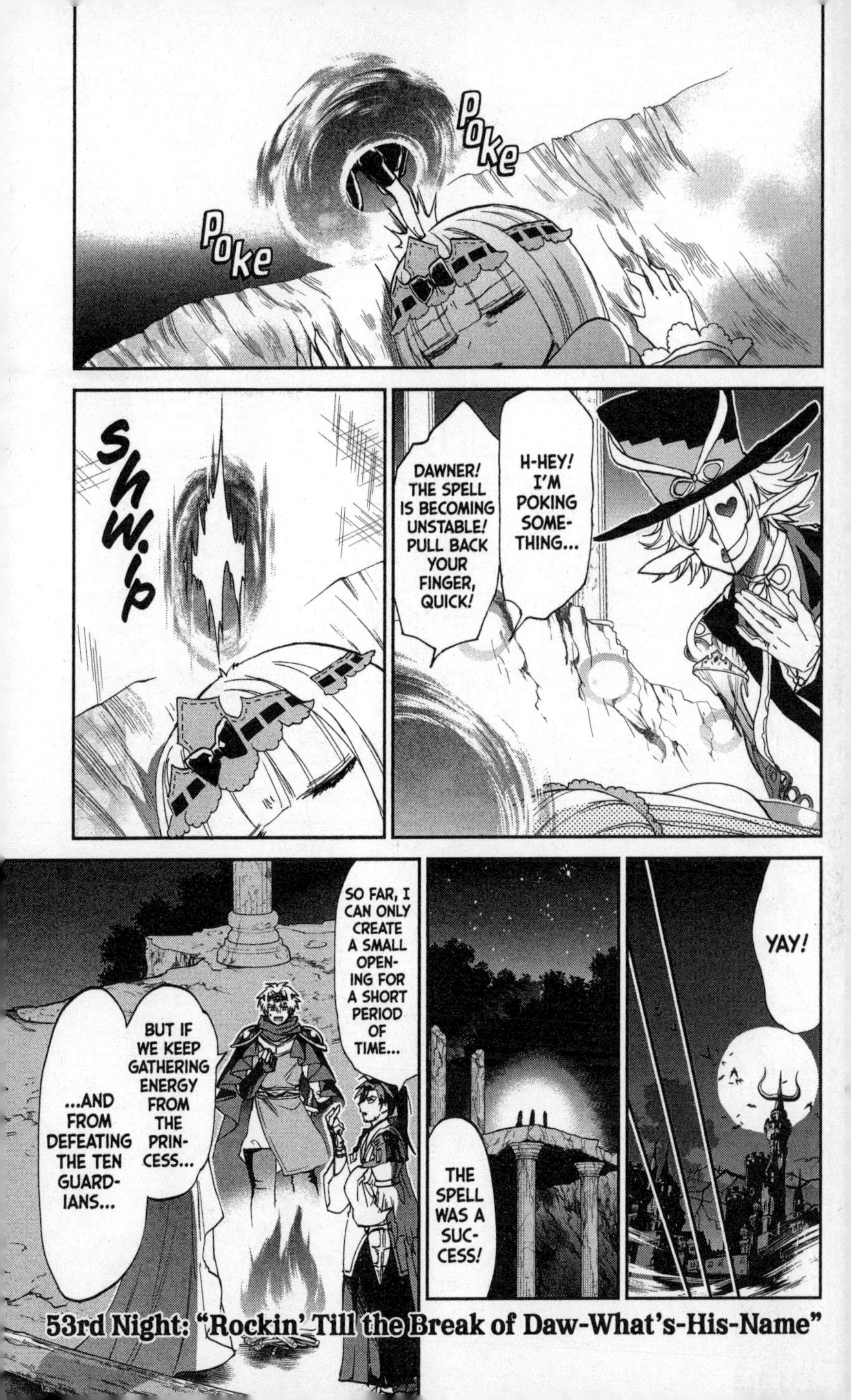
Poke
Poke
H-HEY! I'M POKING SOME-THING...
DAWNER! THE SPELL IS BECOMING UNSTABLE! PULL BACK YOUR FINGER, QUICK!
SHWIP
YAY!
THE SPELL WAS A SUC-CESS!
SO FAR, I CAN ONLY CREATE A SMALL OPEN-ING FOR A SHORT PERIOD OF TIME...
BUT IF WE KEEP GATHERING ENERGY FROM THE PRIN-CESS...
...AND FROM DEFEATING THE TEN GUARD-IANS...

53rd Night: "Rockin' Till the Break of Daw-What's-His-Name"

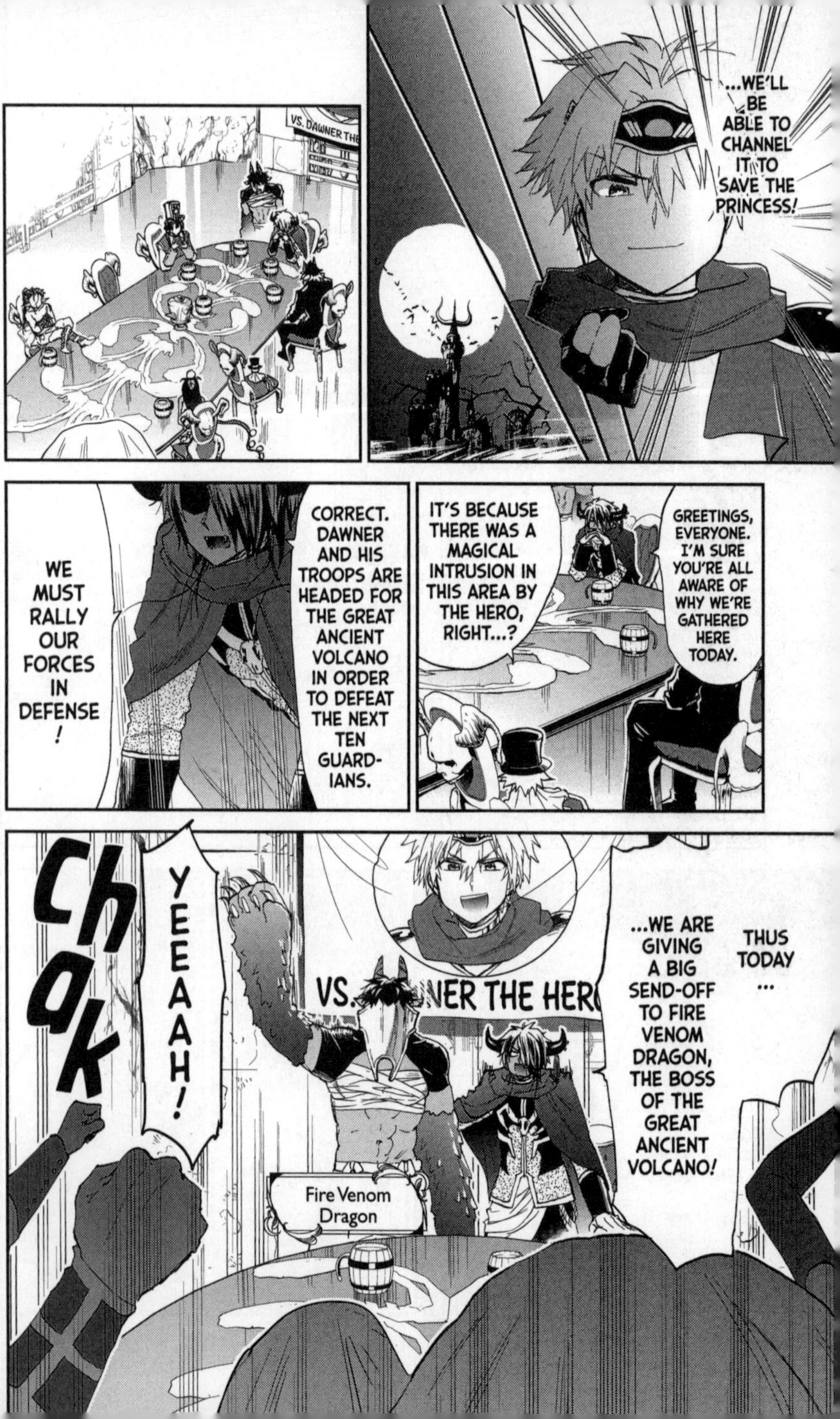
...WE'LL BE ABLE TO CHANNEL IT TO SAVE THE PRINCESS!
VS. DAWNER THE
GREETINGS, EVERYONE. I'M SURE YOU'RE ALL AWARE OF WHY WE'RE GATHERED HERE TODAY.
IT'S BECAUSE THERE WAS A MAGICAL INTRUSION IN THIS AREA BY THE HERO, RIGHT...?
CORRECT. DAWNER AND HIS TROOPS ARE HEADED FOR THE GREAT ANCIENT VOLCANO IN ORDER TO DEFEAT THE NEXT TEN GUARDIANS.
WE MUST RALLY OUR FORCES IN DEFENSE!
THUS TODAY...
...WE ARE GIVING A BIG SEND-OFF TO FIRE VENOM DRAGON, THE BOSS OF THE GREAT ANCIENT VOLCANO!
VS. NER THE HER
YEEAAH!
Chok
Fire Venom Dragon

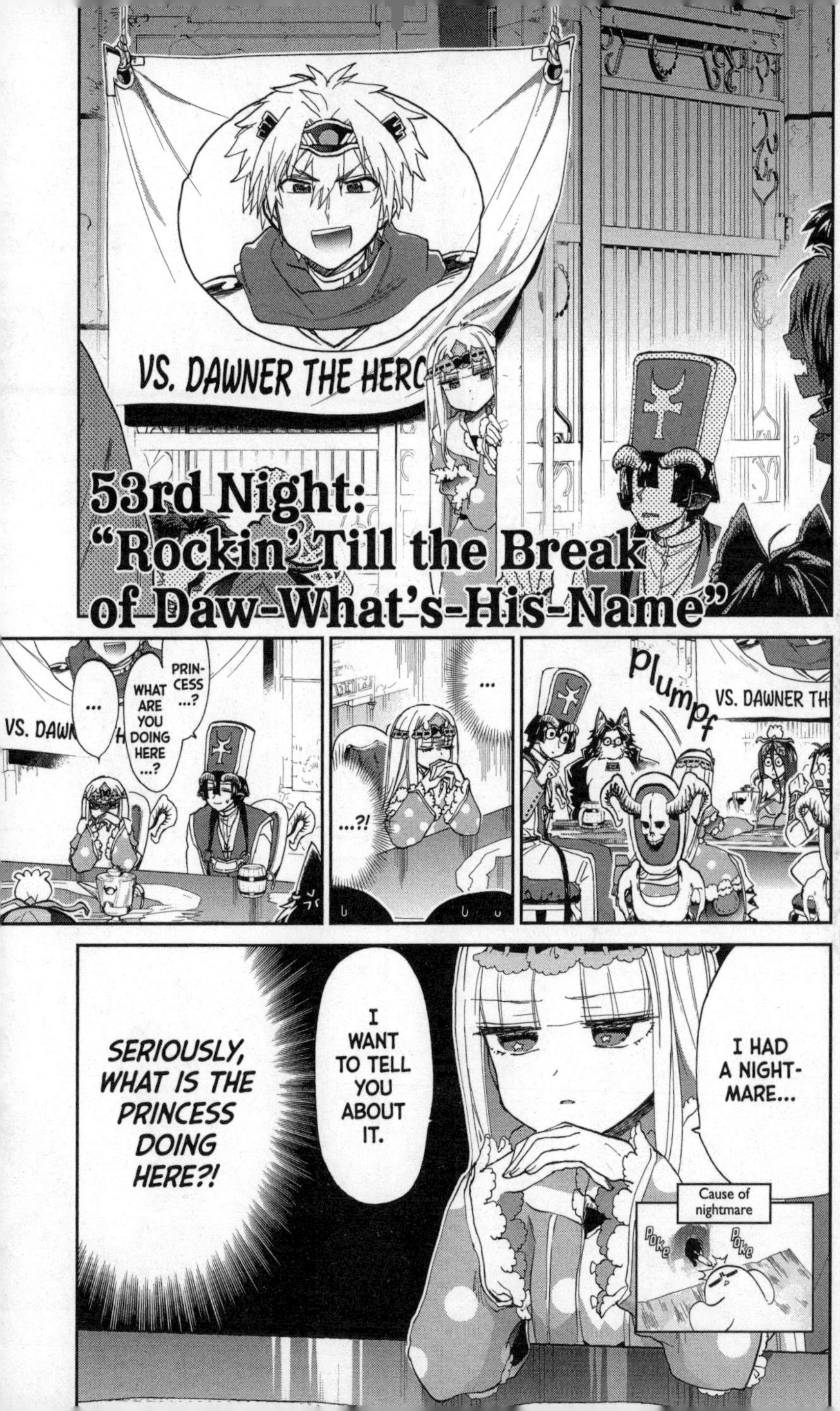
VS. DAWNER THE HERO
53rd Night: "Rockin' Till the Break of Daw-What's-His-Name"
Plumpf
VS. DAWNER TH
...
...?!
PRIN-CESS ...?
...
WHAT ARE YOU DOING HERE ...?
VS. DAWN
I HAD A NIGHT-MARE...
I WANT TO TELL YOU ABOUT IT.
SERIOUSLY, WHAT IS THE PRINCESS DOING HERE?!
Cause of nightmare
Poke
Poke

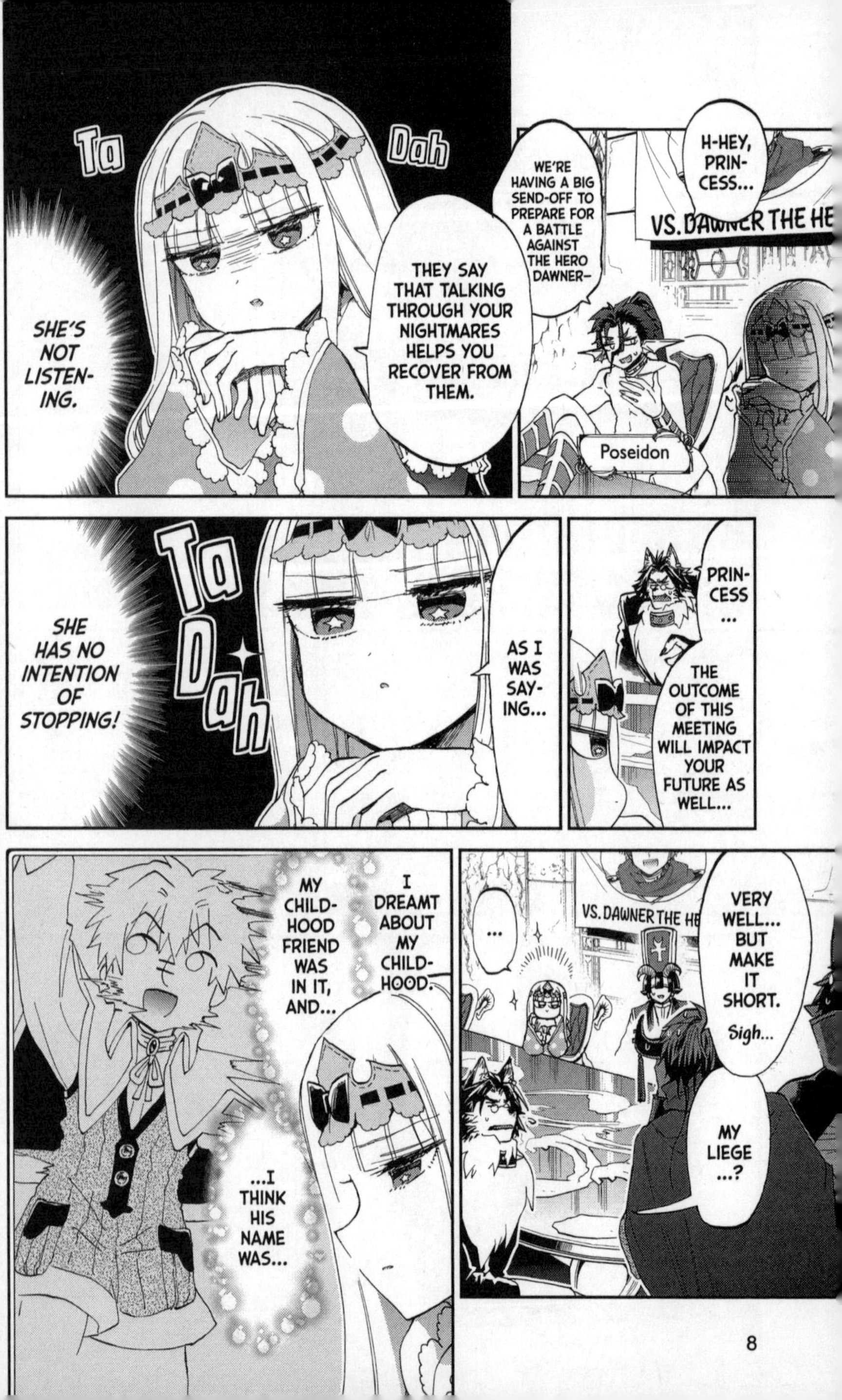
H-HEY, PRINCESS...
VS. DAWNER THE HE
WE'RE HAVING A BIG SEND-OFF TO PREPARE FOR A BATTLE AGAINST THE HERO DAWNER–
Poseidon
Ta Dah
THEY SAY THAT TALKING THROUGH YOUR NIGHTMARES HELPS YOU RECOVER FROM THEM.
SHE'S NOT LISTENING.
PRINCESS...
THE OUTCOME OF THIS MEETING WILL IMPACT YOUR FUTURE AS WELL...
AS I WAS SAYING...
Ta Dah
SHE HAS NO INTENTION OF STOPPING!
VERY WELL... BUT MAKE IT SHORT.
Sigh...
MY LIEGE...?
VS. DAWNER THE HE
...
I DREAMT ABOUT MY CHILDHOOD.
MY CHILDHOOD FRIEND WAS IN IT, AND...
...I THINK HIS NAME WAS...

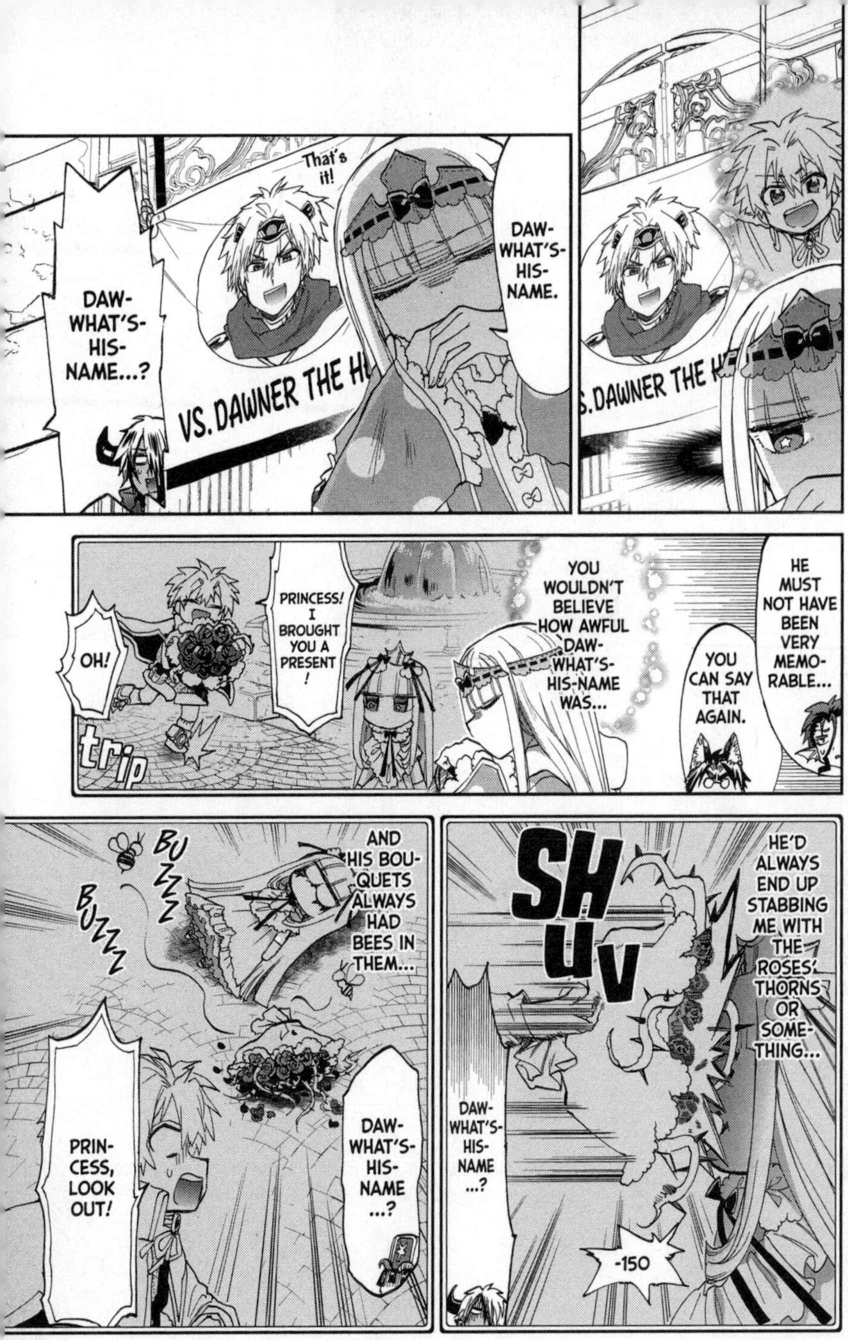
S.DAWNER THE H
DAW-WHAT'S-HIS-NAME.
That's it!
DAW-WHAT'S-HIS-NAME...?
VS.DAWNER THE H
HE MUST NOT HAVE BEEN VERY MEMORABLE...
YOU CAN SAY THAT AGAIN.
YOU WOULDN'T BELIEVE HOW AWFUL DAW-WHAT'S-HIS-NAME WAS...
PRINCESS! I BROUGHT YOU A PRESENT!
OH!
trip
HE'D ALWAYS END UP STABBING ME WITH THE ROSES' THORNS OR SOMETHING...
SHUV
DAW-WHAT'S-HIS-NAME...?
-150
AND HIS BOUQUETS ALWAYS HAD BEES IN THEM...
BUZZZ
BUZZZ
DAW-WHAT'S-HIS-NAME...?
PRINCESS, LOOK OUT!

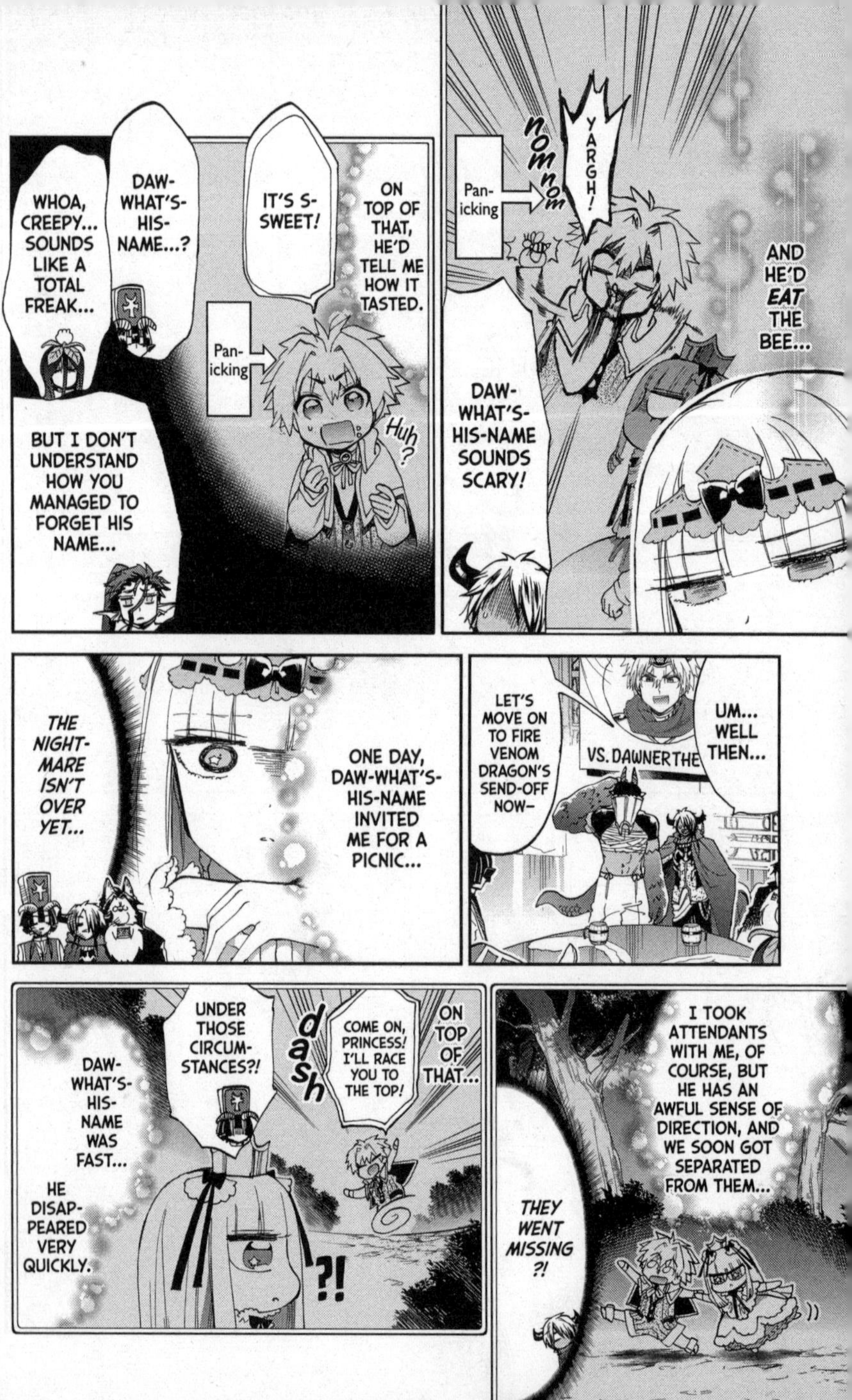
AND HE'D EAT THE BEE...
YARGH!
nom nom
Pan-icking
DAW-WHAT'S-HIS-NAME SOUNDS SCARY!
ON TOP OF THAT, HE'D TELL ME HOW IT TASTED.
IT'S S-SWEET!
Pan-icking
Huh?
DAW-WHAT'S-HIS-NAME...?
WHOA, CREEPY... SOUNDS LIKE A TOTAL FREAK...
BUT I DON'T UNDERSTAND HOW YOU MANAGED TO FORGET HIS NAME...
UM... WELL THEN...
LET'S MOVE ON TO FIRE VENOM DRAGON'S SEND-OFF NOW—
VS. DAWNER THE
ONE DAY, DAW-WHAT'S-HIS-NAME INVITED ME FOR A PICNIC...
THE NIGHTMARE ISN'T OVER YET...
I TOOK ATTENDANTS WITH ME, OF COURSE, BUT HE HAS AN AWFUL SENSE OF DIRECTION, AND WE SOON GOT SEPARATED FROM THEM...
THEY WENT MISSING?!
ON TOP OF THAT...
COME ON, PRINCESS! I'LL RACE YOU TO THE TOP!
dash
UNDER THOSE CIRCUMSTANCES?!
DAW-WHAT'S-HIS-NAME WAS FAST...
HE DISAPPEARED VERY QUICKLY.
?!

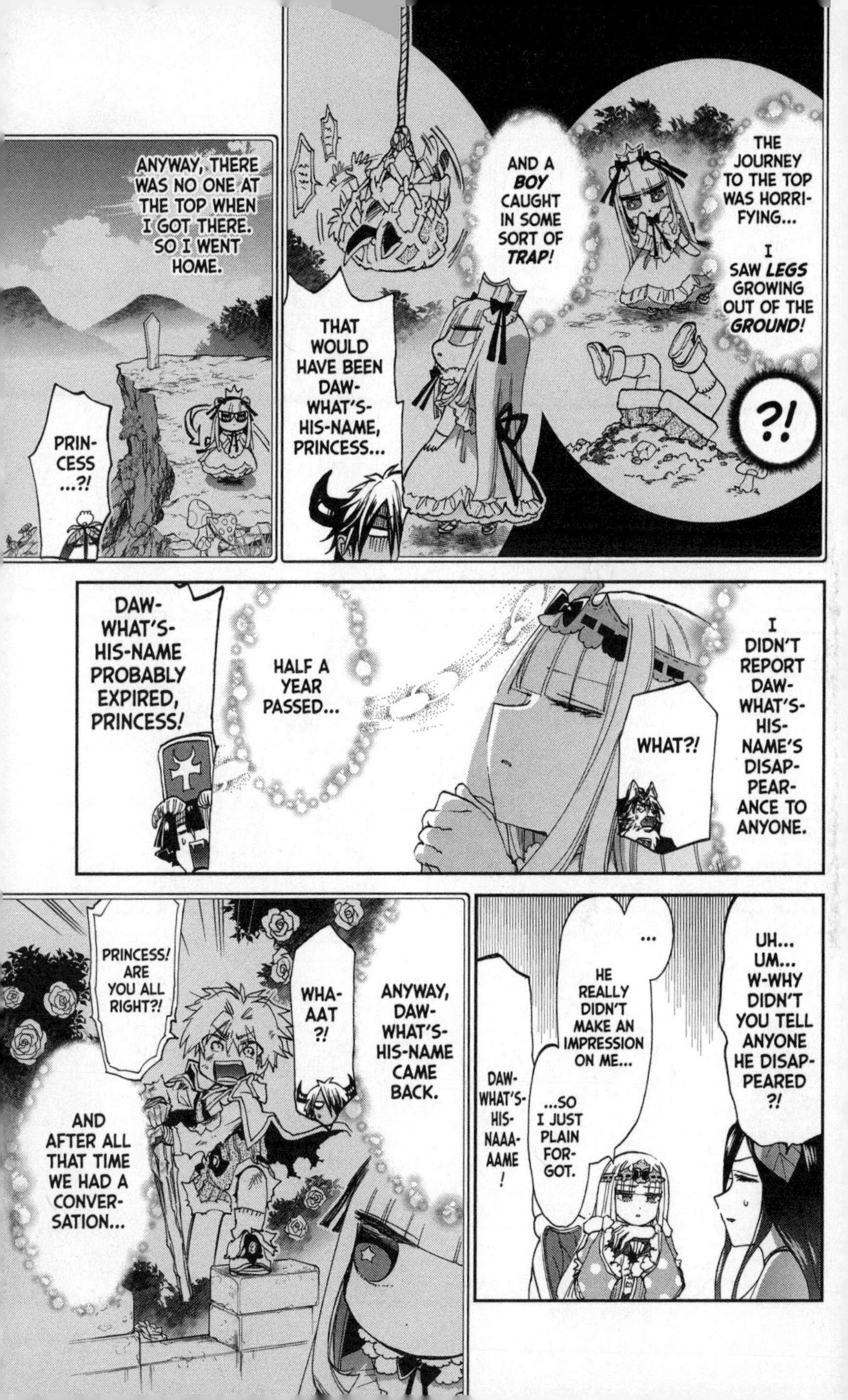
THE JOURNEY TO THE TOP WAS HORRIFYING...
I SAW *LEGS* GROWING OUT OF THE *GROUND!*
?!
AND A *BOY* CAUGHT IN SOME SORT OF *TRAP!*
THAT WOULD HAVE BEEN DAW-WHAT'S-HIS-NAME, PRINCESS...
ANYWAY, THERE WAS NO ONE AT THE TOP WHEN I GOT THERE. SO I WENT HOME.
PRINCESS...?!
I DIDN'T REPORT DAW-WHAT'S-HIS-NAME'S DISAPPEARANCE TO ANYONE.
WHAT?!
HALF A YEAR PASSED...
DAW-WHAT'S-HIS-NAME PROBABLY EXPIRED, PRINCESS!
UH... UM... W-WHY DIDN'T YOU TELL ANYONE HE DISAPPEARED?!
...
HE REALLY DIDN'T MAKE AN IMPRESSION ON ME...
...SO I JUST PLAIN FORGOT.
DAW-WHAT'S-HIS-NAAAAAME!
ANYWAY, DAW-WHAT'S-HIS-NAME CAME BACK.
WHAAAT?!
PRINCESS! ARE YOU ALL RIGHT?!
AND AFTER ALL THAT TIME WE HAD A CONVERSATION...

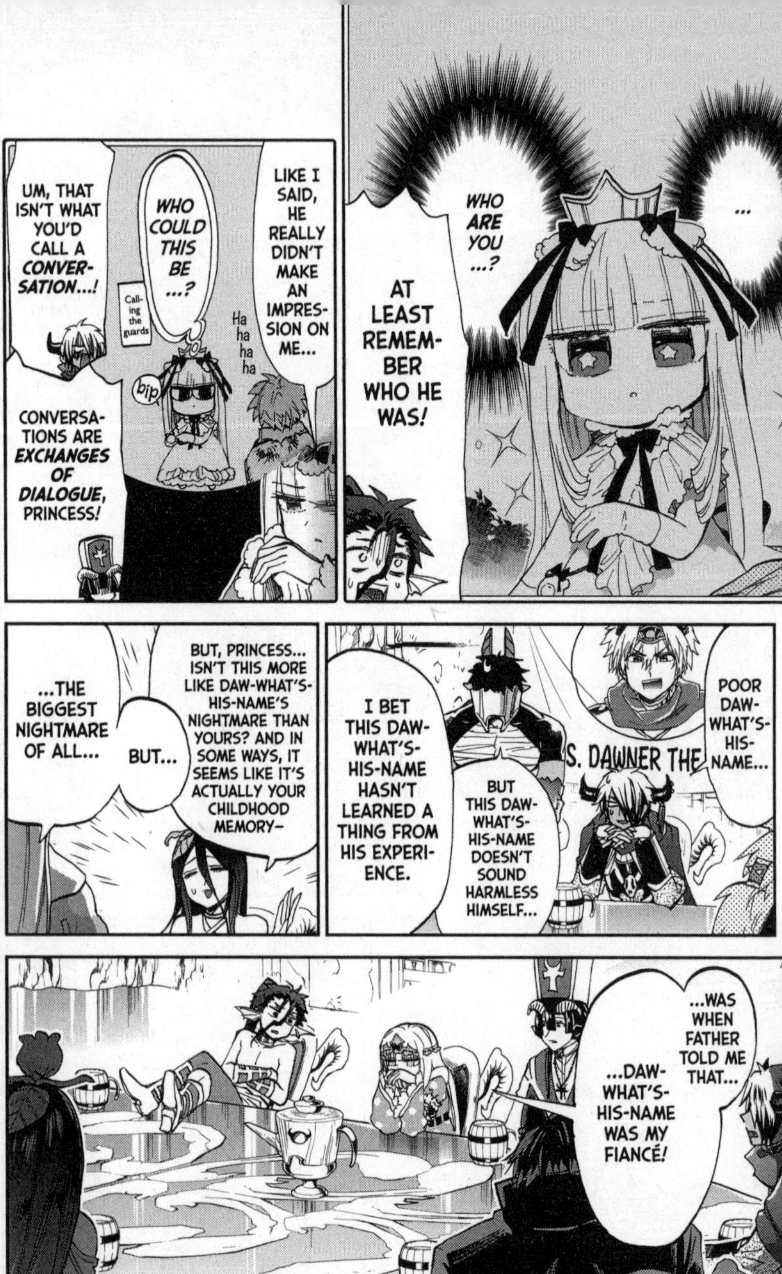
...
WHO ARE YOU ...?
AT LEAST REMEMBER WHO HE WAS!
LIKE I SAID, HE REALLY DIDN'T MAKE AN IMPRESSION ON ME...
Ha ha ha ha
WHO COULD THIS BE ...?
Calling the guards
bip
UM, THAT ISN'T WHAT YOU'D CALL A CONVERSATION...!
CONVERSATIONS ARE EXCHANGES OF DIALOGUE, PRINCESS!
POOR DAW-WHAT'S-HIS-NAME...
S. DAWNER THE
I BET THIS DAW-WHAT'S-HIS-NAME HASN'T LEARNED A THING FROM HIS EXPERIENCE.
BUT THIS DAW-WHAT'S-HIS-NAME DOESN'T SOUND HARMLESS HIMSELF...
BUT, PRINCESS... ISN'T THIS MORE LIKE DAW-WHAT'S-HIS-NAME'S NIGHTMARE THAN YOURS? AND IN SOME WAYS, IT SEEMS LIKE IT'S ACTUALLY YOUR CHILDHOOD MEMORY–
BUT...
...THE BIGGEST NIGHTMARE OF ALL...
...WAS WHEN FATHER TOLD ME THAT...
...DAW-WHAT'S-HIS-NAME WAS MY FIANCÉ!

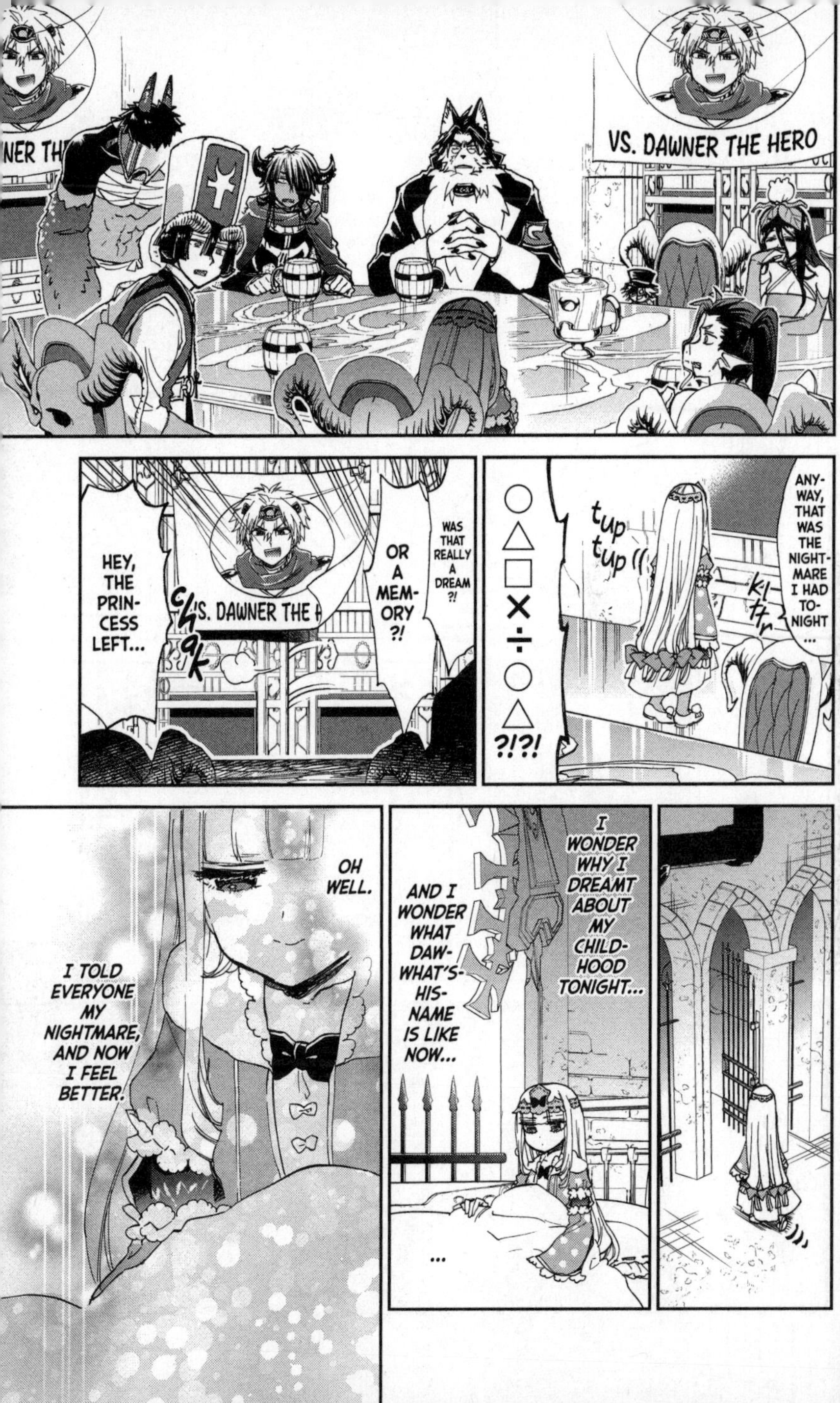
VS. DAWNER THE HERO
NER TH
ANYWAY, THAT WAS THE NIGHTMARE I HAD TONIGHT...
tup tup
kl ttr
○△□×÷○△ ?!?!
WAS THAT REALLY A DREAM ?!
OR A MEMORY ?!
HEY, THE PRINCESS LEFT...
VS. DAWNER THE H
chak
I WONDER WHY I DREAMT ABOUT MY CHILDHOOD TONIGHT...
AND I WONDER WHAT DAW-WHAT'S-HIS-NAME IS LIKE NOW...
...
OH WELL.
I TOLD EVERYONE MY NIGHTMARE, AND NOW I FEEL BETTER.

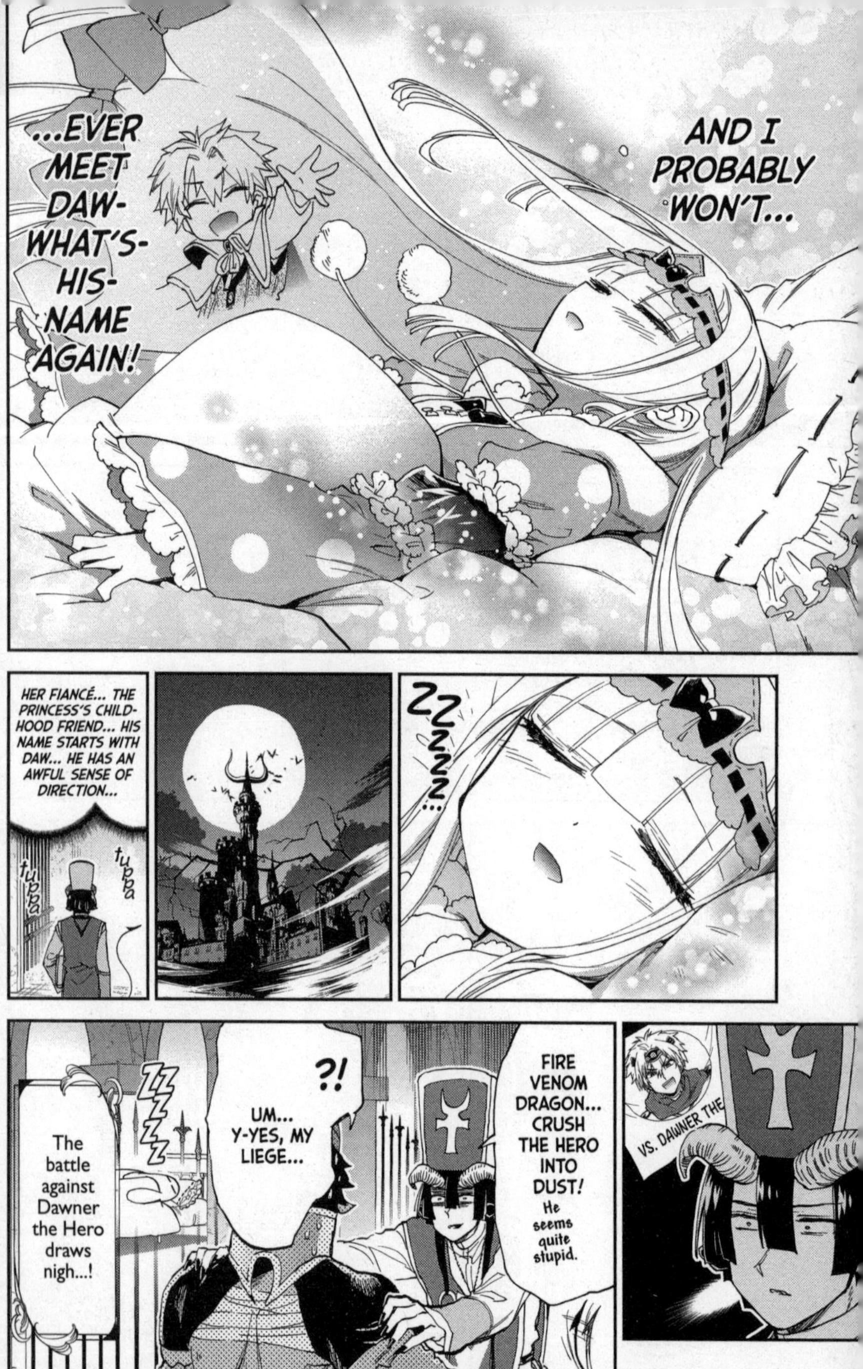
AND I PROBABLY WON'T...
...EVER MEET DAW-WHAT'S-HIS-NAME AGAIN!
ZZZZZ...
HER FIANCÉ... THE PRINCESS'S CHILDHOOD FRIEND... HIS NAME STARTS WITH DAW... HE HAS AN AWFUL SENSE OF DIRECTION...
tuppa
tuppa
VS. DAWNER THE
FIRE VENOM DRAGON... CRUSH THE HERO INTO DUST!
He seems quite stupid.
?!
UM... Y-YES, MY LIEGE...
ZZZZZ
The battle against Dawner the Hero draws nigh...!

Daw-what's-his-name

Brightness: ☆☆☆☆☆☆☆☆☆☆
Toughness: ☆☆☆☆☆☆☆☆☆☆

He has a promising future ahead of him.

▼

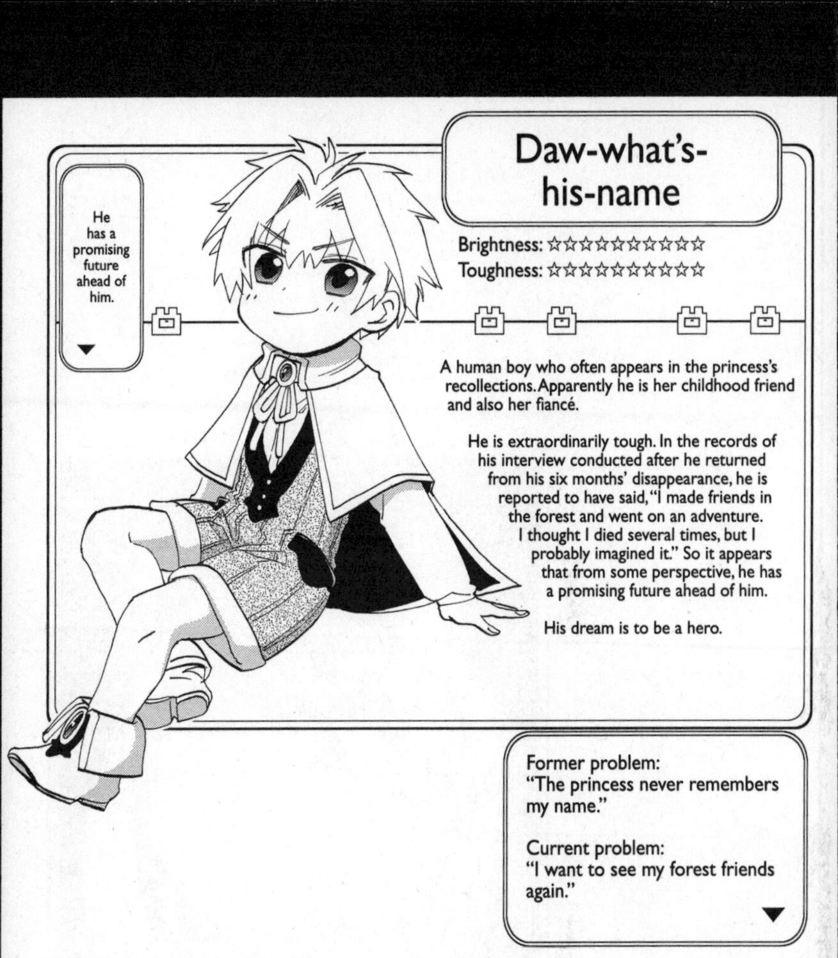

A human boy who often appears in the princess's recollections. Apparently he is her childhood friend and also her fiancé.

He is extraordinarily tough. In the records of his interview conducted after he returned from his six months' disappearance, he is reported to have said, "I made friends in the forest and went on an adventure. I thought I died several times, but I probably imagined it." So it appears that from some perspective, he has a promising future ahead of him.

His dream is to be a hero.

Former problem:
"The princess never remembers my name."

Current problem:
"I want to see my forest friends again."

▼

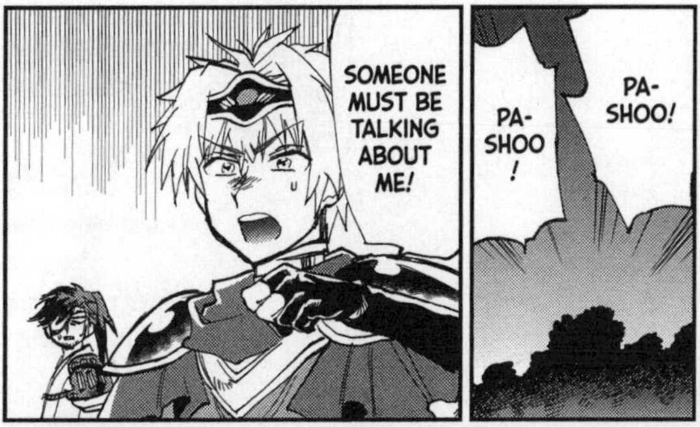
PA-SHOO!
PA-SHOO!
SOMEONE MUST BE TALKING ABOUT ME!

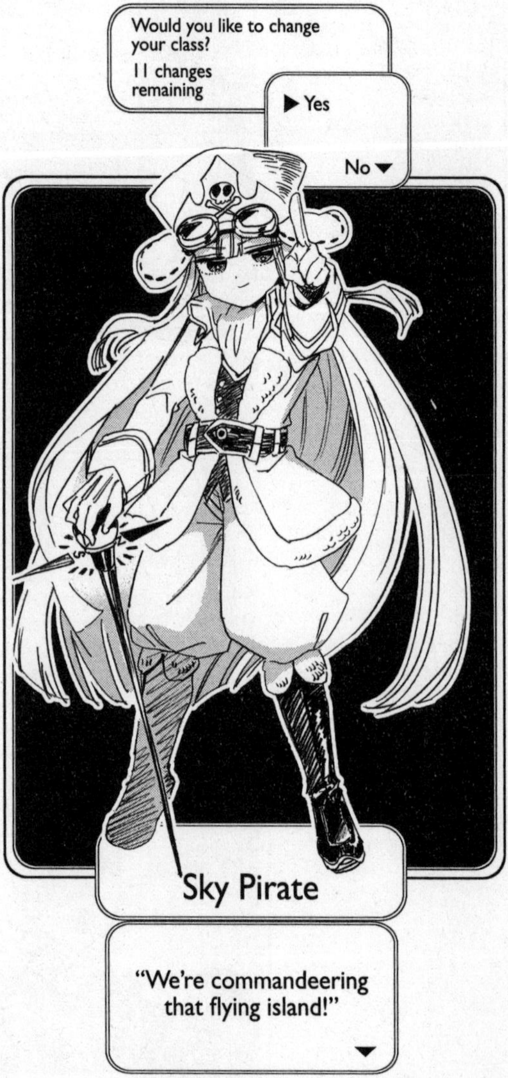
Would you like to change your class?
11 changes remaining
▶ Yes
No ▼
Sky Pirate
"We're commandeering that flying island!"

54th Night: It's Like Female Bonding

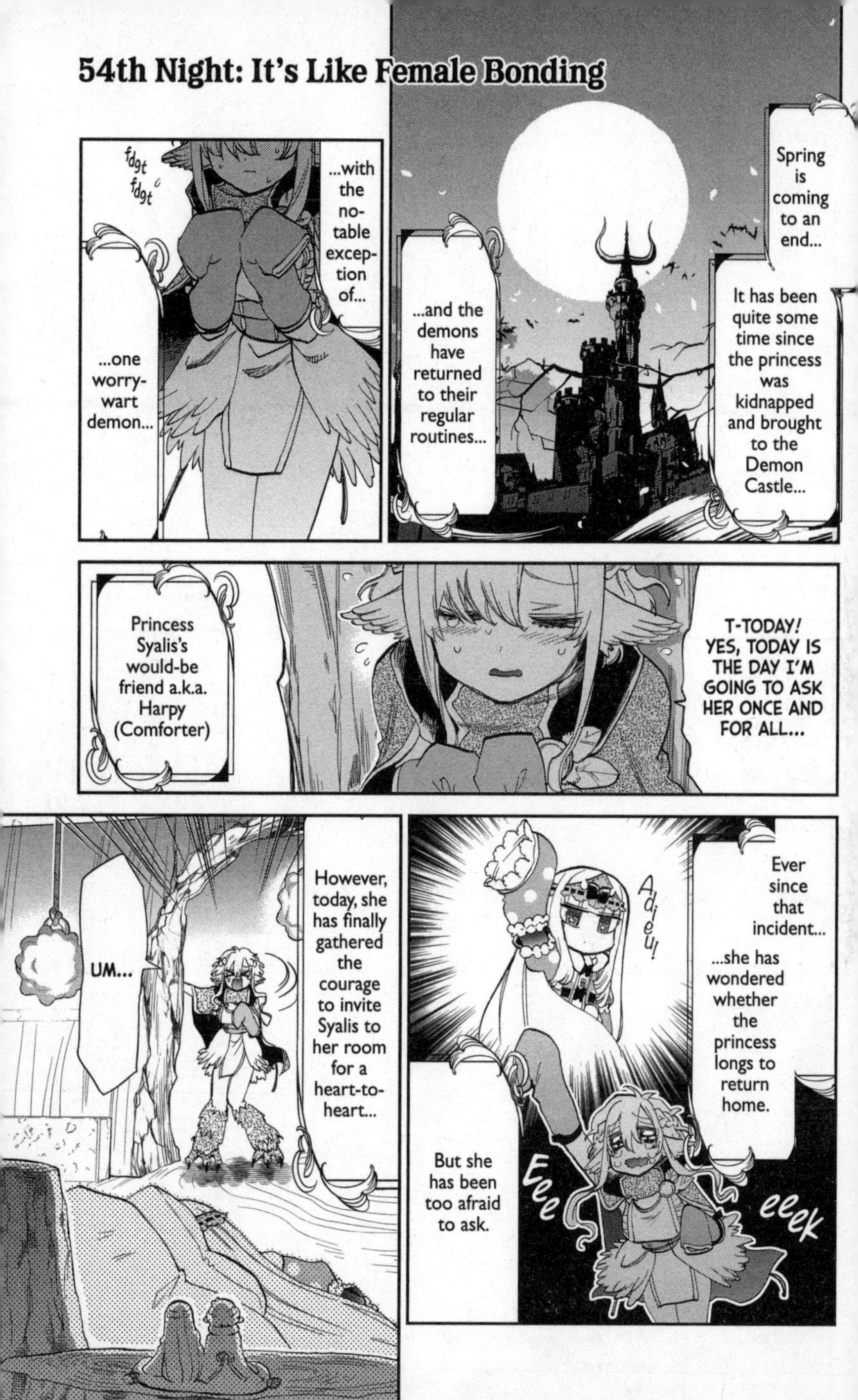
Spring is coming to an end...
It has been quite some time since the princess was kidnapped and brought to the Demon Castle...
...and the demons have returned to their regular routines...
...with the notable exception of...
fdgt fdgt
...one worry-wart demon...
T-TODAY! YES, TODAY IS THE DAY I'M GOING TO ASK HER ONCE AND FOR ALL...
Princess Syalis's would-be friend a.k.a. Harpy (Comforter)
Ever since that incident...
...she has wondered whether the princess longs to return home.
Adieu!
Eeeeeek
But she has been too afraid to ask.
However, today, she has finally gathered the courage to invite Syalis to her room for a heart-to-heart...
UM...

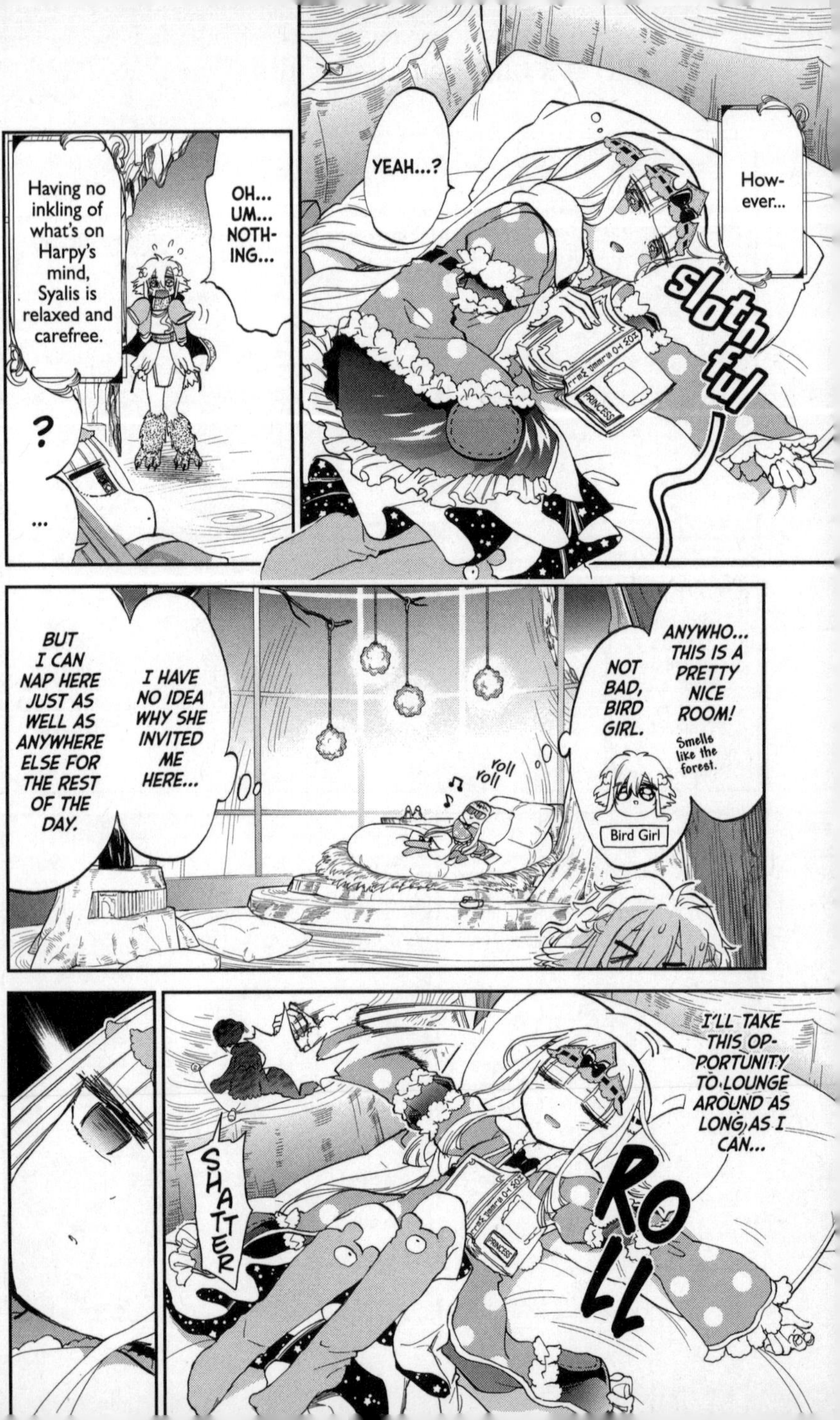
How-ever...
YEAH...?
slothful
Having no inkling of what's on Harpy's mind, Syalis is relaxed and carefree.
OH... UM... NOTH-ING...
?
...
ANYWHO... THIS IS A PRETTY NICE ROOM!
Smells like the forest.
NOT BAD, BIRD GIRL.
Bird Girl
roll roll
I HAVE NO IDEA WHY SHE INVITED ME HERE...
BUT I CAN NAP HERE JUST AS WELL AS ANYWHERE ELSE FOR THE REST OF THE DAY.
I'LL TAKE THIS OP-PORTUNITY TO LOUNGE AROUND AS LONG AS I CAN...
ROLL
SHATTER
PRINCESS

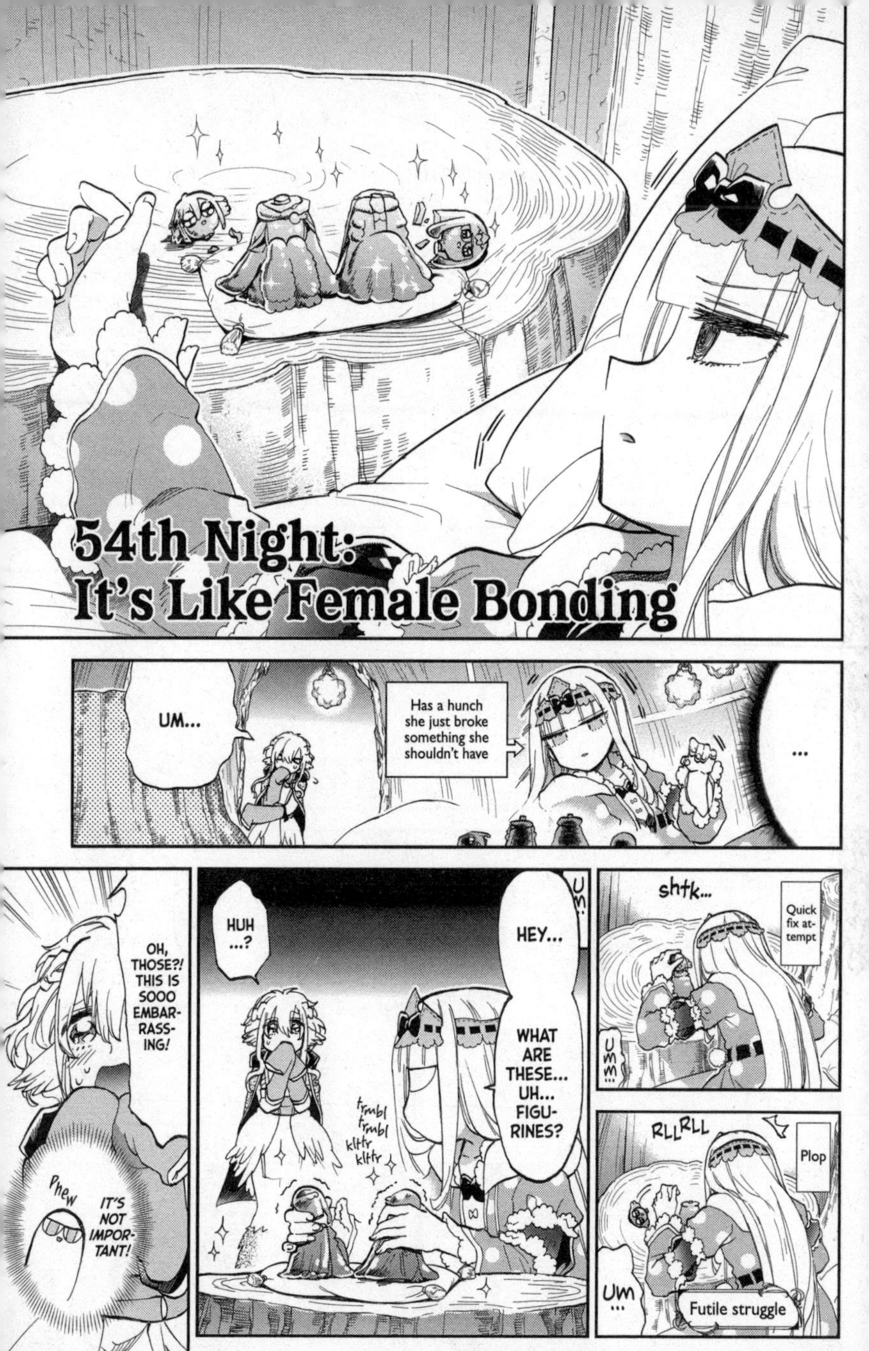
54th Night:
It's Like Female Bonding
...
Has a hunch she just broke something she shouldn't have
UM...
Quick fix attempt
shtk...
UMM...
Plop
RLLRLL
UM...
Futile struggle
UM...
HEY... WHAT ARE THESE... UH... FIGURINES?
HUH ...?
trmbl trmbl klttr klttr
OH, THOSE?! THIS IS SOOO EMBARRASSING!
Phew
IT'S NOT IMPORTANT!

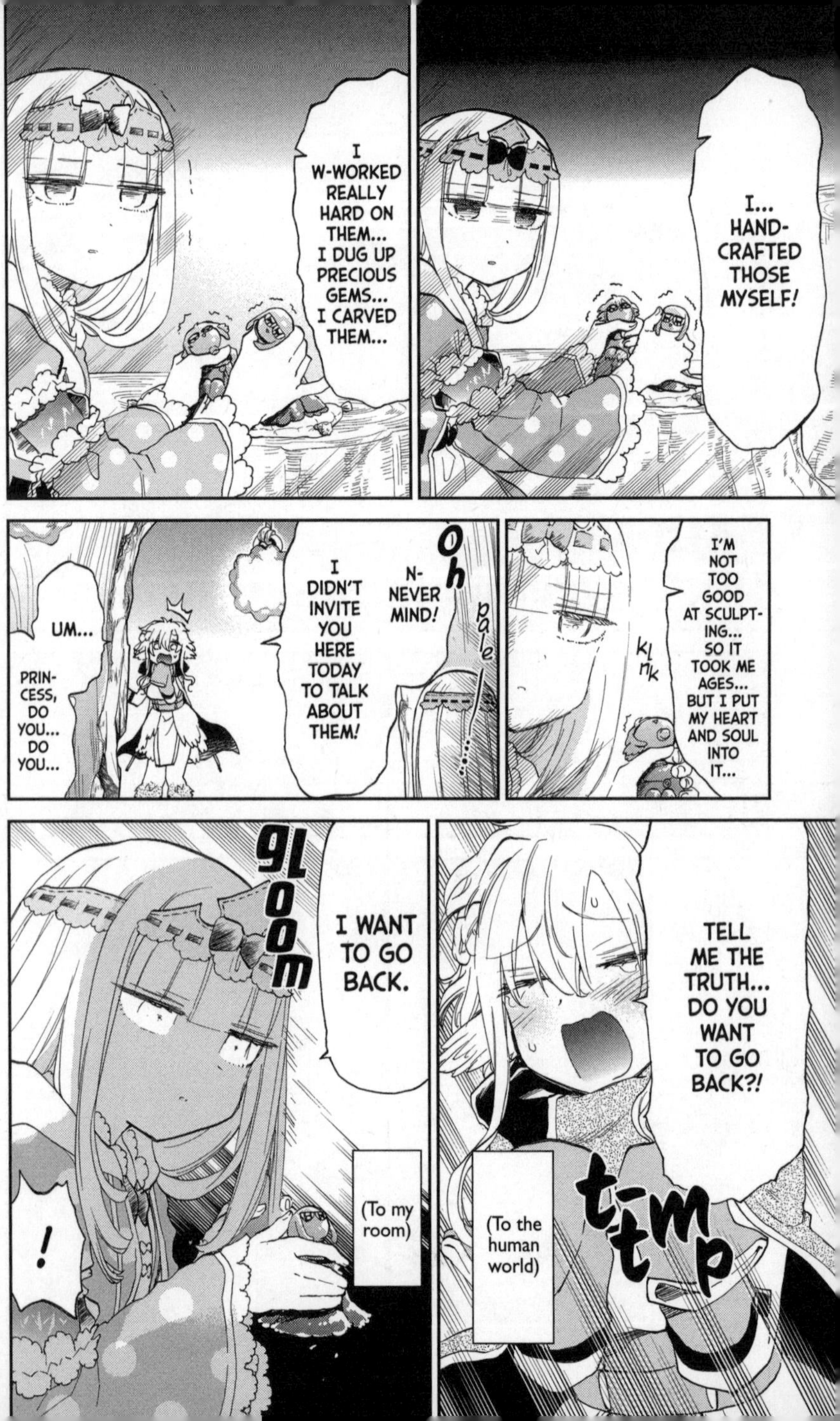
I... HAND-CRAFTED THOSE MYSELF!
I W-WORKED REALLY HARD ON THEM... I DUG UP PRECIOUS GEMS... I CARVED THEM...
I'M NOT TOO GOOD AT SCULPTING... SO IT TOOK ME AGES... BUT I PUT MY HEART AND SOUL INTO IT...
oh
pale
N-NEVER MIND!
I DIDN'T INVITE YOU HERE TODAY TO TALK ABOUT THEM!
UM...
PRINCESS, DO YOU... DO YOU...
TELL ME THE TRUTH... DO YOU WANT TO GO BACK?!
(To the human world)
t-tmp
gloom
I WANT TO GO BACK.
(To my room)
!

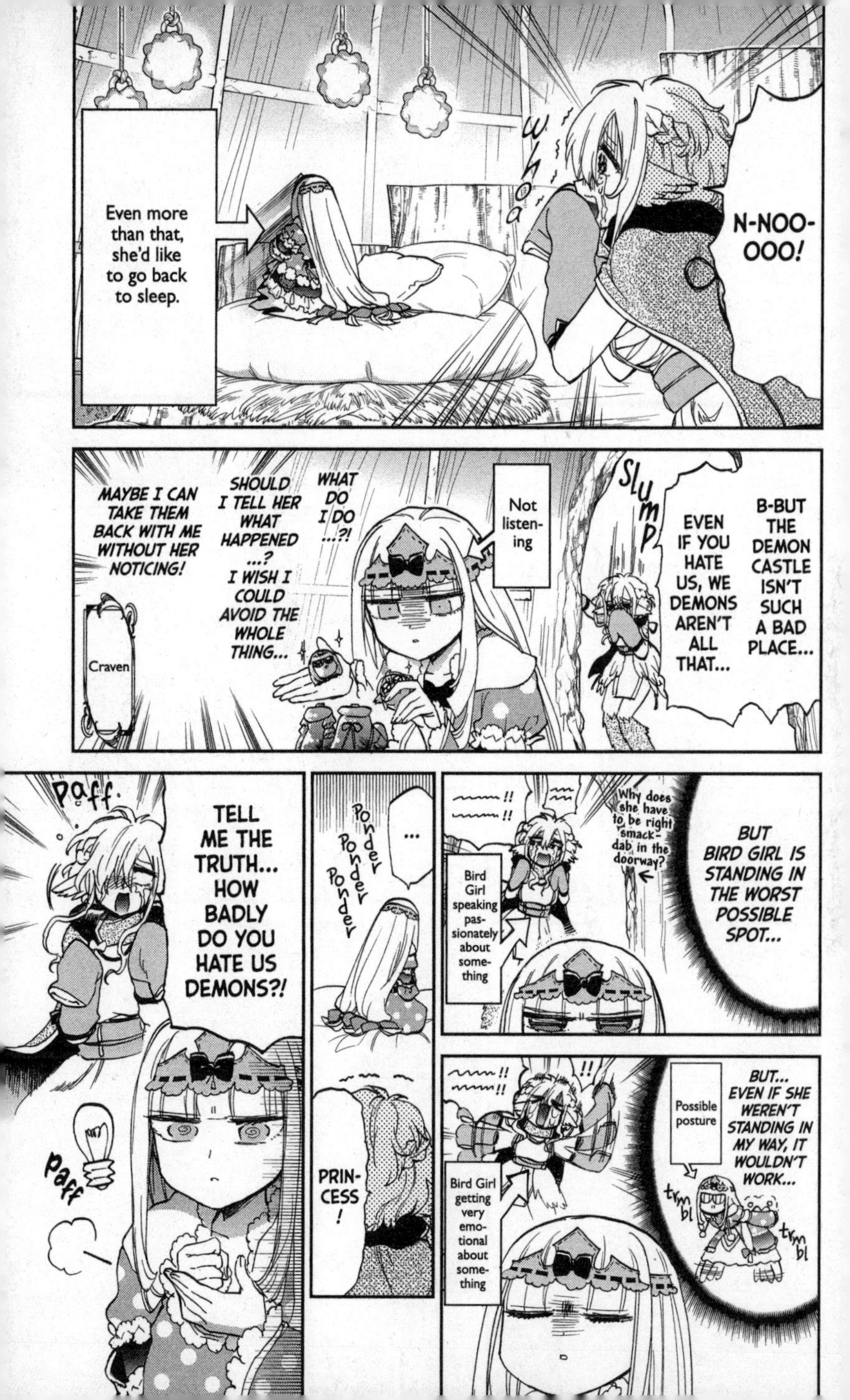
N-NOO-OOO!
whoa
Even more than that, she'd like to go back to sleep.
B-BUT THE DEMON CASTLE ISN'T SUCH A BAD PLACE...
EVEN IF YOU HATE US, WE DEMONS AREN'T ALL THAT...
Slump
Not listen-ing
WHAT DO I DO...?!
SHOULD I TELL HER WHAT HAPPENED...? I WISH I COULD AVOID THE WHOLE THING...
MAYBE I CAN TAKE THEM BACK WITH ME WITHOUT HER NOTICING!
Craven
BUT BIRD GIRL IS STANDING IN THE WORST POSSIBLE SPOT...
Why does she have to be right smack-dab in the doorway?
Bird Girl speaking pas-sionately about some-thing
BUT... EVEN IF SHE WEREN'T STANDING IN MY WAY, IT WOULDN'T WORK...
Possible posture
trmbl
trmbl
!!
Bird Girl getting very emo-tional about some-thing
...
Ponder Ponder Ponder
PRIN-CESS!
TELL ME THE TRUTH... HOW BADLY DO YOU HATE US DEMONS?!
Paff
Paff

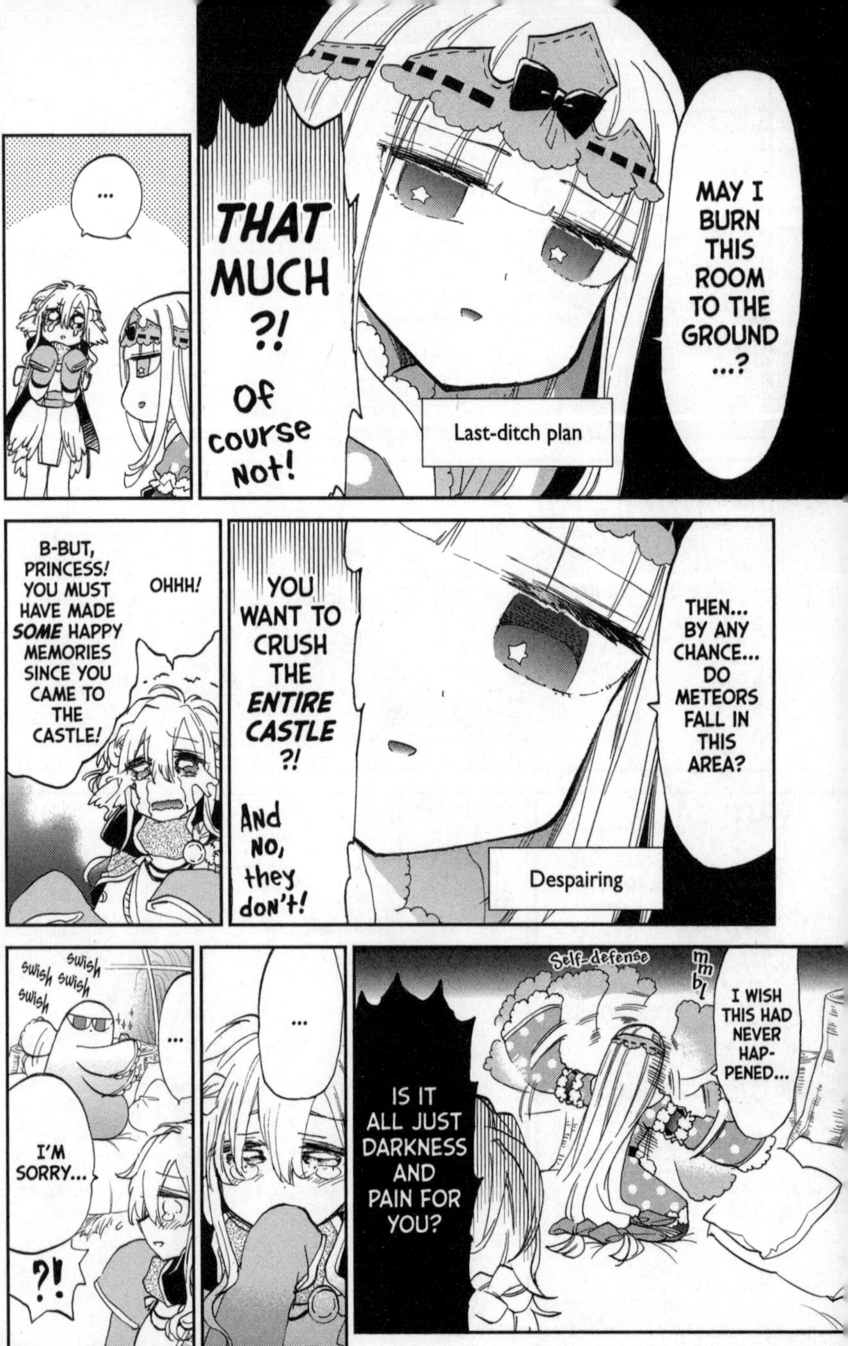
MAY I BURN THIS ROOM TO THE GROUND ...?
Last-ditch plan
THAT MUCH ?!
Of course not!
...
THEN... BY ANY CHANCE... DO METEORS FALL IN THIS AREA?
Despairing
YOU WANT TO CRUSH THE *ENTIRE CASTLE* ?!
And no, they don't!
OHHH!
B-BUT, PRINCESS! YOU MUST HAVE MADE *SOME* HAPPY MEMORIES SINCE YOU CAME TO THE CASTLE!
I WISH THIS HAD NEVER HAP-PENED...
mmbl
Self-defense
IS IT ALL JUST DARKNESS AND PAIN FOR YOU?
...
swish swish swish swish
...
I'M SORRY...
?!

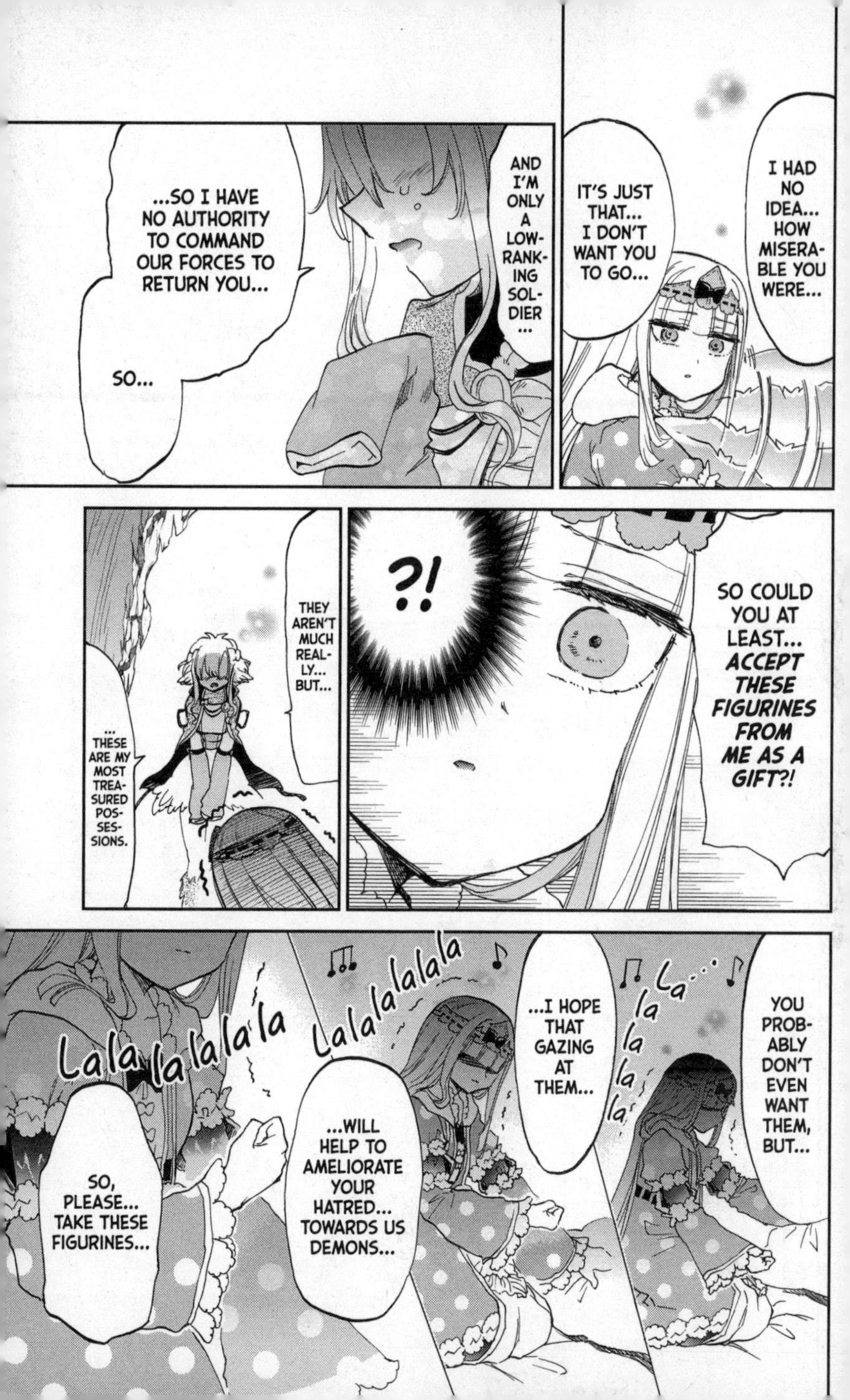
I HAD NO IDEA... HOW MISERABLE YOU WERE...
IT'S JUST THAT... I DON'T WANT YOU TO GO...
AND I'M ONLY A LOW-RANKING SOLDIER...
...SO I HAVE NO AUTHORITY TO COMMAND OUR FORCES TO RETURN YOU...
SO...
?!
SO COULD YOU AT LEAST... ACCEPT THESE FIGURINES FROM ME AS A GIFT?!
THEY AREN'T MUCH REALLY... BUT...
...THESE ARE MY MOST TREASURED POSSESSIONS.
YOU PROBABLY DON'T EVEN WANT THEM, BUT...
La la la la la la
...I HOPE THAT GAZING AT THEM...
Lalalalalala
...WILL HELP TO AMELIORATE YOUR HATRED... TOWARDS US DEMONS...
Lala la la la la
SO, PLEASE... TAKE THESE FIGURINES...

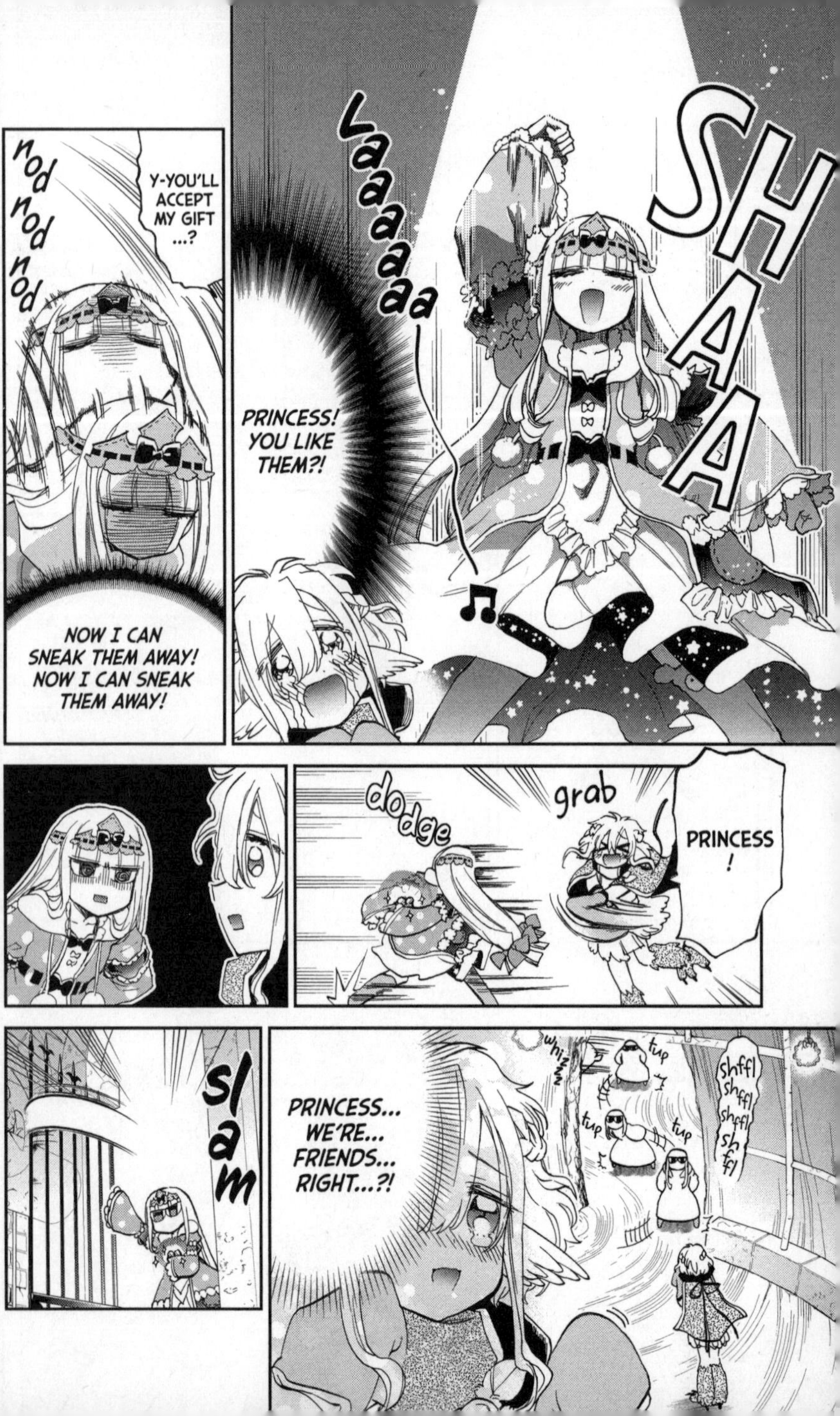
SHAAA
Laaaaaaa
PRINCESS! YOU LIKE THEM?!
Y-YOU'LL ACCEPT MY GIFT ...?
nod nod nod
NOW I CAN SNEAK THEM AWAY! NOW I CAN SNEAK THEM AWAY!
PRINCESS!
grab
dodge
shffl shffl shffl shffl
tup
tup
tup
PRINCESS... WE'RE... FRIENDS... RIGHT...?!
slam

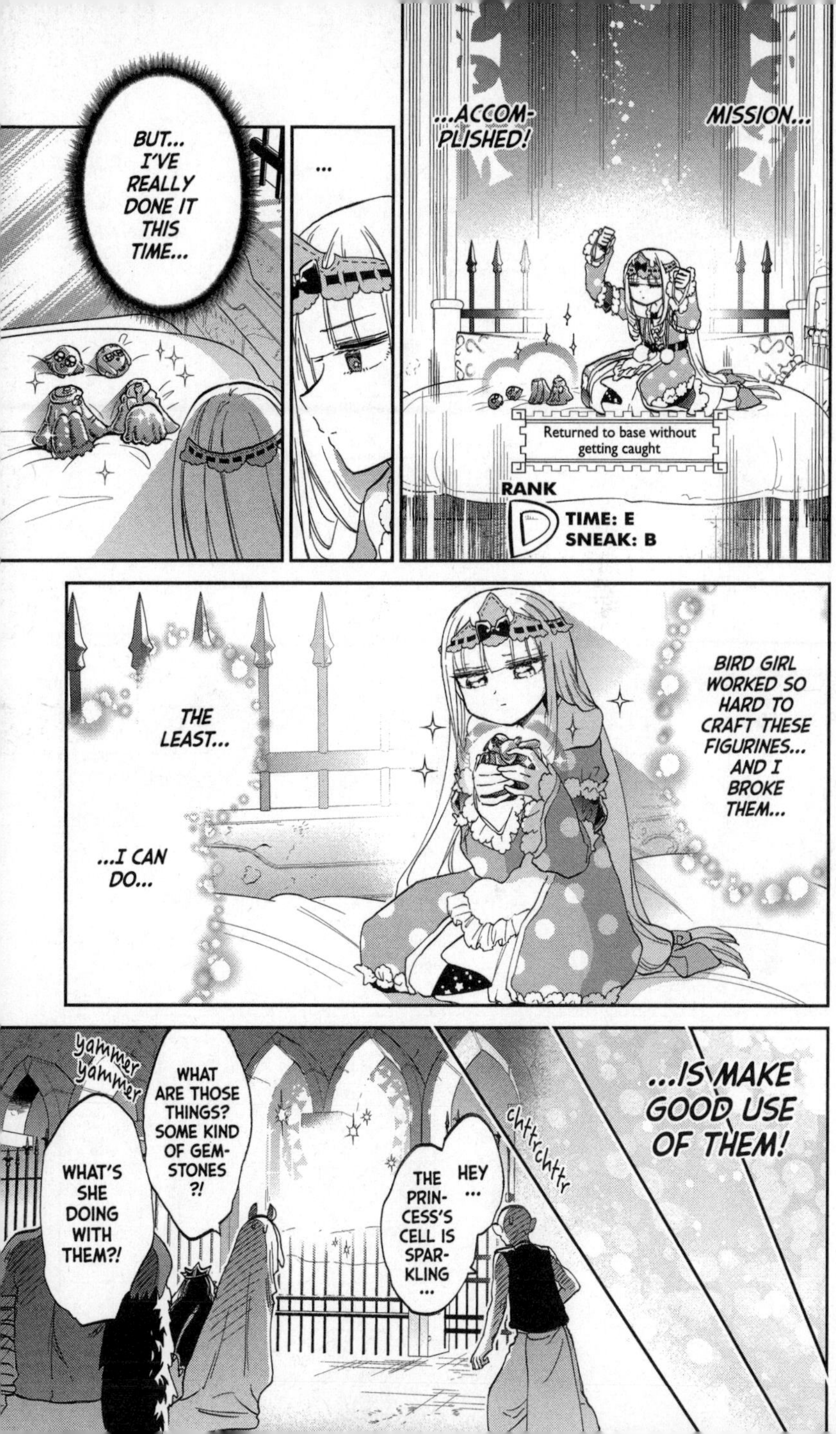

MISSION...
...ACCOM-PLISHED!
Returned to base without getting caught
RANK
D
TIME: E
SNEAK: B
...
BUT... I'VE REALLY DONE IT THIS TIME...
BIRD GIRL WORKED SO HARD TO CRAFT THESE FIGURINES... AND I BROKE THEM...
THE LEAST...
...I CAN DO...
...IS MAKE GOOD USE OF THEM!
chttrchttr
HEY...
THE PRIN-CESS'S CELL IS SPAR-KLING...
yammer yammer
WHAT ARE THOSE THINGS? SOME KIND OF GEM-STONES?!
WHAT'S SHE DOING WITH THEM?!

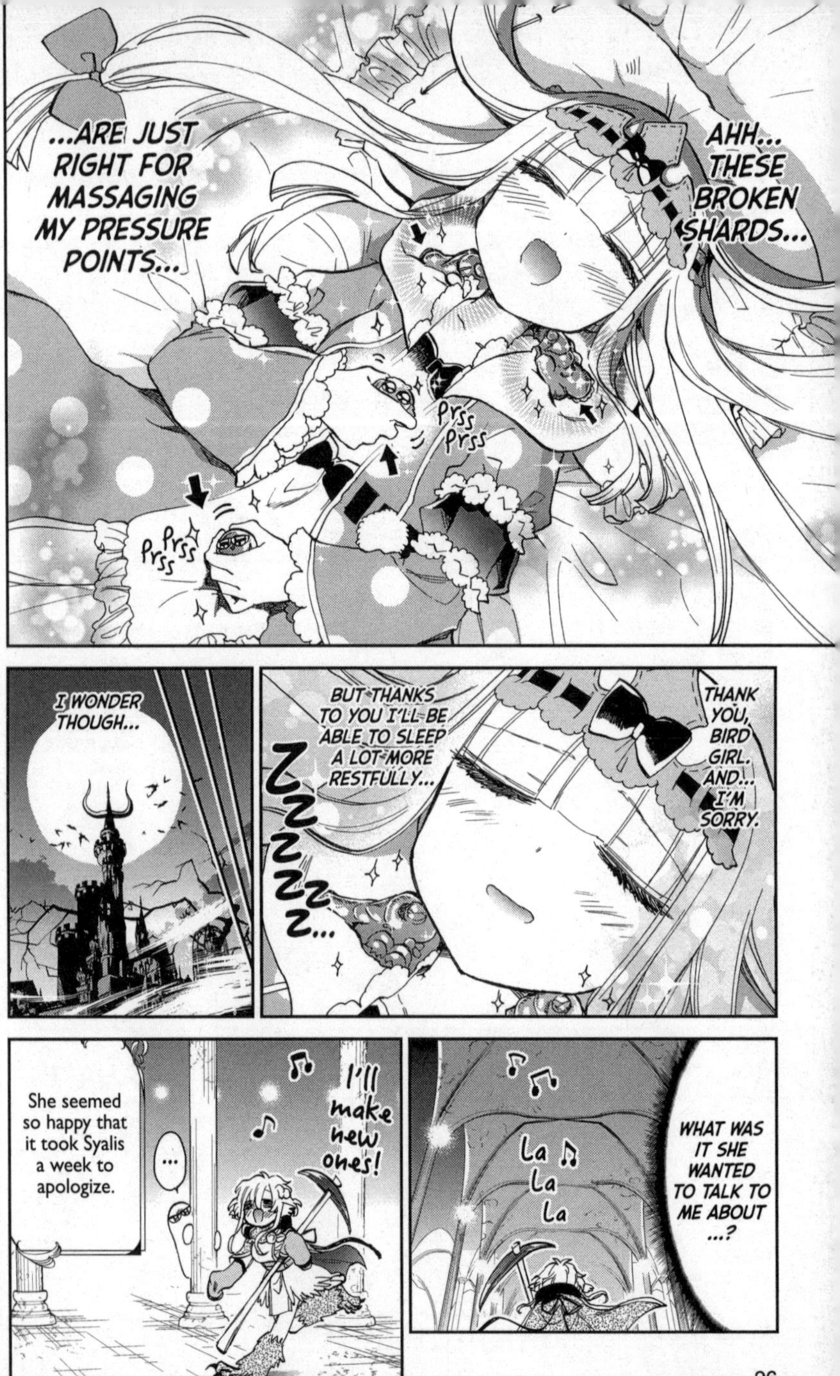
AHH... THESE BROKEN SHARDS...
...ARE JUST RIGHT FOR MASSAGING MY PRESSURE POINTS...
Prss Prss
Prss Prss
THANK YOU, BIRD GIRL. AND... I'M SORRY.
BUT THANKS TO YOU I'LL BE ABLE TO SLEEP A LOT MORE RESTFULLY...
ZZZZZZZ...
I WONDER THOUGH...
WHAT WAS IT SHE WANTED TO TALK TO ME ABOUT ...?
La La La
I'll make new ones!
...
She seemed so happy that it took Syalis a week to apologize.

Wild Bird Species Zone
Free Birds Airport

Residents: ☆☆☆

Freedom: ☆☆☆☆☆☆☆

The area for the wild bird species consists of a huge tree that penetrates the Demon Castle and a massive birdcage that has become a roost for Firefly Bats. Most of the wild bird species have departed to fly around outside, so this spot has pretty much become a demon condo.

It is sparsely populated, so the Harpy siblings have a lot of space. The entire area sways during strong winds, so there has been talk of demolishing or renovating it.

Major Residents
- Harpy
- Cursed Musician
- Flocks of Firefly Bats
- Lucky Lucky Owl

▼

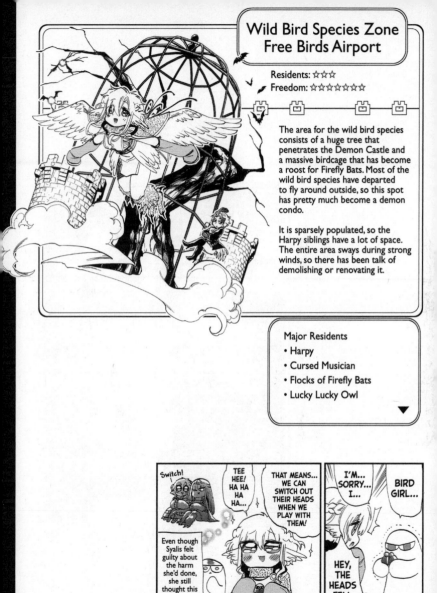

BIRD GIRL...
I'M... SORRY... I...
HEY, THE HEADS FELL OFF!
THAT MEANS... WE CAN SWITCH OUT THEIR HEADS WHEN WE PLAY WITH THEM!
TEE HEE! HA HA HA HA...
Switch!
Even though Syalis felt guilty about the harm she'd done, she still thought this girl was too easily cheered up.

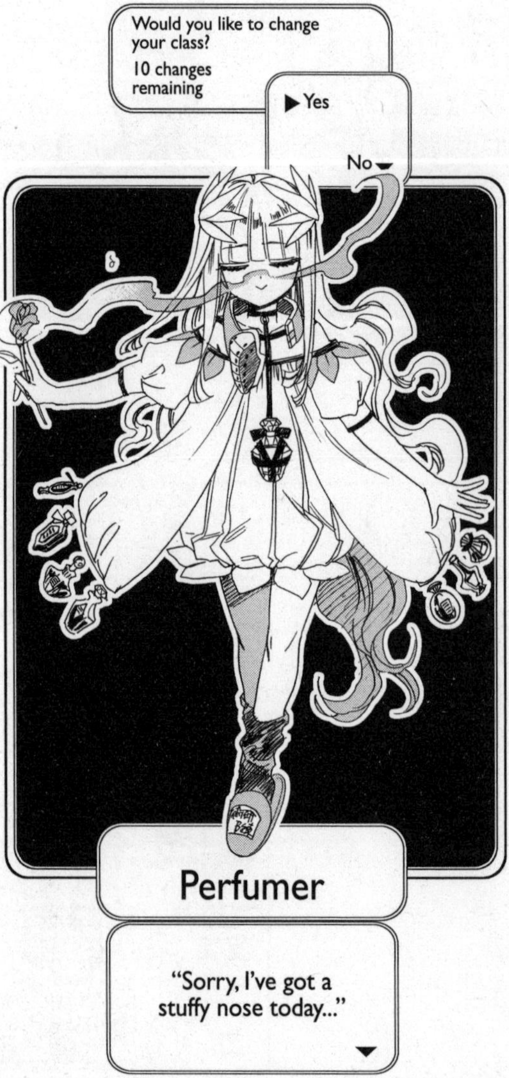
Would you like to change your class?
10 changes remaining
▶Yes
No
Perfumer
"Sorry, I've got a stuffy nose today..."

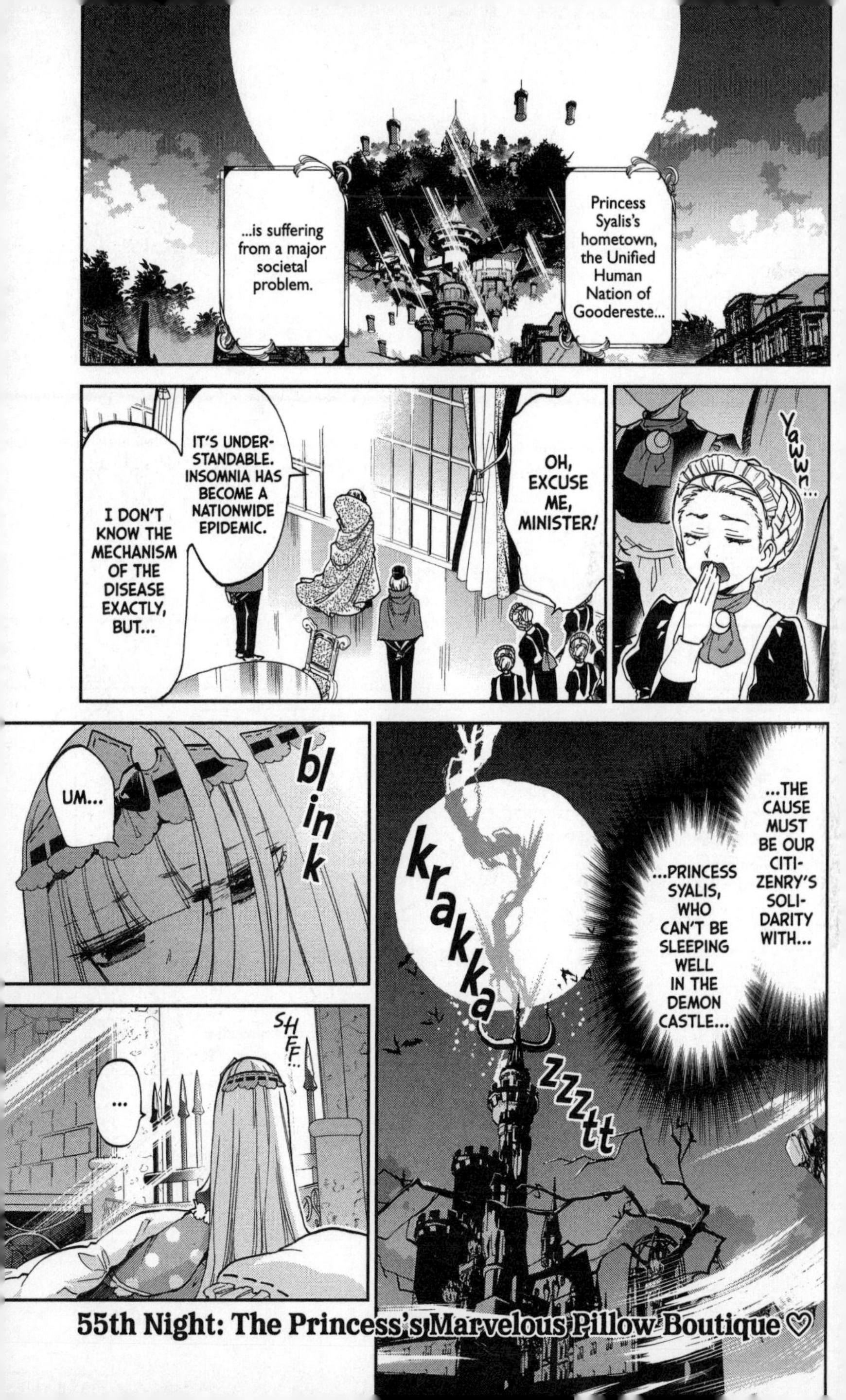
Princess Syalis's hometown, the Unified Human Nation of Goodereste...
...is suffering from a major societal problem.
Yawwn...
OH, EXCUSE ME, MINISTER!
IT'S UNDER-STANDABLE. INSOMNIA HAS BECOME A NATIONWIDE EPIDEMIC.
I DON'T KNOW THE MECHANISM OF THE DISEASE EXACTLY, BUT...
...THE CAUSE MUST BE OUR CITI-ZENRY'S SOLI-DARITY WITH...
...PRINCESS SYALIS, WHO CAN'T BE SLEEPING WELL IN THE DEMON CASTLE...
krakka
zzztt
UM...
blink
SHFF...
...

55th Night: The Princess's Marvelous Pillow Boutique ♡

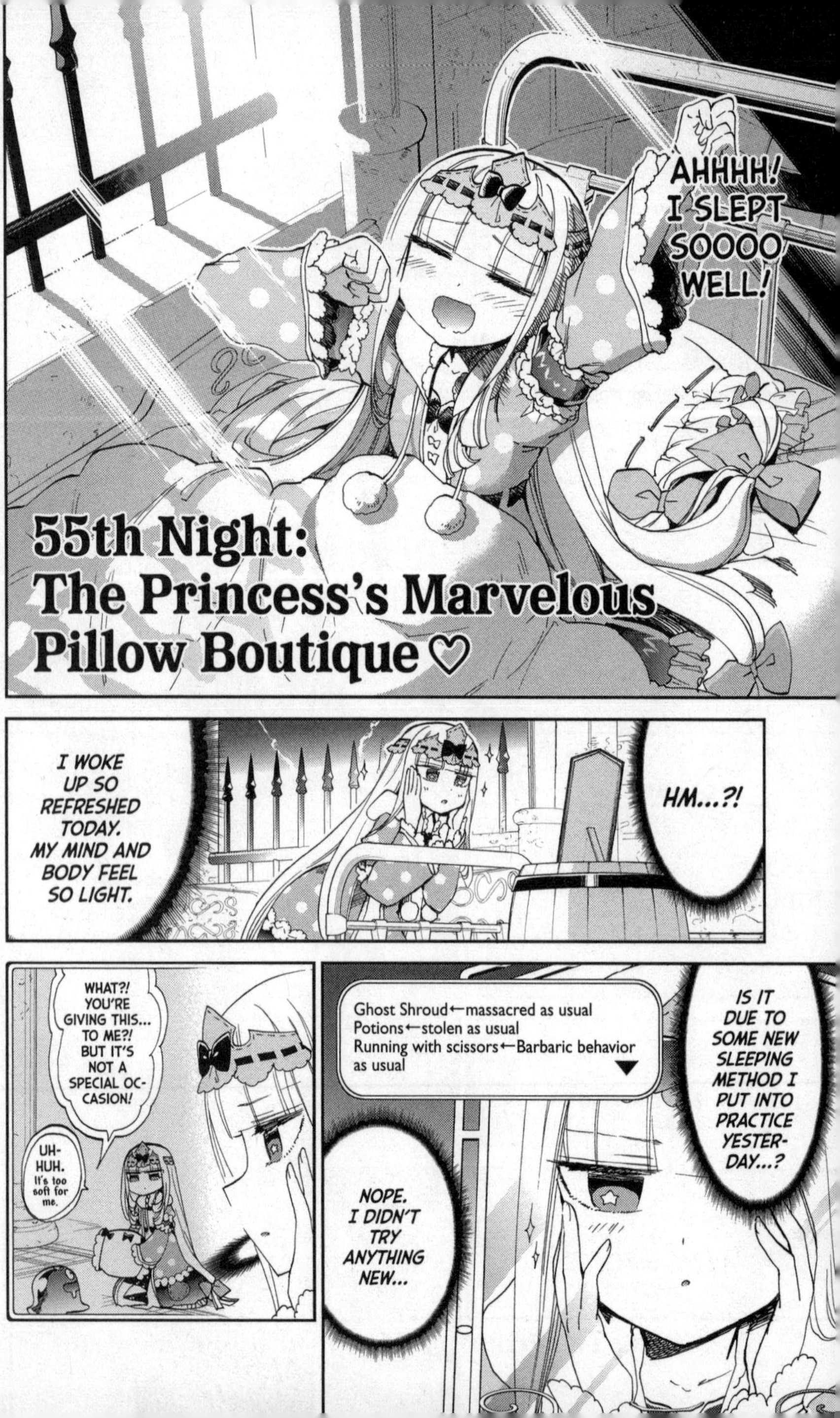
AHHHH! I SLEPT SOOOO WELL!
55th Night: The Princess's Marvelous Pillow Boutique ♡
HM...?!
I WOKE UP SO REFRESHED TODAY. MY MIND AND BODY FEEL SO LIGHT.
IS IT DUE TO SOME NEW SLEEPING METHOD I PUT INTO PRACTICE YESTER-DAY...?
Ghost Shroud←massacred as usual
Potions←stolen as usual
Running with scissors←Barbaric behavior as usual
NOPE. I DIDN'T TRY ANYTHING NEW...
WHAT?! YOU'RE GIVING THIS... TO ME?! BUT IT'S NOT A SPECIAL OC-CASION!
UH-HUH.
It's too soft for me.

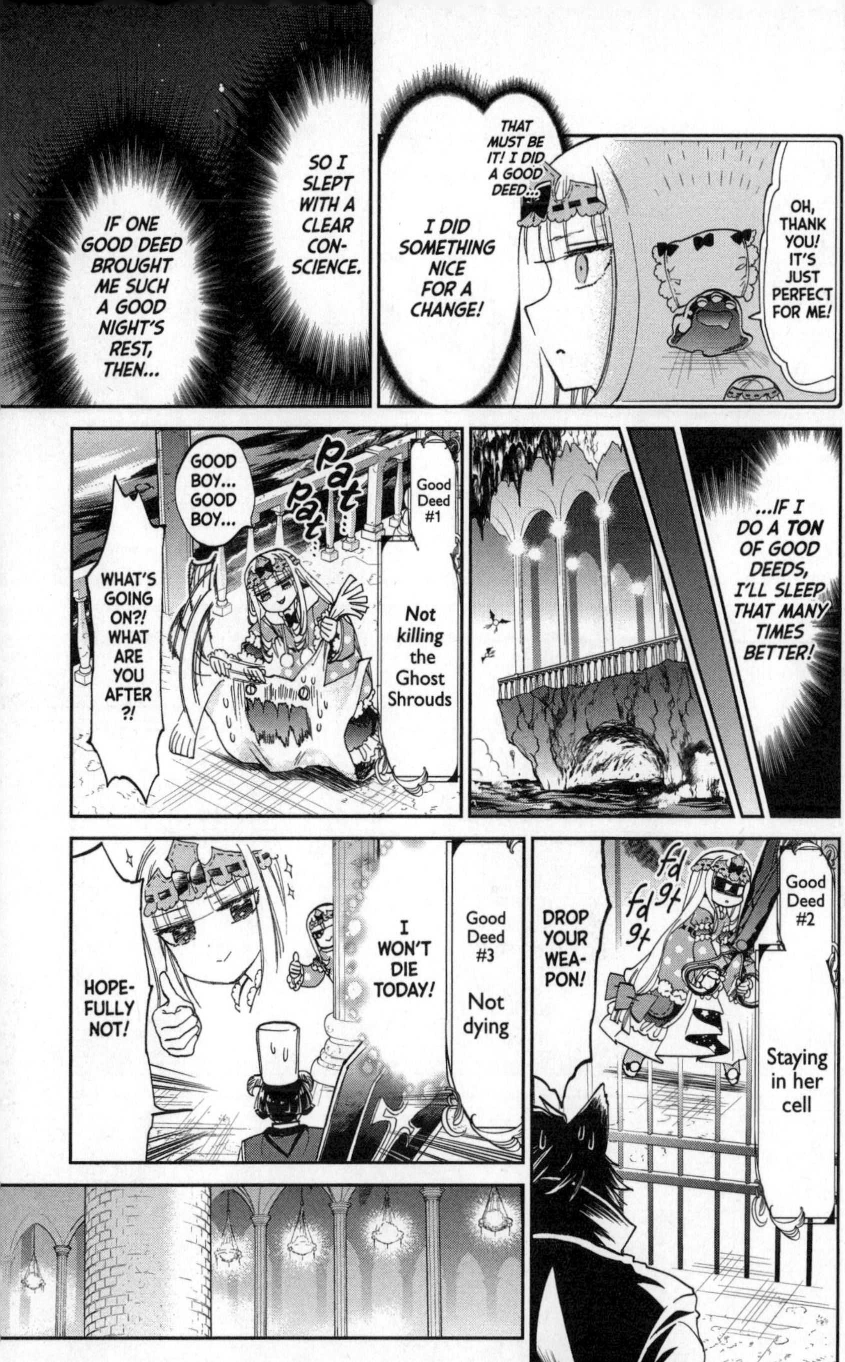
OH, THANK YOU! IT'S JUST PERFECT FOR ME!
THAT MUST BE IT! I DID A GOOD DEED...
I DID SOMETHING NICE FOR A CHANGE!
SO I SLEPT WITH A CLEAR CON-SCIENCE.
IF ONE GOOD DEED BROUGHT ME SUCH A GOOD NIGHT'S REST, THEN...
...IF I DO A TON OF GOOD DEEDS, I'LL SLEEP THAT MANY TIMES BETTER!
Good Deed #1
Not killing the Ghost Shrouds
pat pat
GOOD BOY... GOOD BOY...
WHAT'S GOING ON?! WHAT ARE YOU AFTER?!
Good Deed #2
Staying in her cell
DROP YOUR WEA-PON!
Good Deed #3
Not dying
I WON'T DIE TODAY!
HOPE-FULLY NOT!

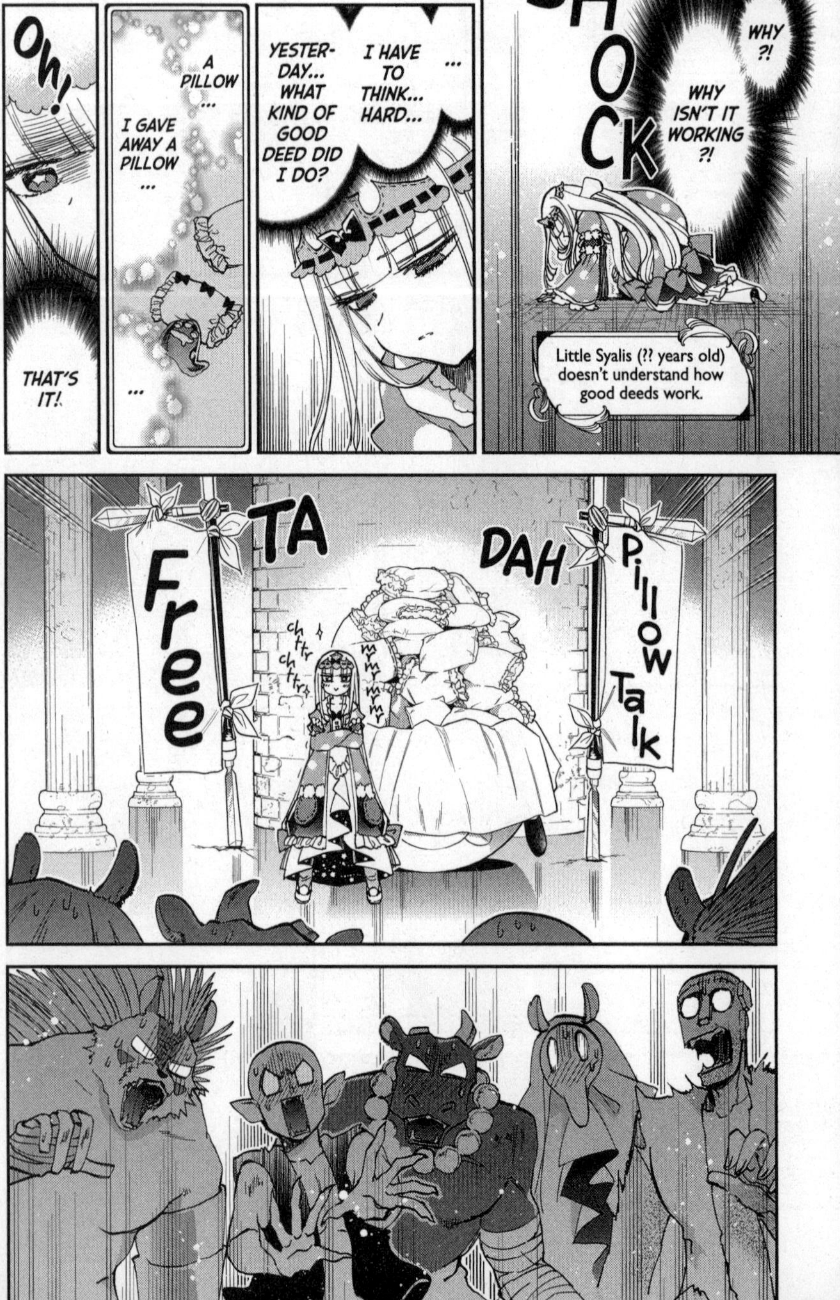
SHOCK
WHY ?!
WHY ISN'T IT WORKING ?!
Little Syalis (?? years old) doesn't understand how good deeds work.
...
I HAVE TO THINK... HARD...
YESTER-DAY... WHAT KIND OF GOOD DEED DID I DO?
A PILLOW ...
I GAVE AWAY A PILLOW ...
...
Oh!
THAT'S IT!
TA
DAH
Free
Pillow Talk
chttr chttr
mrmr mrmr

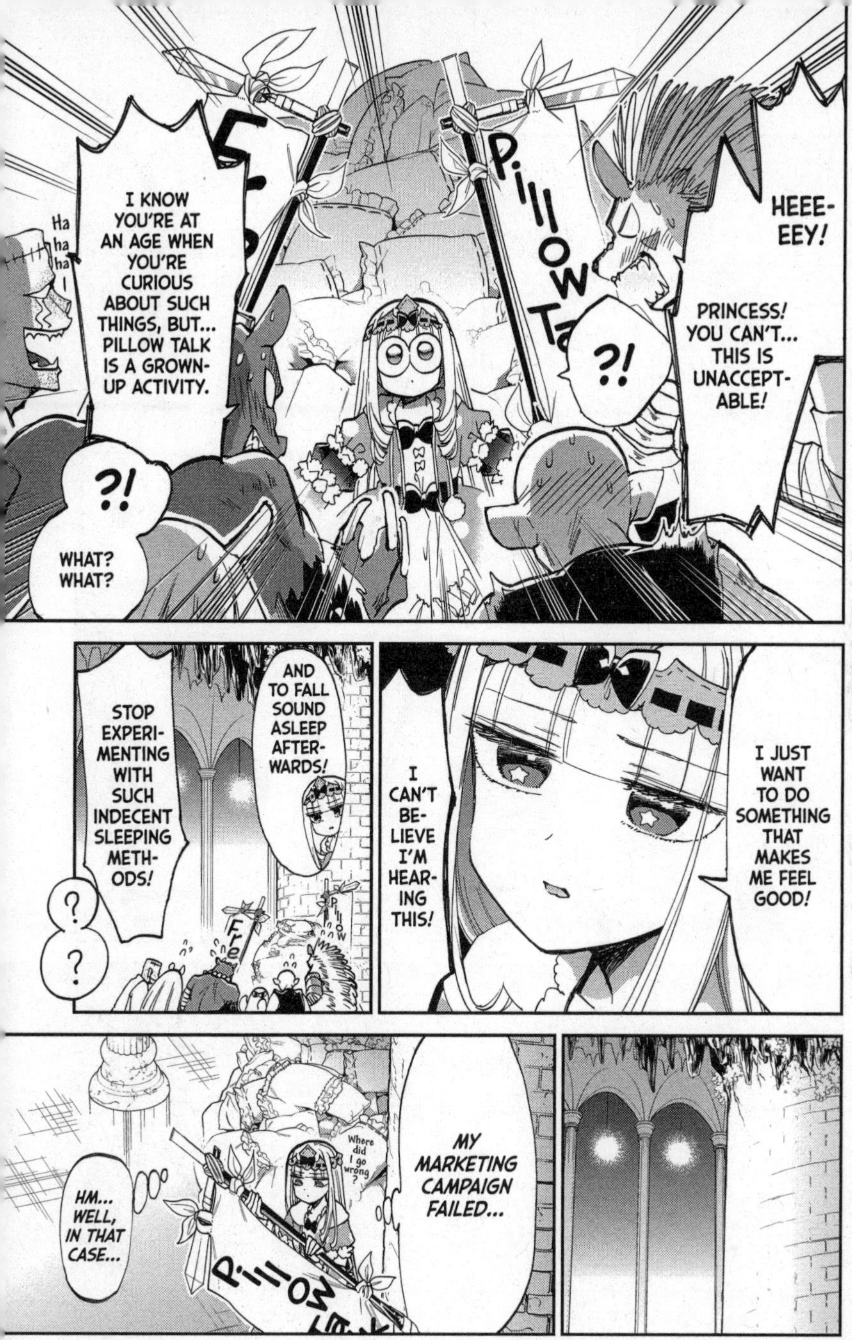
HEEE-EEY!
PRINCESS! YOU CAN'T... THIS IS UNACCEPTABLE!
?!
Pillow Ta
I KNOW YOU'RE AT AN AGE WHEN YOU'RE CURIOUS ABOUT SUCH THINGS, BUT... PILLOW TALK IS A GROWN-UP ACTIVITY.
Ha ha ha!
?!
WHAT? WHAT?
I JUST WANT TO DO SOMETHING THAT MAKES ME FEEL GOOD!
I CAN'T BELIEVE I'M HEARING THIS!
AND TO FALL SOUND ASLEEP AFTERWARDS!
STOP EXPERIMENTING WITH SUCH INDECENT SLEEPING METHODS!
? ?
MY MARKETING CAMPAIGN FAILED...
Where did I go wrong?
HM... WELL, IN THAT CASE...

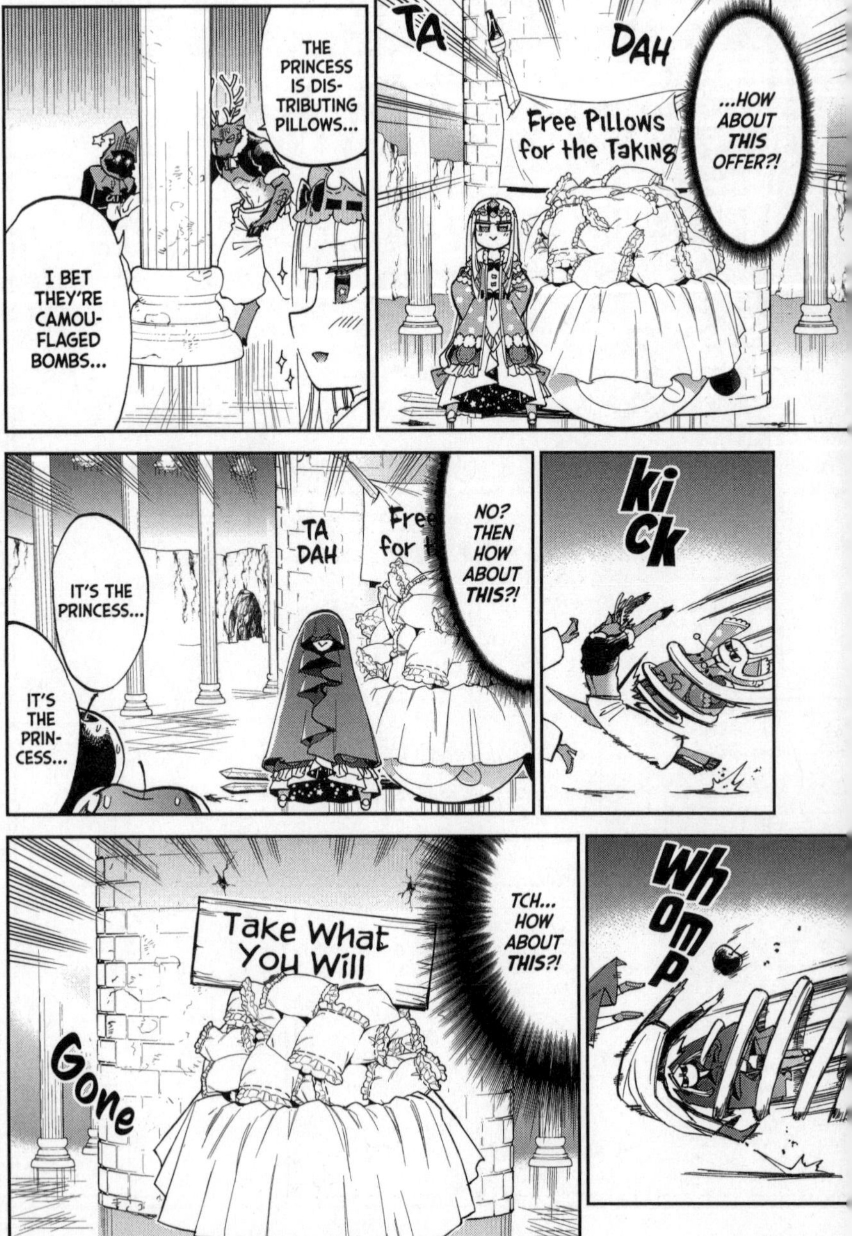

TA
DAH
...HOW ABOUT THIS OFFER?!
Free Pillows for the Taking
THE PRINCESS IS DISTRIBUTING PILLOWS...
I BET THEY'RE CAMOUFLAGED BOMBS...
kick
NO? THEN HOW ABOUT THIS?!
TA DAH
IT'S THE PRINCESS...
IT'S THE PRINCESS...
Whomp
TCH... HOW ABOUT THIS?!
Take What You Will
Gone

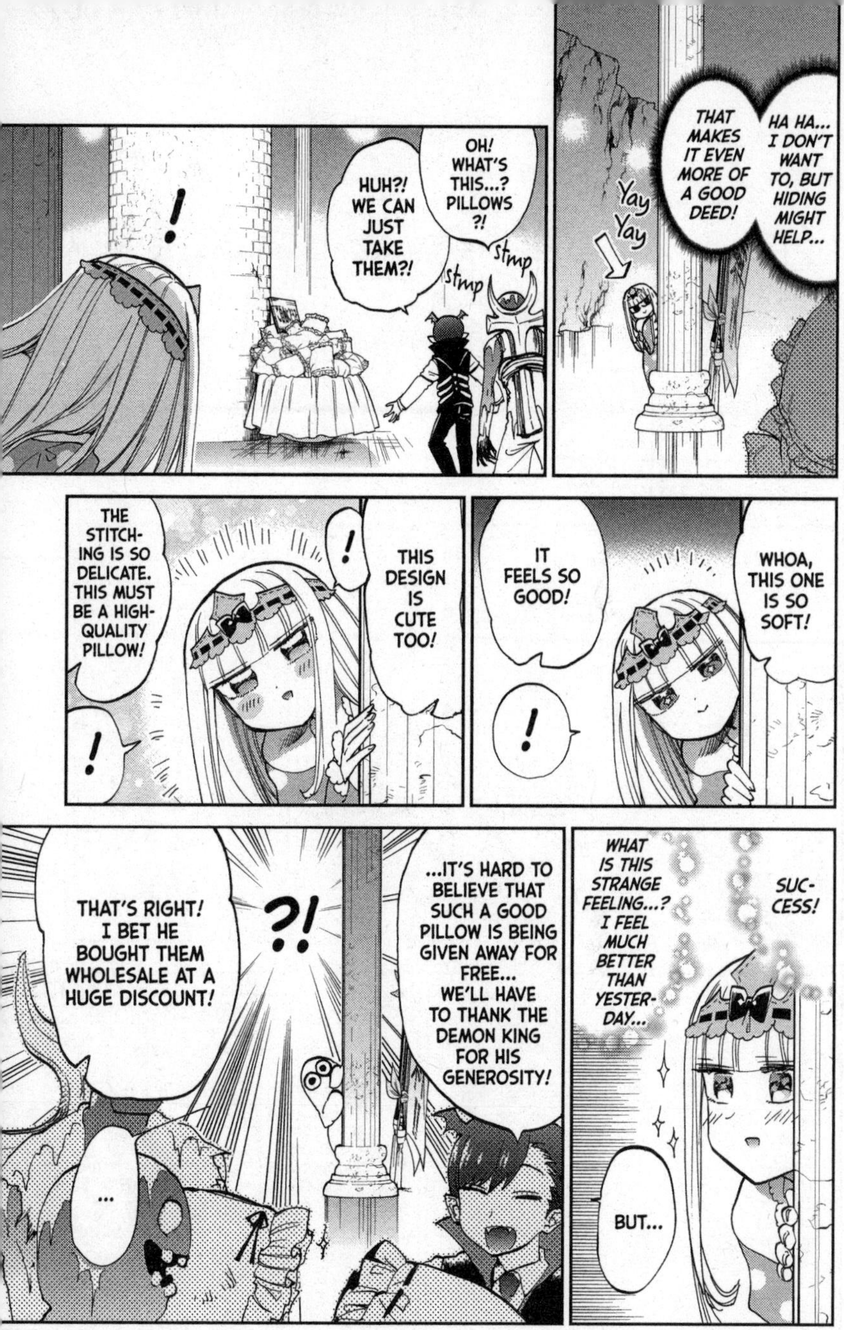
HA HA... I DON'T WANT TO, BUT HIDING MIGHT HELP...
THAT MAKES IT EVEN MORE OF A GOOD DEED!
Yay Yay
OH! WHAT'S THIS...? PILLOWS?!
HUH?! WE CAN JUST TAKE THEM?!
stmp
stmp
!
WHOA, THIS ONE IS SO SOFT!
IT FEELS SO GOOD!
!
THIS DESIGN IS CUTE TOO!
!
THE STITCH-ING IS SO DELICATE. THIS MUST BE A HIGH-QUALITY PILLOW!
!
SUC-CESS!
WHAT IS THIS STRANGE FEELING...? I FEEL MUCH BETTER THAN YESTER-DAY...
BUT...
...IT'S HARD TO BELIEVE THAT SUCH A GOOD PILLOW IS BEING GIVEN AWAY FOR FREE... WE'LL HAVE TO THANK THE DEMON KING FOR HIS GENEROSITY!
?!
THAT'S RIGHT! I BET HE BOUGHT THEM WHOLESALE AT A HUGE DISCOUNT!
...

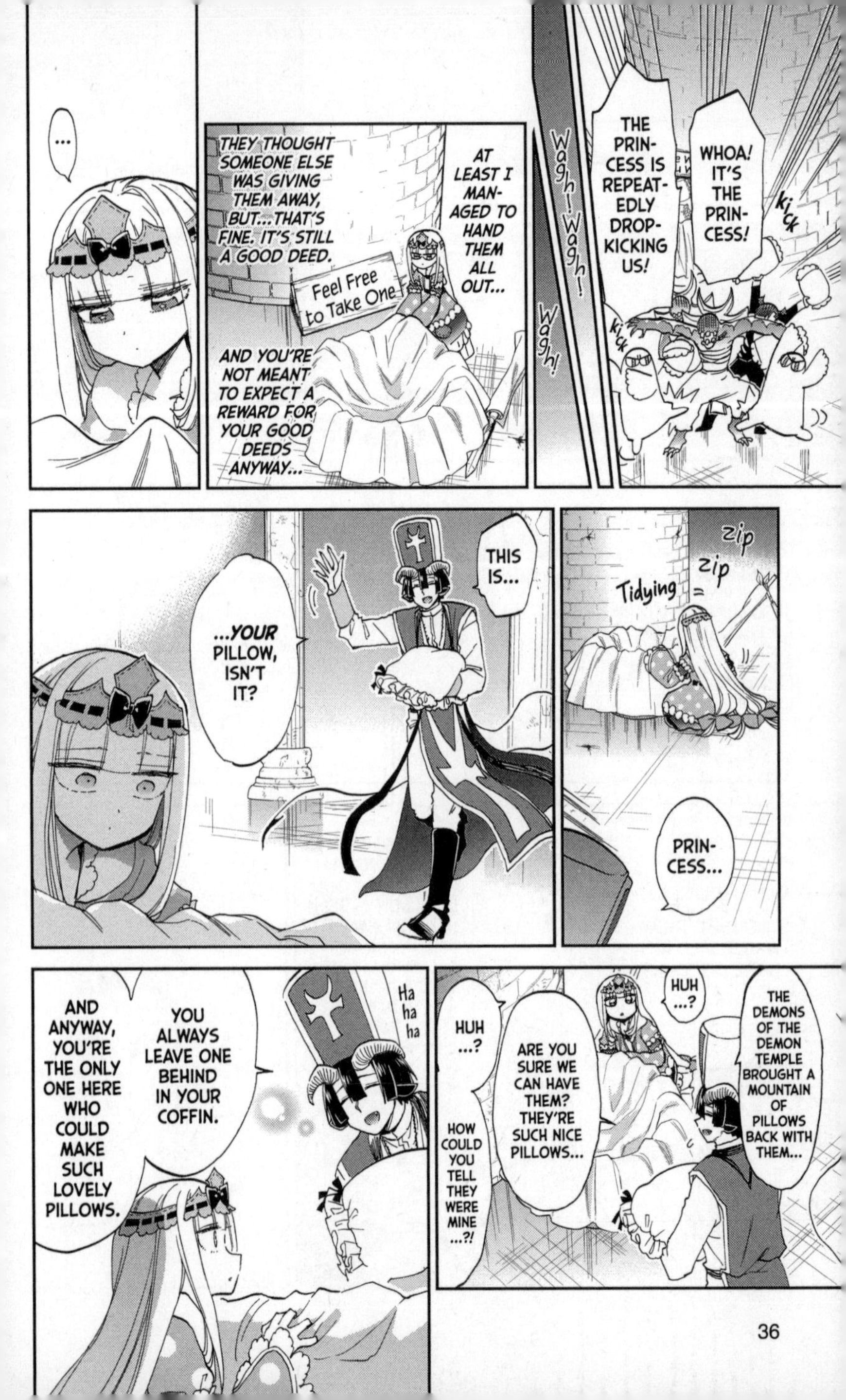
WHOA! IT'S THE PRINCESS!
THE PRINCESS IS REPEATEDLY DROP-KICKING US!
kick
kick
Wagh! Wagh!
Wagh!
AT LEAST I MANAGED TO HAND THEM ALL OUT...
THEY THOUGHT SOMEONE ELSE WAS GIVING THEM AWAY, BUT... THAT'S FINE. IT'S STILL A GOOD DEED.
Feel Free to Take One
AND YOU'RE NOT MEANT TO EXPECT A REWARD FOR YOUR GOOD DEEDS ANYWAY...
...
zip
zip
Tidying
PRINCESS...
THIS IS...
...YOUR PILLOW, ISN'T IT?
THE DEMONS OF THE DEMON TEMPLE BROUGHT A MOUNTAIN OF PILLOWS BACK WITH THEM...
HUH ...?
ARE YOU SURE WE CAN HAVE THEM? THEY'RE SUCH NICE PILLOWS...
HUH ...?
HOW COULD YOU TELL THEY WERE MINE ...?!
Ha ha ha
YOU ALWAYS LEAVE ONE BEHIND IN YOUR COFFIN.
AND ANYWAY, YOU'RE THE ONLY ONE HERE WHO COULD MAKE SUCH LOVELY PILLOWS.

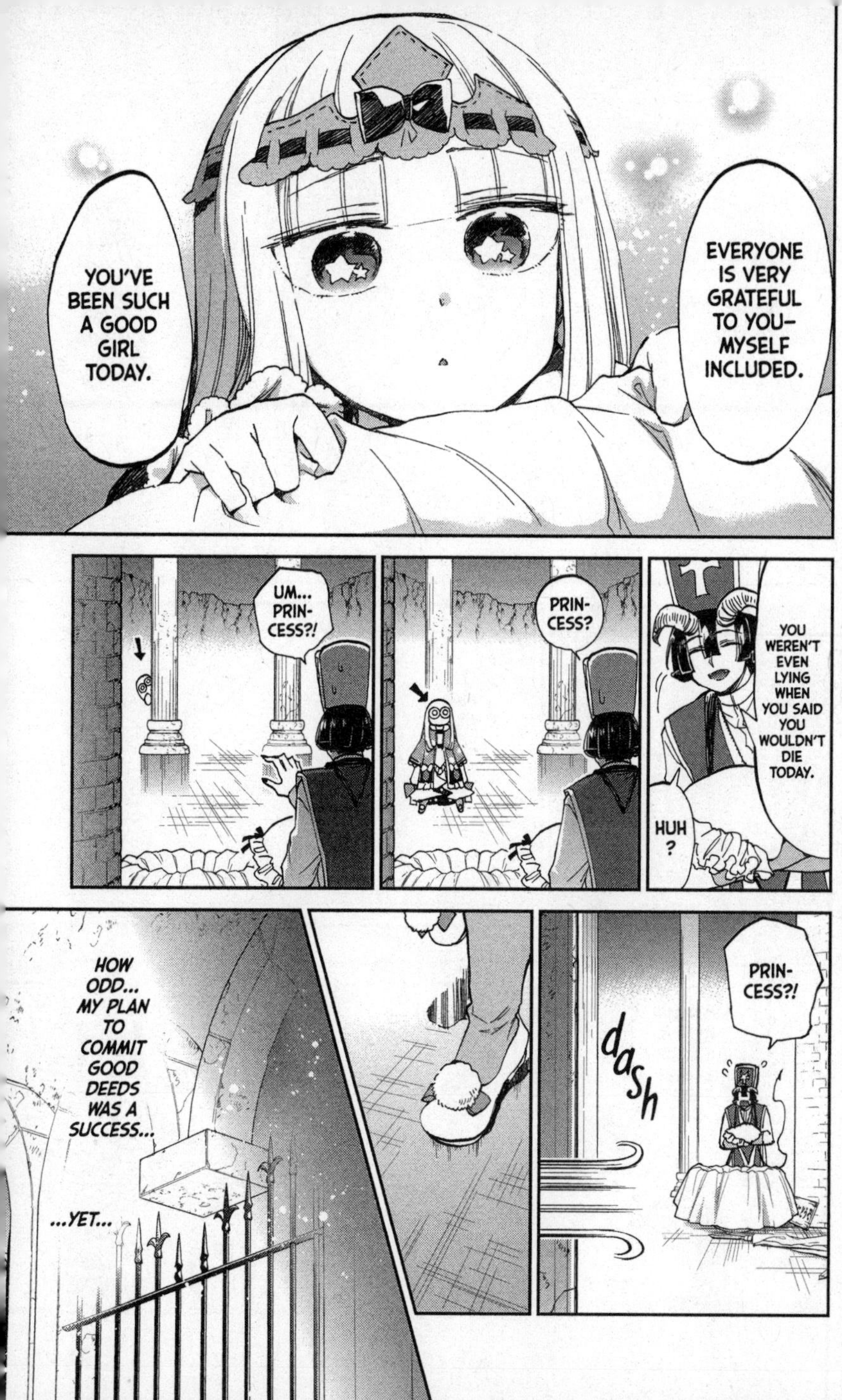
EVERYONE IS VERY GRATEFUL TO YOU—MYSELF INCLUDED.
YOU'VE BEEN SUCH A GOOD GIRL TODAY.
YOU WEREN'T EVEN LYING WHEN YOU SAID YOU WOULDN'T DIE TODAY.
HUH?
PRIN-CESS?
UM... PRIN-CESS?!
PRIN-CESS?!
dash
HOW ODD... MY PLAN TO COMMIT GOOD DEEDS WAS A SUCCESS...
...YET...

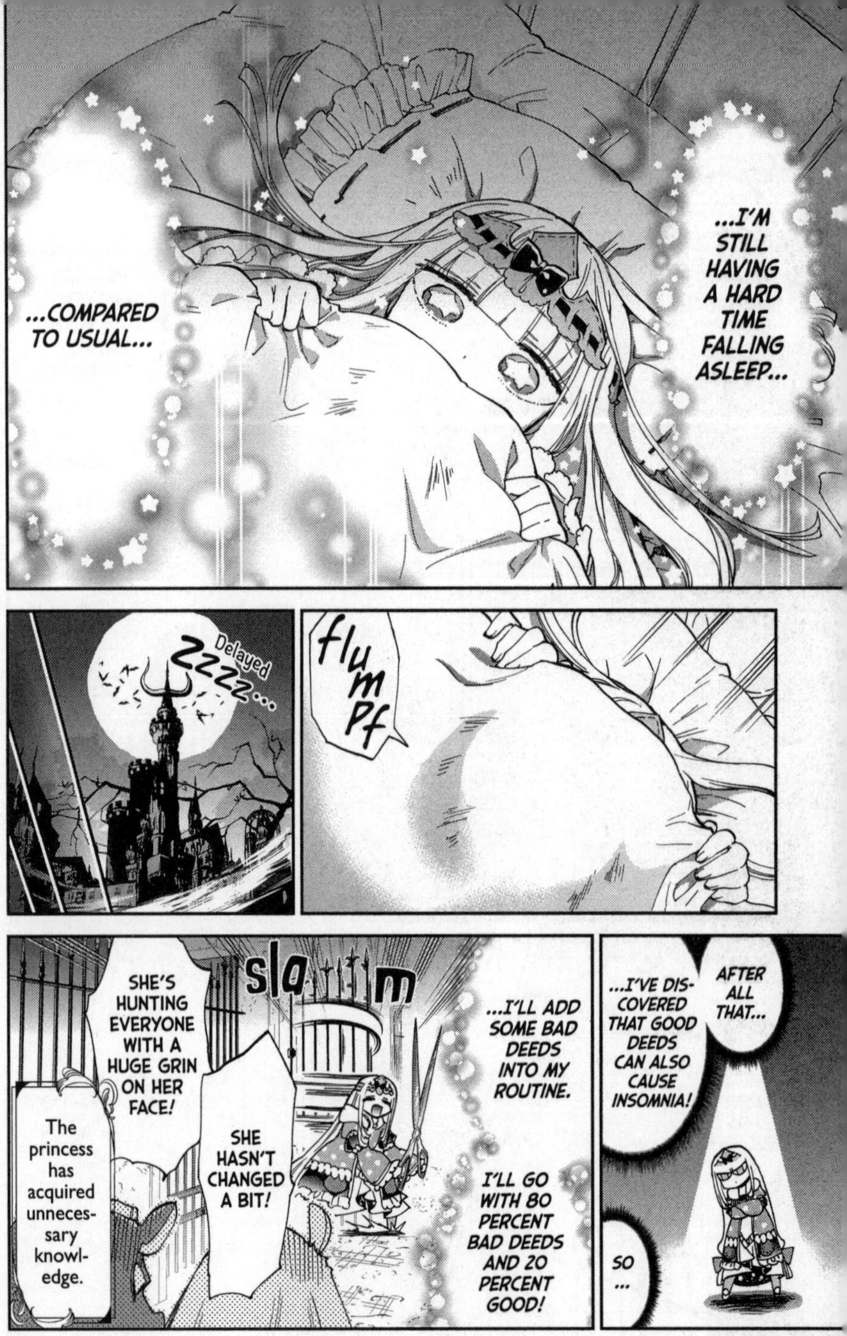
...I'M STILL HAVING A HARD TIME FALLING ASLEEP...
...COMPARED TO USUAL...
flumpf
Delayed Zzzz...
AFTER ALL THAT...
...I'VE DISCOVERED THAT GOOD DEEDS CAN ALSO CAUSE INSOMNIA!
SO ...
...I'LL ADD SOME BAD DEEDS INTO MY ROUTINE.
I'LL GO WITH 80 PERCENT BAD DEEDS AND 20 PERCENT GOOD!
slam
SHE'S HUNTING EVERYONE WITH A HUGE GRIN ON HER FACE!
SHE HASN'T CHANGED A BIT!
The princess has acquired unnecessary knowledge.

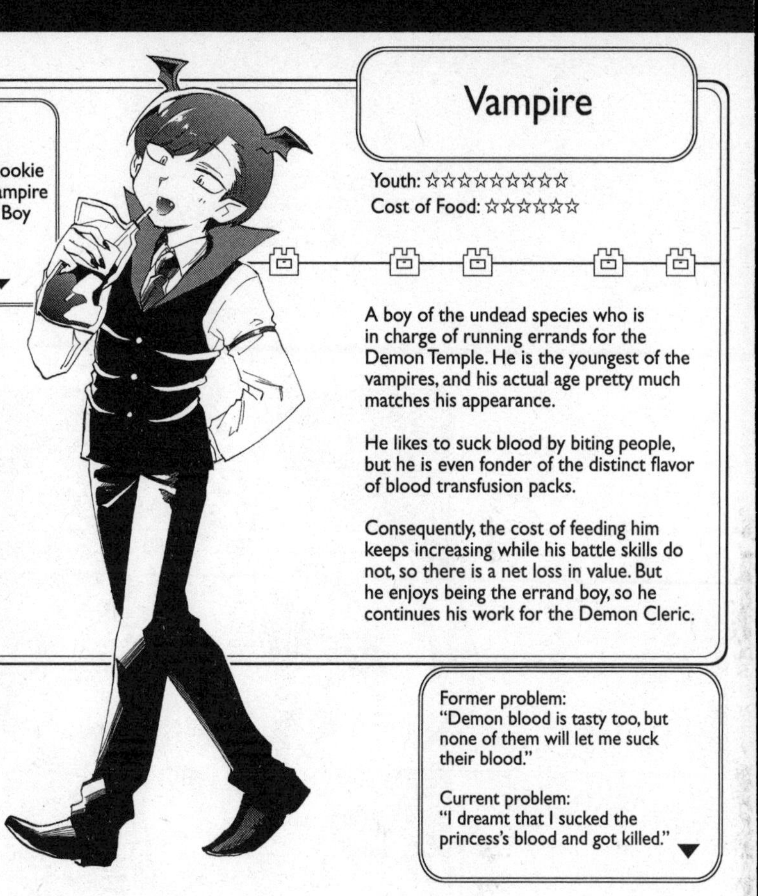

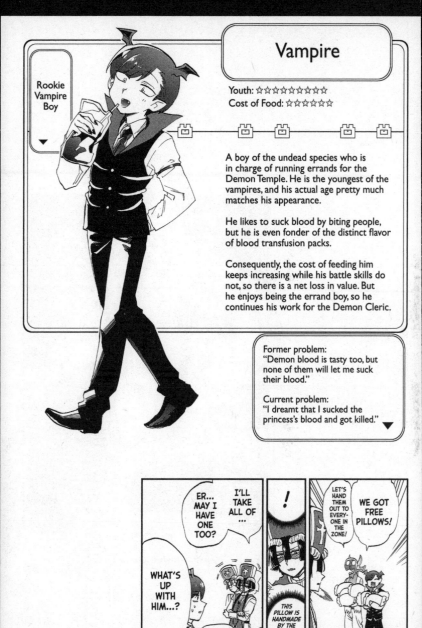

Rookie Vampire Boy

Vampire

Youth: ☆☆☆☆☆☆☆☆☆☆
Cost of Food: ☆☆☆☆☆☆

A boy of the undead species who is in charge of running errands for the Demon Temple. He is the youngest of the vampires, and his actual age pretty much matches his appearance.

He likes to suck blood by biting people, but he is even fonder of the distinct flavor of blood transfusion packs.

Consequently, the cost of feeding him keeps increasing while his battle skills do not, so there is a net loss in value. But he enjoys being the errand boy, so he continues his work for the Demon Cleric.

Former problem:
"Demon blood is tasty too, but none of them will let me suck their blood."

Current problem:
"I dreamt that I sucked the princess's blood and got killed."

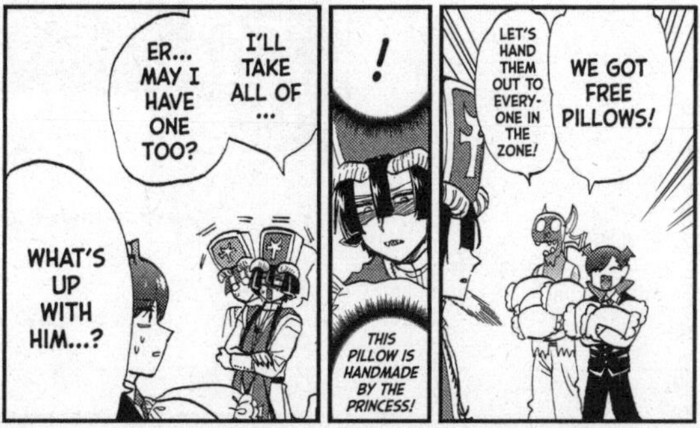
WE GOT FREE PILLOWS!
LET'S HAND THEM OUT TO EVERYONE IN THE ZONE!
!
THIS PILLOW IS HANDMADE BY THE PRINCESS!
I'LL TAKE ALL OF ...
ER... MAY I HAVE ONE TOO?
WHAT'S UP WITH HIM...?

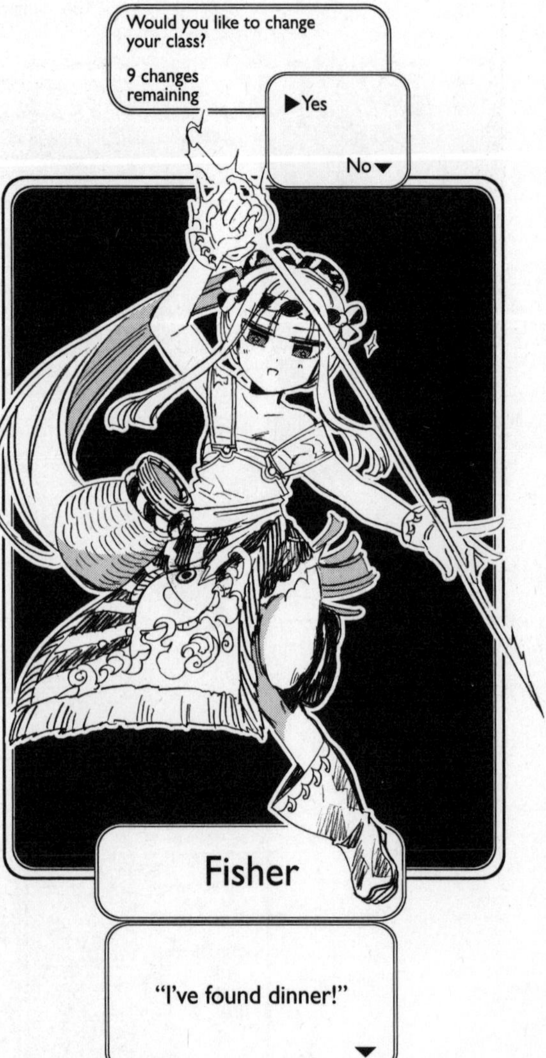
Would you like to change your class?
9 changes remaining
▶Yes
No▼
Fisher
"I've found dinner!"

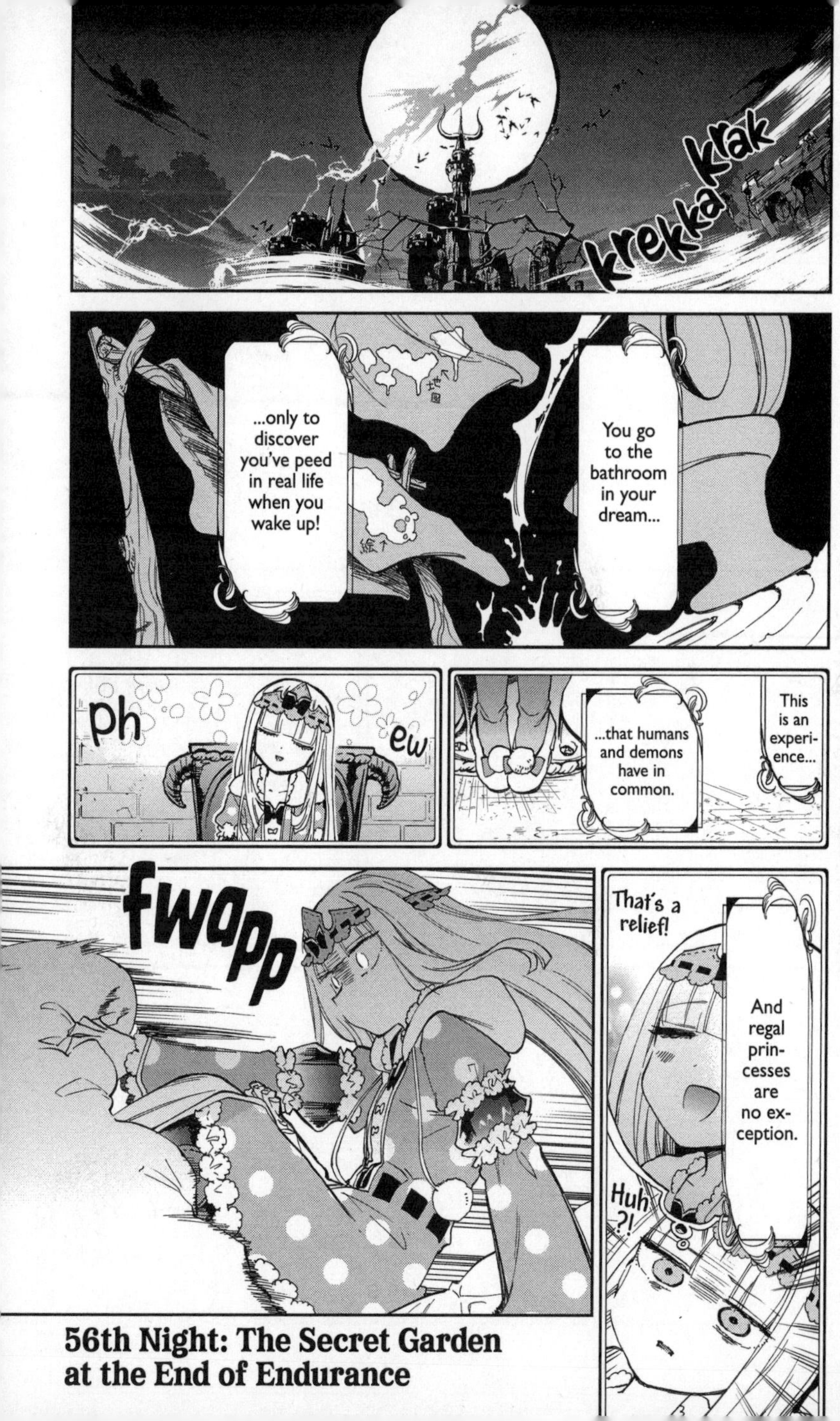
krekka krak
You go to the bathroom in your dream...
...only to discover you've peed in real life when you wake up!
This is an experience...
...that humans and demons have in common.
ph
ew
And regal princesses are no exception.
That's a relief!
fwapp
Huh ?!

56th Night: The Secret Garden at the End of Endurance

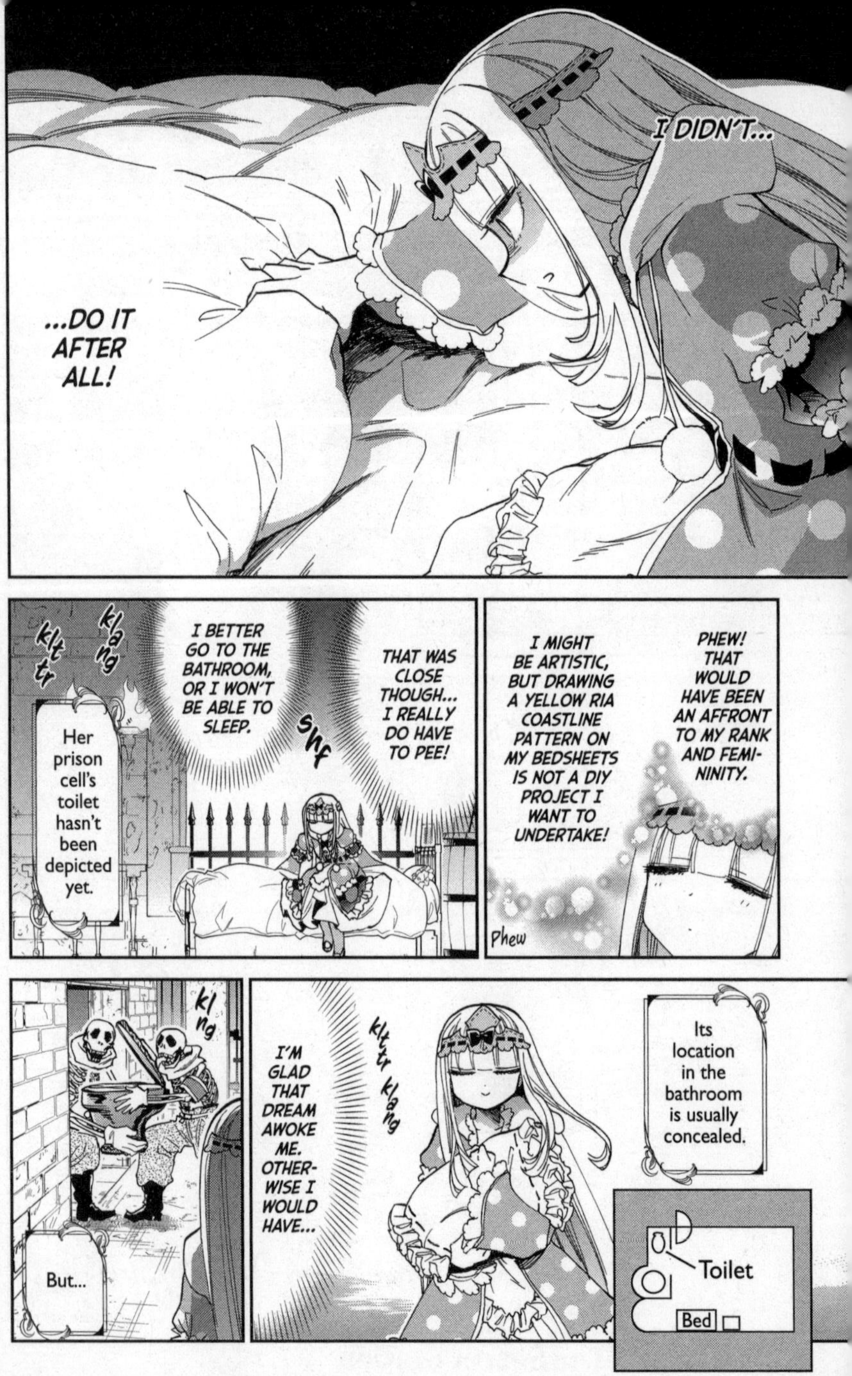
I DIDN'T...
...DO IT AFTER ALL!
PHEW! THAT WOULD HAVE BEEN AN AFFRONT TO MY RANK AND FEMININITY.
I MIGHT BE ARTISTIC, BUT DRAWING A YELLOW RIA COASTLINE PATTERN ON MY BEDSHEETS IS NOT A DIY PROJECT I WANT TO UNDERTAKE!
Phew
THAT WAS CLOSE THOUGH... I REALLY DO HAVE TO PEE!
snf
I BETTER GO TO THE BATHROOM, OR I WON'T BE ABLE TO SLEEP.
klang
kltr
Her prison cell's toilet hasn't been depicted yet.
Its location in the bathroom is usually concealed.
Toilet
Bed
klttr klang
I'M GLAD THAT DREAM AWOKE ME. OTHERWISE I WOULD HAVE...
klng
But...

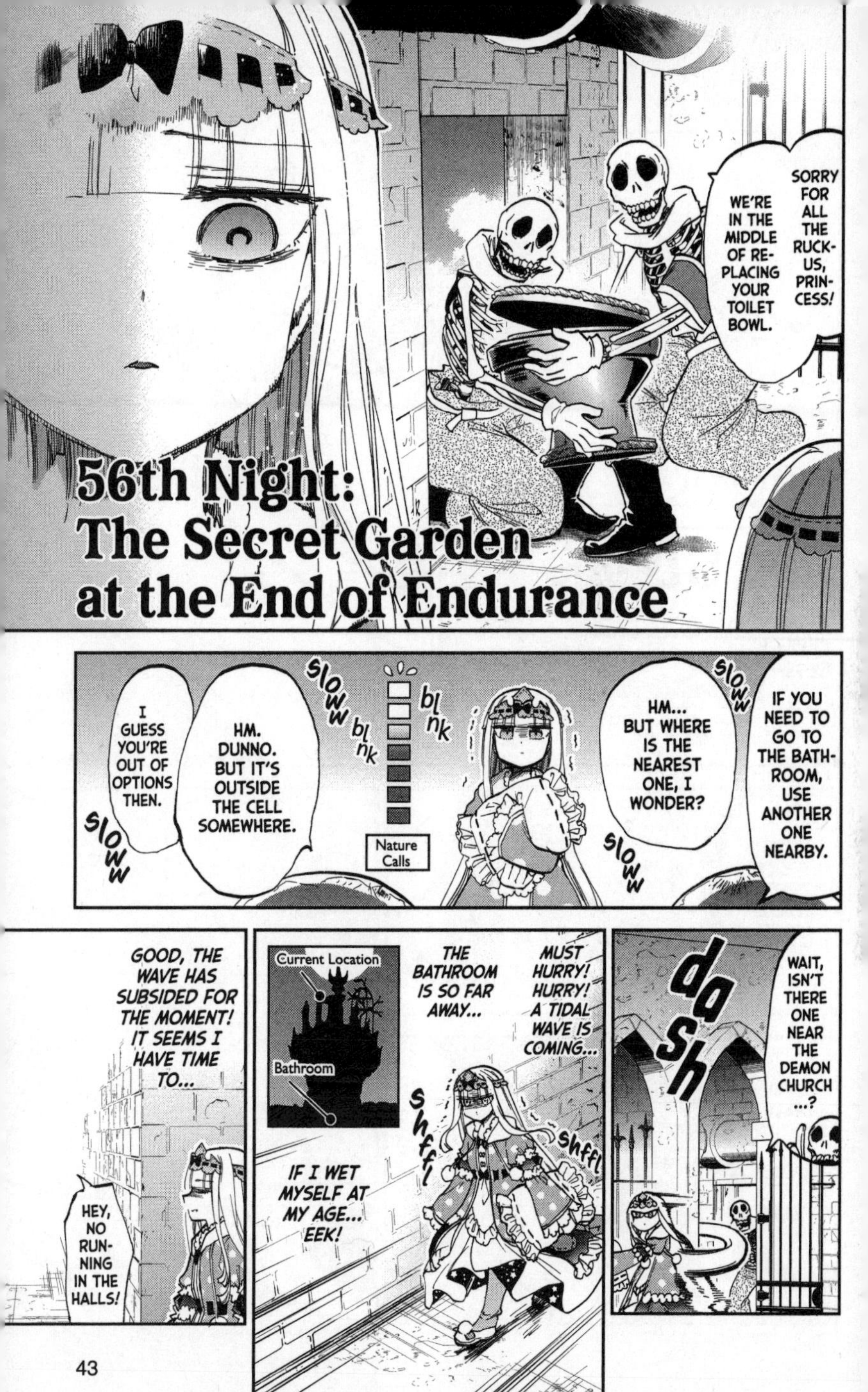
SORRY FOR ALL THE RUCKUS, PRINCESS!
WE'RE IN THE MIDDLE OF REPLACING YOUR TOILET BOWL.
56th Night: The Secret Garden at the End of Endurance
IF YOU NEED TO GO TO THE BATHROOM, USE ANOTHER ONE NEARBY.
slow
HM... BUT WHERE IS THE NEAREST ONE, I WONDER?
slow
blnk
blnk
Nature Calls
slow
HM. DUNNO. BUT IT'S OUTSIDE THE CELL SOMEWHERE.
I GUESS YOU'RE OUT OF OPTIONS THEN.
slow
WAIT, ISN'T THERE ONE NEAR THE DEMON CHURCH ...?
dash
MUST HURRY! HURRY! A TIDAL WAVE IS COMING...
THE BATHROOM IS SO FAR AWAY...
Current Location
Bathroom
shffl
shffl
IF I WET MYSELF AT MY AGE... EEK!
GOOD, THE WAVE HAS SUBSIDED FOR THE MOMENT! IT SEEMS I HAVE TIME TO...
HEY, NO RUNNING IN THE HALLS!

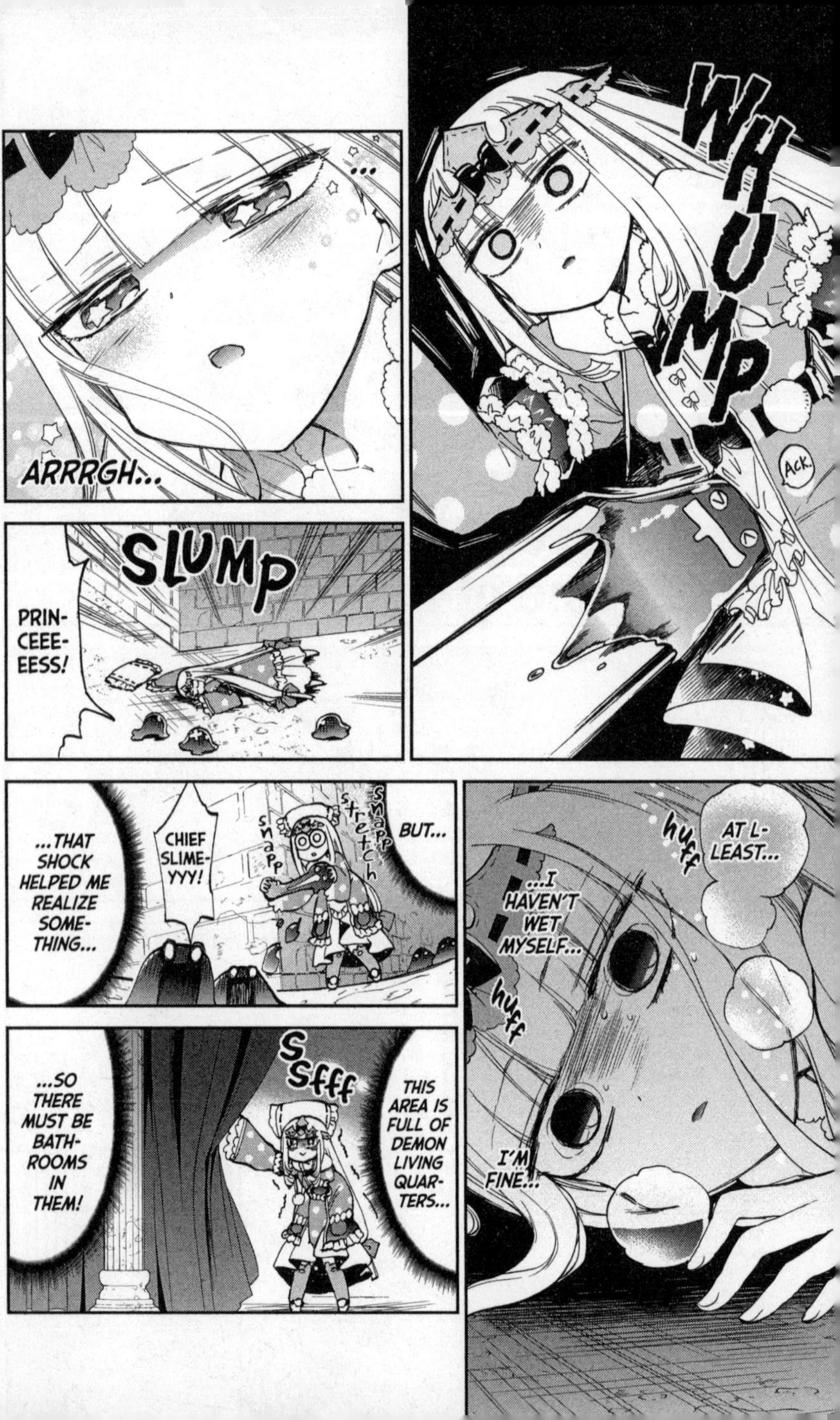
WHUMP
Ack.
...
ARRRGH...
SLUMP
PRIN-CEEE-EESS!
huff
AT L-LEAST...
...I HAVEN'T WET MYSELF...
huff
I'M FINE...
BUT...
snapp
stretch
snapp
CHIEF SLIME-YYY!
...THAT SHOCK HELPED ME REALIZE SOME-THING...
Ssfff
THIS AREA IS FULL OF DEMON LIVING QUAR-TERS...
...SO THERE MUST BE BATH-ROOMS IN THEM!

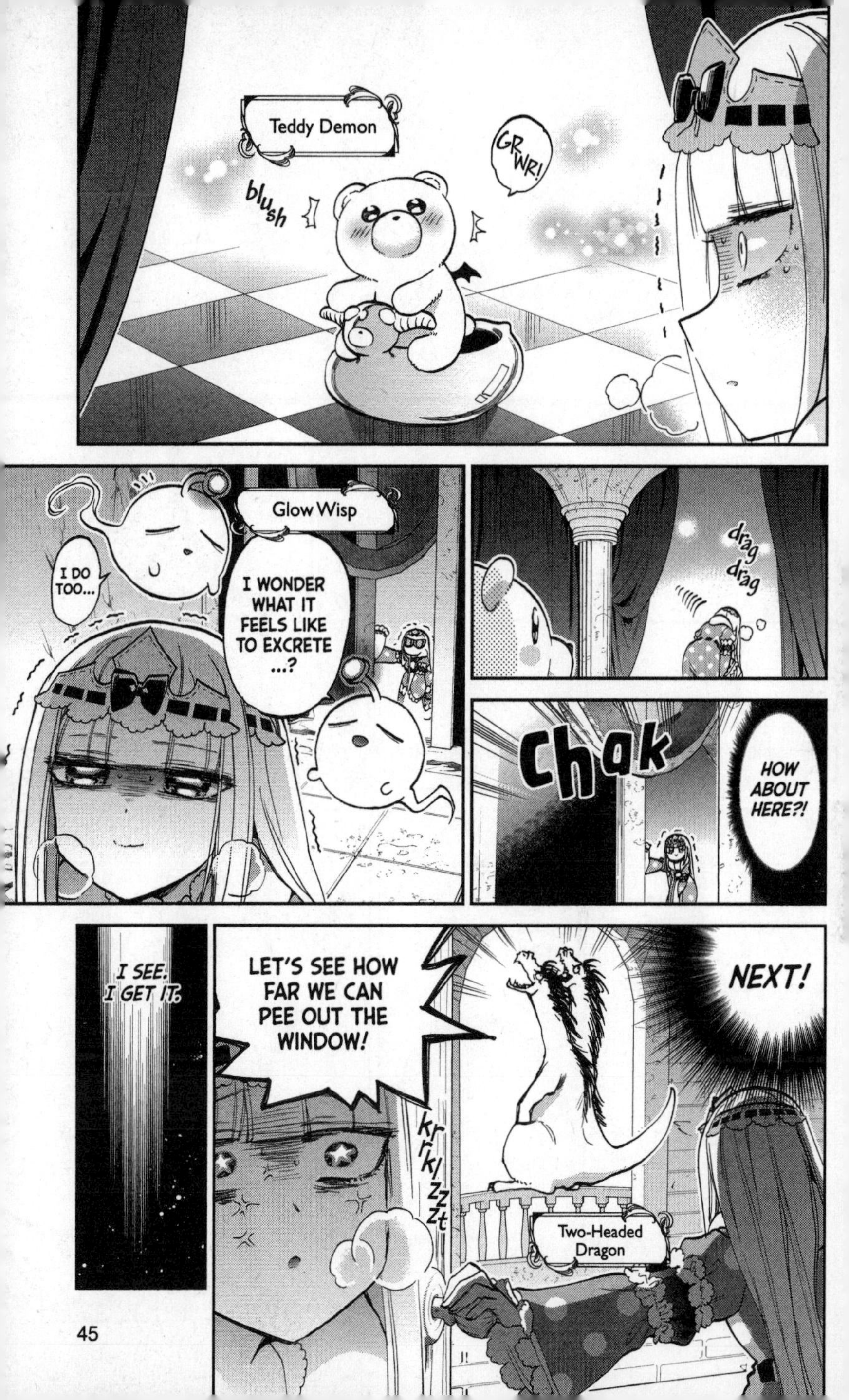

Teddy Demon
GRWR!
blush
drag drag
Chak
HOW ABOUT HERE?!
Glow Wisp
I WONDER WHAT IT FEELS LIKE TO EXCRETE ...?
I DO TOO...
NEXT!
Two-Headed Dragon
LET'S SEE HOW FAR WE CAN PEE OUT THE WINDOW!
krrklzzzt
I SEE. I GET IT.

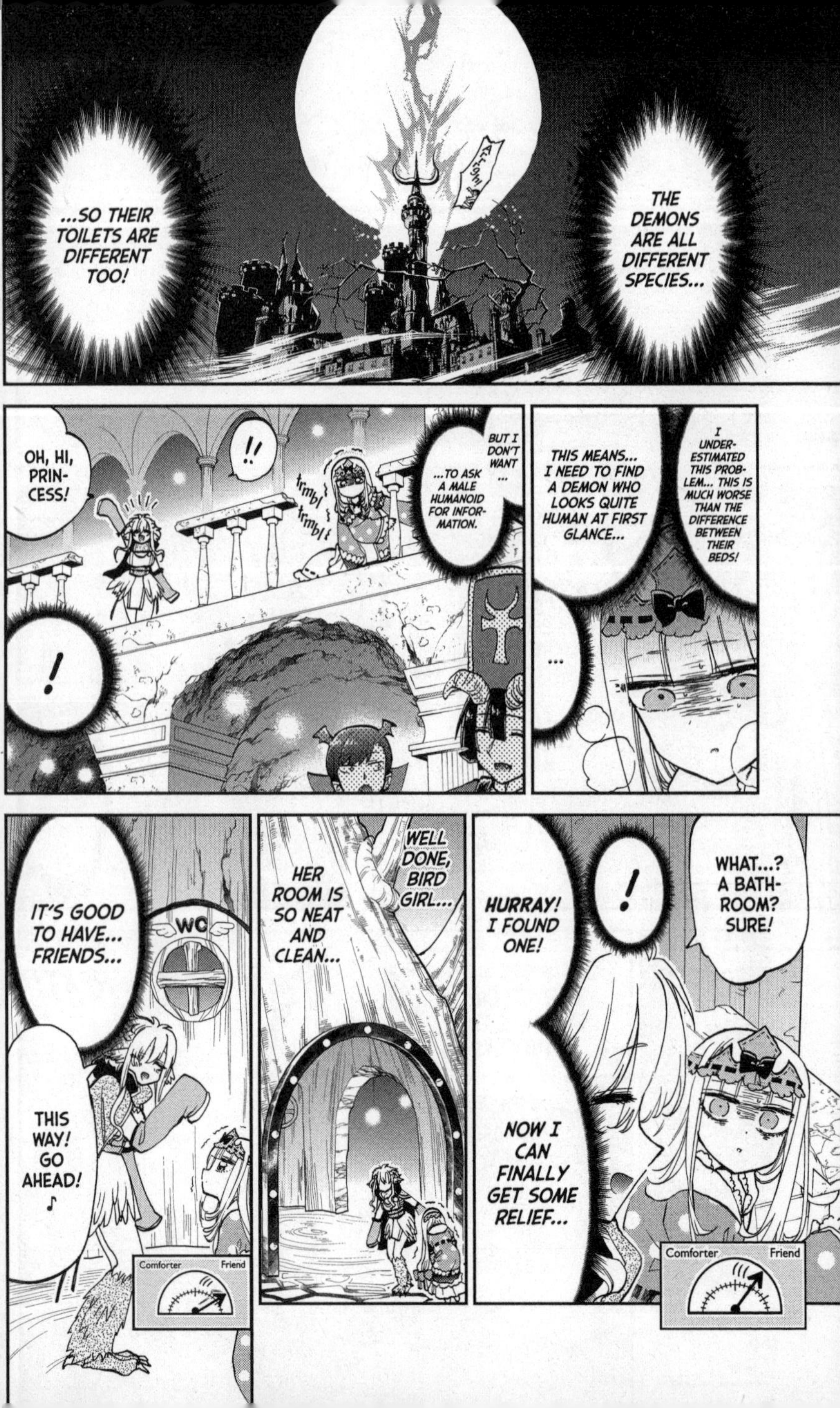
THE DEMONS ARE ALL DIFFERENT SPECIES...
...SO THEIR TOILETS ARE DIFFERENT TOO!
I UNDERESTIMATED THIS PROBLEM... THIS IS MUCH WORSE THAN THE DIFFERENCE BETWEEN THEIR BEDS!
THIS MEANS... I NEED TO FIND A DEMON WHO LOOKS QUITE HUMAN AT FIRST GLANCE...
...
BUT I DON'T WANT...
...TO ASK A MALE HUMANOID FOR INFORMATION.
!!
trmbl trmbl
OH, HI, PRINCESS!
!
WHAT...? A BATHROOM? SURE!
!
HURRAY! I FOUND ONE!
NOW I CAN FINALLY GET SOME RELIEF...
Comforter
Friend
WELL DONE, BIRD GIRL...
HER ROOM IS SO NEAT AND CLEAN...
IT'S GOOD TO HAVE... FRIENDS...
WC
THIS WAY! GO AHEAD! ♪
Comforter
Friend

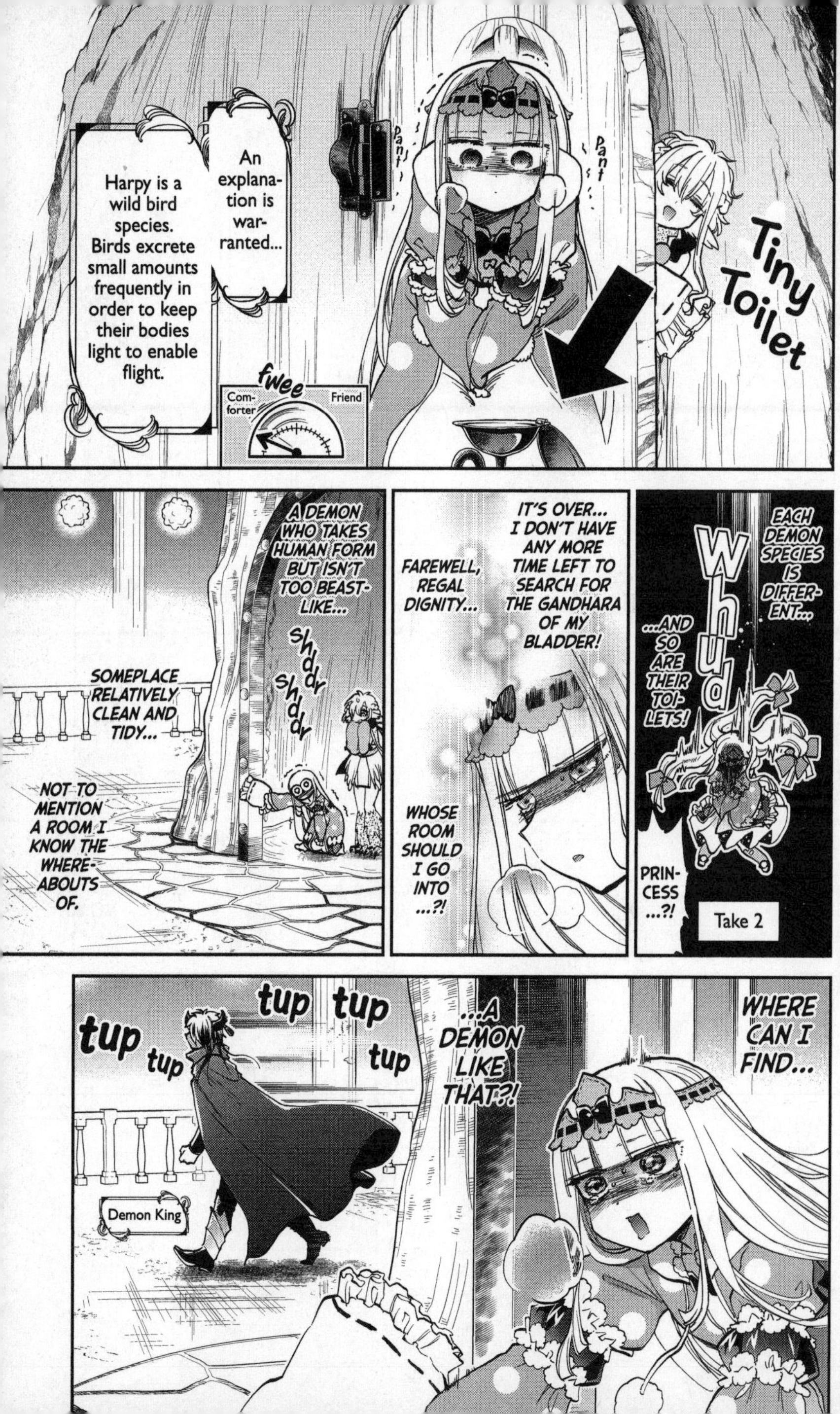
Tiny Toilet
Pant
Pant
An explanation is warranted...
Harpy is a wild bird species. Birds excrete small amounts frequently in order to keep their bodies light to enable flight.
fwee
Com-forter
Friend
EACH DEMON SPECIES IS DIFFERENT...
...AND SO ARE THEIR TOILETS!
Whud
PRINCESS...?!
Take 2
IT'S OVER... I DON'T HAVE ANY MORE TIME LEFT TO SEARCH FOR THE GANDHARA OF MY BLADDER!
FAREWELL, REGAL DIGNITY...
WHOSE ROOM SHOULD I GO INTO...?!
A DEMON WHO TAKES HUMAN FORM BUT ISN'T TOO BEAST-LIKE...
shddr shddr
SOMEPLACE RELATIVELY CLEAN AND TIDY...
NOT TO MENTION A ROOM I KNOW THE WHEREABOUTS OF.
WHERE CAN I FIND...
...A DEMON LIKE THAT?!
tup tup
tup
tup tup
Demon King

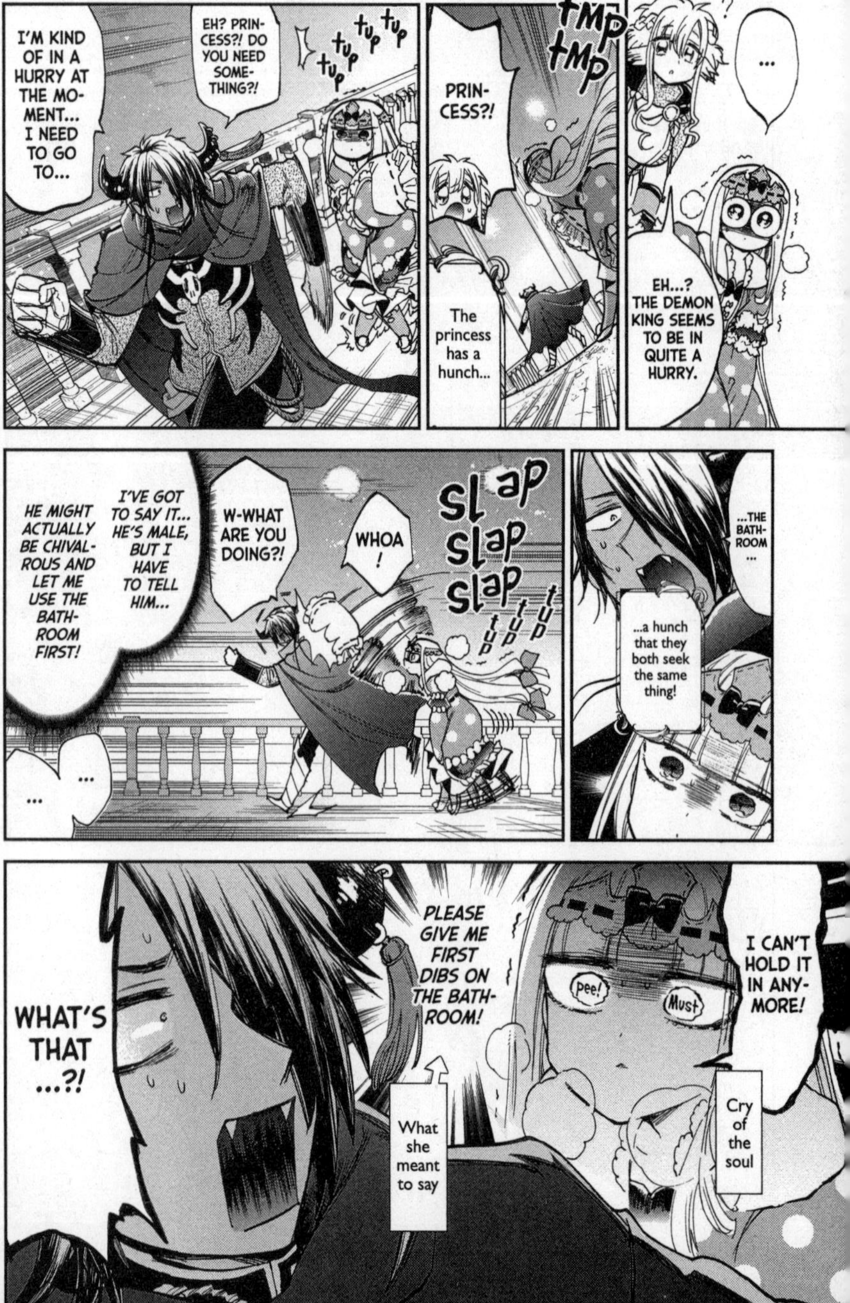
?
...
EH...? THE DEMON KING SEEMS TO BE IN QUITE A HURRY.
TMP TMP
PRINCESS?!
The princess has a hunch...
EH? PRINCESS?! DO YOU NEED SOMETHING?!
tup tup tup tup
I'M KIND OF IN A HURRY AT THE MOMENT... I NEED TO GO TO...
...THE BATHROOM...
...a hunch that they both seek the same thing!
SLAP SLAP SLAP
tup tup tup
WHOA!
W-WHAT ARE YOU DOING?!
I'VE GOT TO SAY IT... HE'S MALE, BUT I HAVE TO TELL HIM...
HE MIGHT ACTUALLY BE CHIVALROUS AND LET ME USE THE BATHROOM FIRST!
... ...
I CAN'T HOLD IT IN ANYMORE!
Cry of the soul
Must pee!
PLEASE GIVE ME FIRST DIBS ON THE BATHROOM!
What she meant to say
WHAT'S THAT...?!

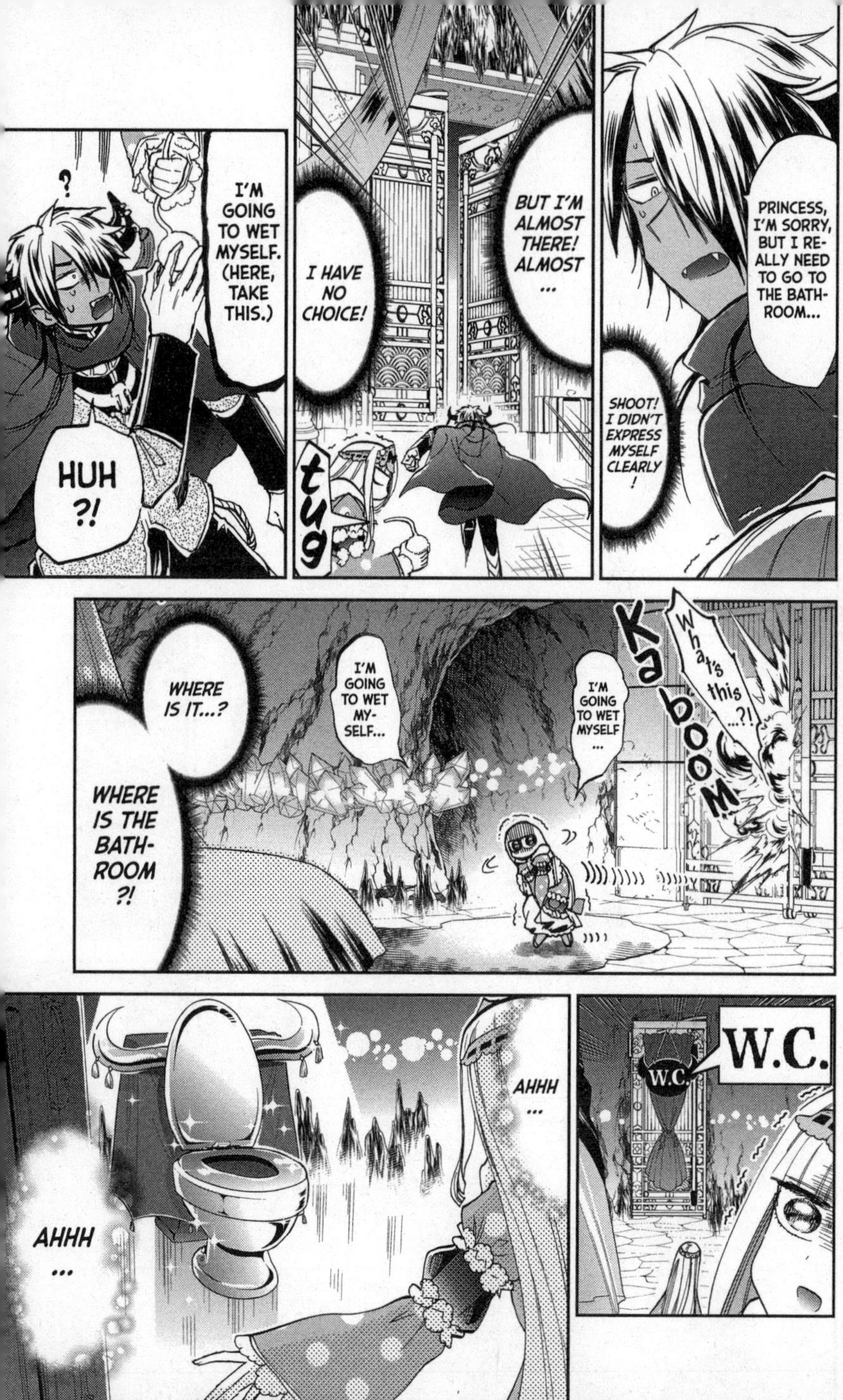
PRINCESS, I'M SORRY, BUT I REALLY NEED TO GO TO THE BATHROOM...
SHOOT! I DIDN'T EXPRESS MYSELF CLEARLY!
BUT I'M ALMOST THERE! ALMOST...
I HAVE NO CHOICE!
tug
I'M GOING TO WET MYSELF. (HERE, TAKE THIS.)
?
HUH?!
Kaboom
What's this...?!
I'M GOING TO WET MYSELF...
I'M GOING TO WET MYSELF...
WHERE IS IT...?
WHERE IS THE BATHROOM?!
W.C.
W.C.
AHHH...
AHHH...

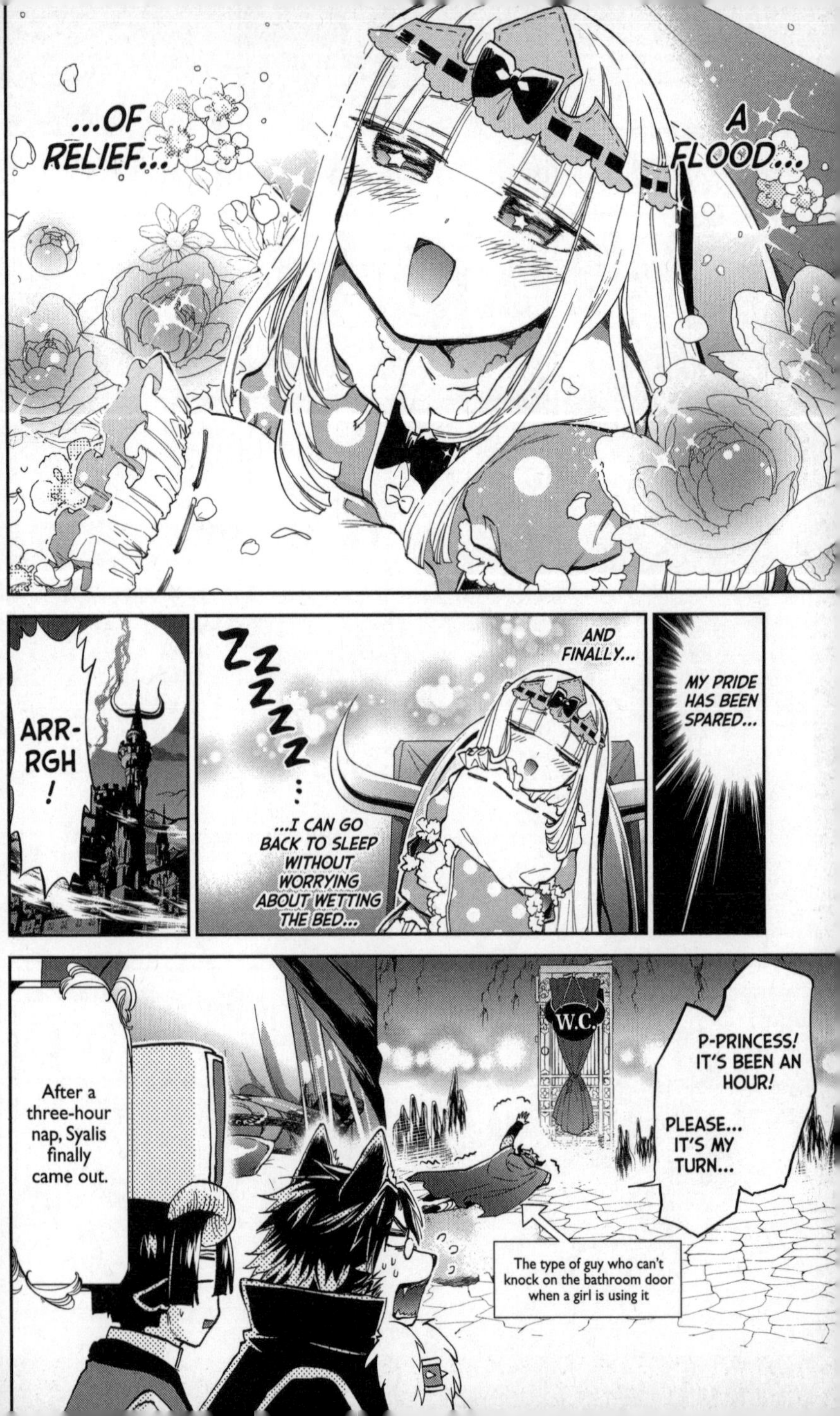
A FLOOD...
...OF RELIEF...
MY PRIDE HAS BEEN SPARED...
AND FINALLY...
ZZZZZ...
...I CAN GO BACK TO SLEEP WITHOUT WORRYING ABOUT WETTING THE BED...
ARR-RGH!
P-PRINCESS! IT'S BEEN AN HOUR!
PLEASE... IT'S MY TURN...
W.C.
The type of guy who can't knock on the bathroom door when a girl is using it
After a three-hour nap, Syalis finally came out.

Demon Castle Renovation Unit

Work Efficiency: ☆☆☆☆
End Results: ☆☆☆☆☆☆☆☆☆☆☆

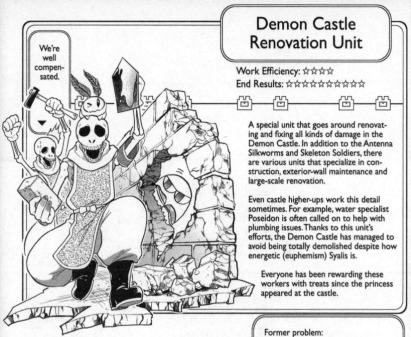

We're well compensated.

A special unit that goes around renovating and fixing all kinds of damage in the Demon Castle. In addition to the Antenna Silkworms and Skeleton Soldiers, there are various units that specialize in construction, exterior-wall maintenance and large-scale renovation.

Even castle higher-ups work this detail sometimes. For example, water specialist Poseidon is often called on to help with plumbing issues. Thanks to this unit's efforts, the Demon Castle has managed to avoid being totally demolished despite how energetic (euphemism) Syalis is.

Everyone has been rewarding these workers with treats since the princess appeared at the castle.

Former problem:
"We'd like to go and renovate the Old Demon Castle too, but we're afraid we'll get reprimanded!"

Current problem:
"What? The princess did it **again**?!"

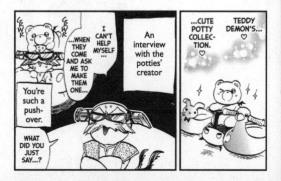

TEDDY DEMON'S... ♡
...CUTE POTTY COLLECTION. ♡
An interview with the potties' creator
I CAN'T HELP MYSELF...
...WHEN THEY COME AND ASK ME TO MAKE THEM ONE...
GRWR
GRWR
You're such a push-over.
WHAT DID YOU JUST SAY...?

Would you like to change your class?

8 changes remaining

▶Yes

No ▼

Teacher

"I can only draw red circles with this."

▼

57th Night: No One Did Anything Wrong ♡

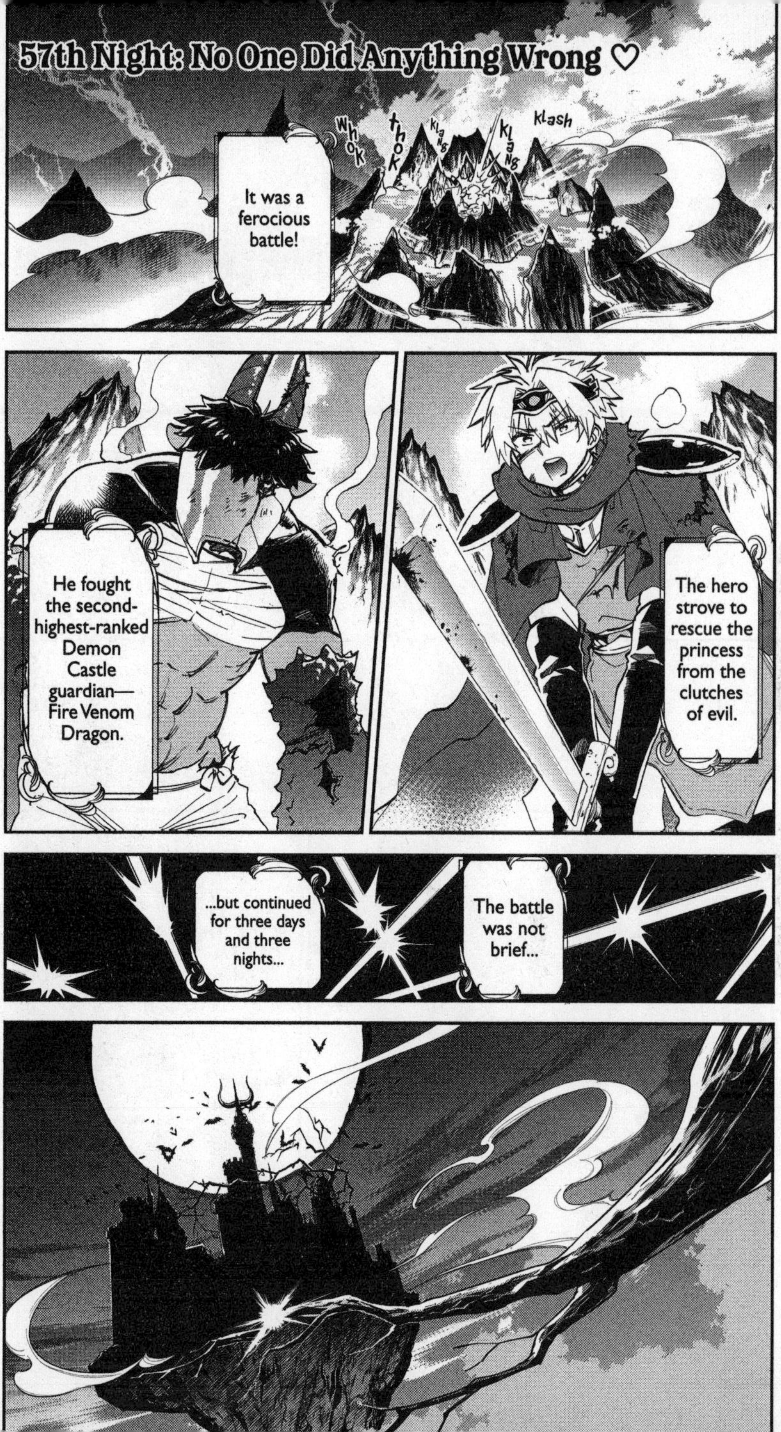
klash
klang
klang
thok
whok
It was a ferocious battle!
The hero strove to rescue the princess from the clutches of evil.
He fought the second-highest-ranked Demon Castle guardian—Fire Venom Dragon.
The battle was not brief...
...but continued for three days and three nights...

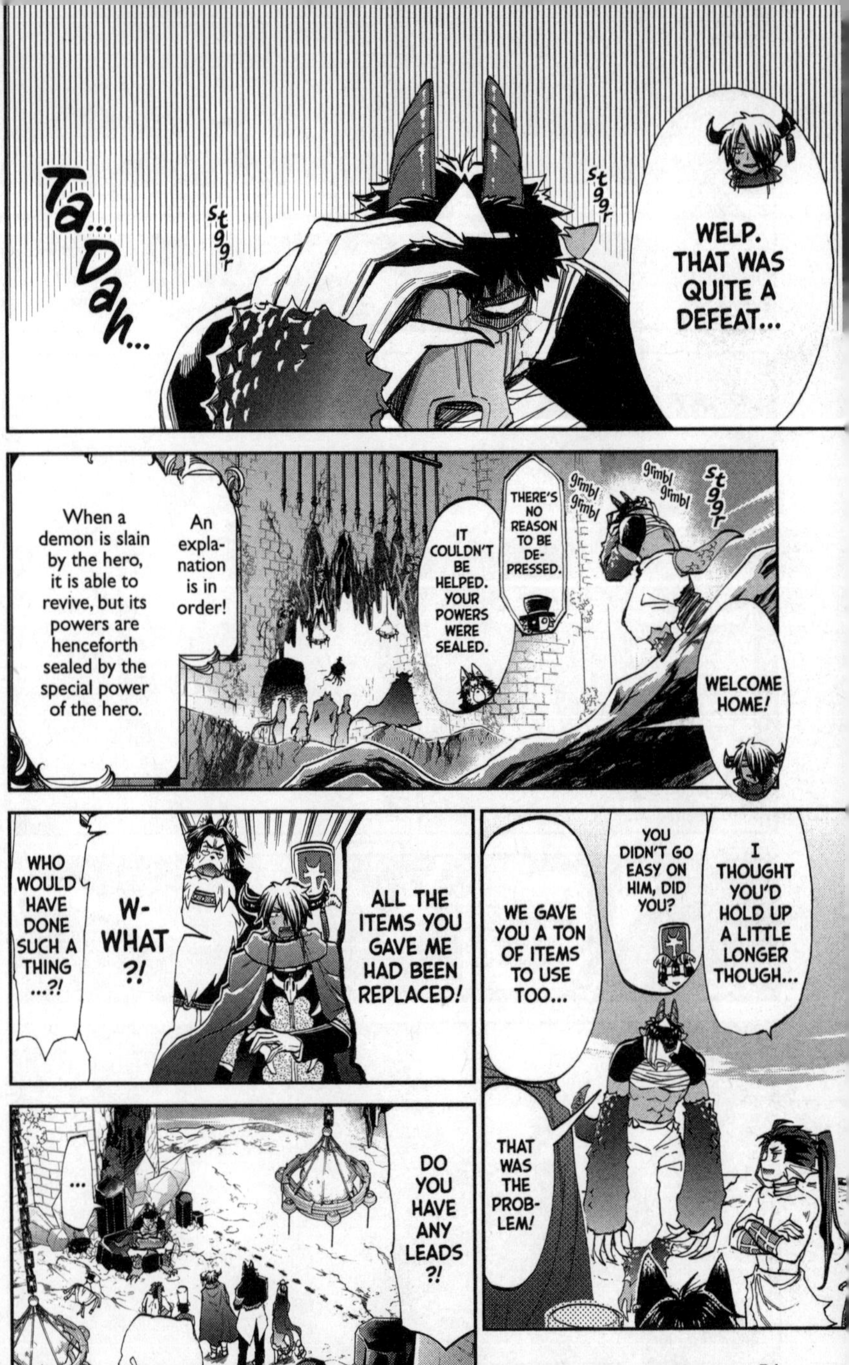
WELP. THAT WAS QUITE A DEFEAT...
stggr
stggr
Ta... Dah...
stggr
grmbl grmbl
grmbl grmbl
WELCOME HOME!
THERE'S NO REASON TO BE DE-PRESSED.
IT COULDN'T BE HELPED. YOUR POWERS WERE SEALED.
An expla-nation is in order!
When a demon is slain by the hero, it is able to revive, but its powers are henceforth sealed by the special power of the hero.
I THOUGHT YOU'D HOLD UP A LITTLE LONGER THOUGH...
YOU DIDN'T GO EASY ON HIM, DID YOU?
WE GAVE YOU A TON OF ITEMS TO USE TOO...
THAT WAS THE PROB-LEM!
ALL THE ITEMS YOU GAVE ME HAD BEEN REPLACED!
W-WHAT?!
WHO WOULD HAVE DONE SUCH A THING...?!
DO YOU HAVE ANY LEADS?!
...

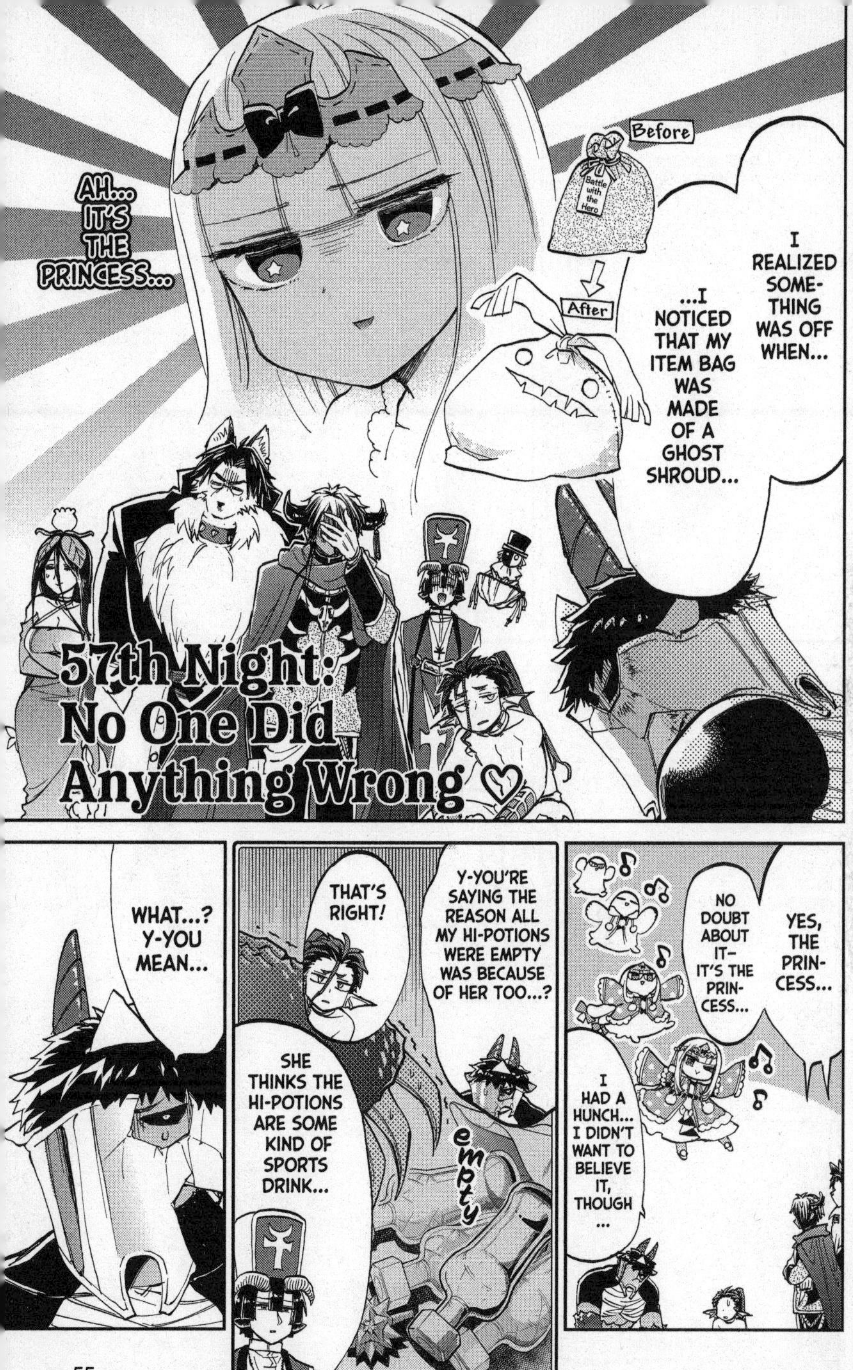
I REALIZED SOMETHING WAS OFF WHEN...
...I NOTICED THAT MY ITEM BAG WAS MADE OF A GHOST SHROUD...
Before
Battle with the Hero
After
AH... IT'S THE PRINCESS...
57th Night: No One Did Anything Wrong ♡
YES, THE PRINCESS...
NO DOUBT ABOUT IT— IT'S THE PRINCESS...
I HAD A HUNCH... I DIDN'T WANT TO BELIEVE IT, THOUGH...
Y-YOU'RE SAYING THE REASON ALL MY HI-POTIONS WERE EMPTY WAS BECAUSE OF HER TOO...?
THAT'S RIGHT!
SHE THINKS THE HI-POTIONS ARE SOME KIND OF SPORTS DRINK...
empty
WHAT...? Y-YOU MEAN...

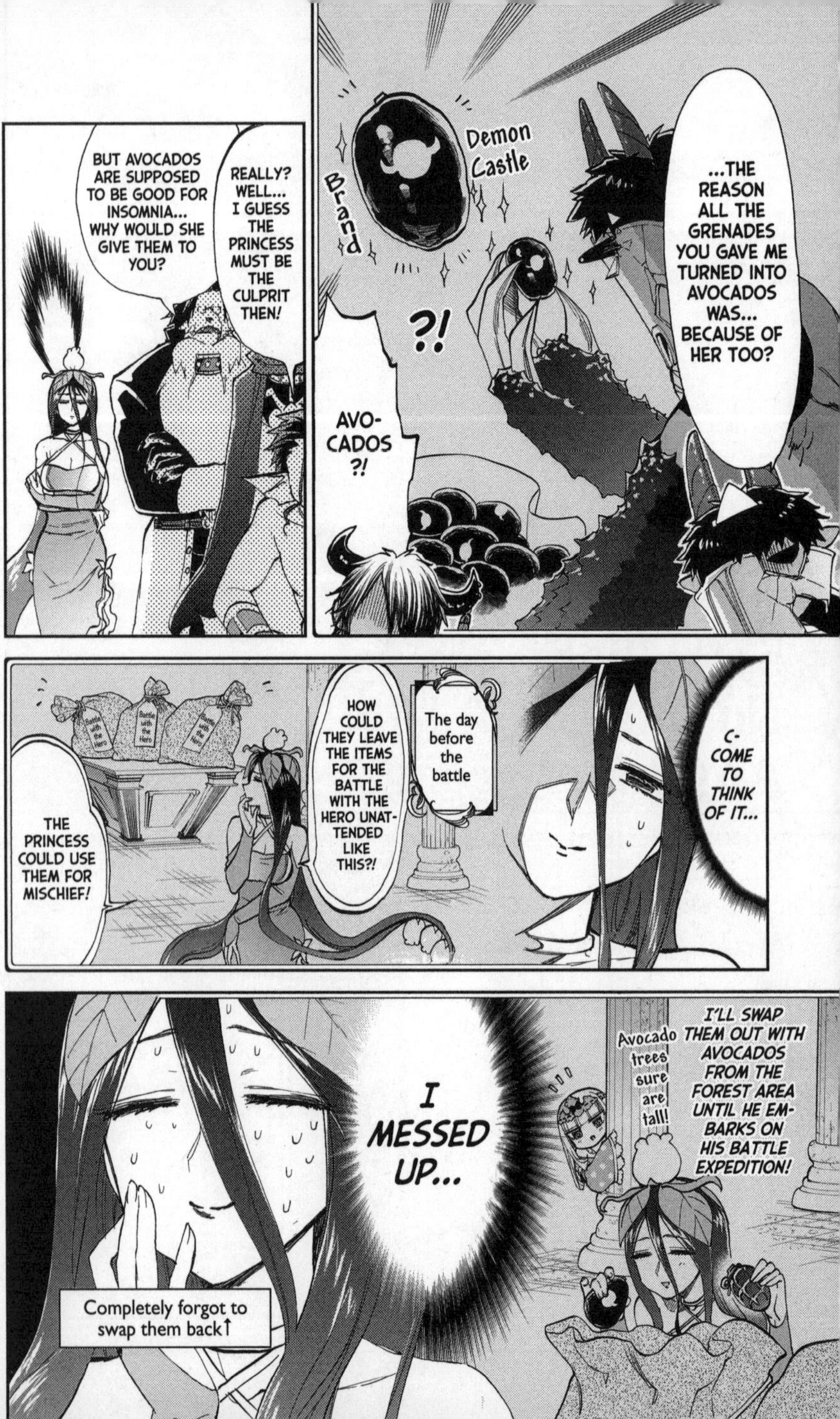
...THE REASON ALL THE GRENADES YOU GAVE ME TURNED INTO AVOCADOS WAS... BECAUSE OF HER TOO?
Demon Castle
Brand
?!
AVOCADOS?!
REALLY? WELL... I GUESS THE PRINCESS MUST BE THE CULPRIT THEN!
BUT AVOCADOS ARE SUPPOSED TO BE GOOD FOR INSOMNIA... WHY WOULD SHE GIVE THEM TO YOU?
C-COME TO THINK OF IT...
The day before the battle
HOW COULD THEY LEAVE THE ITEMS FOR THE BATTLE WITH THE HERO UNATTENDED LIKE THIS?!
Battle with the Hero
Battle with the Hero
Battle with the Hero
THE PRINCESS COULD USE THEM FOR MISCHIEF!
I'LL SWAP THEM OUT WITH AVOCADOS FROM THE FOREST AREA UNTIL HE EMBARKS ON HIS BATTLE EXPEDITION!
Avocado trees sure are tall!
I MESSED UP...
Completely forgot to swap them back↑

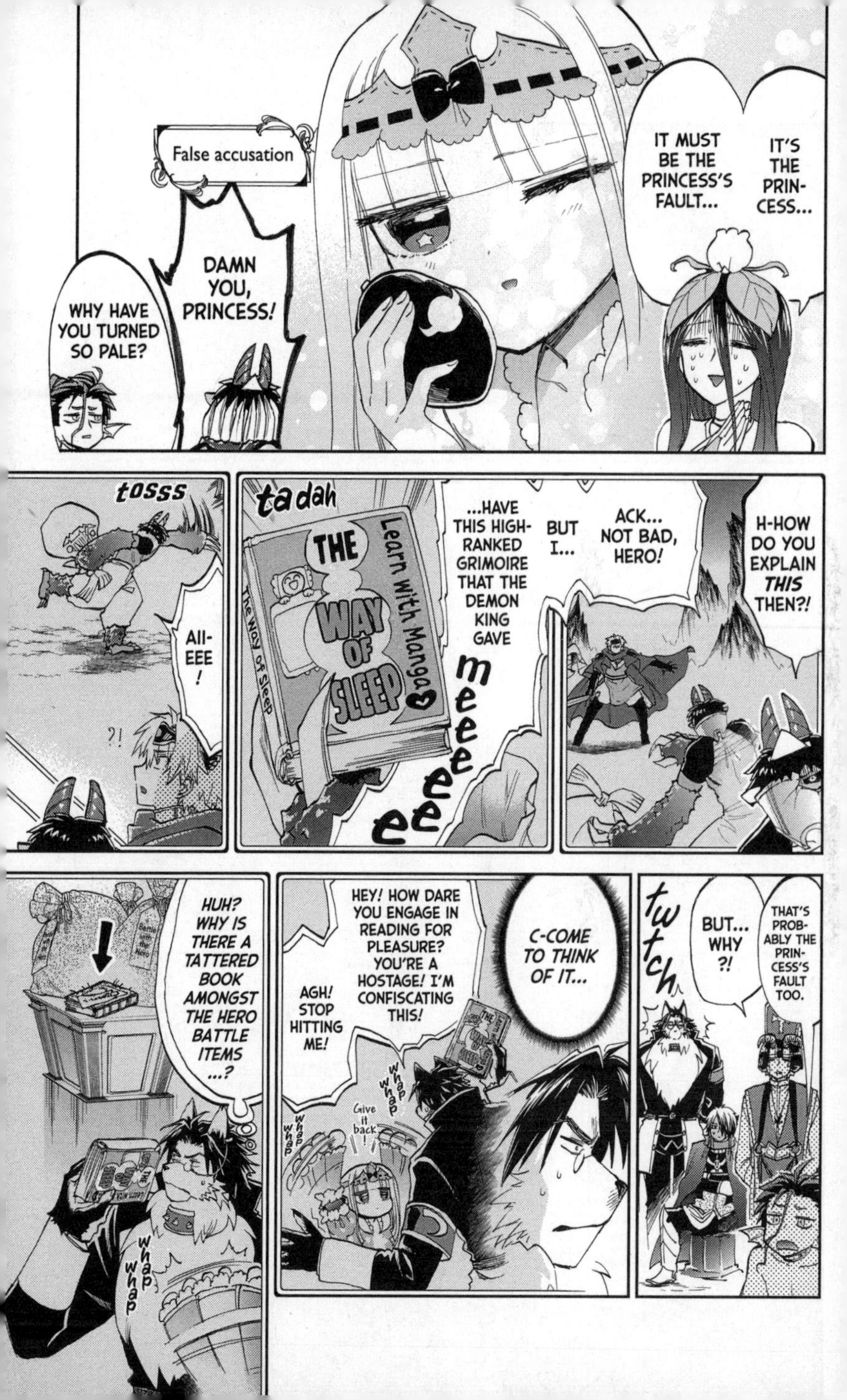
IT'S THE PRINCESS...
IT MUST BE THE PRINCESS'S FAULT...
False accusation
DAMN YOU, PRINCESS!
WHY HAVE YOU TURNED SO PALE?
H-HOW DO YOU EXPLAIN THIS THEN?!
ACK... NOT BAD, HERO!
BUT I...
...HAVE THIS HIGH-RANKED GRIMOIRE THAT THE DEMON KING GAVE
ta dah
THE WAY OF SLEEP
Learn With Manga
The Way of Sleep
meeeeeeee
tosss
AII-EEE!
?!
twtch
THAT'S PROBABLY THE PRINCESS'S FAULT TOO.
BUT... WHY?!
C-COME TO THINK OF IT...
HEY! HOW DARE YOU ENGAGE IN READING FOR PLEASURE? YOU'RE A HOSTAGE! I'M CONFISCATING THIS!
AGH! STOP HITTING ME!
whap whap
Give it back!
whap whap
Battle with the Hero
HUH? WHY IS THERE A TATTERED BOOK AMONGST THE HERO BATTLE ITEMS...?
whap whap

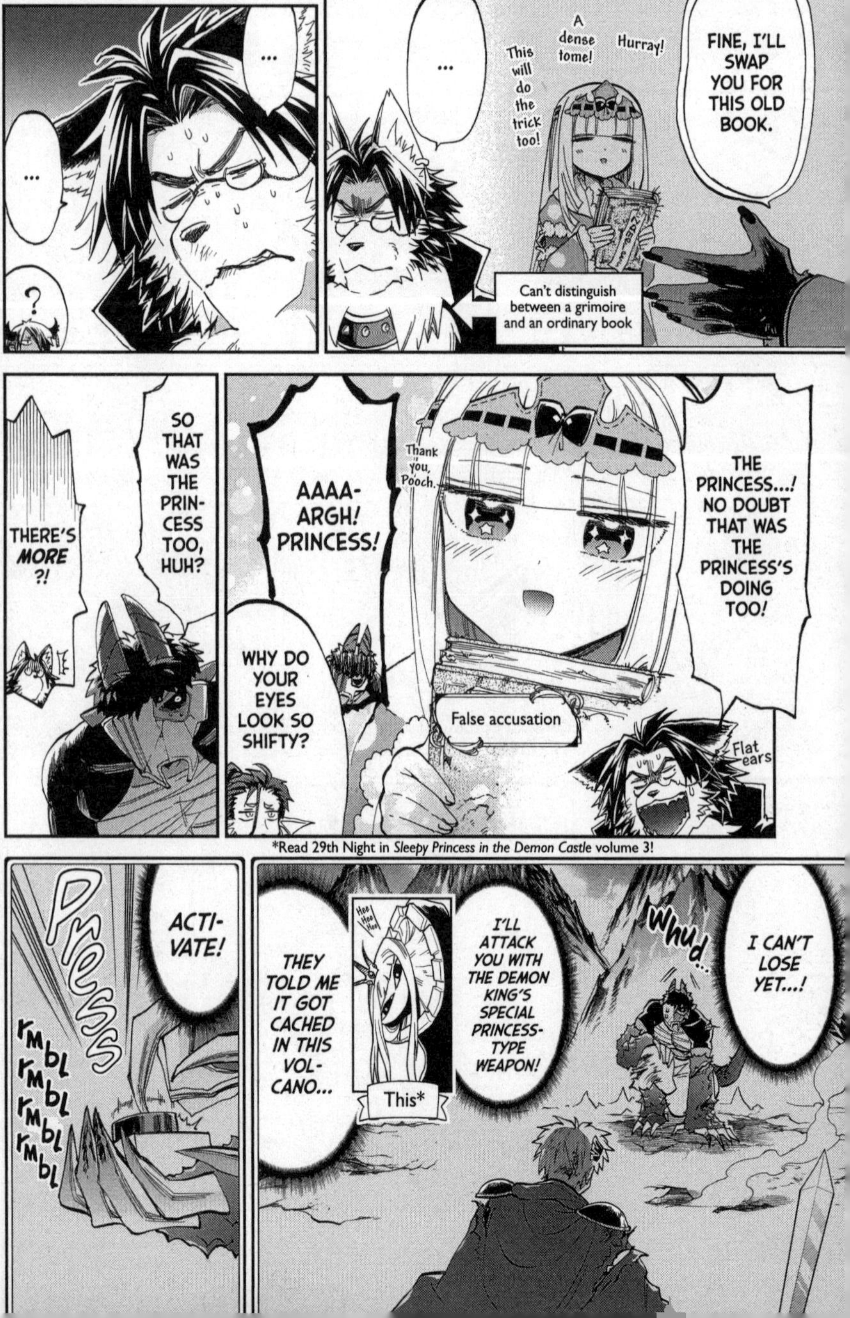
FINE, I'LL SWAP YOU FOR THIS OLD BOOK.
Hurray!
A dense tome!
This will do the trick too!
...
Can't distinguish between a grimoire and an ordinary book
...
...
?
THE PRINCESS...! NO DOUBT THAT WAS THE PRINCESS'S DOING TOO!
Thank you, Pooch.
AAAA-ARGH! PRINCESS!
WHY DO YOUR EYES LOOK SO SHIFTY?
False accusation
Flat ears
SO THAT WAS THE PRINCESS TOO, HUH?
THERE'S *MORE* ?!
I CAN'T LOSE YET...!
whud...
I'LL ATTACK YOU WITH THE DEMON KING'S SPECIAL PRINCESS-TYPE WEAPON!
Hee Hee Hee
THEY TOLD ME IT GOT CACHED IN THIS VOLCANO...
This*
ACTI-VATE!
Press
rmbl rmbl rmbl rmbl

*Read 29th Night in *Sleepy Princess in the Demon Castle* volume 3!

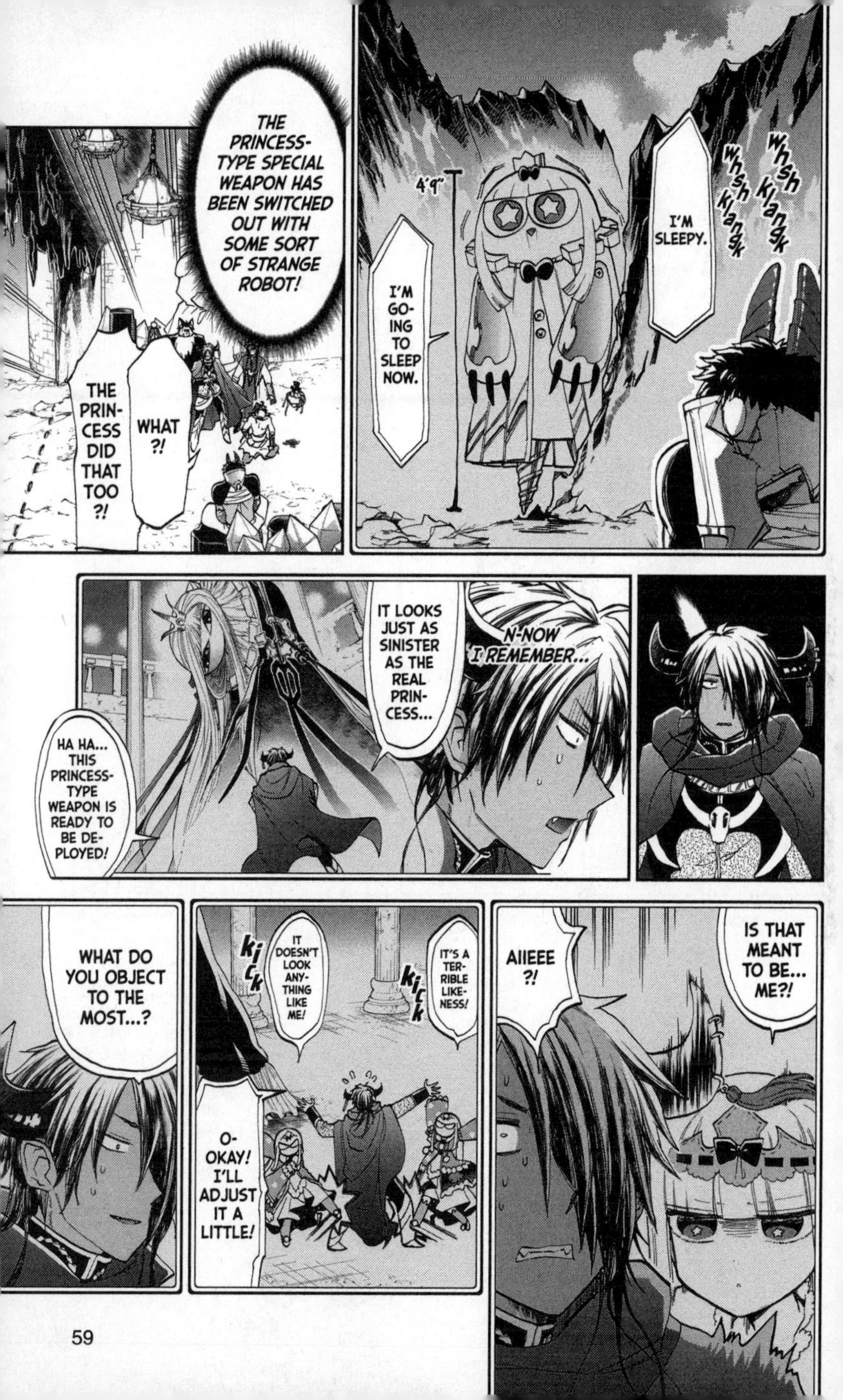
whsh klangk
whsh klangk
I'M SLEEPY.
4'9"
I'M GOING TO SLEEP NOW.
THE PRINCESS-TYPE SPECIAL WEAPON HAS BEEN SWITCHED OUT WITH SOME SORT OF STRANGE ROBOT!
WHAT ?!
THE PRINCESS DID THAT TOO ?!
N-NOW I REMEMBER...
IT LOOKS JUST AS SINISTER AS THE REAL PRINCESS...
HA HA... THIS PRINCESS-TYPE WEAPON IS READY TO BE DEPLOYED!
IS THAT MEANT TO BE... ME?!
AIIEEE ?!
IT'S A TERRIBLE LIKENESS!
kick
IT DOESN'T LOOK ANYTHING LIKE ME!
kick
O-OKAY! I'LL ADJUST IT A LITTLE!
WHAT DO YOU OBJECT TO THE MOST...?

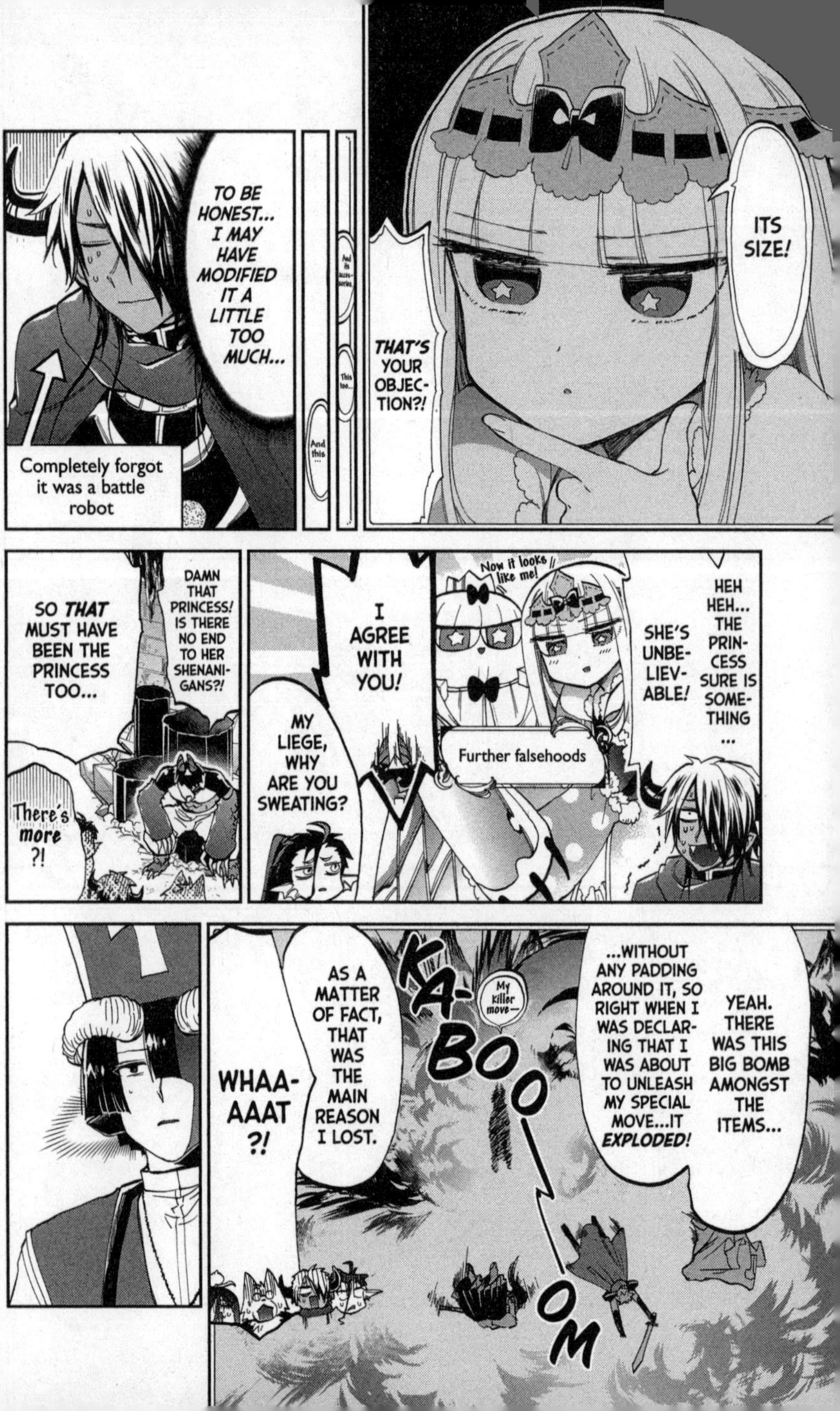
ITS SIZE!
THAT'S YOUR OBJECTION?!
And its accessories.
This too...
And this...
TO BE HONEST... I MAY HAVE MODIFIED IT A LITTLE TOO MUCH...
Completely forgot it was a battle robot
HEH HEH... THE PRINCESS SURE IS SOMETHING...
SHE'S UNBELIEVABLE!
Now it looks like me!
I AGREE WITH YOU!
Further falsehoods
MY LIEGE, WHY ARE YOU SWEATING?
DAMN THAT PRINCESS! IS THERE NO END TO HER SHENANIGANS?!
SO THAT MUST HAVE BEEN THE PRINCESS TOO...
There's more?!
YEAH. THERE WAS THIS BIG BOMB AMONGST THE ITEMS...
...WITHOUT ANY PADDING AROUND IT, SO RIGHT WHEN I WAS DECLARING THAT I WAS ABOUT TO UNLEASH MY SPECIAL MOVE...IT EXPLODED!
My killer move—
KA-BOOO—OM
AS A MATTER OF FACT, THAT WAS THE MAIN REASON I LOST.
WHAAAAAT?!

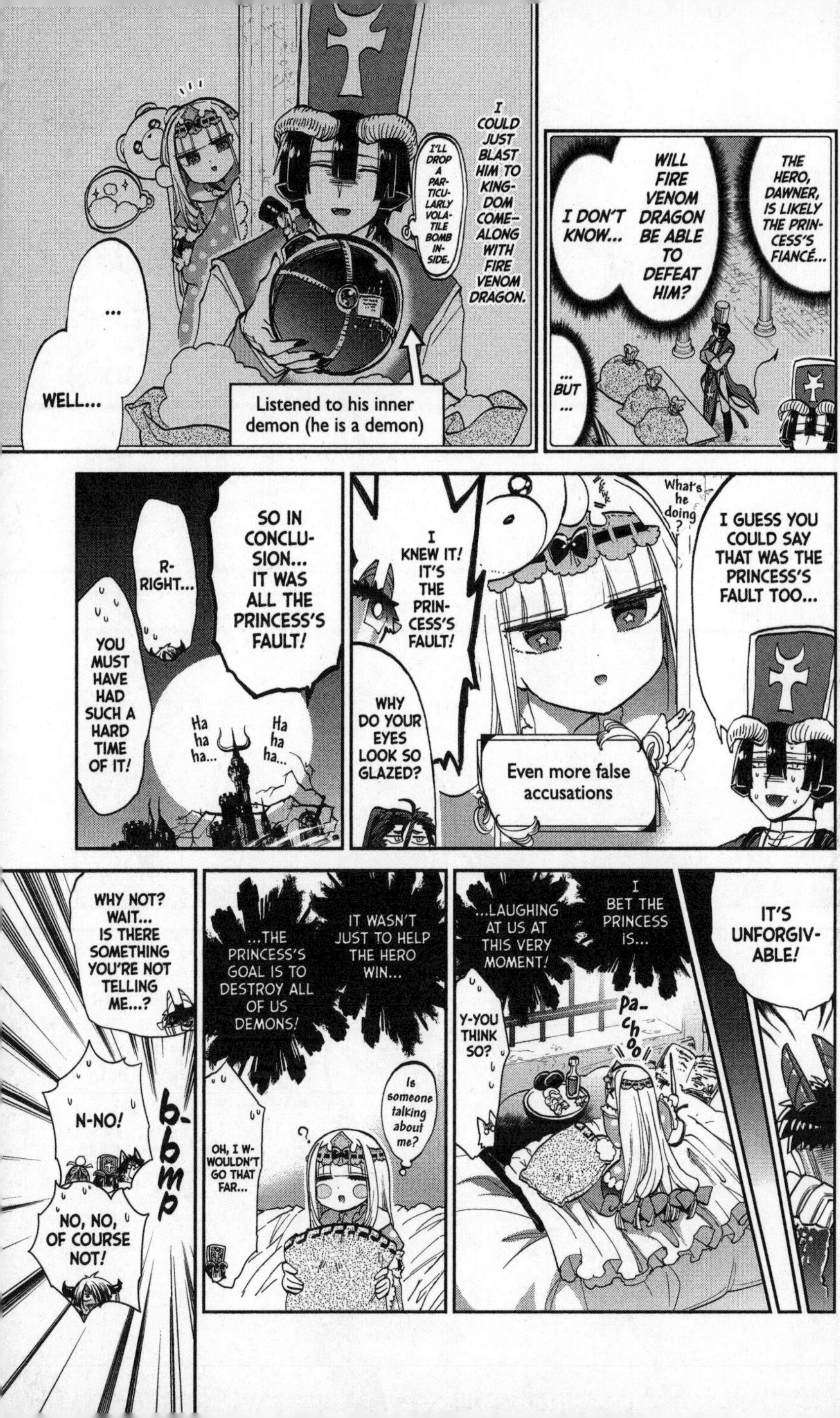
THE HERO, DAWNER, IS LIKELY THE PRINCESS'S FIANCÉ...
WILL FIRE VENOM DRAGON BE ABLE TO DEFEAT HIM?
I DON'T KNOW...
...BUT ...
I COULD JUST BLAST HIM TO KINGDOM COME—ALONG WITH FIRE VENOM DRAGON.
I'LL DROP A PARTICULARLY VOLATILE BOMB INSIDE.
...
WELL...
Listened to his inner demon (he is a demon)
I GUESS YOU COULD SAY THAT WAS THE PRINCESS'S FAULT TOO...
What's he doing?
Even more false accusations
I KNEW IT! IT'S THE PRINCESS'S FAULT!
WHY DO YOUR EYES LOOK SO GLAZED?
SO IN CONCLUSION... IT WAS ALL THE PRINCESS'S FAULT!
R-RIGHT...
YOU MUST HAVE HAD SUCH A HARD TIME OF IT!
Ha ha ha...
Ha ha ha...
IT'S UNFORGIVABLE!
I BET THE PRINCESS IS...
...LAUGHING AT US AT THIS VERY MOMENT!
Y-YOU THINK SO?
Pa-choo
IT WASN'T JUST TO HELP THE HERO WIN...
...THE PRINCESS'S GOAL IS TO DESTROY ALL OF US DEMONS!
Is someone talking about me?
OH, I W-WOULDN'T GO THAT FAR...
WHY NOT? WAIT... IS THERE SOMETHING YOU'RE NOT TELLING ME...?
N-NO!
b-bmp
NO, NO, OF COURSE NOT!

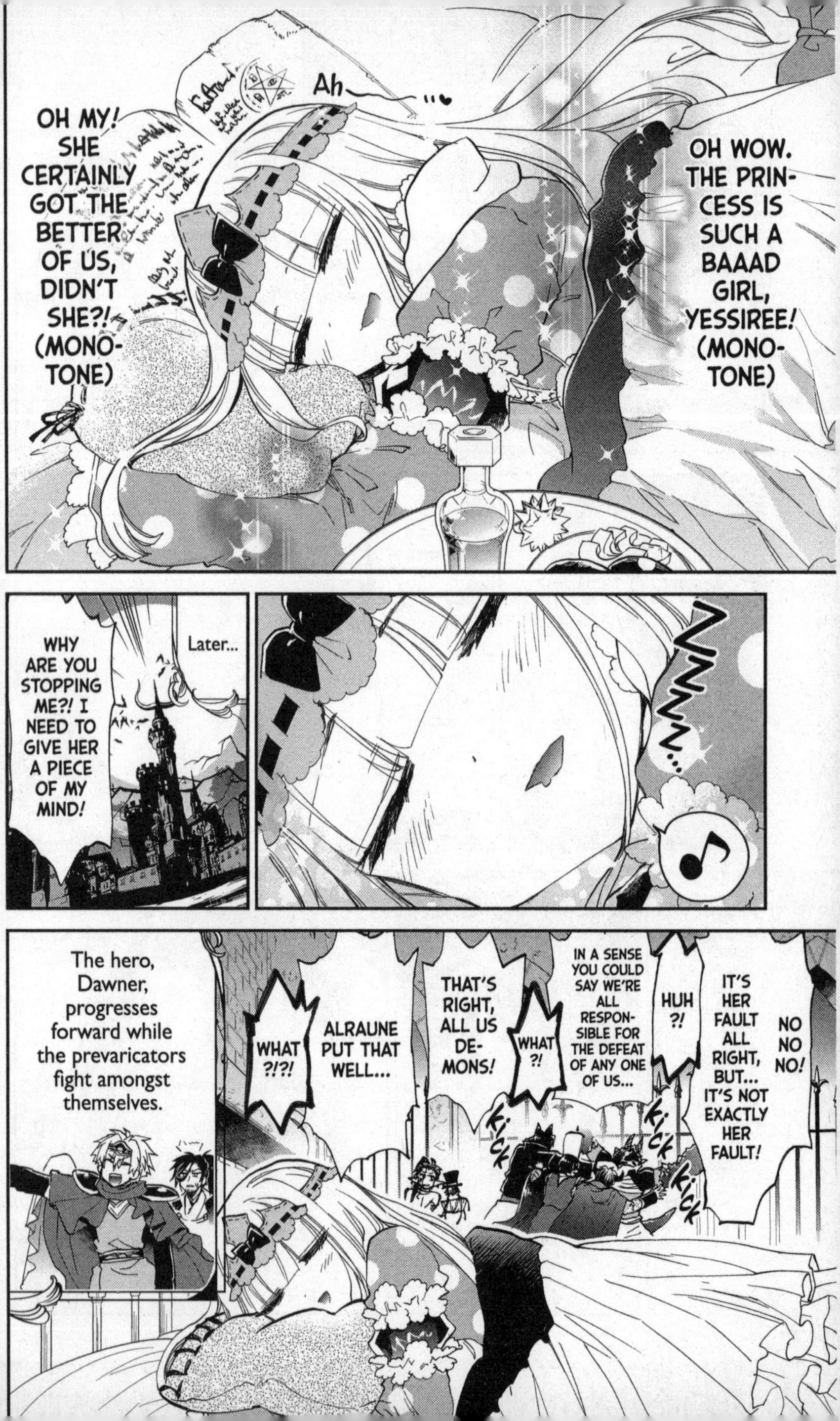
Ah~...♥
OH WOW. THE PRIN-CESS IS SUCH A BAAAD GIRL, YESSIREE! (MONO-TONE)
OH MY! SHE CERTAINLY GOT THE BETTER OF US, DIDN'T SHE?! (MONO-TONE)
ZZZZZ...
♪
Later...
WHY ARE YOU STOPPING ME?! I NEED TO GIVE HER A PIECE OF MY MIND!
NO NO NO!
IT'S HER FAULT ALL RIGHT, BUT... IT'S NOT EXACTLY HER FAULT!
HUH ?!
IN A SENSE YOU COULD SAY WE'RE ALL RESPON-SIBLE FOR THE DEFEAT OF ANY ONE OF US...
WHAT ?!
THAT'S RIGHT, ALL US DE-MONS!
ALRAUNE PUT THAT WELL...
WHAT ?!?!
KICK
KICK
KICK
The hero, Dawner, progresses forward while the prevaricators fight amongst themselves.

Fire Venom Dragon

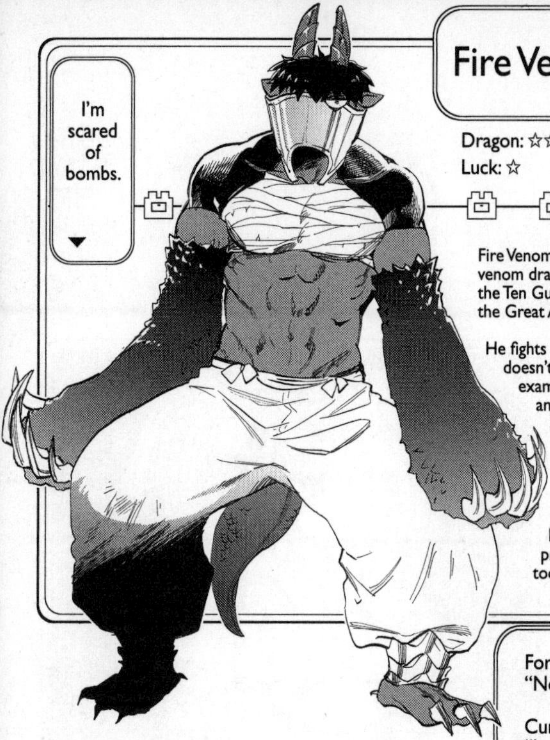

Dragon: ☆☆
Luck: ☆

I'm scared of bombs.

Fire Venom Dragon is a demon of the fire venom dragon species. He is a member of the Ten Guardians as well as the boss of the Great Ancient Volcano Zone.

He fights by spewing fire and venom. He doesn't forgive or forget easily. For example, he bears a grudge against anyone who ever said, "But you don't look like a dragon." He has a very powerful venom gland inside his mouth, so he protects his face with a shield to prevent accidents.

He used to go by his actual proper name, but it sounded too much like the name of a fish.

Former problem:
"Nothing!"

Current problem:
"I can't believe Dawner sealed away so much of my power!"

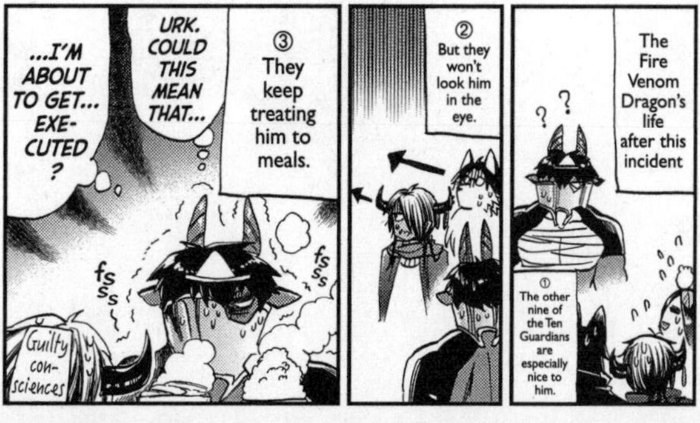
The Fire Venom Dragon's life after this incident
? ?
① The other nine of the Ten Guardians are especially nice to him.
② But they won't look him in the eye.
③ They keep treating him to meals.
URK. COULD THIS MEAN THAT...
...I'M ABOUT TO GET... EXE-CUTED?
fsss
fsss
Guilty consciences

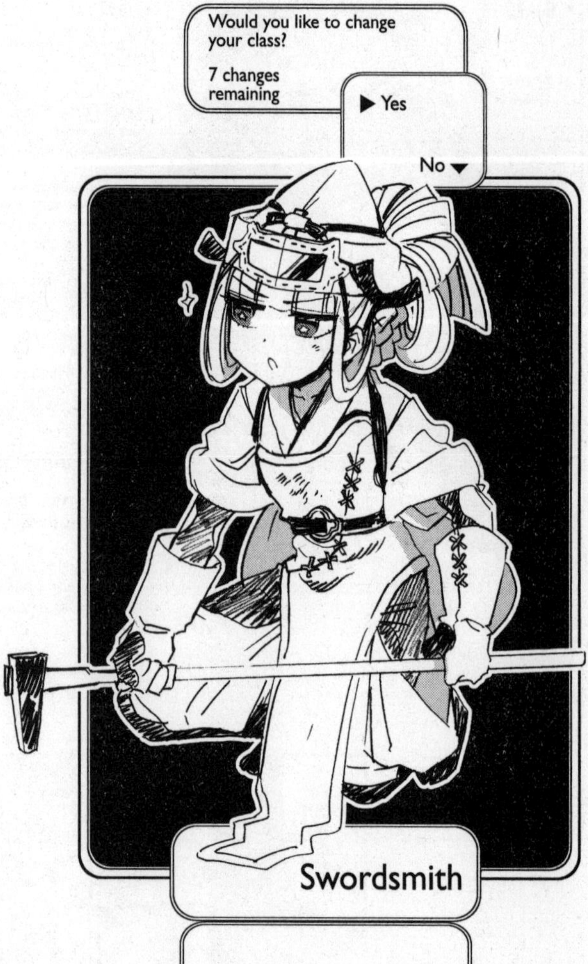
Would you like to change your class?
7 changes remaining
▶ Yes
No
Swordsmith
"This is very challenging..."

58th Night: From the Mouths of Princesses

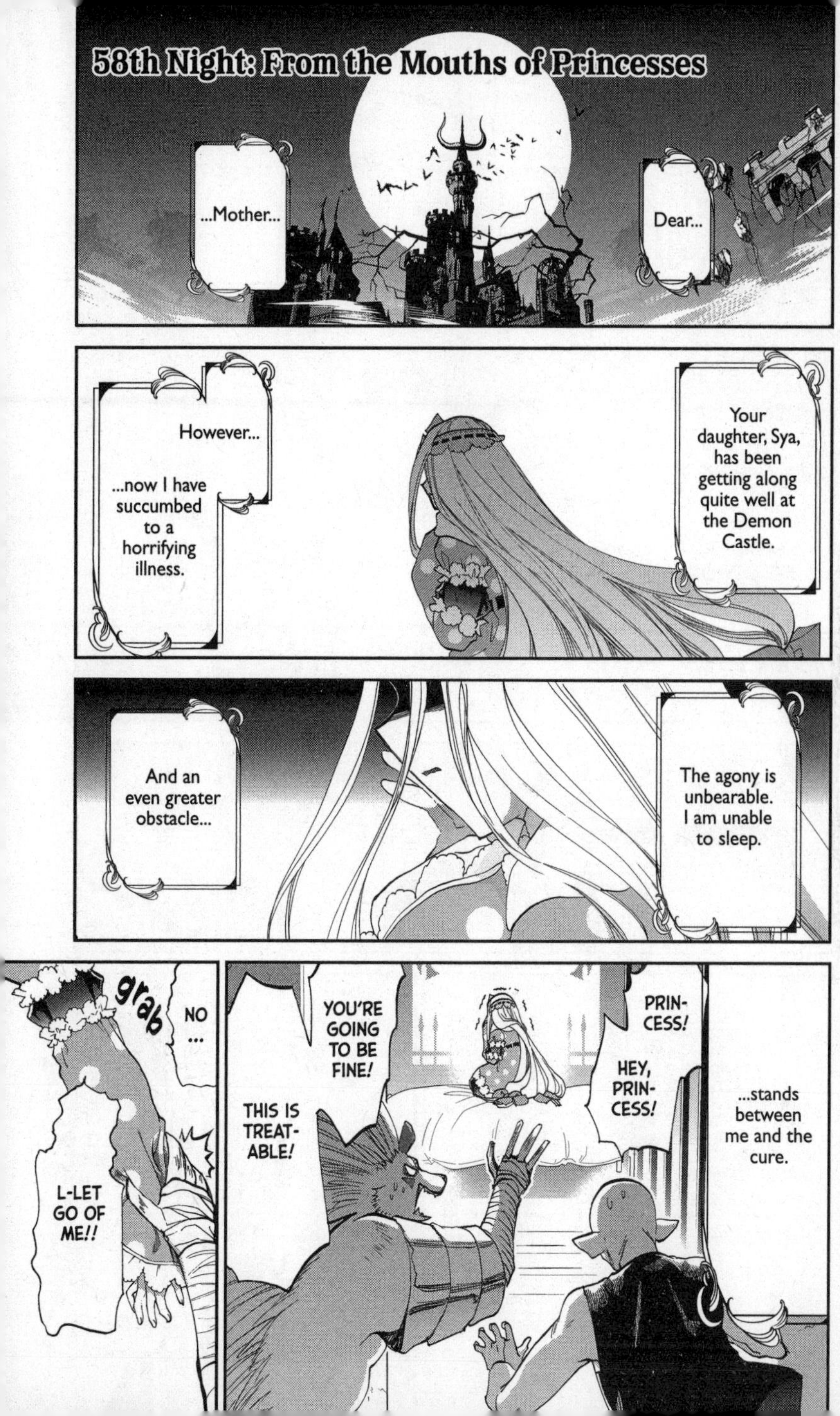
Dear...
...Mother...
Your daughter, Sya, has been getting along quite well at the Demon Castle.
However...
...now I have succumbed to a horrifying illness.
The agony is unbearable. I am unable to sleep.
And an even greater obstacle...
...stands between me and the cure.
PRIN-CESS!
HEY, PRIN-CESS!
YOU'RE GOING TO BE FINE!
THIS IS TREAT-ABLE!
grab
NO ...
L-LET GO OF ME!!

58th Night: From the Mouths of Princesses

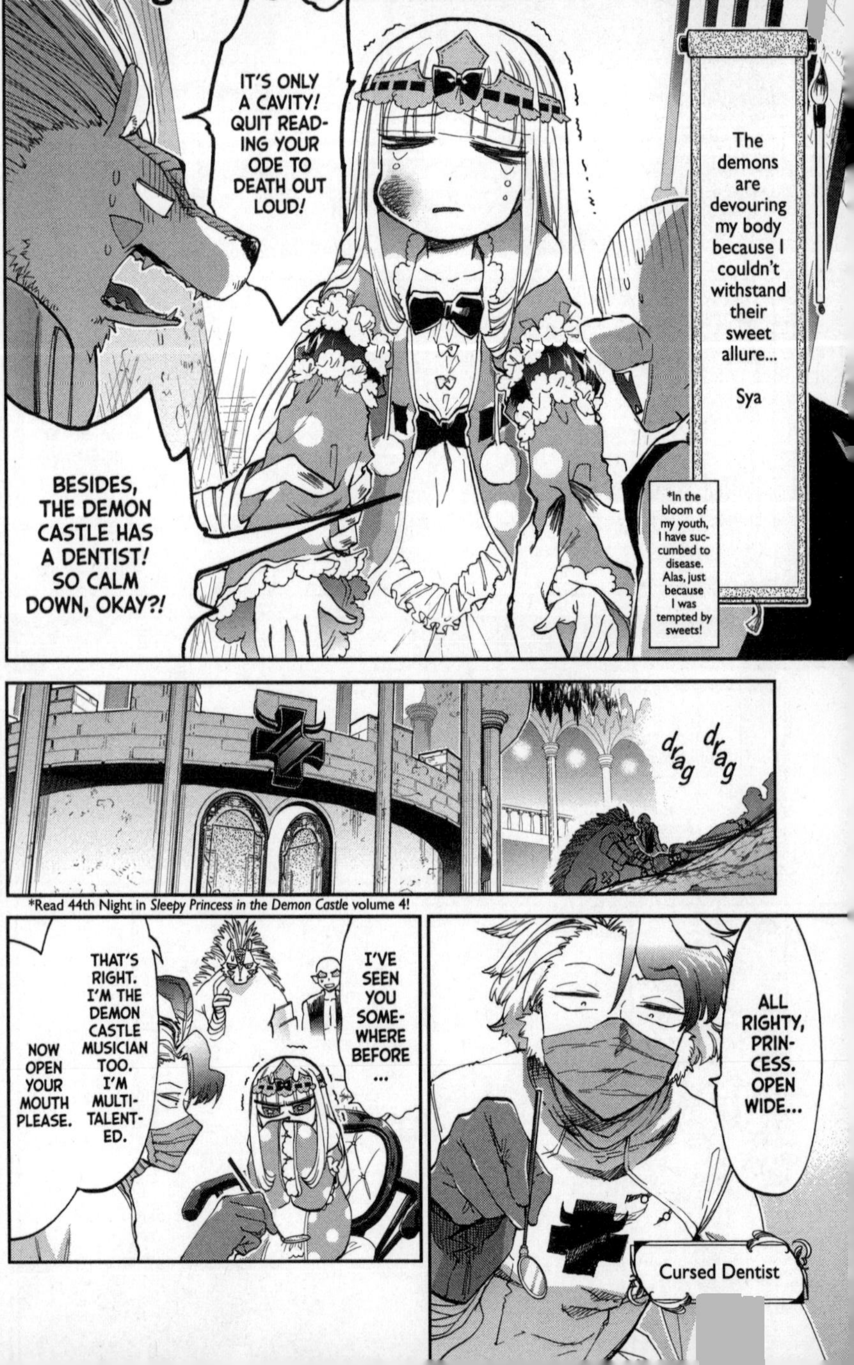
The demons are devouring my body because I couldn't withstand their sweet allure...
Sya
*In the bloom of my youth, I have succumbed to disease. Alas, just because I was tempted by sweets!
IT'S ONLY A CAVITY! QUIT READING YOUR ODE TO DEATH OUT LOUD!
BESIDES, THE DEMON CASTLE HAS A DENTIST! SO CALM DOWN, OKAY?!
drag drag
*Read 44th Night in *Sleepy Princess in the Demon Castle* volume 4!
ALL RIGHTY, PRINCESS. OPEN WIDE...
Cursed Dentist
I'VE SEEN YOU SOMEWHERE BEFORE...
THAT'S RIGHT. I'M THE DEMON CASTLE MUSICIAN TOO. I'M MULTI-TALENTED.
NOW OPEN YOUR MOUTH PLEASE.

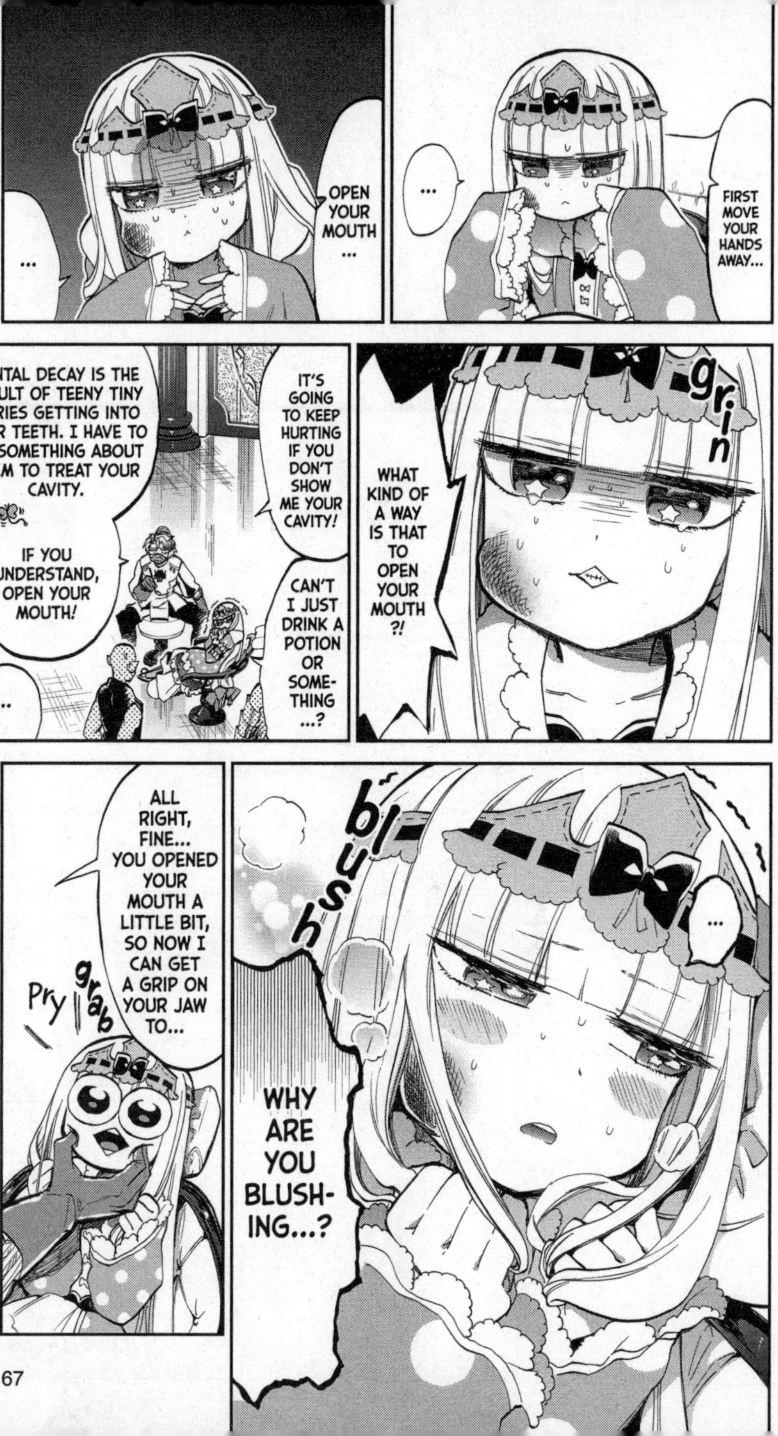
FIRST MOVE YOUR HANDS AWAY...
...
OPEN YOUR MOUTH ...
...
grin
WHAT KIND OF A WAY IS THAT TO OPEN YOUR MOUTH ?!
IT'S GOING TO KEEP HURTING IF YOU DON'T SHOW ME YOUR CAVITY!
DENTAL DECAY IS THE RESULT OF TEENY TINY FAIRIES GETTING INTO YOUR TEETH. I HAVE TO DO SOMETHING ABOUT THEM TO TREAT YOUR CAVITY.
CAN'T I JUST DRINK A POTION OR SOME-THING ...?
IF YOU UNDERSTAND, OPEN YOUR MOUTH!
...
...
blush
WHY ARE YOU BLUSH-ING...?
ALL RIGHT, FINE... YOU OPENED YOUR MOUTH A LITTLE BIT, SO NOW I CAN GET A GRIP ON YOUR JAW TO...
grab
Pry

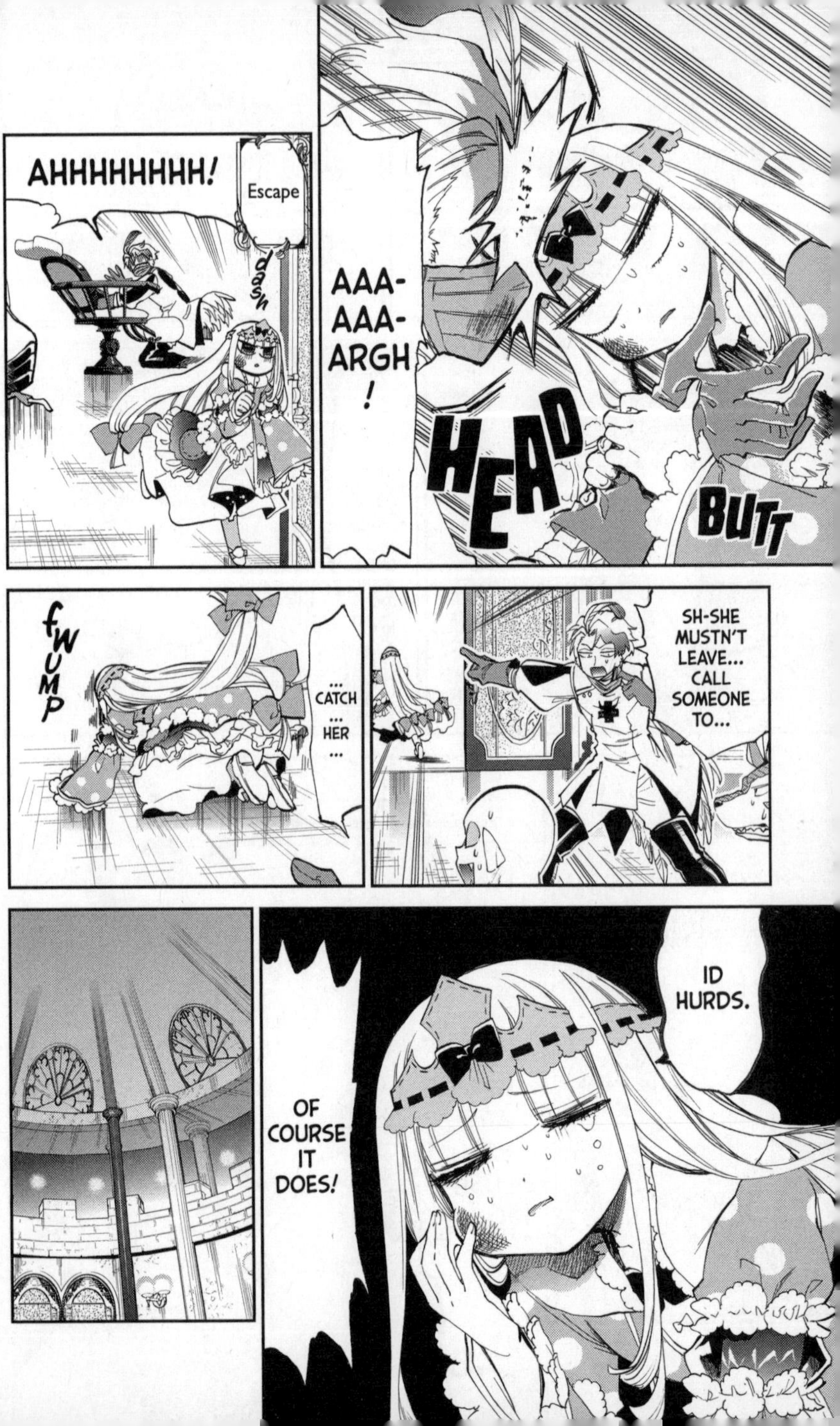
AAA-AAA-ARGH!
HEAD
BUTT
AHHHHHHHH!
Escape
dash
SH-SHE MUSTN'T LEAVE... CALL SOMEONE TO...
... CATCH ... HER ...
fWUMP
ID HURDS.
OF COURSE IT DOES!

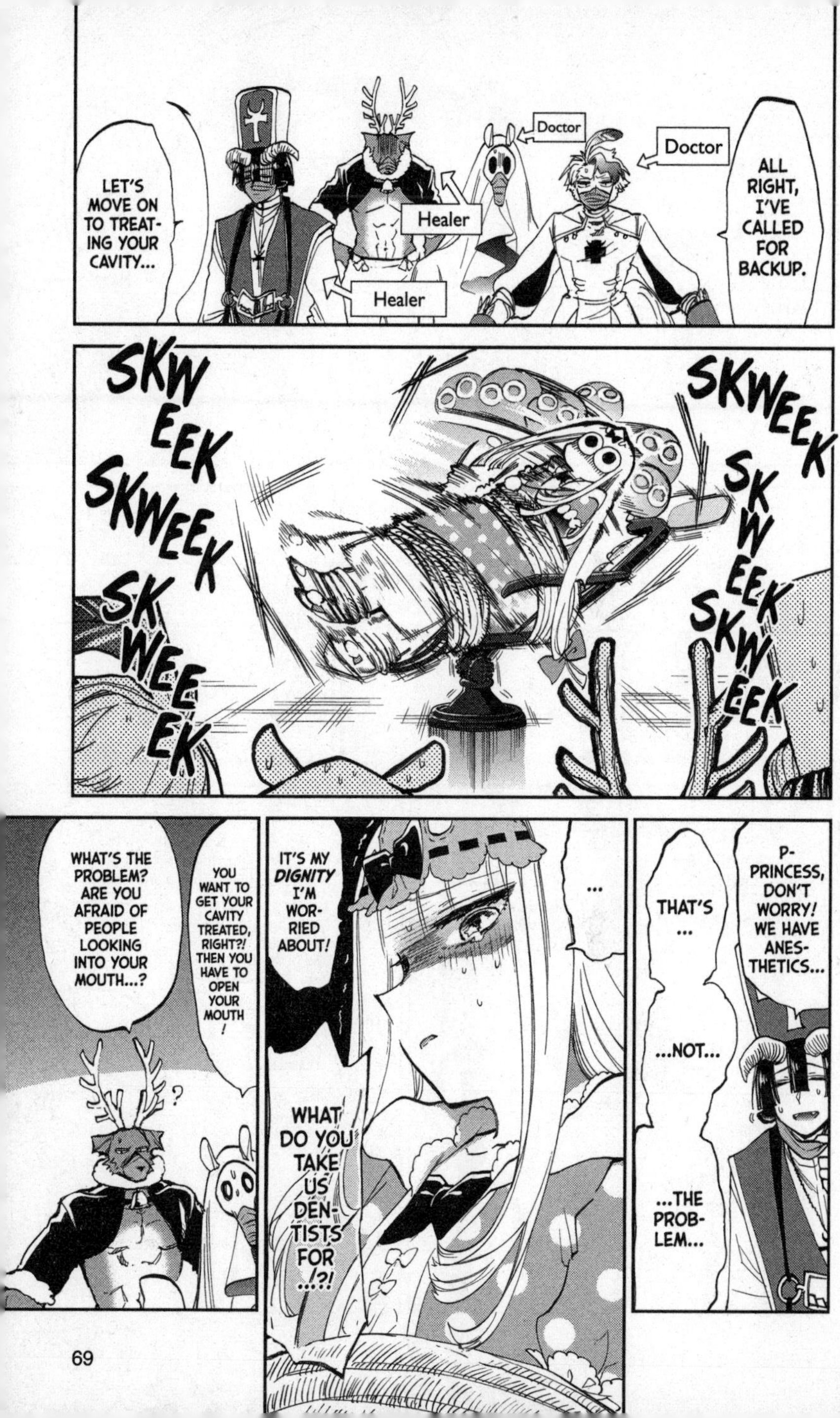

ALL RIGHT, I'VE CALLED FOR BACKUP.
Doctor
Doctor
Healer
Healer
LET'S MOVE ON TO TREATING YOUR CAVITY...
SKWEEK
SKWEEK
SKWEEK
SKWEEK
SKWEEK
SKWEEK
P-PRINCESS, DON'T WORRY! WE HAVE ANESTHETICS...
THAT'S...
...NOT...
...THE PROBLEM...
...
IT'S MY *DIGNITY* I'M WORRIED ABOUT!
WHAT DO YOU TAKE US DENTISTS FOR...!?!
YOU WANT TO GET YOUR CAVITY TREATED, RIGHT?! THEN YOU HAVE TO OPEN YOUR MOUTH!
WHAT'S THE PROBLEM? ARE YOU AFRAID OF PEOPLE LOOKING INTO YOUR MOUTH...?
?

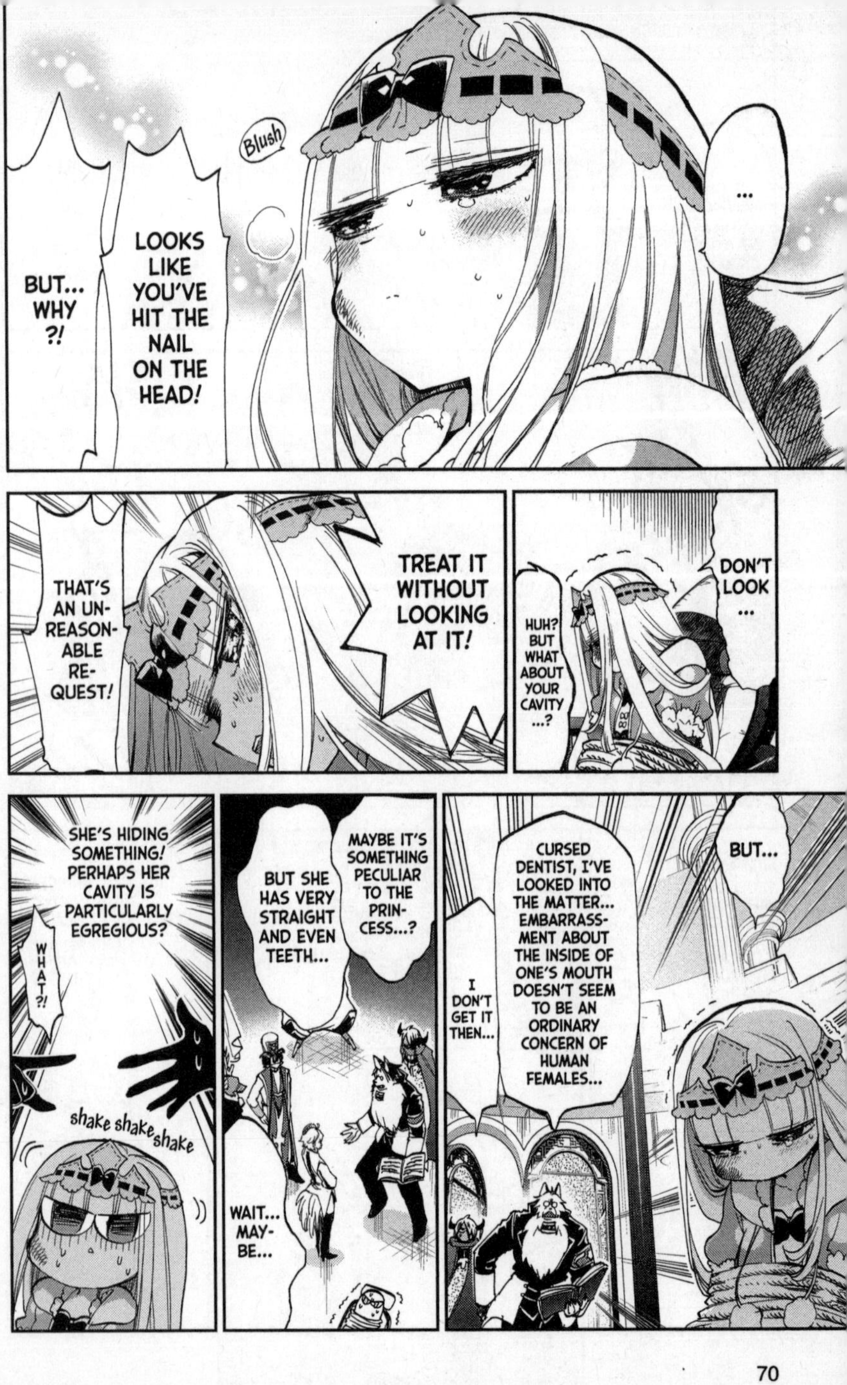
...
Blush
LOOKS LIKE YOU'VE HIT THE NAIL ON THE HEAD!
BUT... WHY ?!
DON'T LOOK ...
HUH? BUT WHAT ABOUT YOUR CAVITY ...?
TREAT IT WITHOUT LOOKING AT IT!
THAT'S AN UN-REASON-ABLE RE-QUEST!
BUT...
CURSED DENTIST, I'VE LOOKED INTO THE MATTER... EMBARRASS-MENT ABOUT THE INSIDE OF ONE'S MOUTH DOESN'T SEEM TO BE AN ORDINARY CONCERN OF HUMAN FEMALES...
I DON'T GET IT THEN...
MAYBE IT'S SOMETHING PECULIAR TO THE PRIN-CESS...?
BUT SHE HAS VERY STRAIGHT AND EVEN TEETH...
WAIT... MAY-BE...
SHE'S HIDING SOMETHING! PERHAPS HER CAVITY IS PARTICULARLY EGREGIOUS?
WHAT?!
shake shake shake

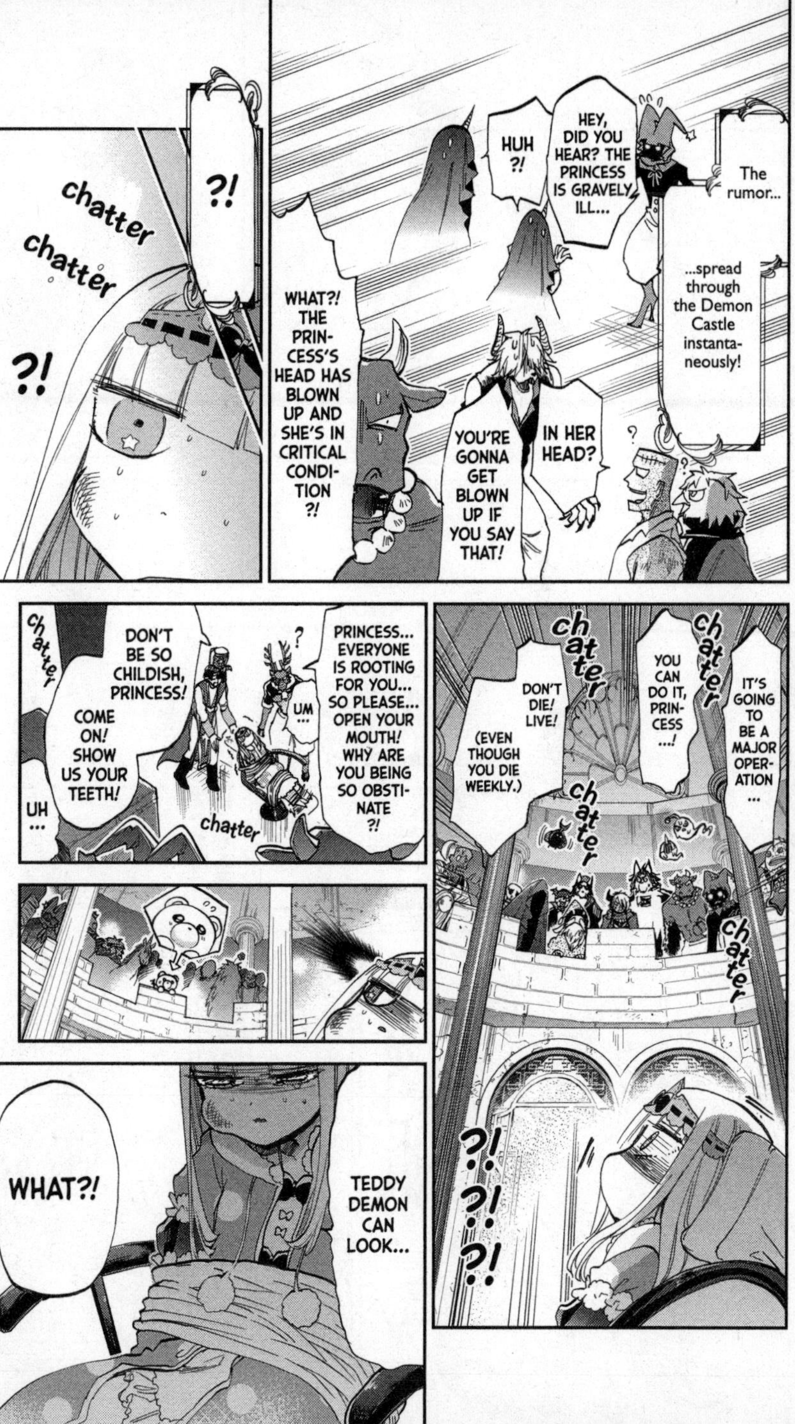
The rumor...
...spread through the Demon Castle instantaneously!
HEY, DID YOU HEAR? THE PRINCESS IS GRAVELY ILL...
HUH ?!
IN HER HEAD?
YOU'RE GONNA GET BLOWN UP IF YOU SAY THAT!
WHAT?! THE PRINCESS'S HEAD HAS BLOWN UP AND SHE'S IN CRITICAL CONDITION ?!
?!
chatter
chatter
?!
IT'S GOING TO BE A MAJOR OPERATION ...
chatter
YOU CAN DO IT, PRINCESS ...!
chatter
DON'T DIE! LIVE!
(EVEN THOUGH YOU DIE WEEKLY.)
chatter
chatter
?!?!?!?!
PRINCESS... EVERYONE IS ROOTING FOR YOU... SO PLEASE... OPEN YOUR MOUTH! WHY ARE YOU BEING SO OBSTINATE ?!
?
UM ...
DON'T BE SO CHILDISH, PRINCESS!
chatter
COME ON! SHOW US YOUR TEETH!
UH ...
chatter
TEDDY DEMON CAN LOOK...
WHAT?!

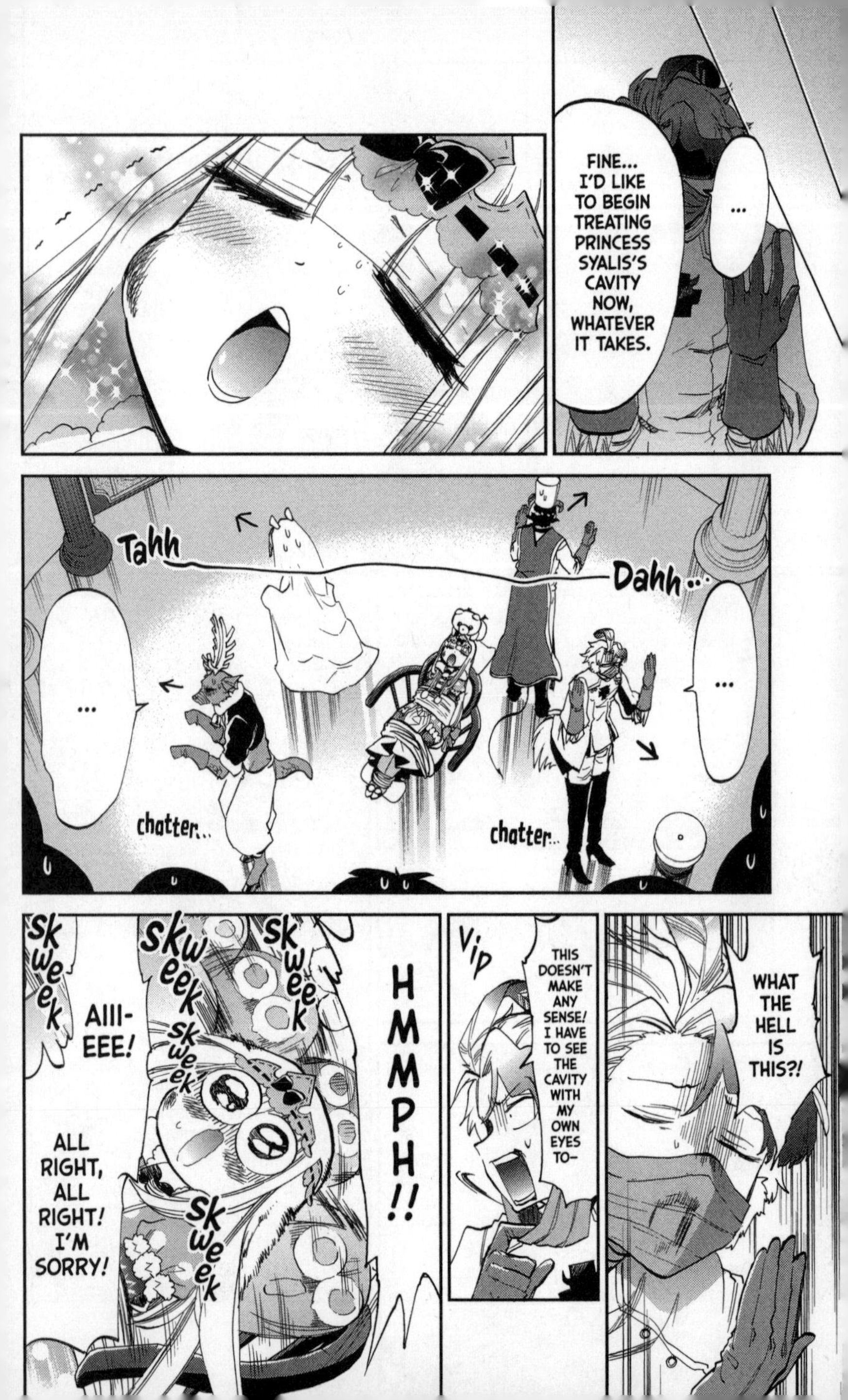
...
FINE... I'D LIKE TO BEGIN TREATING PRINCESS SYALIS'S CAVITY NOW, WHATEVER IT TAKES.
Tahh
Dahh...
...
chatter...
...
chatter...
WHAT THE HELL IS THIS?!
Vip
THIS DOESN'T MAKE ANY SENSE! I HAVE TO SEE THE CAVITY WITH MY OWN EYES TO—
HMMPH!!
skweek
skweek
skweek
skweek
skweek
AIII-EEE!
ALL RIGHT, ALL RIGHT! I'M SORRY!

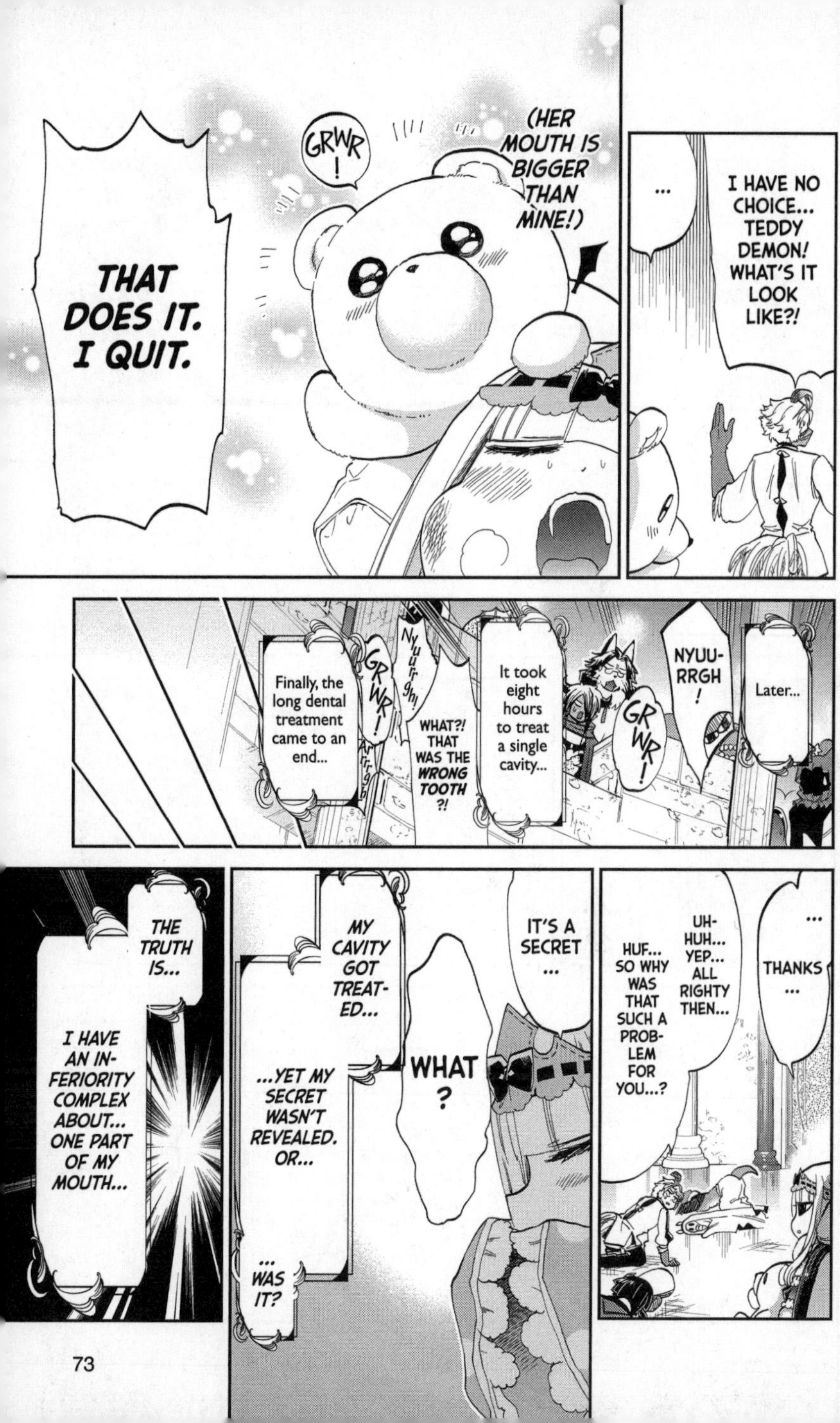
...
I HAVE NO CHOICE... TEDDY DEMON! WHAT'S IT LOOK LIKE?!
(HER MOUTH IS BIGGER THAN MINE!)
GRWR !
THAT DOES IT. I QUIT.
Later...
NYUU-RRGH !
GRWR !
It took eight hours to treat a single cavity...
WHAT?! THAT WAS THE WRONG TOOTH ?!
Nyuurrgh!
GRWR !
Arrrgh
Finally, the long dental treatment came to an end...
... THANKS ...
UH-HUH... YEP... ALL RIGHTY THEN...
HUF... SO WHY WAS THAT SUCH A PROBLEM FOR YOU...?
IT'S A SECRET ...
WHAT ?
MY CAVITY GOT TREAT-ED...
...YET MY SECRET WASN'T REVEALED. OR...
... WAS IT?
THE TRUTH IS...
I HAVE AN IN-FERIORITY COMPLEX ABOUT... ONE PART OF MY MOUTH...

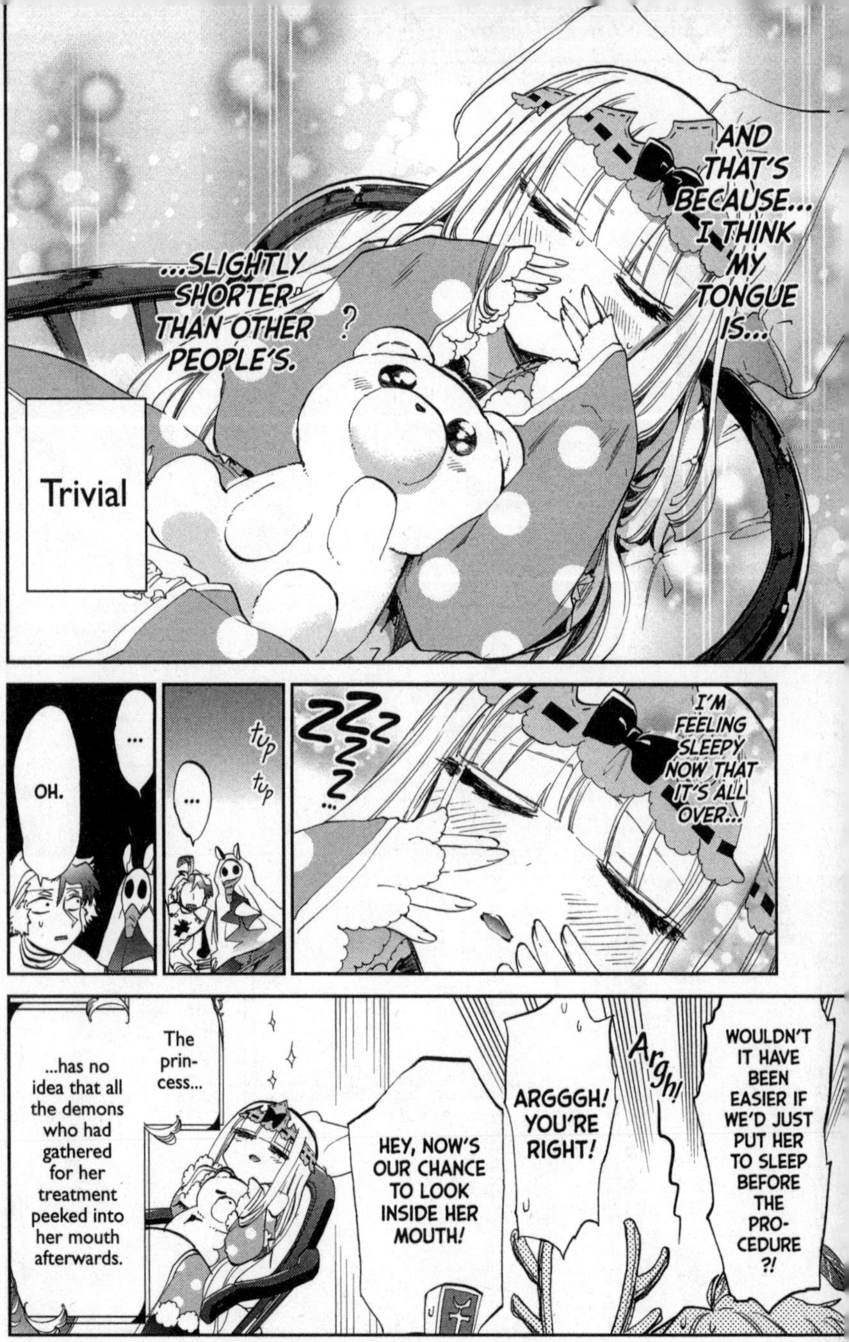

AND THAT'S BECAUSE... I THINK MY TONGUE IS...
?
...SLIGHTLY SHORTER THAN OTHER PEOPLE'S.
Trivial
I'M FEELING SLEEPY NOW THAT IT'S ALL OVER...
ZZZ...
tup tup
...
...
OH.
WOULDN'T IT HAVE BEEN EASIER IF WE'D JUST PUT HER TO SLEEP BEFORE THE PRO-CEDURE?!
Argh!
ARGGGH! YOU'RE RIGHT!
HEY, NOW'S OUR CHANCE TO LOOK INSIDE HER MOUTH!
The prin-cess...
...has no idea that all the demons who had gathered for her treatment peeked into her mouth afterwards.

Tentative Name: Pathogenic Fairy, Tooth Cavity Type

Mysteriousness: ☆☆☆☆☆☆☆

Troublesomeness: ☆☆☆☆☆☆☆☆

A common enemy to both demons and mankind.

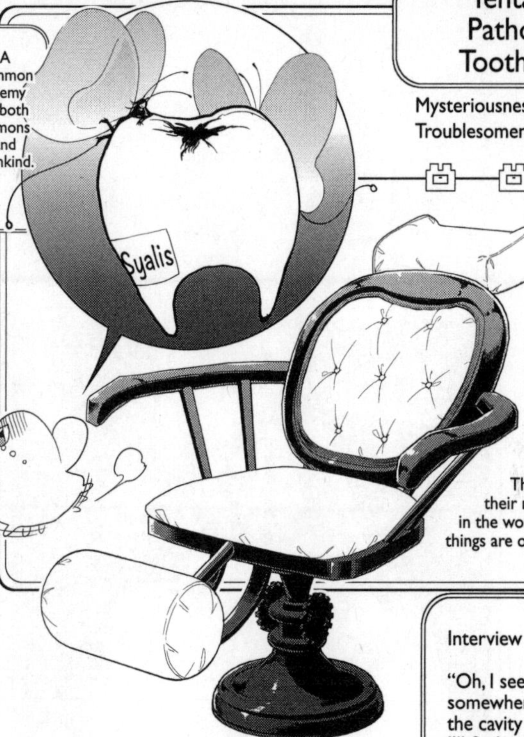
Syalis

A tiny fairy (or something shaped like one) that is the cause of tooth decay in this magically advanced world.

Their bodies can pass through all forms of physical matter, so they must be dealt with through dentistry sorcery. They can be found in both the human and demon worlds, and their characteristics are the same in every region.

The current paradigm is that their main body exists somewhere in the world, and these fairy-looking things are only its terminal units.

Interview with a Patient

"Oh, I see... So the main body exists somewhere else, huh? That means the cavity is that body's fault? Then I'll find and destroy it no matter what it takes...!"

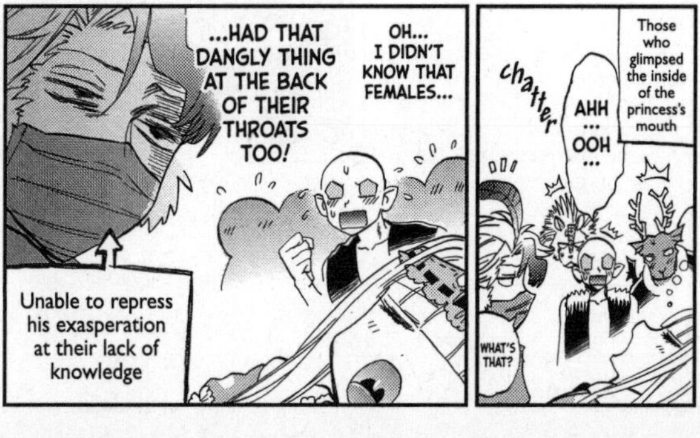
Those who glimpsed the inside of the princess's mouth
chatter
AHH... OOH...
WHAT'S THAT?
OH... I DIDN'T KNOW THAT FEMALES...
...HAD THAT DANGLY THING AT THE BACK OF THEIR THROATS TOO!
Unable to repress his exasperation at their lack of knowledge

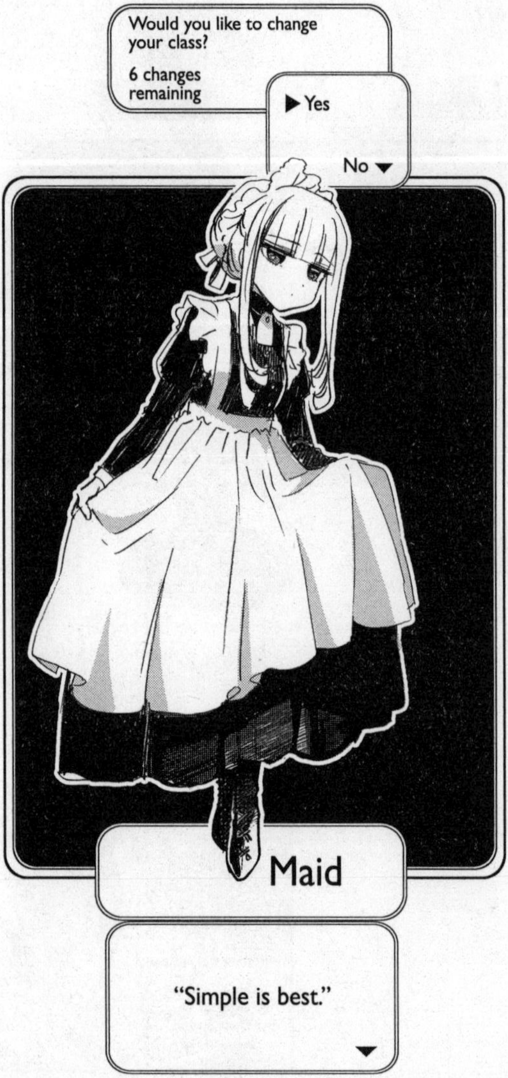
Would you like to change your class?
6 changes remaining
▶ Yes
No ▼
Maid
"Simple is best."

59th Night: Supersized at the Demon Castle

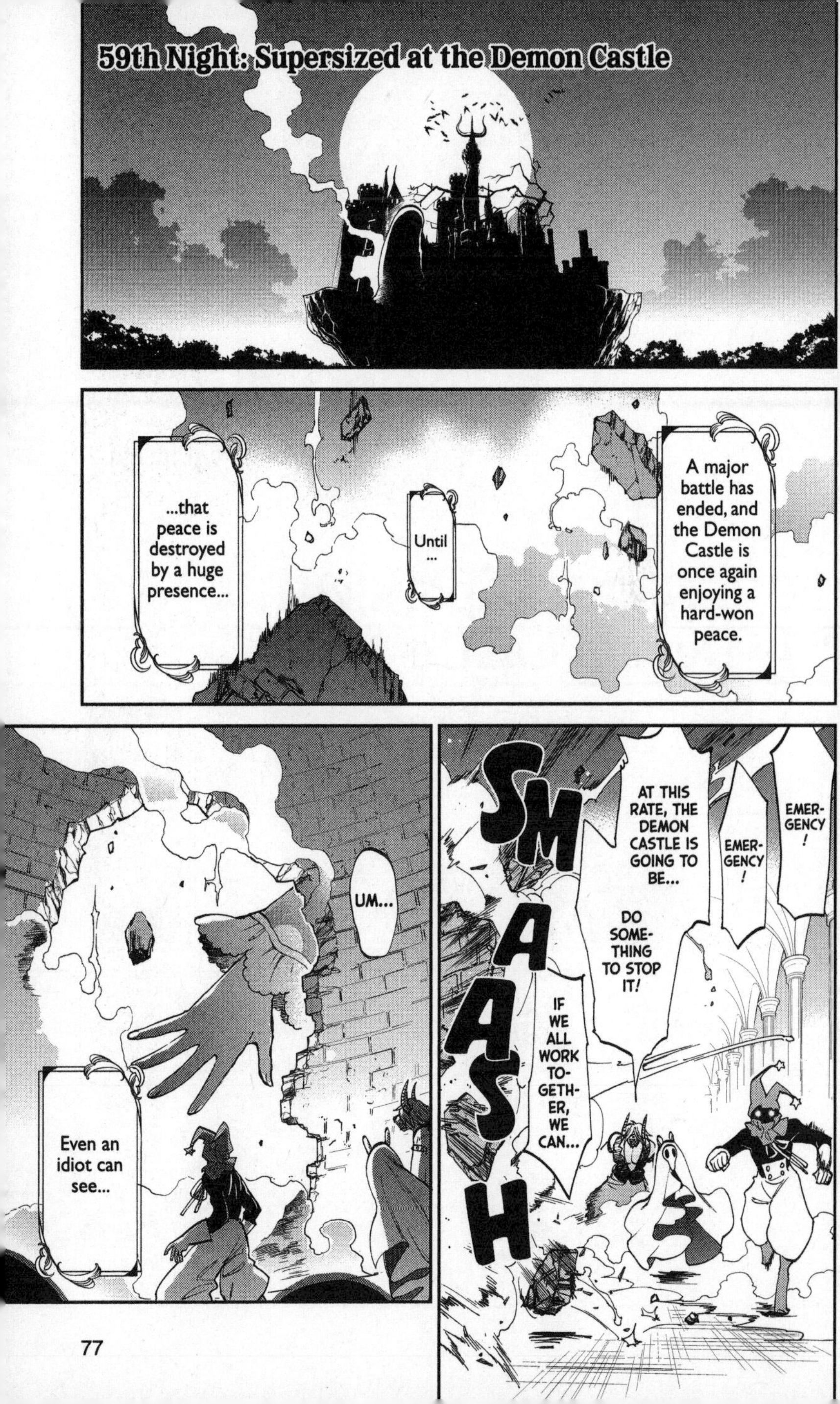
A major battle has ended, and the Demon Castle is once again enjoying a hard-won peace.
Until ...
...that peace is destroyed by a huge presence...
EMERGENCY!
EMERGENCY!
AT THIS RATE, THE DEMON CASTLE IS GOING TO BE...
DO SOMETHING TO STOP IT!
IF WE ALL WORK TOGETHER, WE CAN...
SMAASH
UM...
Even an idiot can see...

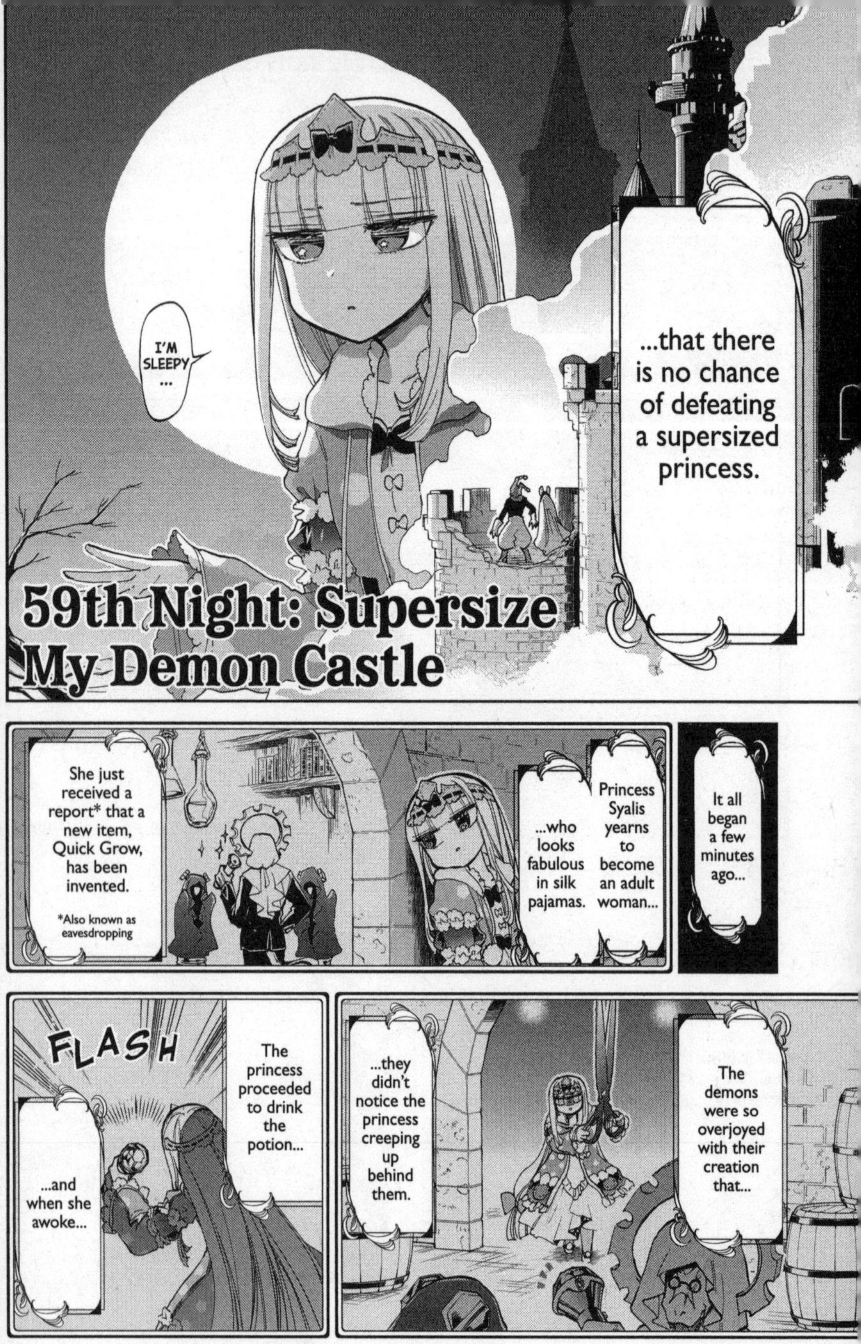
...that there is no chance of defeating a supersized princess.
I'M SLEEPY...
59th Night: Supersize My Demon Castle
It all began a few minutes ago...
Princess Syalis yearns to become an adult woman...
...who looks fabulous in silk pajamas.
She just received a report* that a new item, Quick Grow, has been invented.
*Also known as eavesdropping
The demons were so overjoyed with their creation that...
...they didn't notice the princess creeping up behind them.
The princess proceeded to drink the potion...
FLASH
...and when she awoke...

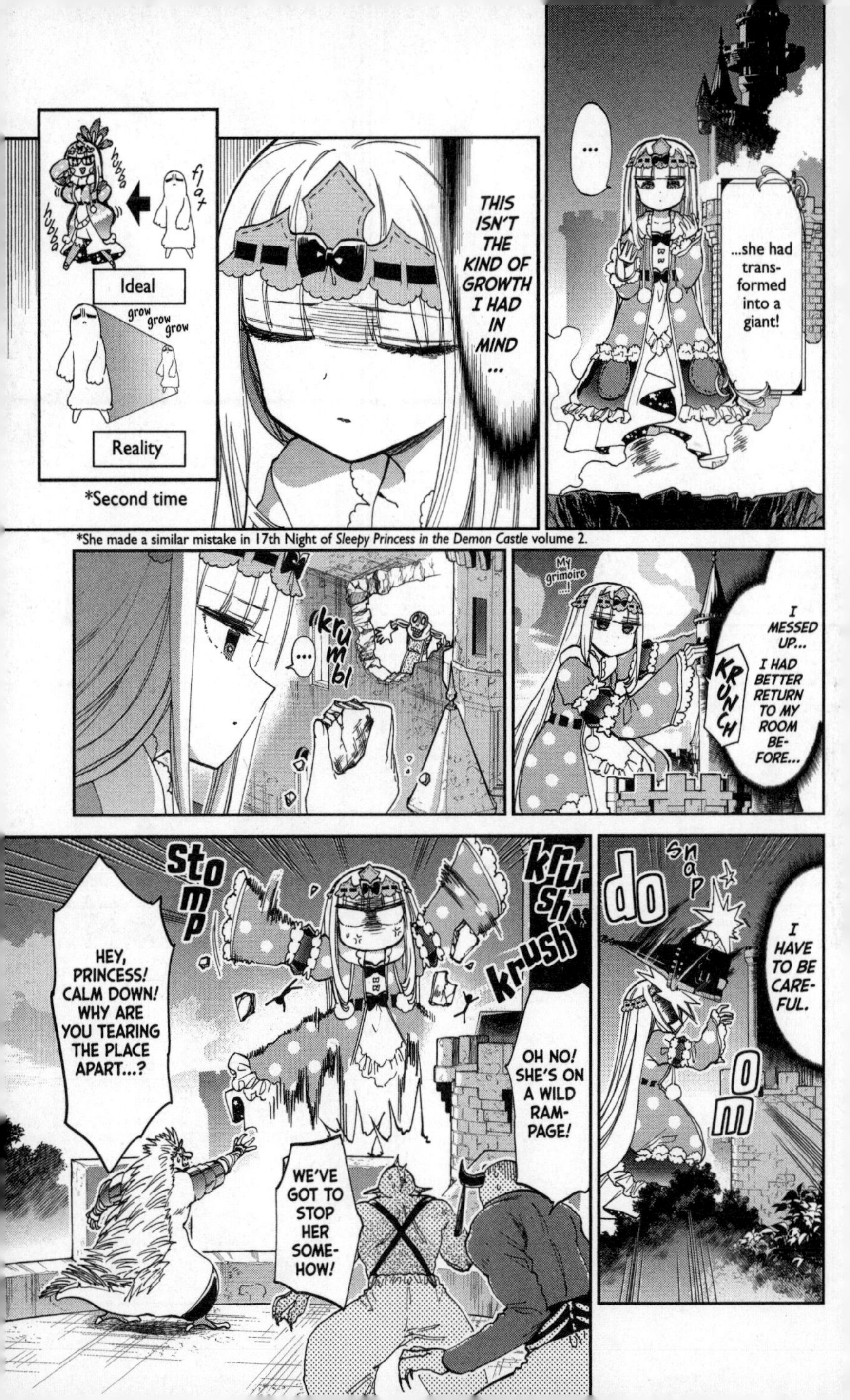
...
...she had transformed into a giant!
THIS ISN'T THE KIND OF GROWTH I HAD IN MIND...
hubba hubba
flat
Ideal
grow grow grow
Reality
*Second time
*She made a similar mistake in 17th Night of Sleepy Princess in the Demon Castle volume 2.
My grimoire...!
I MESSED UP... I HAD BETTER RETURN TO MY ROOM BEFORE...
KRUNCH
krumbl
...
snap
do
om
I HAVE TO BE CAREFUL.
Stomp
krush
krush
HEY, PRINCESS! CALM DOWN! WHY ARE YOU TEARING THE PLACE APART...?
OH NO! SHE'S ON A WILD RAMPAGE!
WE'VE GOT TO STOP HER SOMEHOW!

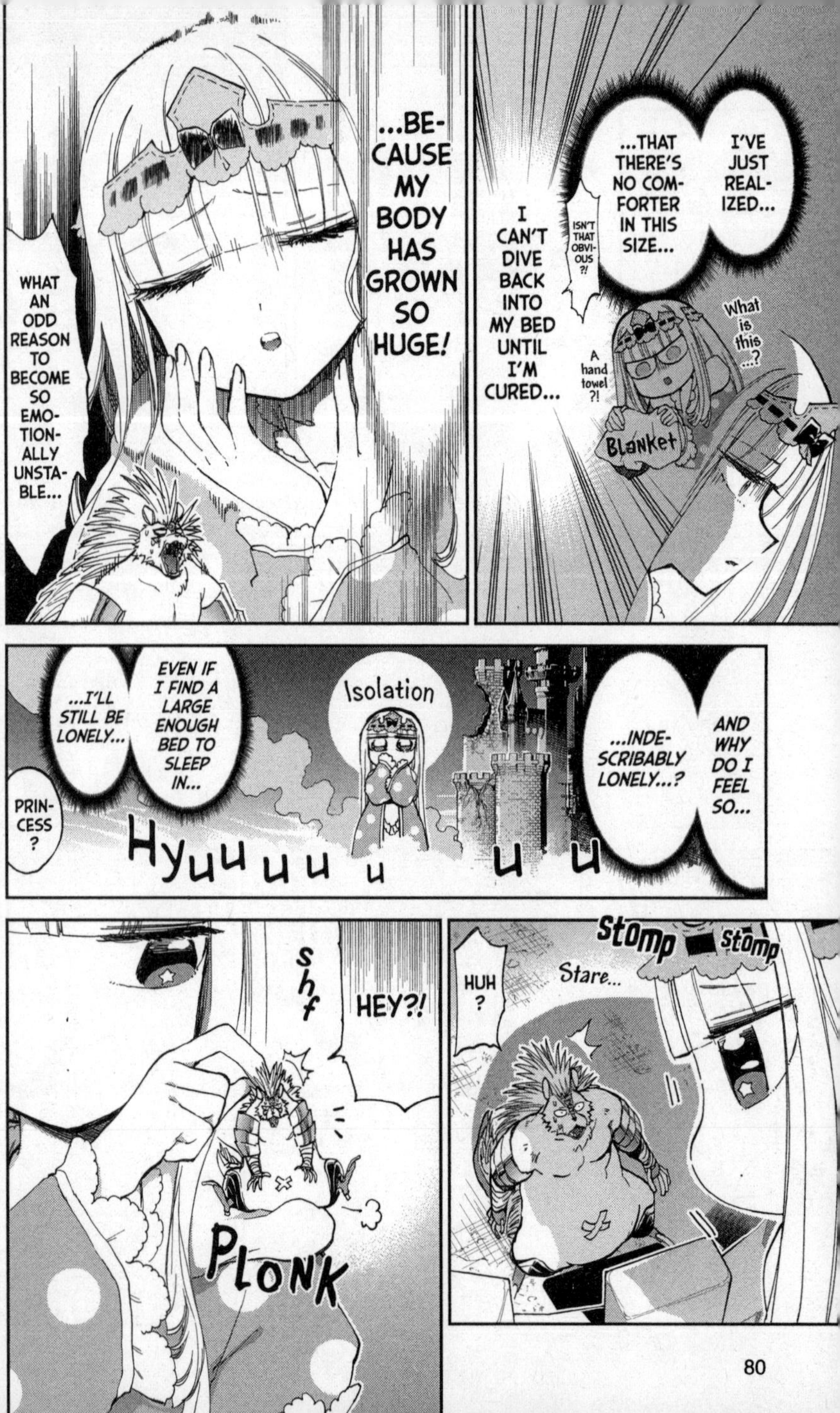
I'VE JUST REALIZED...
...THAT THERE'S NO COMFORTER IN THIS SIZE...
ISN'T THAT OBVIOUS?!
I CAN'T DIVE BACK INTO MY BED UNTIL I'M CURED...
What is this...?
A hand towel?!
Blanket
...BECAUSE MY BODY HAS GROWN SO HUGE!
WHAT AN ODD REASON TO BECOME SO EMOTIONALLY UNSTABLE...
AND WHY DO I FEEL SO...
...INDESCRIBABLY LONELY...?
Isolation
EVEN IF I FIND A LARGE ENOUGH BED TO SLEEP IN...
...I'LL STILL BE LONELY...
PRINCESS?
Hyuuuuuuu
Stomp stomp
Stare...
HUH?
HEY?!
shf
PLONK

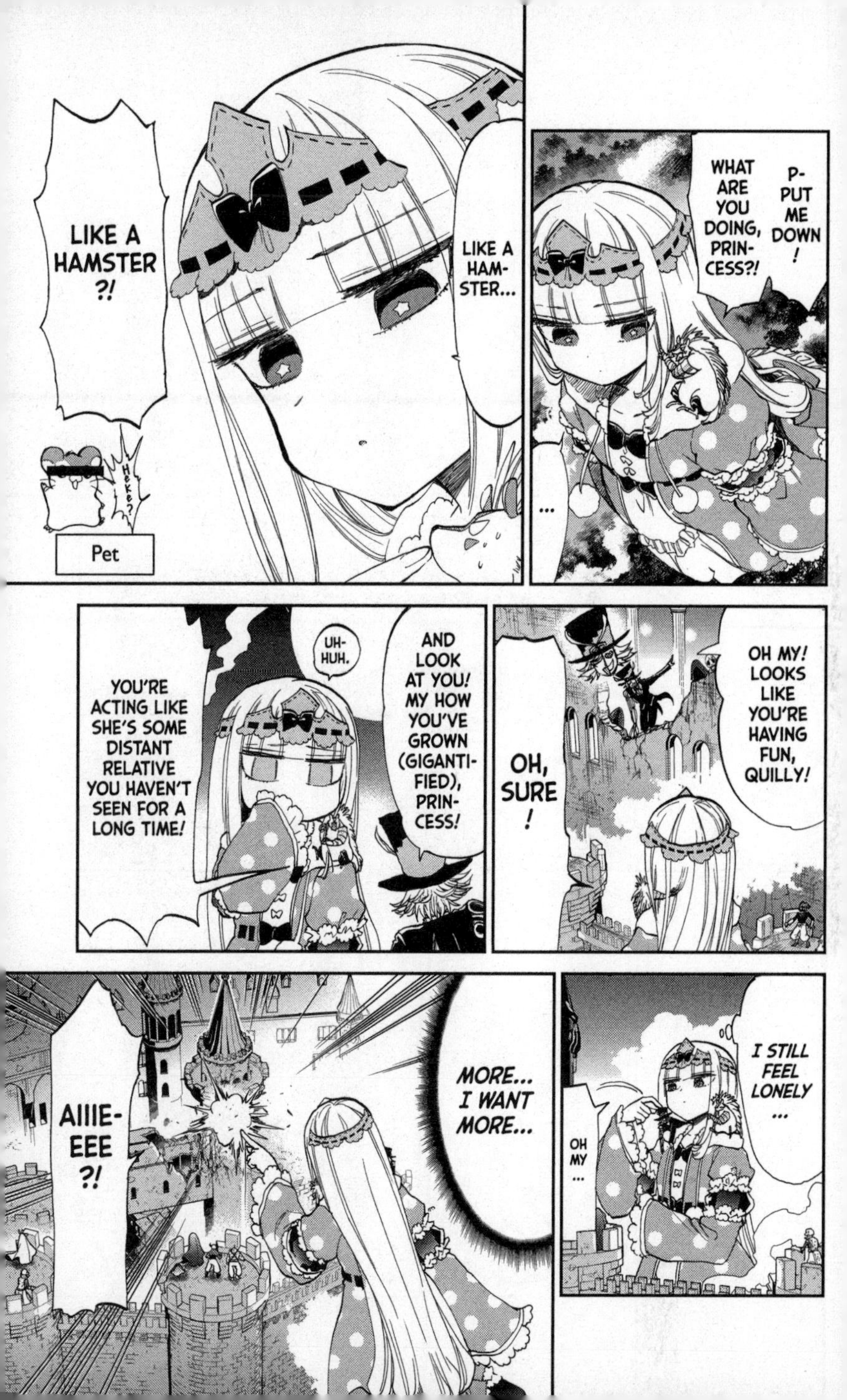
P-PUT ME DOWN!
WHAT ARE YOU DOING, PRINCESS?!
...
LIKE A HAMSTER...
LIKE A HAMSTER?!
Heke?
Pet
OH MY! LOOKS LIKE YOU'RE HAVING FUN, QUILLY!
OH, SURE!
AND LOOK AT YOU! MY HOW YOU'VE GROWN (GIGANTIFIED), PRINCESS!
UH-HUH.
YOU'RE ACTING LIKE SHE'S SOME DISTANT RELATIVE YOU HAVEN'T SEEN FOR A LONG TIME!
I STILL FEEL LONELY...
OH MY...
MORE... I WANT MORE...
AIIIE-EEE?!

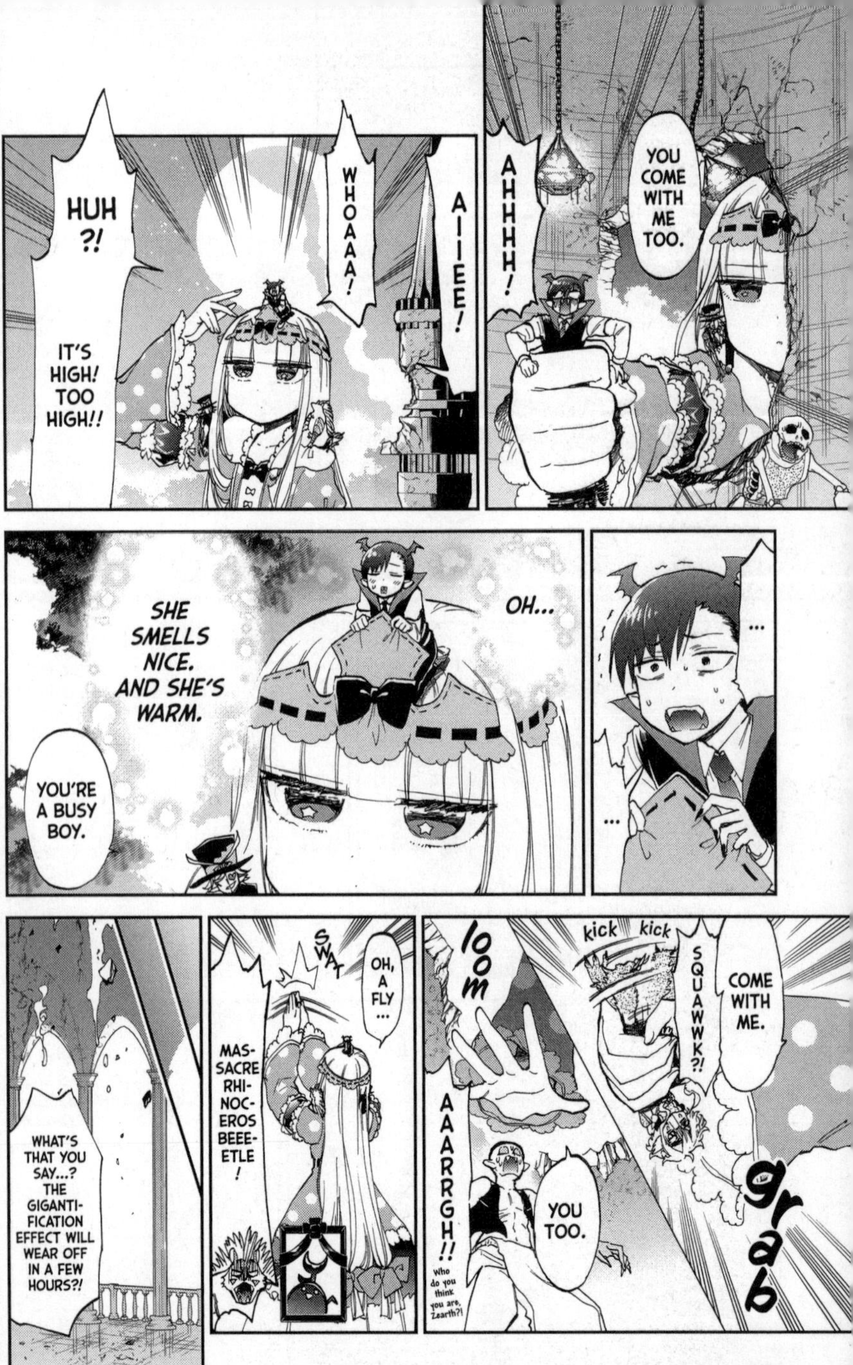
YOU COME WITH ME TOO.
AHHHH!
AIIEEE!
WHOAAA!
HUH?!
IT'S HIGH! TOO HIGH!!
...
...
OH...
SHE SMELLS NICE. AND SHE'S WARM.
YOU'RE A BUSY BOY.
COME WITH ME.
kick kick
SQUAWWK?!
loom
grab
YOU TOO.
AAAARRGH!!
Who do you think you are, Zearth?!
OH, A FLY...
SWAT
MASSACRE RHINOCEROS BEEEETLE!
WHAT'S THAT YOU SAY...? THE GIGANTIFICATION EFFECT WILL WEAR OFF IN A FEW HOURS?!

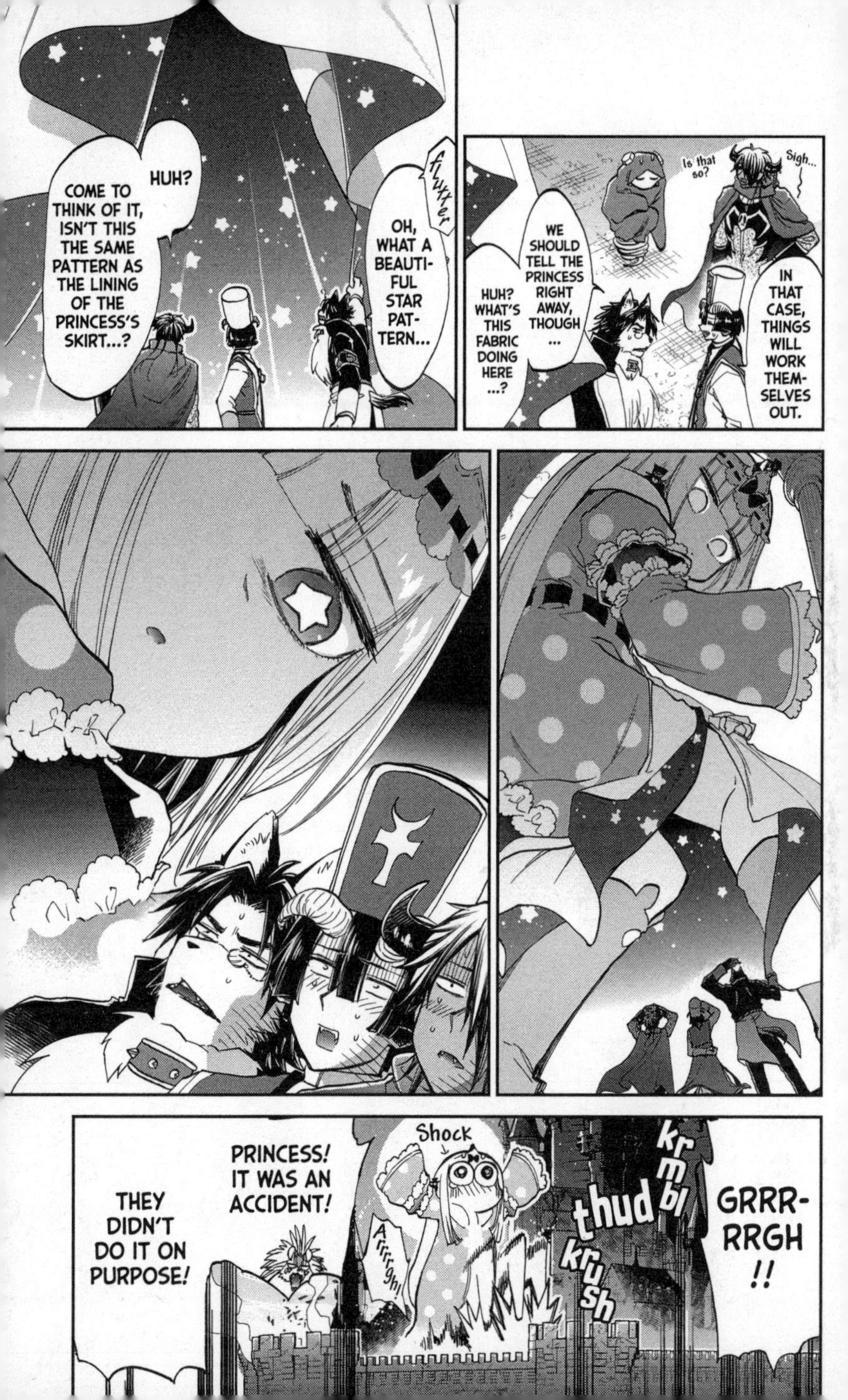
Sigh...
Is that so?
IN THAT CASE, THINGS WILL WORK THEMSELVES OUT.
WE SHOULD TELL THE PRINCESS RIGHT AWAY, THOUGH...
HUH? WHAT'S THIS FABRIC DOING HERE...?
flutter
OH, WHAT A BEAUTIFUL STAR PATTERN...
HUH?
COME TO THINK OF IT, ISN'T THIS THE SAME PATTERN AS THE LINING OF THE PRINCESS'S SKIRT...?
GRRR-RRGH!!
krmbl
thud
krush
Shock
Arrrrgh!
PRINCESS! IT WAS AN ACCIDENT!
THEY DIDN'T DO IT ON PURPOSE!

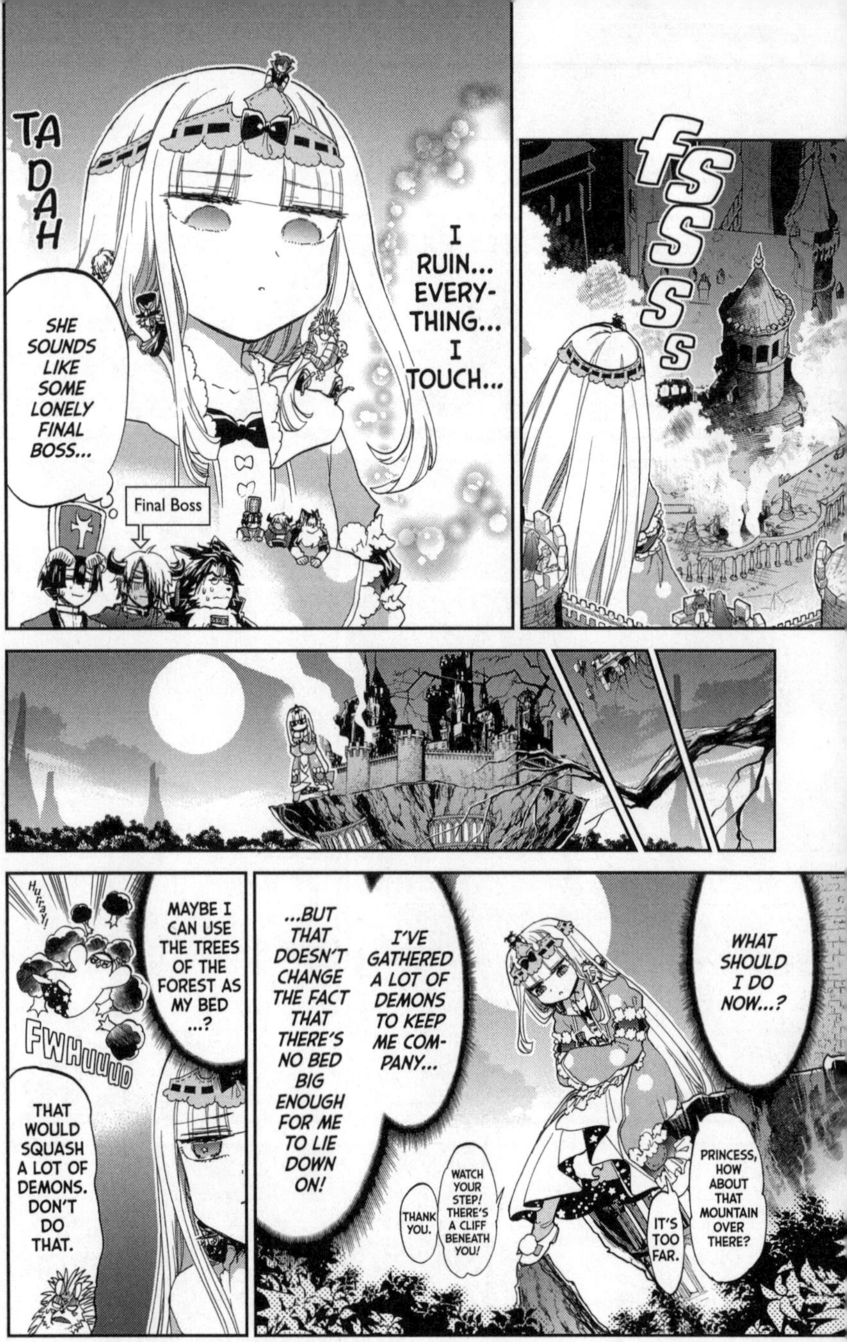
fSSSS
I RUIN... EVERYTHING... I TOUCH...
TADAH
SHE SOUNDS LIKE SOME LONELY FINAL BOSS...
Final Boss
WHAT SHOULD I DO NOW...?
I'VE GATHERED A LOT OF DEMONS TO KEEP ME COMPANY...
...BUT THAT DOESN'T CHANGE THE FACT THAT THERE'S NO BED BIG ENOUGH FOR ME TO LIE DOWN ON!
PRINCESS, HOW ABOUT THAT MOUNTAIN OVER THERE?
IT'S TOO FAR.
WATCH YOUR STEP! THERE'S A CLIFF BENEATH YOU!
THANK YOU.
MAYBE I CAN USE THE TREES OF THE FOREST AS MY BED ...?
Hurray!
FWHUUUD
THAT WOULD SQUASH A LOT OF DEMONS. DON'T DO THAT.

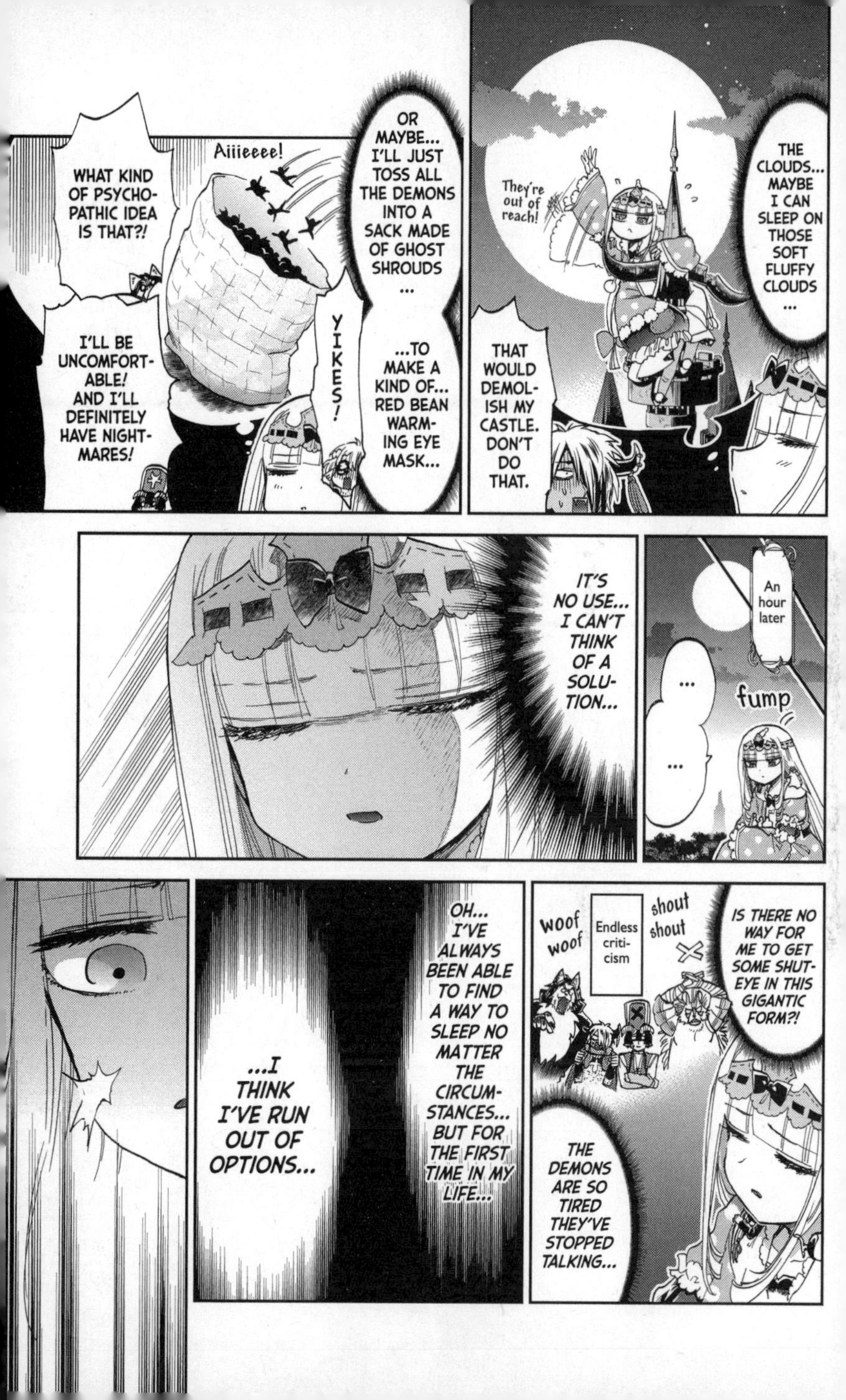
THE CLOUDS... MAYBE I CAN SLEEP ON THOSE SOFT FLUFFY CLOUDS ...
They're out of reach!
THAT WOULD DEMOLISH MY CASTLE. DON'T DO THAT.
OR MAYBE... I'LL JUST TOSS ALL THE DEMONS INTO A SACK MADE OF GHOST SHROUDS ...
...TO MAKE A KIND OF... RED BEAN WARMING EYE MASK...
YIKES!
Aiiieeee!
WHAT KIND OF PSYCHOPATHIC IDEA IS THAT?!
I'LL BE UNCOMFORTABLE! AND I'LL DEFINITELY HAVE NIGHTMARES!
An hour later
...
fump
...
IT'S NO USE... I CAN'T THINK OF A SOLUTION...
IS THERE NO WAY FOR ME TO GET SOME SHUT-EYE IN THIS GIGANTIC FORM?!
shout shout
Endless criticism
woof woof
THE DEMONS ARE SO TIRED THEY'VE STOPPED TALKING...
OH... I'VE ALWAYS BEEN ABLE TO FIND A WAY TO SLEEP NO MATTER THE CIRCUMSTANCES... BUT FOR THE FIRST TIME IN MY LIFE...
...I THINK I'VE RUN OUT OF OPTIONS...

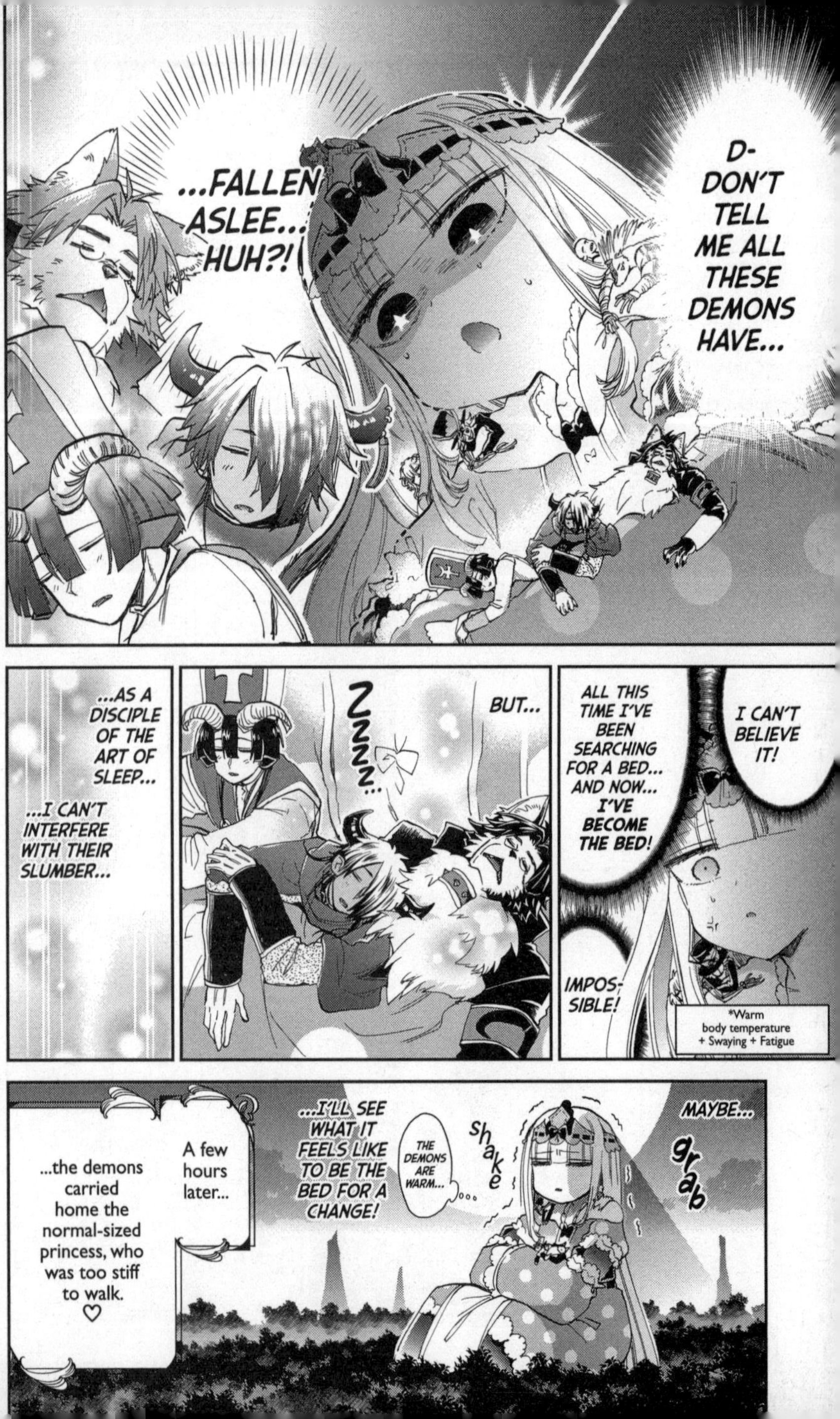
D-DON'T TELL ME ALL THESE DEMONS HAVE...
...FALLEN ASLEE... HUH?!
I CAN'T BELIEVE IT!
ALL THIS TIME I'VE BEEN SEARCHING FOR A BED... AND NOW... I'VE BECOME THE BED!
IMPOS-SIBLE!
*Warm body temperature + Swaying + Fatigue
BUT...
ZZZZ...
...AS A DISCIPLE OF THE ART OF SLEEP...
...I CAN'T INTERFERE WITH THEIR SLUMBER...
MAYBE...
grab
shake
THE DEMONS ARE WARM...
...I'LL SEE WHAT IT FEELS LIKE TO BE THE BED FOR A CHANGE!
A few hours later...
...the demons carried home the normal-sized princess, who was too stiff to walk. ♡

Dr. Gearbolt

Science: ☆☆☆☆☆☆☆☆☆☆
Luck: ☆☆

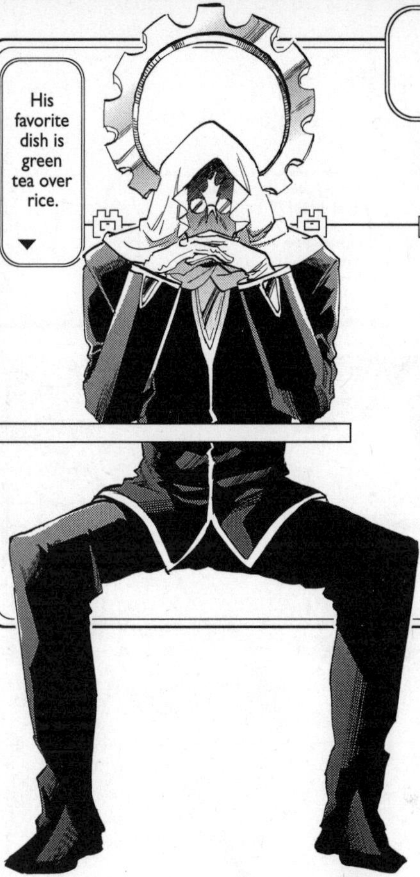

His favorite dish is green tea over rice.

The Demon Castle's professional inventor. Although he is a member of the beast species, parts of his body are mechanized, so he can also be considered a member of the mechanical species. He would never fight on the front lines himself, but his mechanical inventions can be found not only in the Demon Castle but in every dungeon in the region—consequently, in a manner of speaking, he has battled the hero more often than anyone else.

The "Wonder Dog Fur Dryer" he invented upon the orders of the Demon King was a huge hit and has been mass-produced to manage the furry pelts of many demons.

Former problem:
"I have trouble conversing with my son."

Current problem:
"M-O-T-H-E-R won't accept the fact that it is malfunctioning."

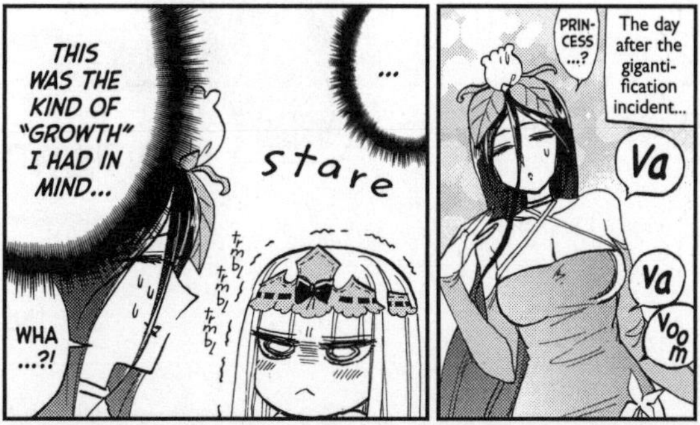
The day after the giganti-fication incident...
PRIN-CESS ...?
Va
Va
Voom
...
stare
THIS WAS THE KIND OF "GROWTH" I HAD IN MIND...
trmbl trmbl trmbl
WHA ...?!

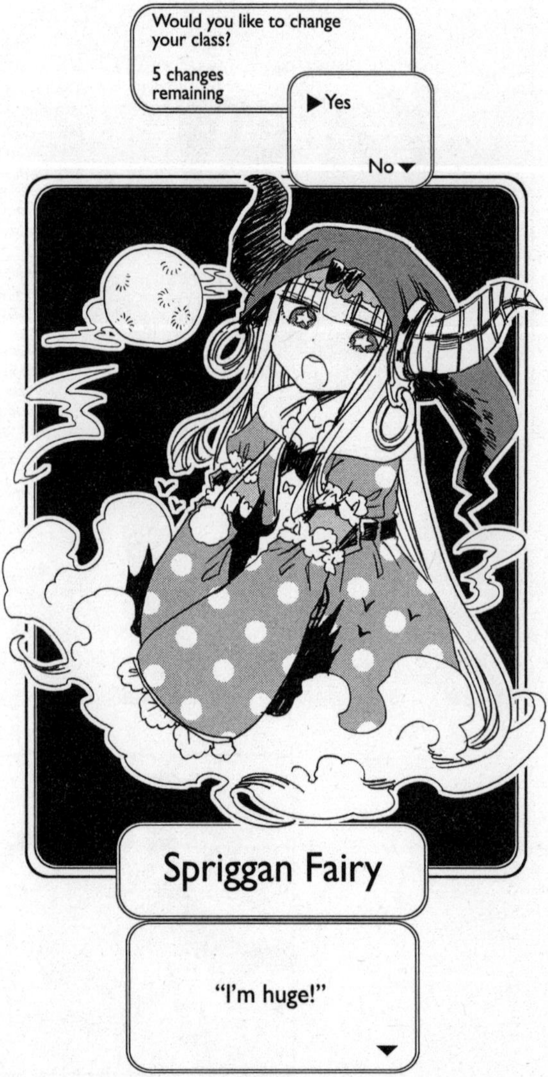
Would you like to change your class?
5 changes remaining
▶Yes
No
Spriggan Fairy
"I'm huge!"

60th Night: No Fair Calling In a Grown-Up!

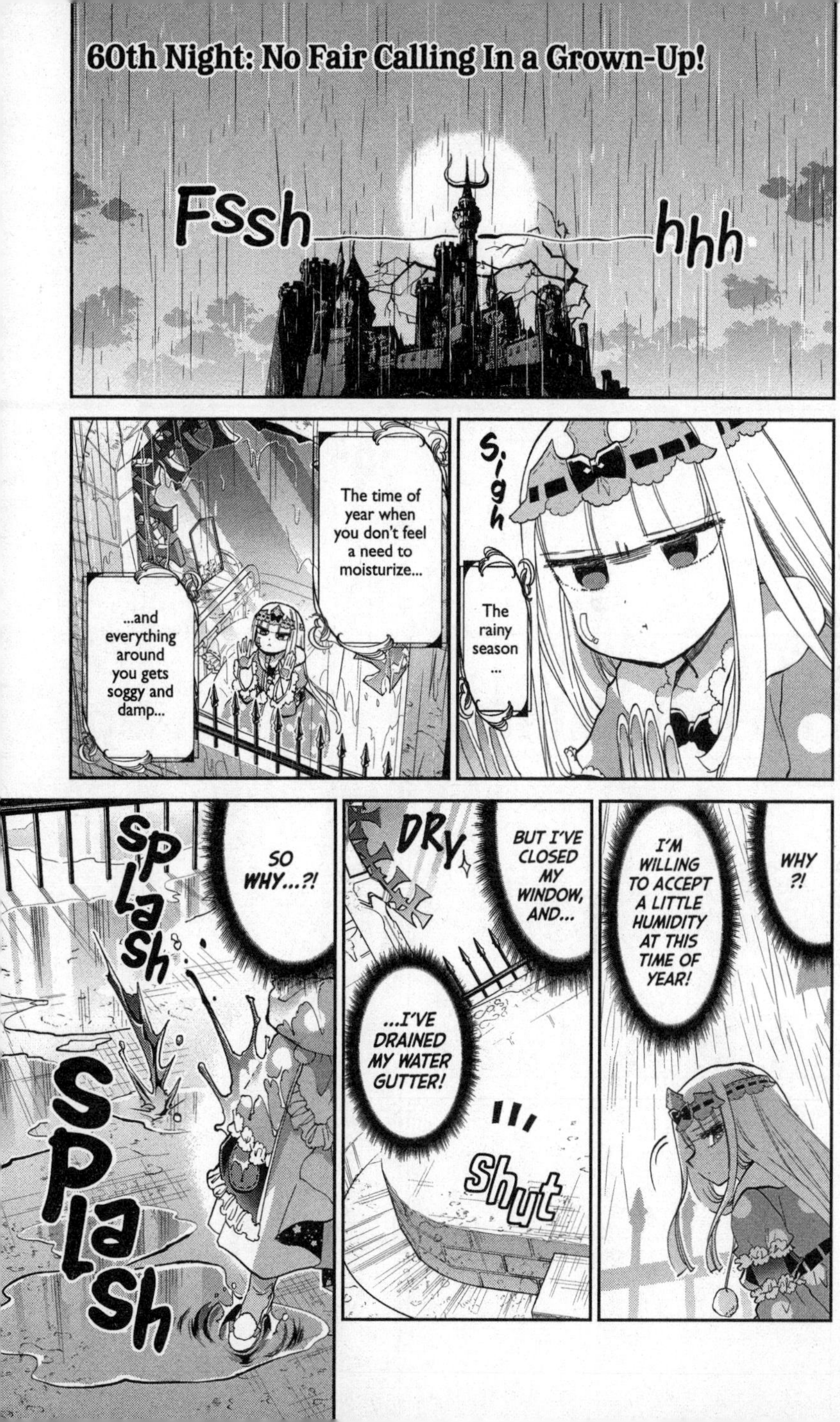

Fssh———hhh
Sigh
The rainy season...
The time of year when you don't feel a need to moisturize...
...and everything around you gets soggy and damp...
WHY?!
I'M WILLING TO ACCEPT A LITTLE HUMIDITY AT THIS TIME OF YEAR!
BUT I'VE CLOSED MY WINDOW, AND...
DRY
...I'VE DRAINED MY WATER GUTTER!
Shut
SO WHY...?!
Splash
Splash

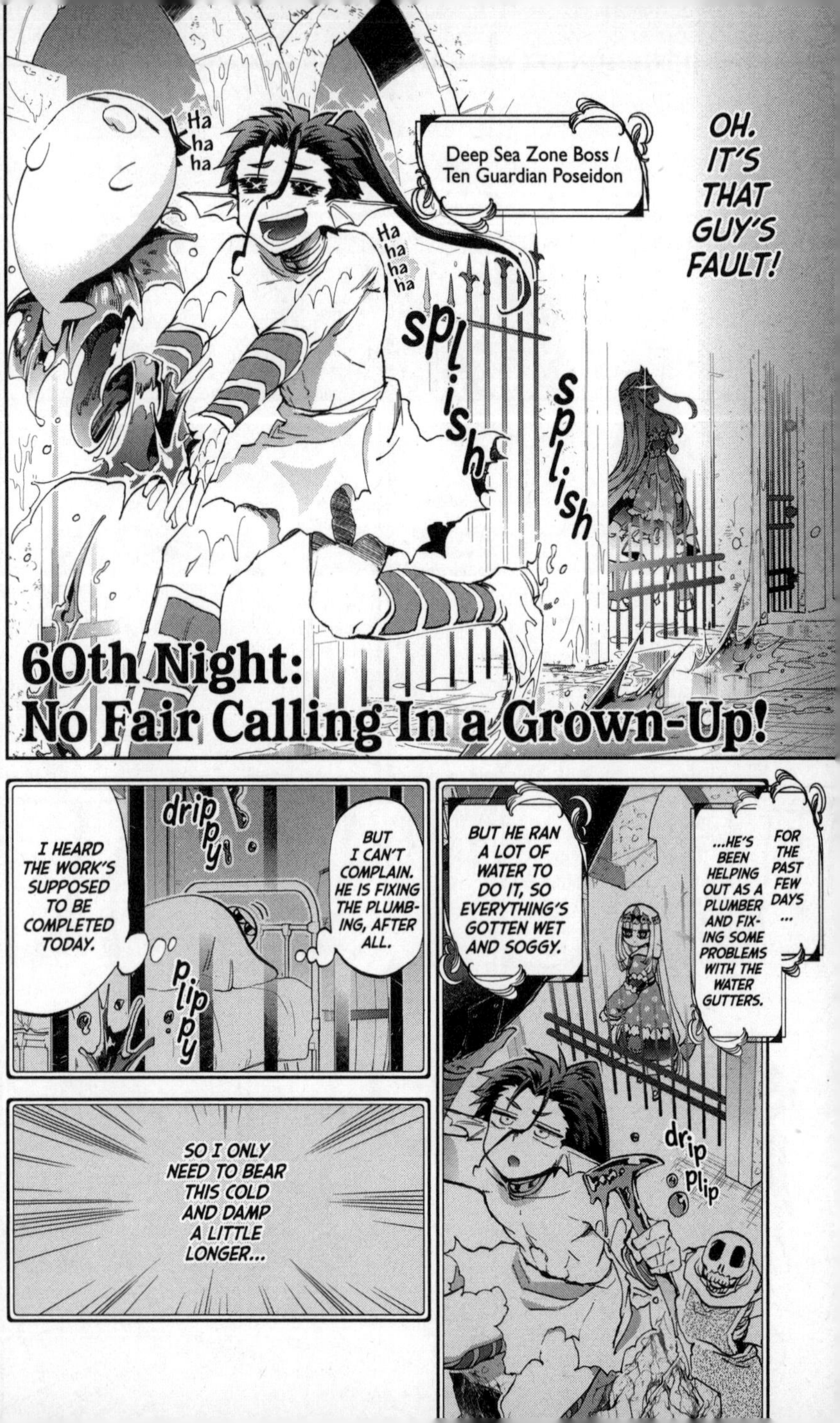
OH. IT'S THAT GUY'S FAULT!
Deep Sea Zone Boss / Ten Guardian Poseidon
splish
splish
Ha ha ha ha
Ha ha ha
60th Night: No Fair Calling In a Grown-Up!
FOR THE PAST FEW DAYS...
...HE'S BEEN HELPING OUT AS A PLUMBER AND FIX-ING SOME PROBLEMS WITH THE WATER GUTTERS.
BUT HE RAN A LOT OF WATER TO DO IT, SO EVERYTHING'S GOTTEN WET AND SOGGY.
drip plip
BUT I CAN'T COMPLAIN. HE IS FIXING THE PLUMB-ING, AFTER ALL.
drippy
I HEARD THE WORK'S SUPPOSED TO BE COMPLETED TODAY.
plippy
SO I ONLY NEED TO BEAR THIS COLD AND DAMP A LITTLE LONGER...

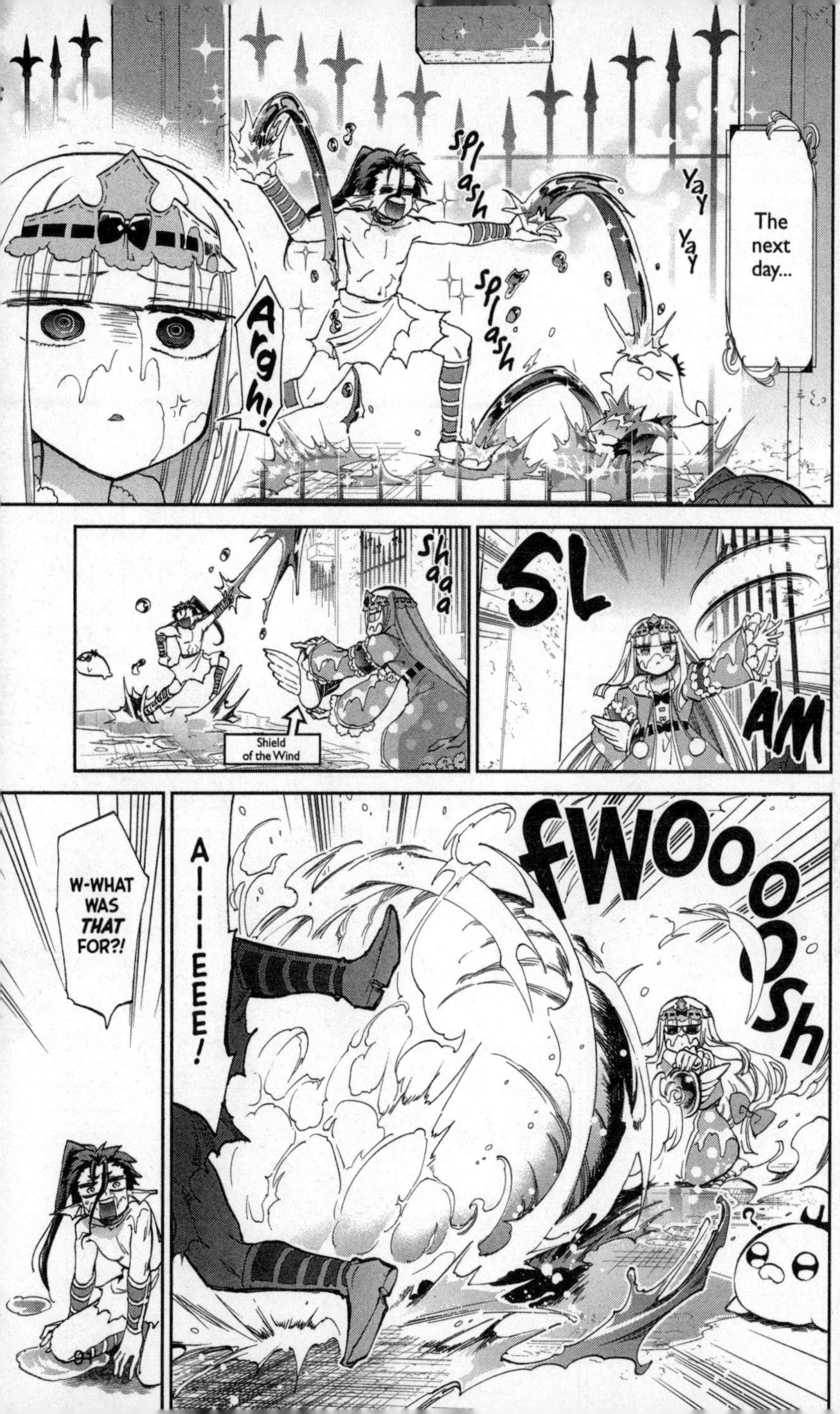
The next day...
Yay Yay
splash
splash
Argh!
SLAM
shaaa
Shield of the Wind
FWOOOOSH
AIIIEEE!
W-WHAT WAS *THAT* FOR?!

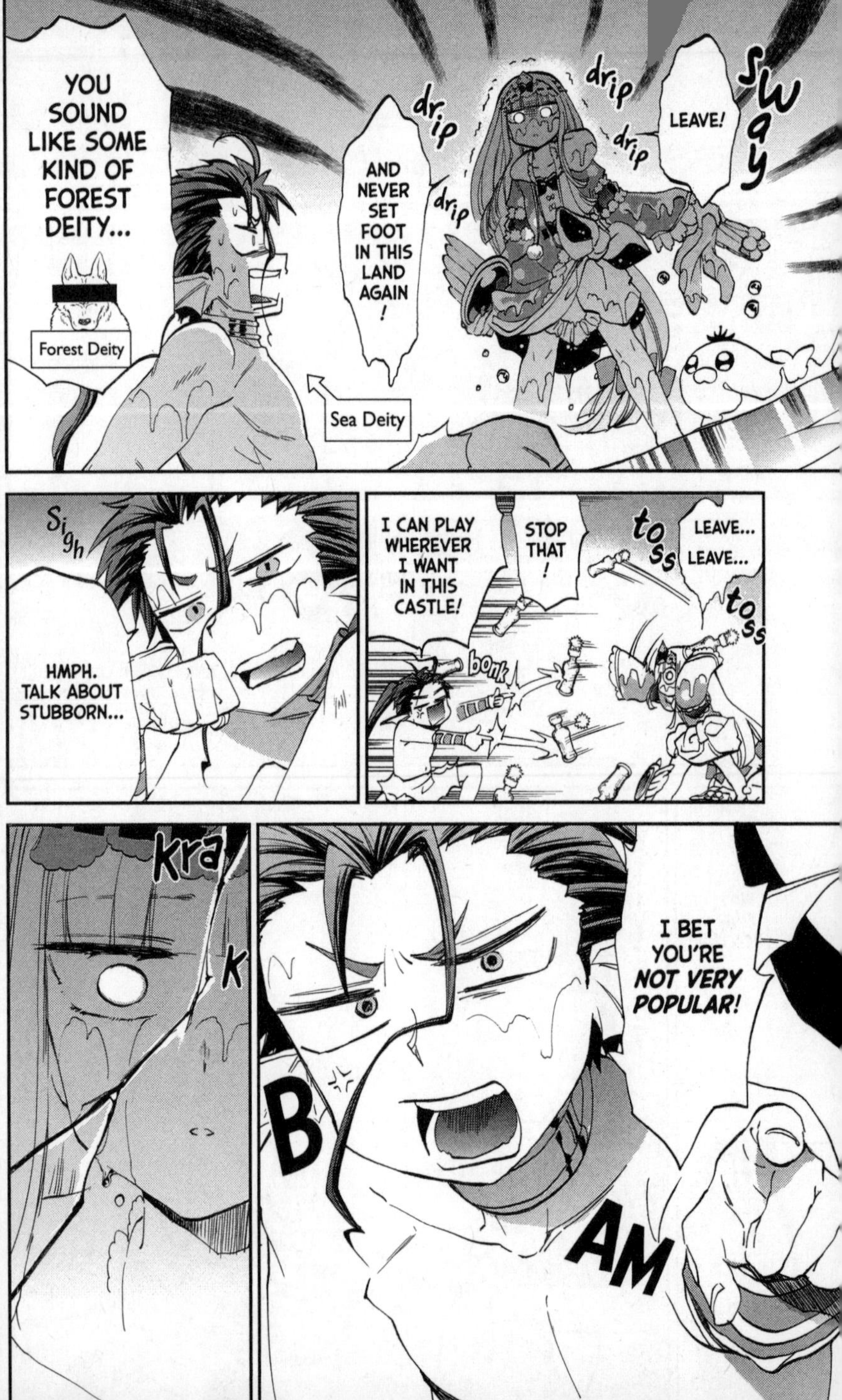
sway
LEAVE!
drip
drip
drip
drip
AND NEVER SET FOOT IN THIS LAND AGAIN!
Sea Deity
YOU SOUND LIKE SOME KIND OF FOREST DEITY...
Forest Deity
LEAVE... LEAVE...
toss
toss
STOP THAT!
I CAN PLAY WHEREVER I WANT IN THIS CASTLE!
bonk
Sigh
HMPH. TALK ABOUT STUBBORN...
I BET YOU'RE *NOT VERY POPULAR!*
BAM
krak

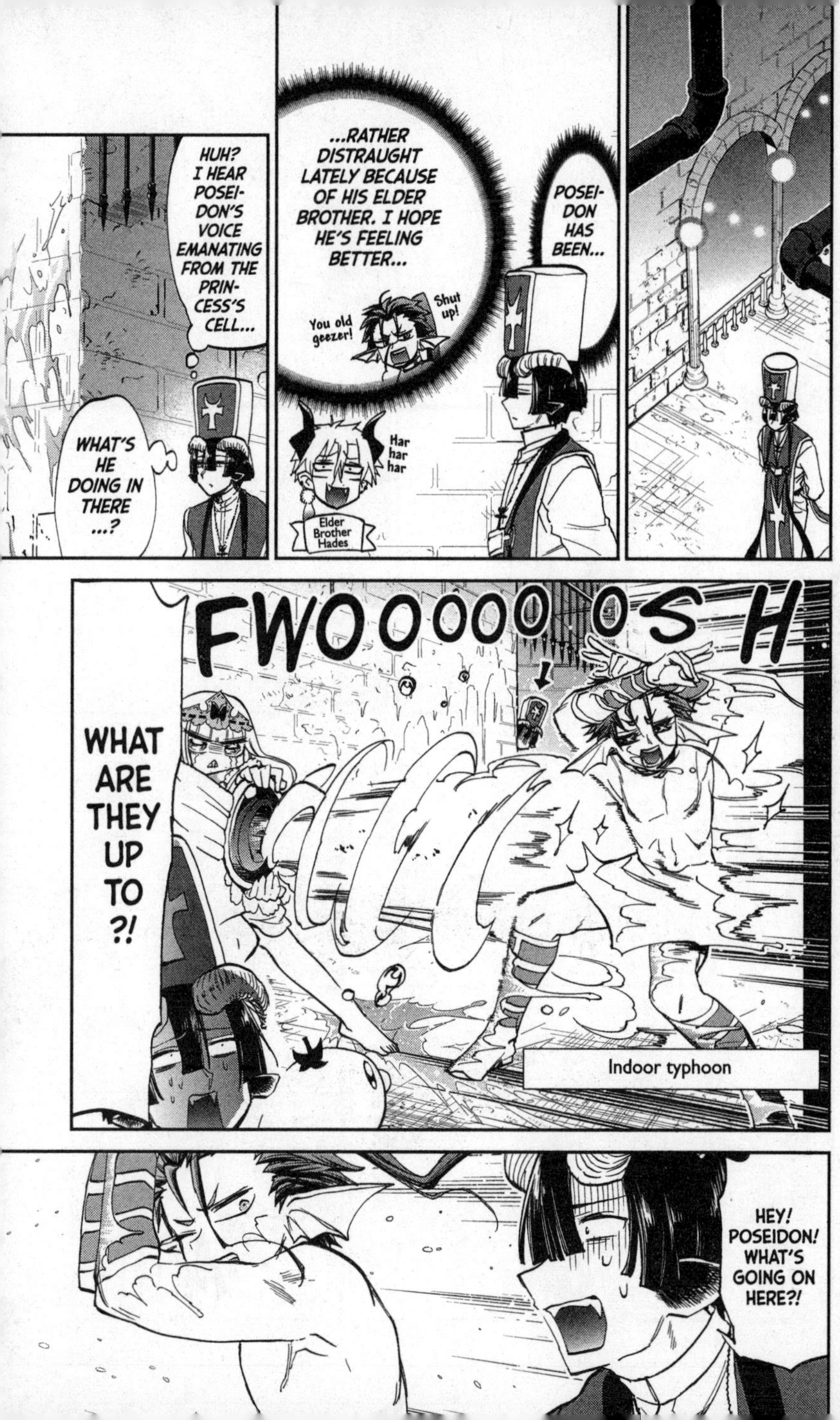
POSEIDON HAS BEEN...
...RATHER DISTRAUGHT LATELY BECAUSE OF HIS ELDER BROTHER. I HOPE HE'S FEELING BETTER...
Shut up!
You old geezer!
Har har har
Elder Brother Hades
HUH? I HEAR POSEIDON'S VOICE EMANATING FROM THE PRINCESS'S CELL...
WHAT'S HE DOING IN THERE ...?
FWOOOOOOSH
WHAT ARE THEY UP TO?!
Indoor typhoon
HEY! POSEIDON! WHAT'S GOING ON HERE?!

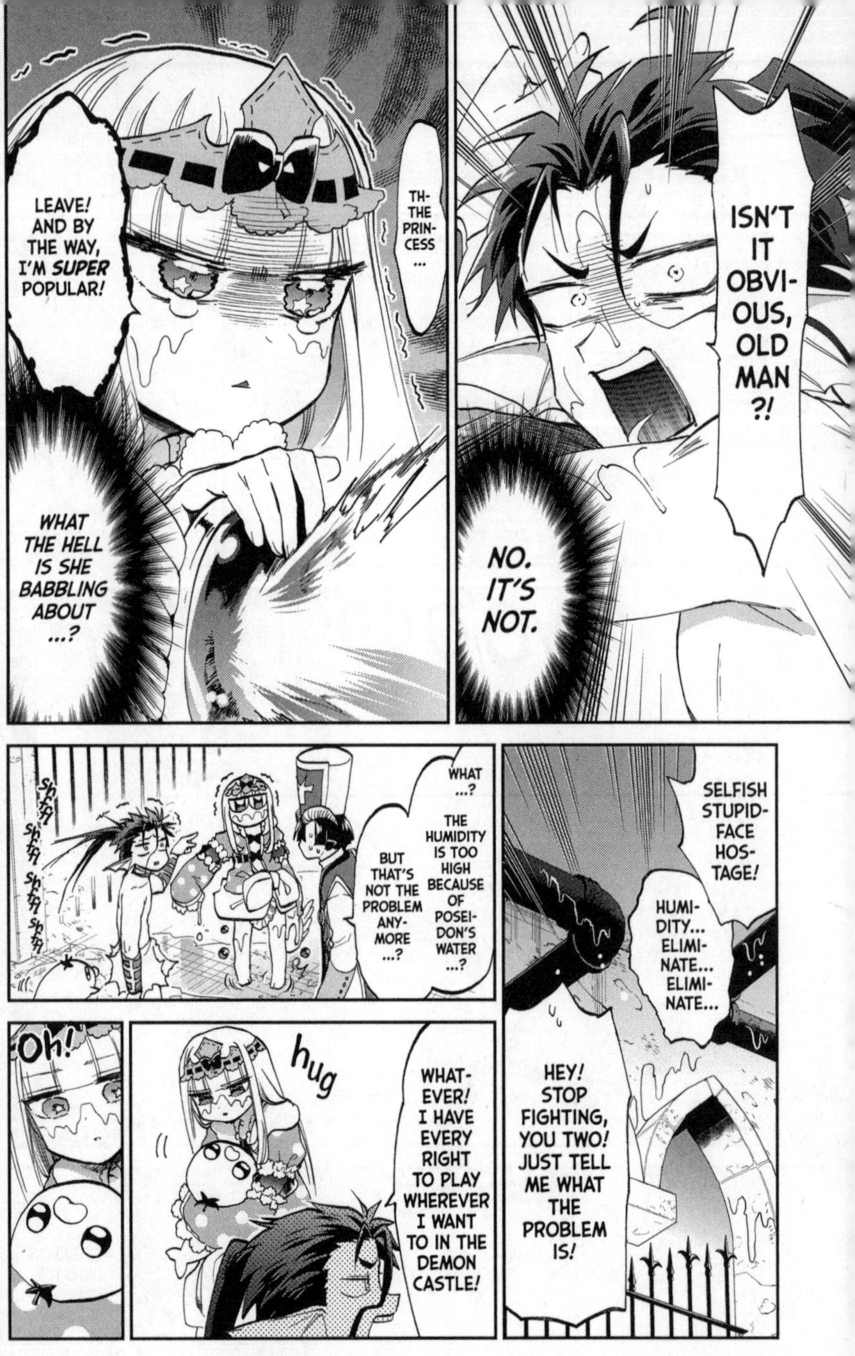
ISN'T IT OBVIOUS, OLD MAN?!
NO. IT'S NOT.
TH-THE PRINCESS...
LEAVE! AND BY THE WAY, I'M *SUPER* POPULAR!
WHAT THE HELL IS SHE BABBLING ABOUT...?
SELFISH STUPID-FACE HOSTAGE!
HUMIDITY... ELIMINATE... ELIMINATE...
HEY! STOP FIGHTING, YOU TWO! JUST TELL ME WHAT THE PROBLEM IS!
WHAT...?
THE HUMIDITY IS TOO HIGH BECAUSE OF POSEIDON'S WATER...?
BUT THAT'S NOT THE PROBLEM ANYMORE...?
shffl shffl shffl shffl
hug
WHATEVER! I HAVE EVERY RIGHT TO PLAY WHEREVER I WANT TO IN THE DEMON CASTLE!
Oh!

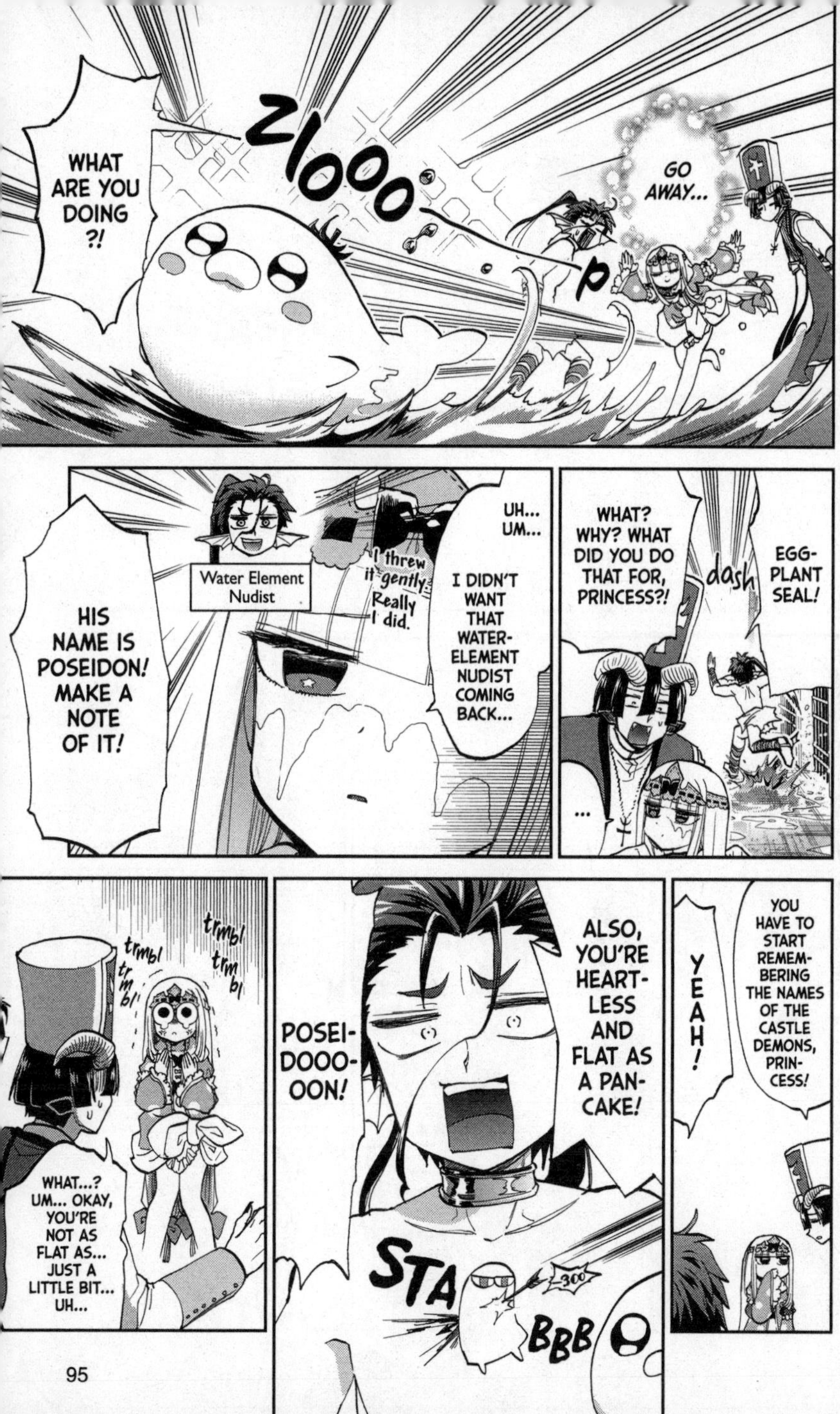
GO AWAY...
ZLOOOP
WHAT ARE YOU DOING ?!
EGG-PLANT SEAL!
dash
WHAT? WHY? WHAT DID YOU DO THAT FOR, PRINCESS?!
...
UH... UM...
I DIDN'T WANT THAT WATER-ELEMENT NUDIST COMING BACK...
I threw it gently. Really I did.
Water Element Nudist
HIS NAME IS POSEIDON! MAKE A NOTE OF IT!
YOU HAVE TO START REMEMBERING THE NAMES OF THE CASTLE DEMONS, PRINCESS!
YEAH!
ALSO, YOU'RE HEARTLESS AND FLAT AS A PANCAKE!
POSEI-DOOOOON!
STABBB
300
trmbl trmbl trmbl trmbl
WHAT...? UM... OKAY, YOU'RE NOT AS FLAT AS... JUST A LITTLE BIT... UH...

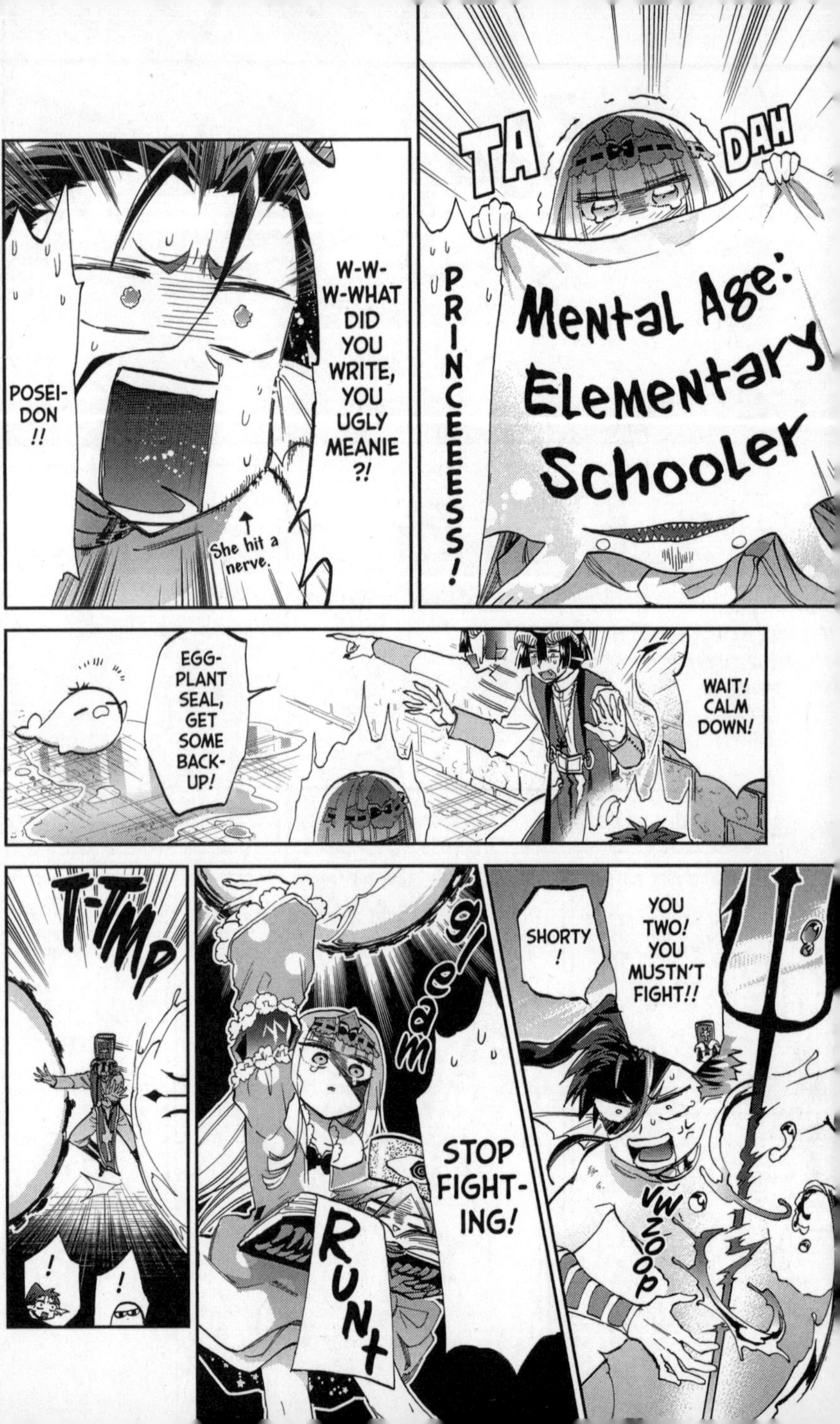
TA
DAH
PRINCEEEESS!
Mental Age: Elementary Schooler
W-W-W-WHAT DID YOU WRITE, YOU UGLY MEANIE?!
POSEI-DON!!
She hit a nerve.
WAIT! CALM DOWN!
EGG-PLANT SEAL, GET SOME BACK-UP!
YOU TWO! YOU MUSTN'T FIGHT!!
SHORTY!
VWZOOP
gleam
STOP FIGHT-ING!
RUNT
T-TMP
!
!

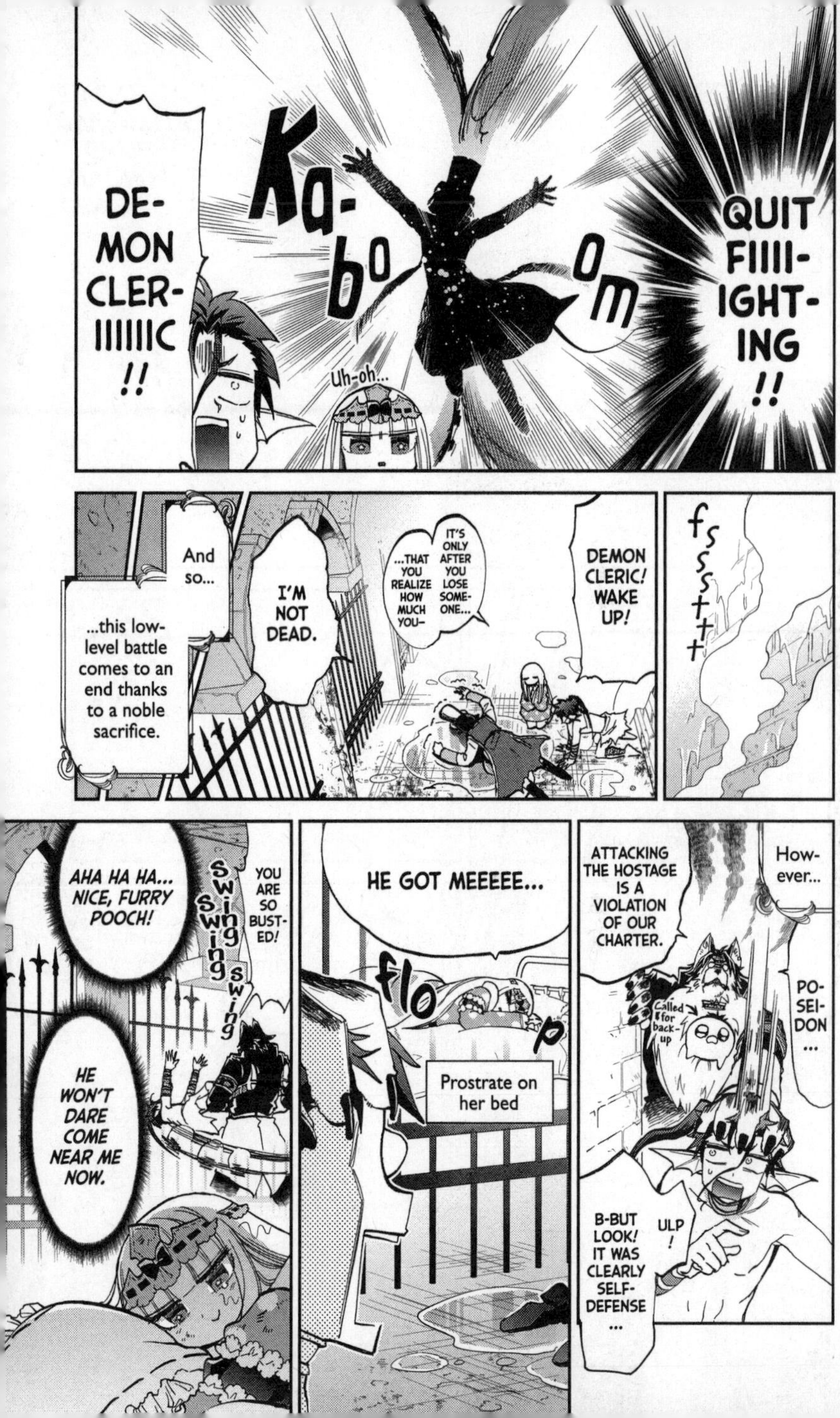
QUIT FIIIII-IGHT-ING!!
Ka-boom
DE-MON CLER-IIIIIIC!!
Uh-oh...
fsssttt
DEMON CLERIC! WAKE UP!
IT'S ONLY AFTER YOU LOSE SOME-ONE...
...THAT YOU REALIZE HOW MUCH YOU—
I'M NOT DEAD.
And so...
...this low-level battle comes to an end thanks to a noble sacrifice.
How-ever...
ATTACKING THE HOSTAGE IS A VIOLATION OF OUR CHARTER.
PO-SEI-DON...
Called for back-up
ULP!
B-BUT LOOK! IT WAS CLEARLY SELF-DEFENSE...
HE GOT MEEEEE...
flop
Prostrate on her bed
YOU ARE SO BUST-ED!
swing swing swing
AHA HA HA... NICE, FURRY POOCH!
HE WON'T DARE COME NEAR ME NOW.

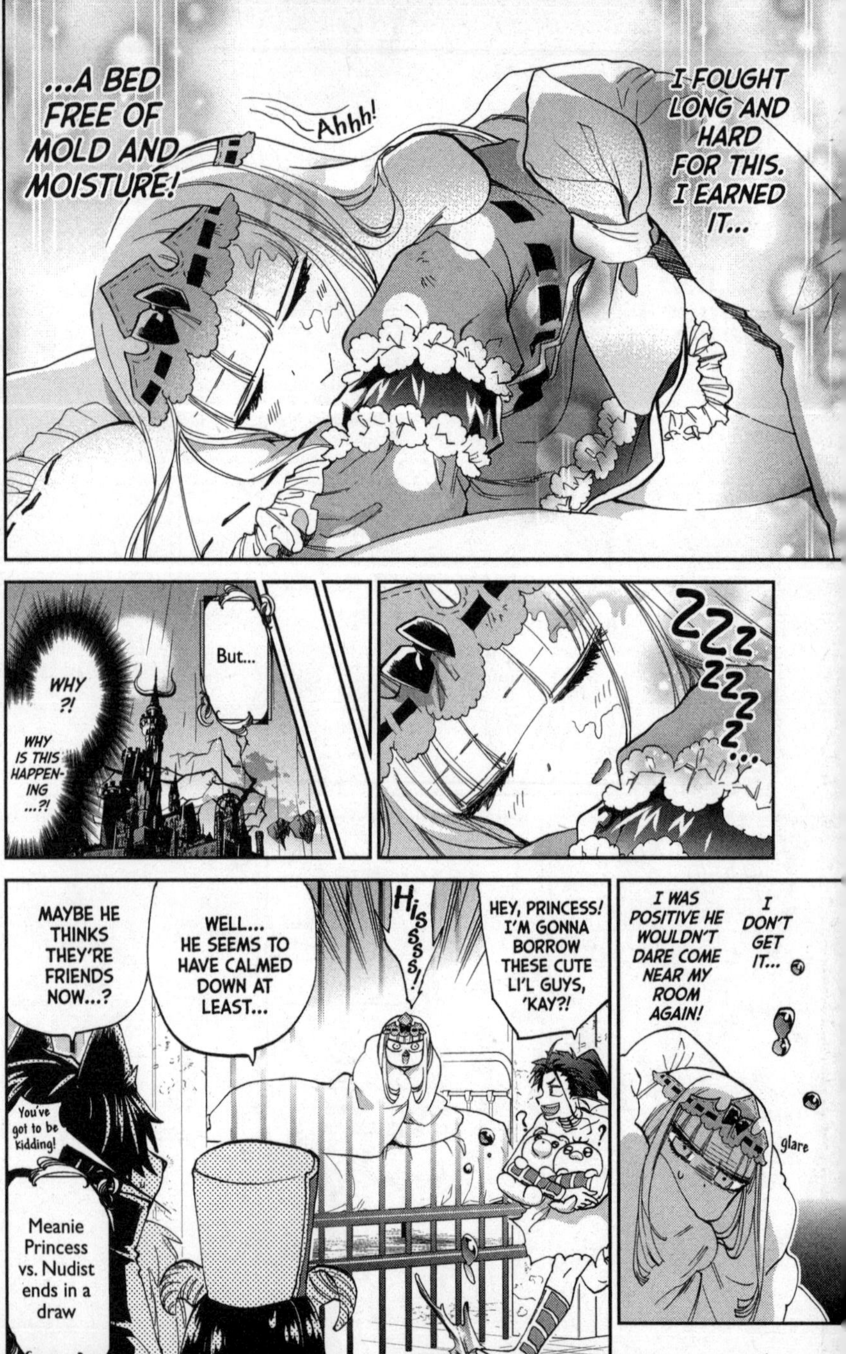
I FOUGHT LONG AND HARD FOR THIS. I EARNED IT...
Ahhh!
...A BED FREE OF MOLD AND MOISTURE!
ZZZ ZZZZ...
But...
WHY?!
WHY IS THIS HAPPENING...?!
I DON'T GET IT...
I WAS POSITIVE HE WOULDN'T DARE COME NEAR MY ROOM AGAIN!
glare
HEY, PRINCESS! I'M GONNA BORROW THESE CUTE LI'L GUYS, 'KAY?!
Hissss!
WELL... HE SEEMS TO HAVE CALMED DOWN AT LEAST...
MAYBE HE THINKS THEY'RE FRIENDS NOW...?
You've got to be kidding!
Meanie Princess vs. Nudist ends in a draw

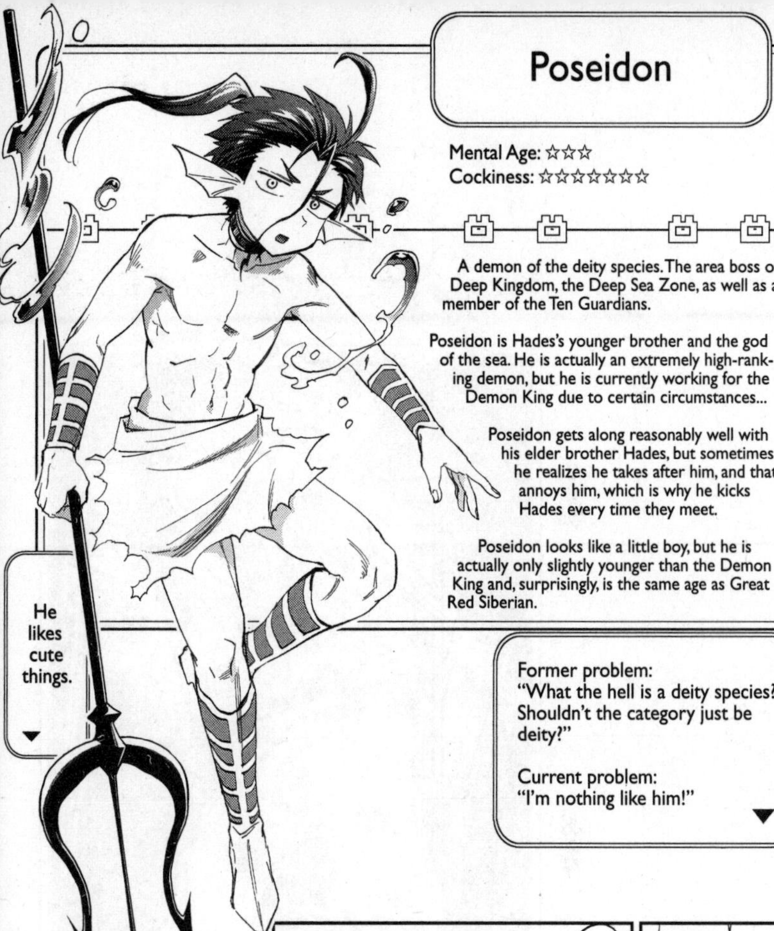

Poseidon

Mental Age: ☆☆☆
Cockiness: ☆☆☆☆☆☆☆☆

A demon of the deity species. The area boss of Deep Kingdom, the Deep Sea Zone, as well as a member of the Ten Guardians.

Poseidon is Hades's younger brother and the god of the sea. He is actually an extremely high-ranking demon, but he is currently working for the Demon King due to certain circumstances...

Poseidon gets along reasonably well with his elder brother Hades, but sometimes he realizes he takes after him, and that annoys him, which is why he kicks Hades every time they meet.

Poseidon looks like a little boy, but he is actually only slightly younger than the Demon King and, surprisingly, is the same age as Great Red Siberian.

He likes cute things.

Former problem:
"What the hell is a deity species? Shouldn't the category just be deity?"

Current problem:
"I'm nothing like him!"

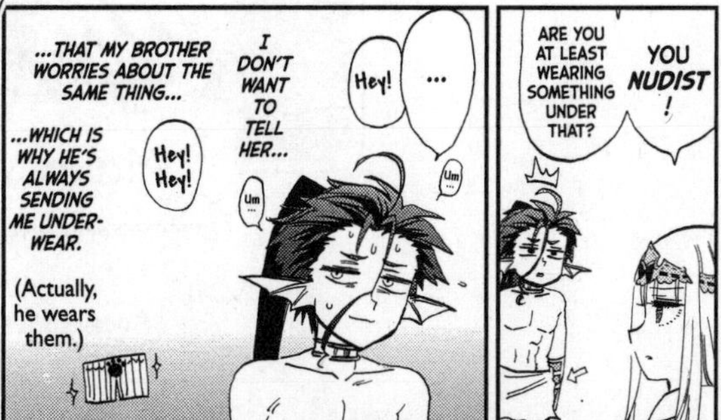
ARE YOU AT LEAST WEARING SOMETHING UNDER THAT?
YOU NUDIST!
...
Hey!
Um...
I DON'T WANT TO TELL HER...
Um...
Hey! Hey!
...THAT MY BROTHER WORRIES ABOUT THE SAME THING...
...WHICH IS WHY HE'S ALWAYS SENDING ME UNDER-WEAR.
(Actually, he wears them.)

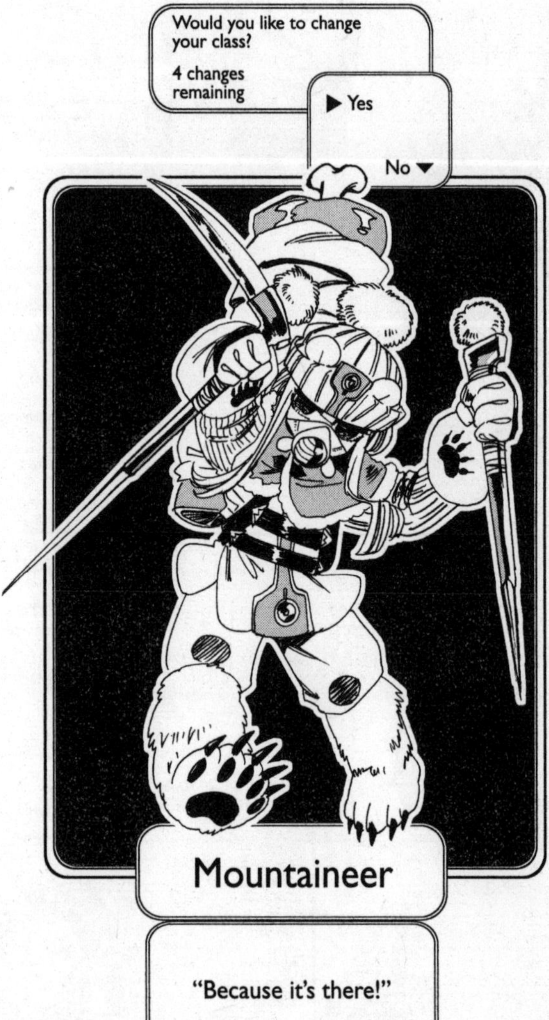
Would you like to change your class?
4 changes remaining
▶ Yes
No ▼
Mountaineer
"Because it's there!"

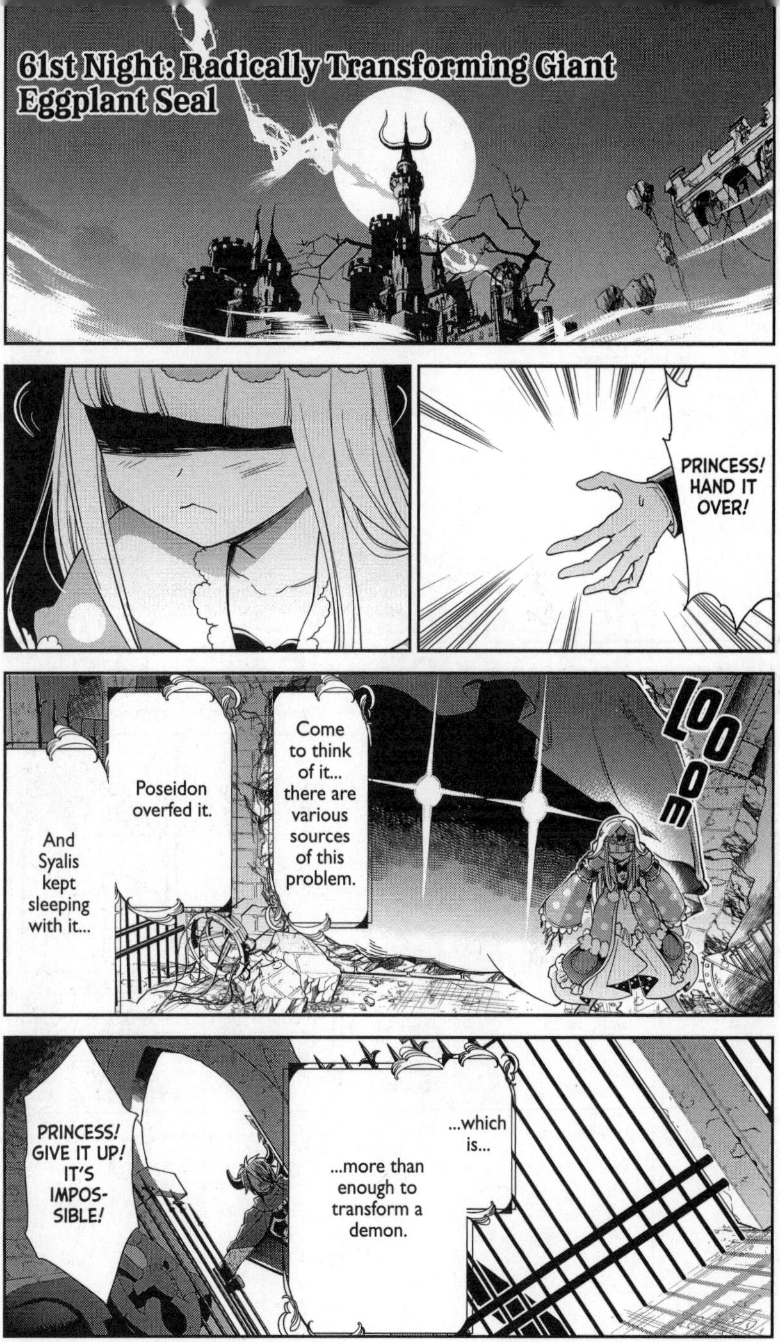
61st Night: Radically Transforming Giant Eggplant Seal
PRINCESS! HAND IT OVER!
LOOOOM
Come to think of it... there are various sources of this problem.
Poseidon overfed it.
And Syalis kept sleeping with it...
...which is...
...more than enough to transform a demon.
PRINCESS! GIVE IT UP! IT'S IMPOSSIBLE!

61st Night: Radically Transforming Giant Eggplant Seal

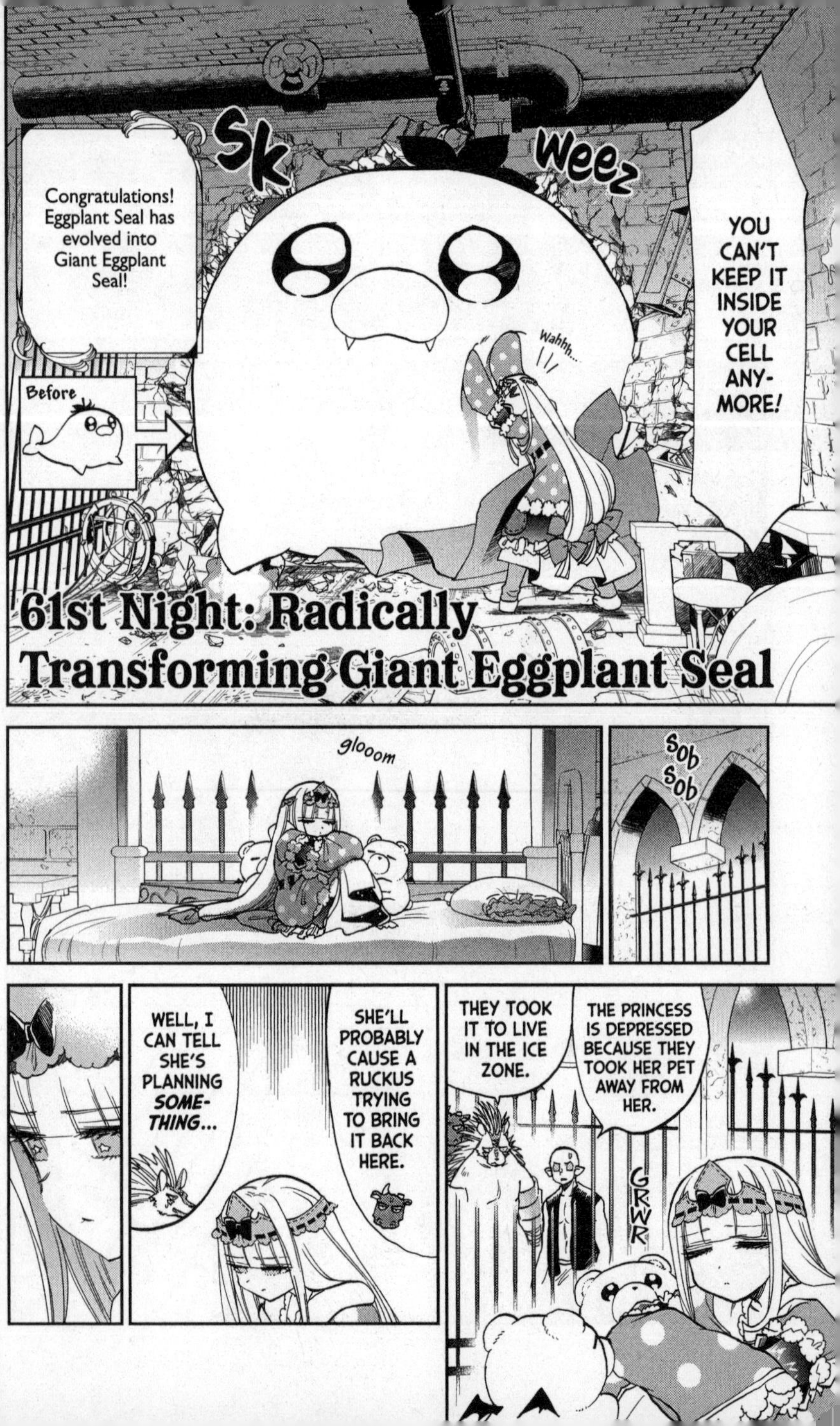
YOU CAN'T KEEP IT INSIDE YOUR CELL ANY-MORE!
Sk weez
Wahhh...
Congratulations! Eggplant Seal has evolved into Giant Eggplant Seal!
Before
Sob sob
glooom
THE PRINCESS IS DEPRESSED BECAUSE THEY TOOK HER PET AWAY FROM HER.
THEY TOOK IT TO LIVE IN THE ICE ZONE.
GRWR
SHE'LL PROBABLY CAUSE A RUCKUS TRYING TO BRING IT BACK HERE.
WELL, I CAN TELL SHE'S PLANNING *SOME-THING...*

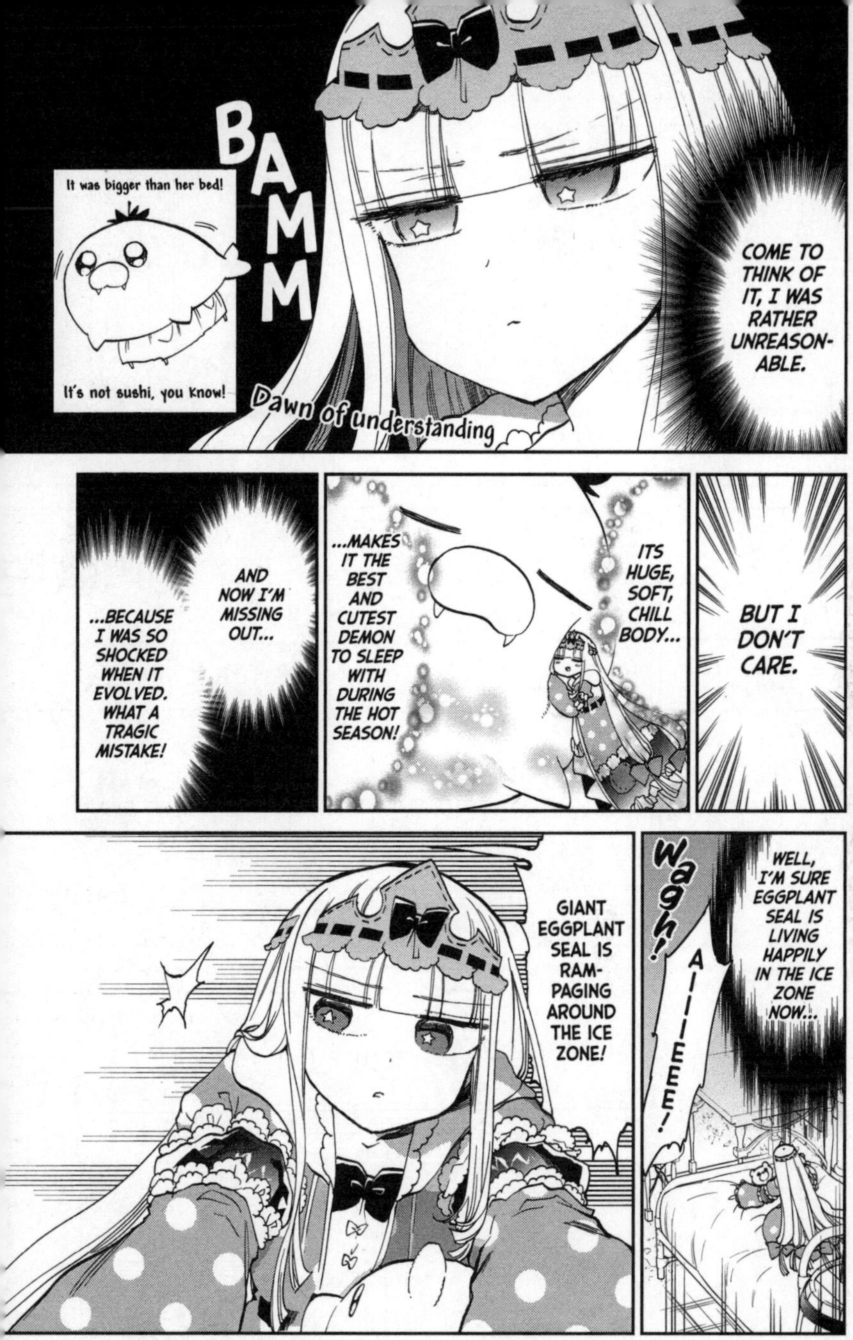

COME TO THINK OF IT, I WAS RATHER UNREASON-ABLE.
BAMM
Dawn of understanding
It was bigger than her bed!
It's not sushi, you know!
BUT I DON'T CARE.
ITS HUGE, SOFT, CHILL BODY...
...MAKES IT THE BEST AND CUTEST DEMON TO SLEEP WITH DURING THE HOT SEASON!
AND NOW I'M MISSING OUT...
...BECAUSE I WAS SO SHOCKED WHEN IT EVOLVED. WHAT A TRAGIC MISTAKE!
WELL, I'M SURE EGGPLANT SEAL IS LIVING HAPPILY IN THE ICE ZONE NOW...
Wagh!
AIIIIEEEE!
GIANT EGGPLANT SEAL IS RAM-PAGING AROUND THE ICE ZONE!

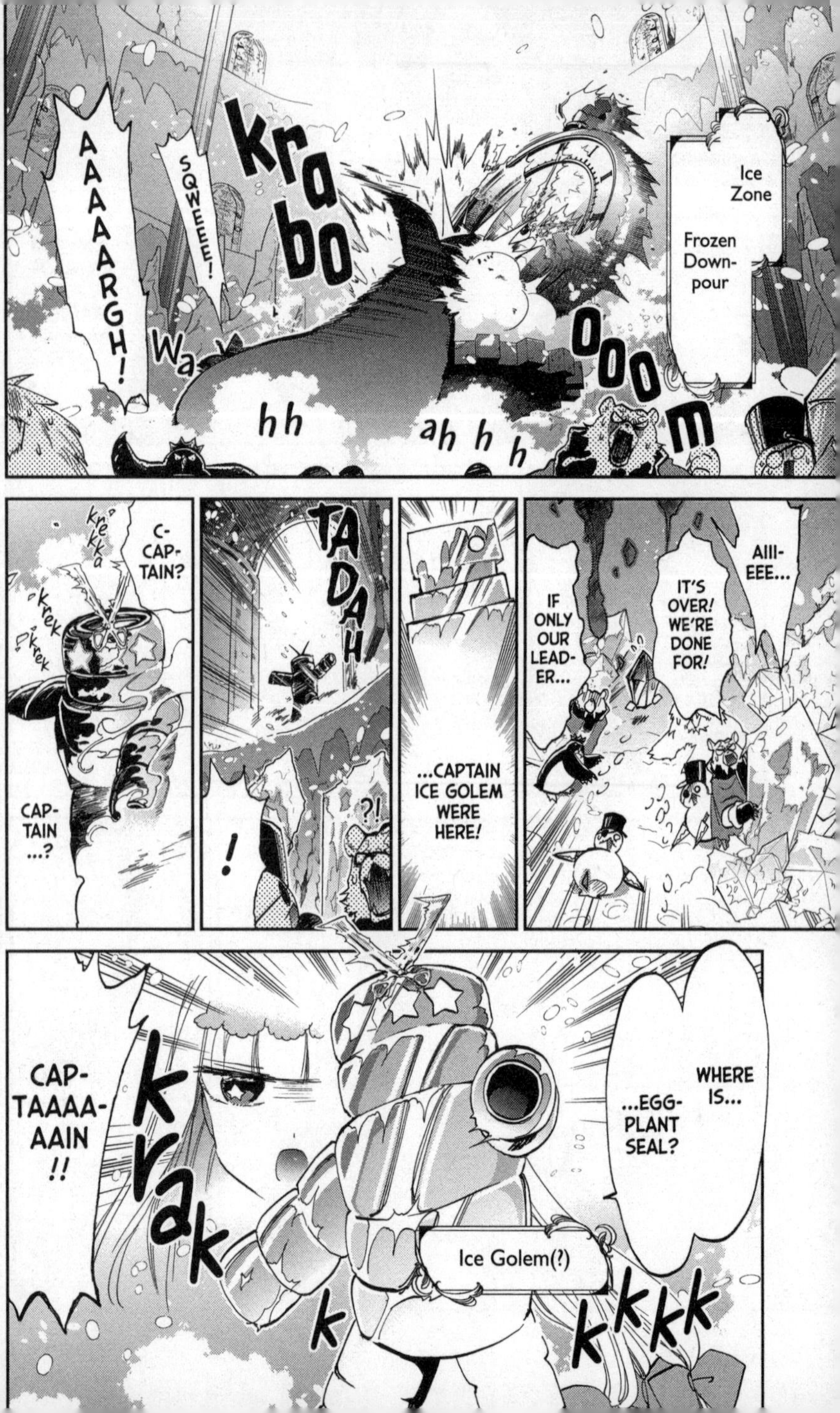
Ice Zone
Frozen Down-pour
kraboOOOm
SQWEEE!
AAAAAARGH!
Wa hh ah h h h
AIII-EEE...
IT'S OVER! WE'RE DONE FOR!
IF ONLY OUR LEADER...
...CAPTAIN ICE GOLEM WERE HERE!
TADAH
?!
!
krekka
C-CAPTAIN?
krek krek
CAPTAIN...?
WHERE IS...
...EGG-PLANT SEAL?
Ice Golem(?)
krak
kkkk
CAPTAAAAAAIN!!

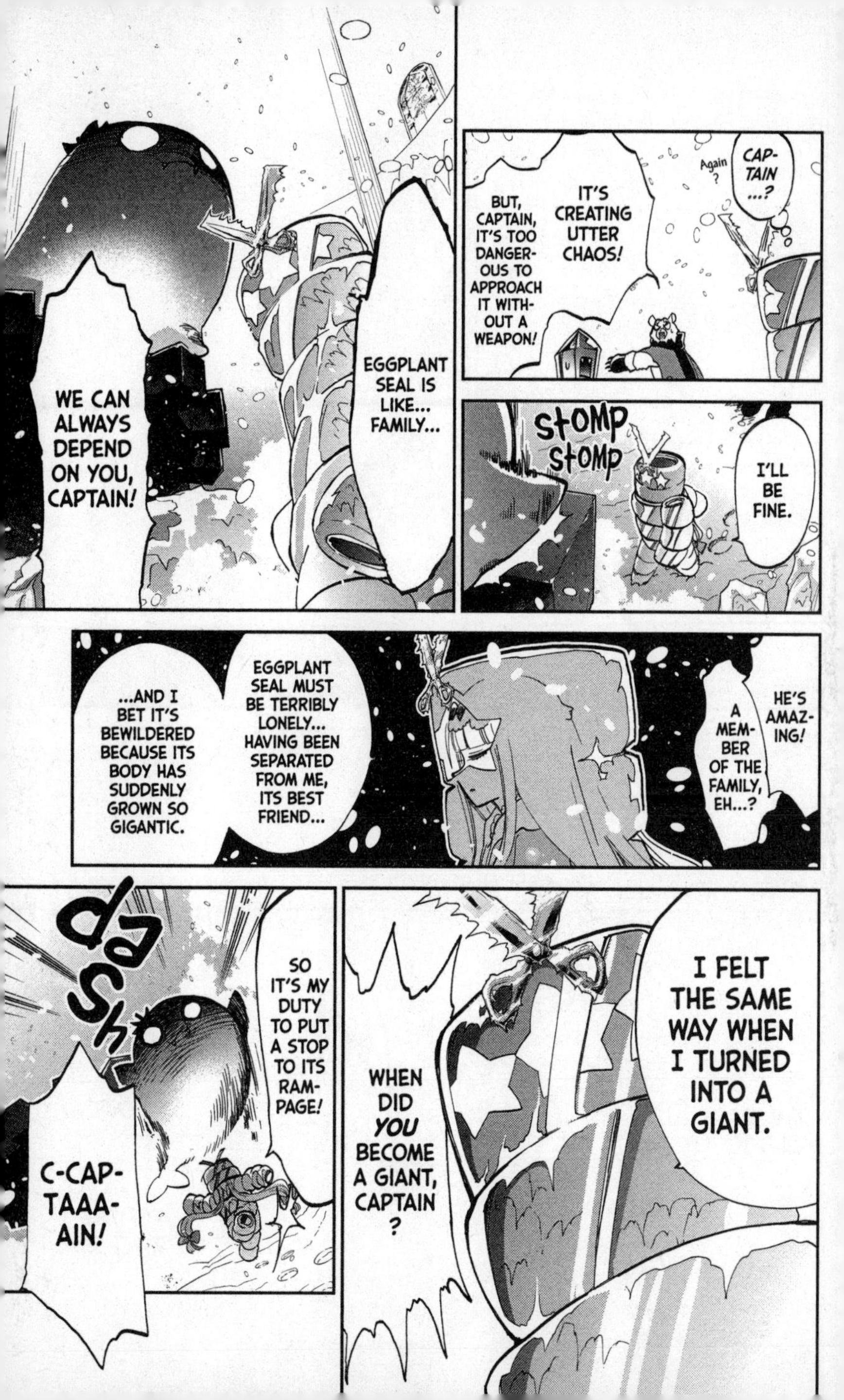
CAPTAIN...?
Again?
IT'S CREATING UTTER CHAOS!
BUT, CAPTAIN, IT'S TOO DANGEROUS TO APPROACH IT WITHOUT A WEAPON!
I'LL BE FINE.
STOMP STOMP
EGGPLANT SEAL IS LIKE... FAMILY...
WE CAN ALWAYS DEPEND ON YOU, CAPTAIN!
HE'S AMAZING!
A MEMBER OF THE FAMILY, EH...?
EGGPLANT SEAL MUST BE TERRIBLY LONELY... HAVING BEEN SEPARATED FROM ME, ITS BEST FRIEND...
...AND I BET IT'S BEWILDERED BECAUSE ITS BODY HAS SUDDENLY GROWN SO GIGANTIC.
I FELT THE SAME WAY WHEN I TURNED INTO A GIANT.
WHEN DID *YOU* BECOME A GIANT, CAPTAIN?
SO IT'S MY DUTY TO PUT A STOP TO ITS RAMPAGE!
DASH
C-CAPTAAAAIN!

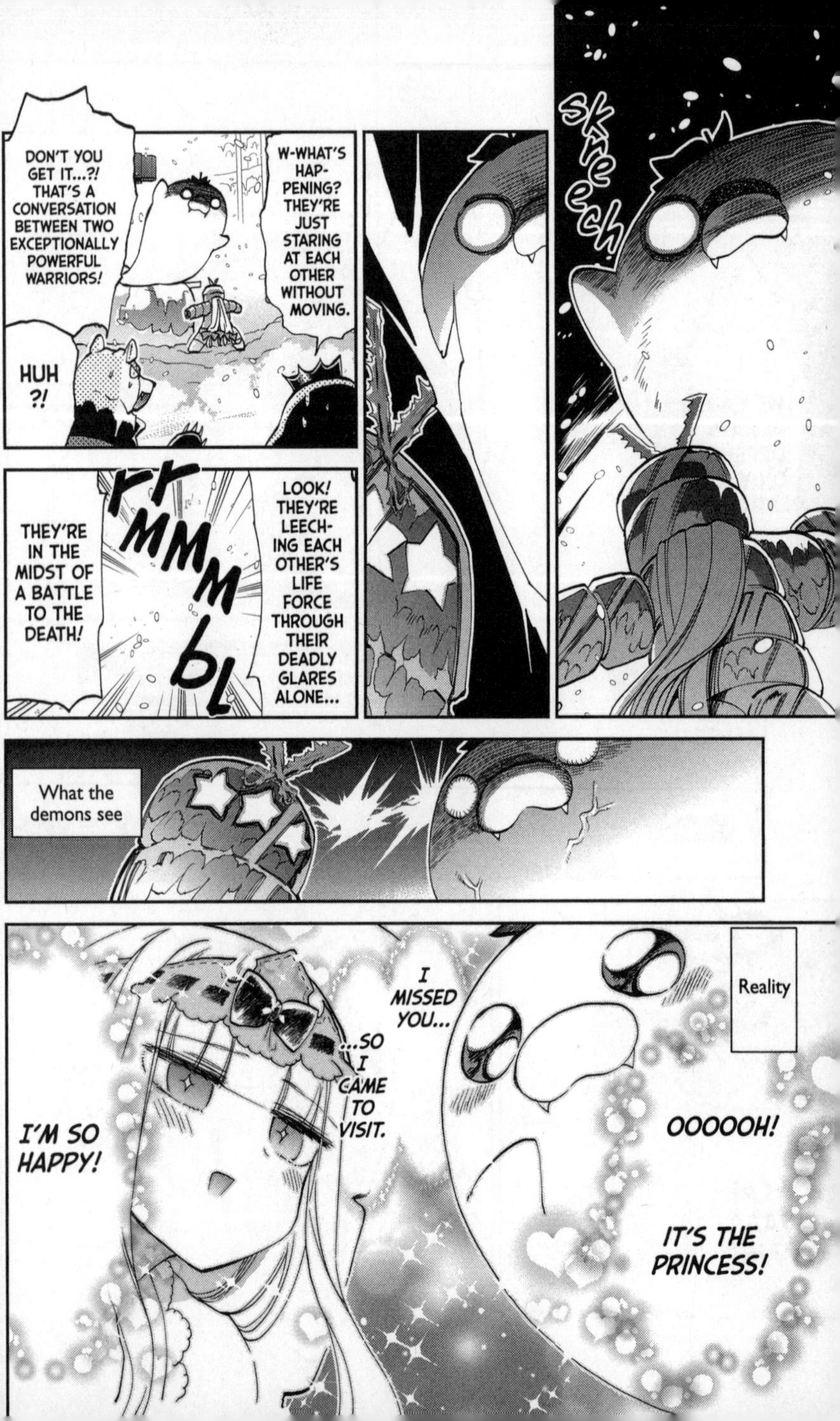

skreech
W-WHAT'S HAPPENING? THEY'RE JUST STARING AT EACH OTHER WITHOUT MOVING.
DON'T YOU GET IT...?! THAT'S A CONVERSATION BETWEEN TWO EXCEPTIONALLY POWERFUL WARRIORS!
HUH?!
LOOK! THEY'RE LEECHING EACH OTHER'S LIFE FORCE THROUGH THEIR DEADLY GLARES ALONE...
rrMMMbl
THEY'RE IN THE MIDST OF A BATTLE TO THE DEATH!
What the demons see
Reality
OOOOOH!
IT'S THE PRINCESS!
I MISSED YOU...
...SO I CAME TO VISIT.
I'M SO HAPPY!

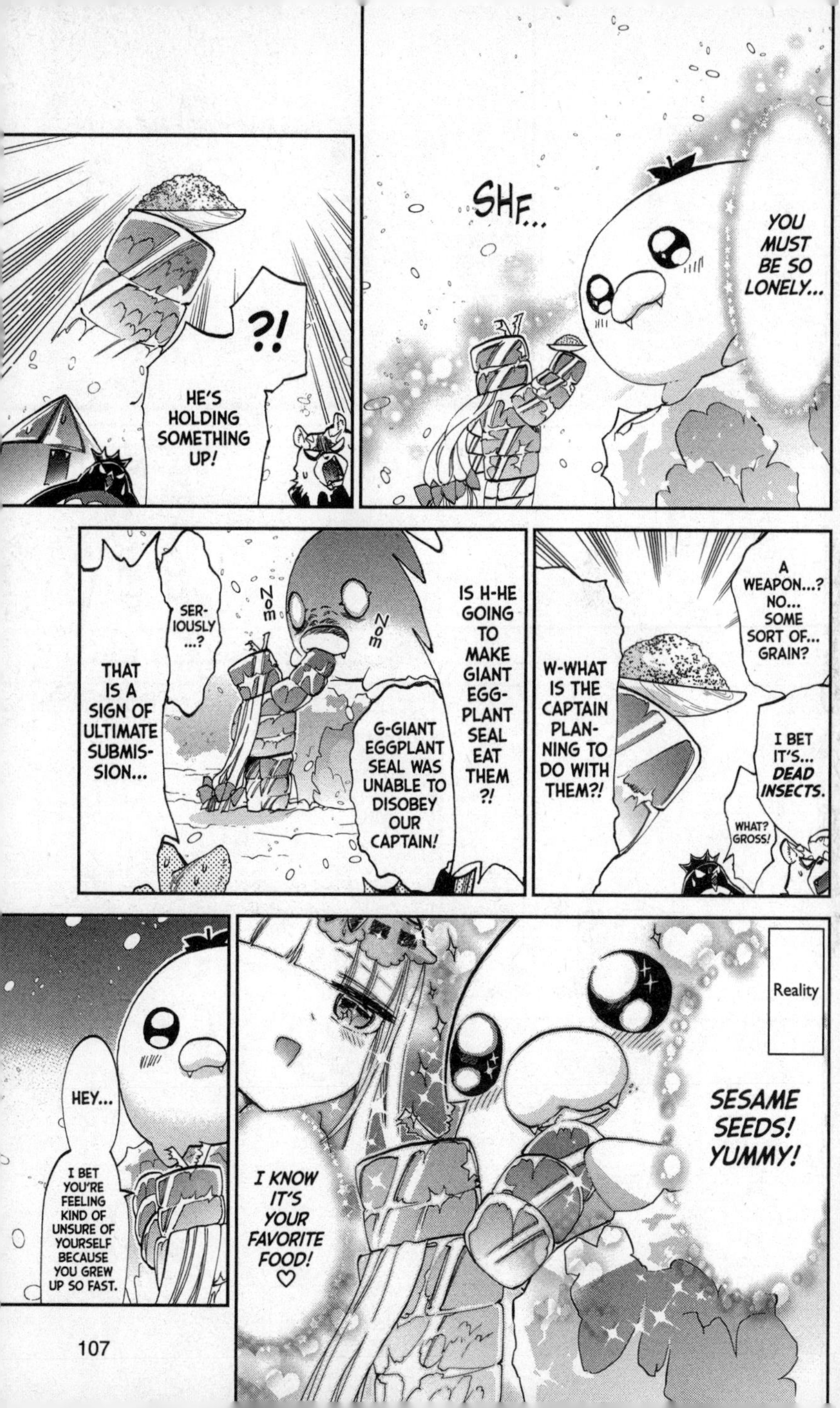
SHF...
YOU MUST BE SO LONELY...
?!
HE'S HOLDING SOMETHING UP!
A WEAPON...? NO... SOME SORT OF... GRAIN?
W-WHAT IS THE CAPTAIN PLAN-NING TO DO WITH THEM?!
I BET IT'S... ***DEAD INSECTS.***
WHAT? GROSS!
IS H-HE GOING TO MAKE GIANT EGG-PLANT SEAL EAT THEM?!
Nom
Nom
G-GIANT EGGPLANT SEAL WAS UNABLE TO DISOBEY OUR CAPTAIN!
SER-IOUSLY ...?
THAT IS A SIGN OF ULTIMATE SUBMIS-SION...
Reality
SESAME SEEDS! YUMMY!
I KNOW IT'S YOUR FAVORITE FOOD! ♡
HEY...
I BET YOU'RE FEELING KIND OF UNSURE OF YOURSELF BECAUSE YOU GREW UP SO FAST.

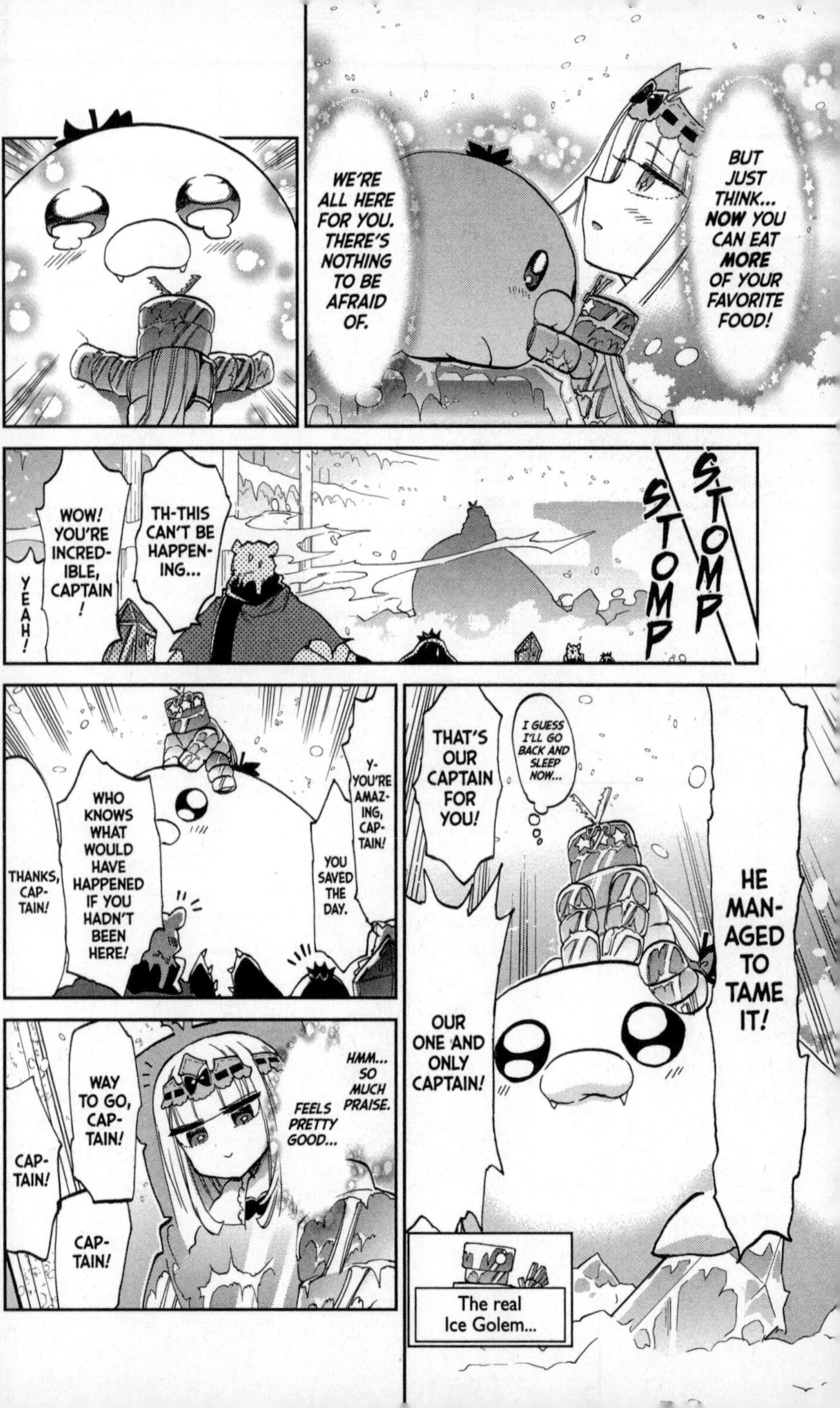
BUT JUST THINK... NOW YOU CAN EAT MORE OF YOUR FAVORITE FOOD!
WE'RE ALL HERE FOR YOU. THERE'S NOTHING TO BE AFRAID OF.
STOMP
STOMP
TH-THIS CAN'T BE HAPPENING...
WOW! YOU'RE INCREDIBLE, CAPTAIN!
YEAH!
HE MANAGED TO TAME IT!
I GUESS I'LL GO BACK AND SLEEP NOW...
THAT'S OUR CAPTAIN FOR YOU!
OUR ONE AND ONLY CAPTAIN!
The real Ice Golem...
Y-YOU'RE AMAZING, CAPTAIN!
YOU SAVED THE DAY.
WHO KNOWS WHAT WOULD HAVE HAPPENED IF YOU HADN'T BEEN HERE!
THANKS, CAPTAIN!
HMM... SO MUCH PRAISE.
FEELS PRETTY GOOD...
WAY TO GO, CAPTAIN!
CAPTAIN!
CAPTAIN!

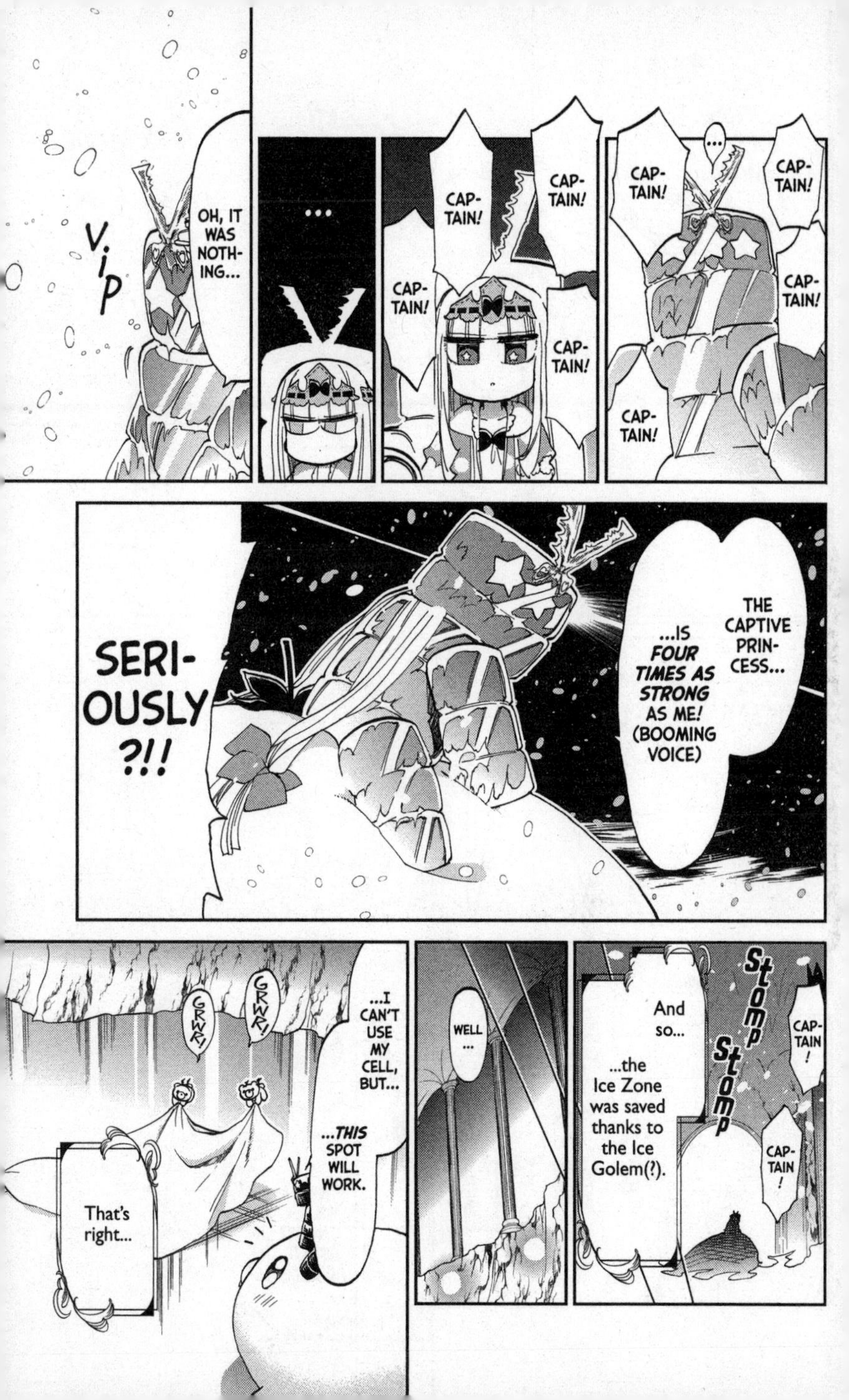
CAP-TAIN!
...
CAP-TAIN!
CAP-TAIN!
CAP-TAIN!
CAP-TAIN!
CAP-TAIN!
CAP-TAIN!
CAP-TAIN!
...
VIP
OH, IT WAS NOTHING...
THE CAPTIVE PRINCESS...
...IS *FOUR TIMES AS STRONG* AS ME! (BOOMING VOICE)
SERIOUSLY?!!
STOMP STOMP STOMP
CAP-TAIN!
CAP-TAIN!
And so...
...the Ice Zone was saved thanks to the Ice Golem(?).
WELL...
...I CAN'T USE MY CELL, BUT...
...*THIS* SPOT WILL WORK.
GRWR!
GRWR!
That's right...

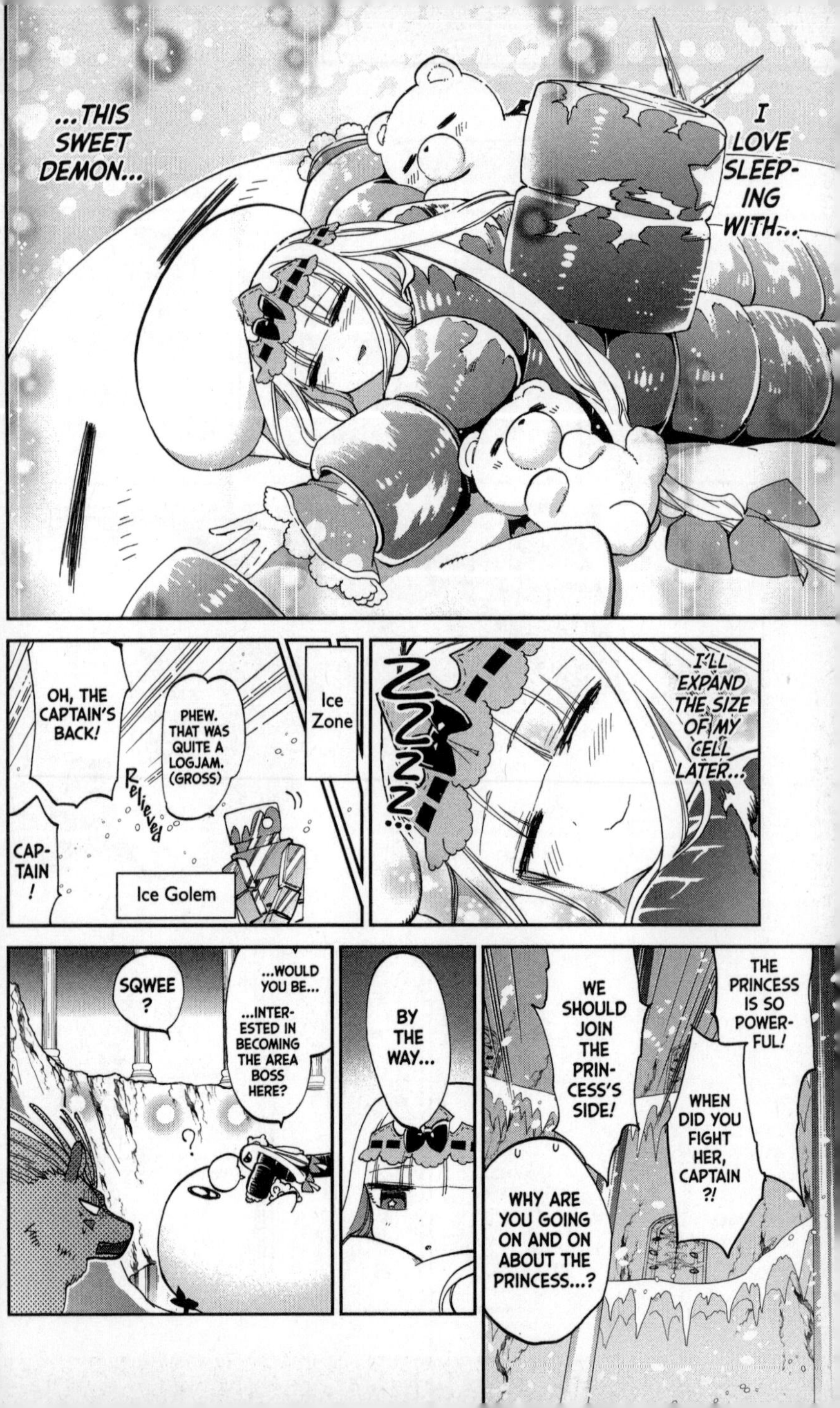
I LOVE SLEEPING WITH...
...THIS SWEET DEMON...
I'LL EXPAND THE SIZE OF MY CELL LATER...
ZZZZ...
Ice Zone
PHEW. THAT WAS QUITE A LOGJAM. (GROSS)
OH, THE CAPTAIN'S BACK!
Relieved
CAPTAIN!
Ice Golem
THE PRINCESS IS SO POWERFUL!
WE SHOULD JOIN THE PRINCESS'S SIDE!
WHEN DID YOU FIGHT HER, CAPTAIN?!
WHY ARE YOU GOING ON AND ON ABOUT THE PRINCESS...?
BY THE WAY...
...WOULD YOU BE...
...INTERESTED IN BECOMING THE AREA BOSS HERE?
SQWEE?

Giant Eggplant Seal

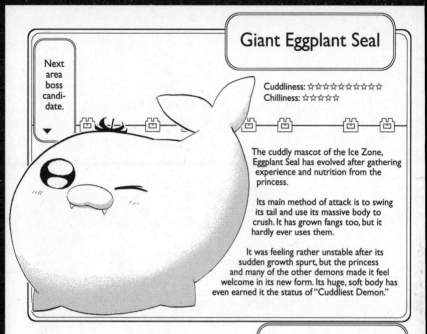

Cuddliness: ☆☆☆☆☆☆☆☆☆☆
Chilliness: ☆☆☆☆☆

Next area boss candidate.

The cuddly mascot of the Ice Zone, Eggplant Seal has evolved after gathering experience and nutrition from the princess.

Its main method of attack is to swing its tail and use its massive body to crush. It has grown fangs too, but it hardly ever uses them.

It was feeling rather unstable after its sudden growth spurt, but the princess and many of the other demons made it feel welcome in its new form. Its huge, soft body has even earned it the status of "Cuddliest Demon."

Former problem:
Staring at you with watery eyes.

Current problem:
Staring at you with watery eyes.

The next day...
HA HA HA HA!
WHOA!
Poseidon is more excited about Eggplant Seal's evolution than anyone.
HA HA HA! THIS IS GREAT!
WHY DON'T YOU COME LIVE IN MY ZONE?
OOH, YOU'RE SO CUD-DLY!
Princess Syalis glares at him through narrowed eyes.

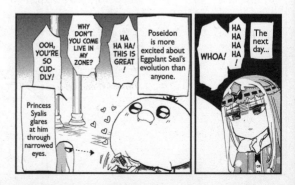

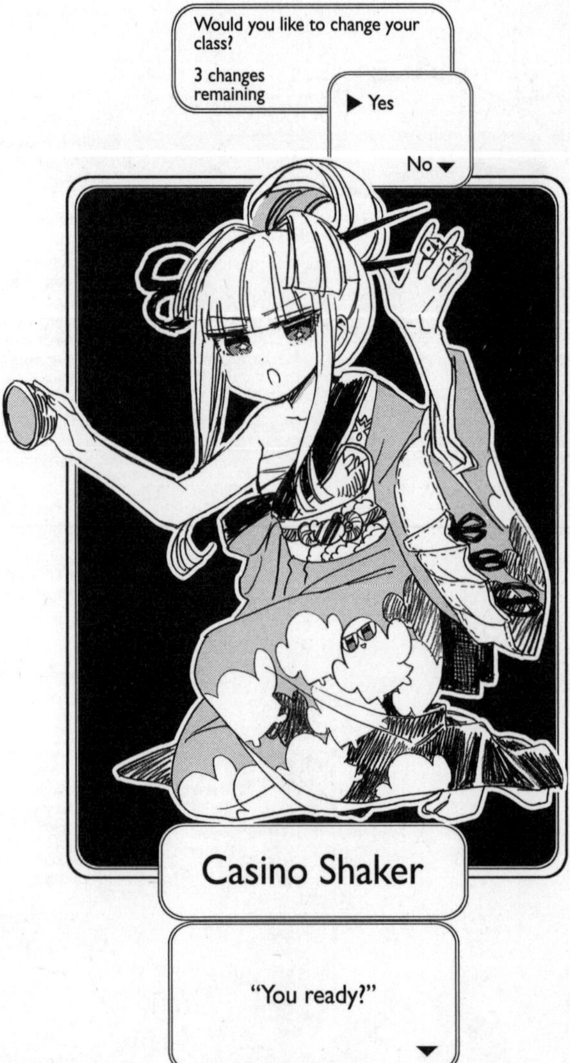
Would you like to change your class?
3 changes remaining
▶ Yes
No
Casino Shaker
"You ready?"

62nd Night: Togetherness with Big Sister Syalis

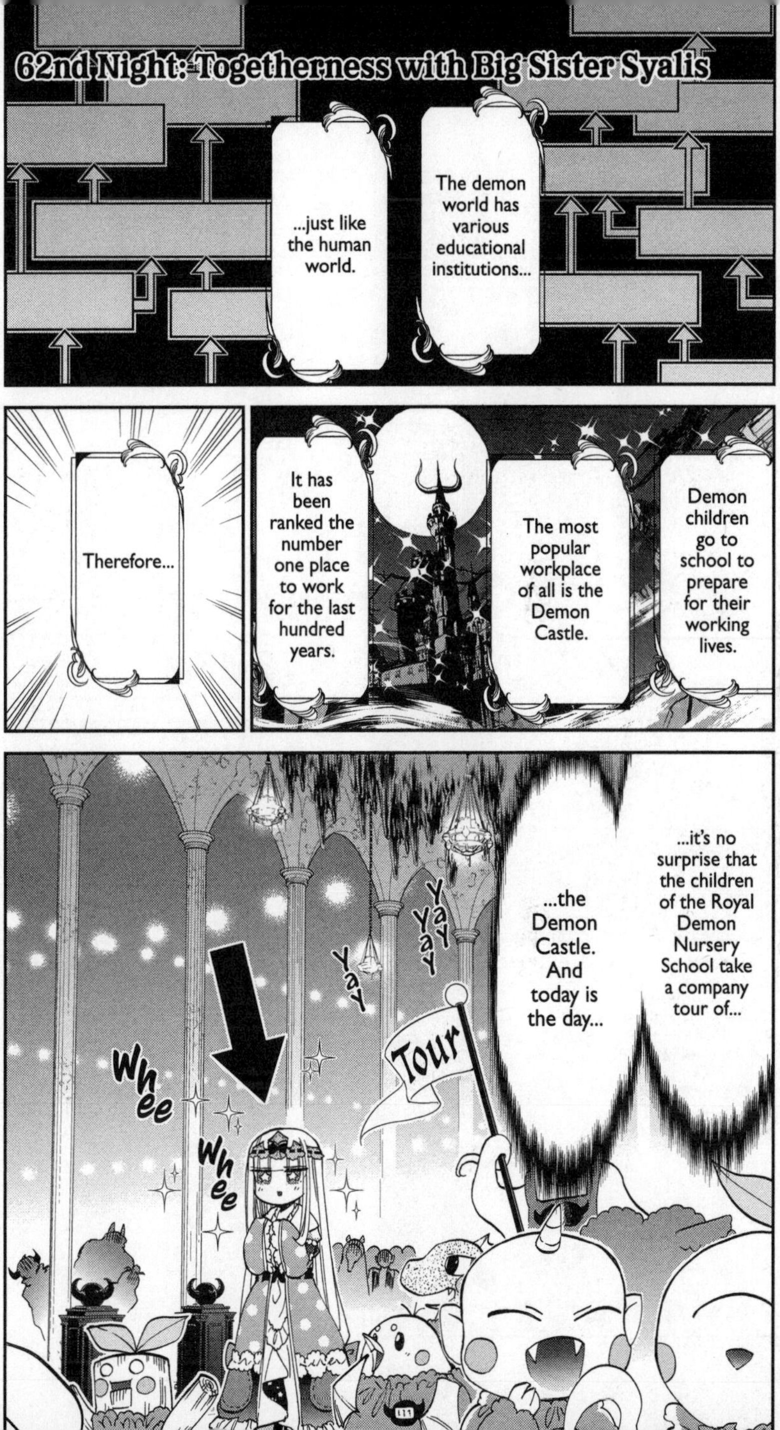
The demon world has various educational institutions...
...just like the human world.
Demon children go to school to prepare for their working lives.
The most popular workplace of all is the Demon Castle.
It has been ranked the number one place to work for the last hundred years.
Therefore...
...it's no surprise that the children of the Royal Demon Nursery School take a company tour of...
...the Demon Castle. And today is the day...
Yay
Yay
Yay
Tour
Whee
Whee

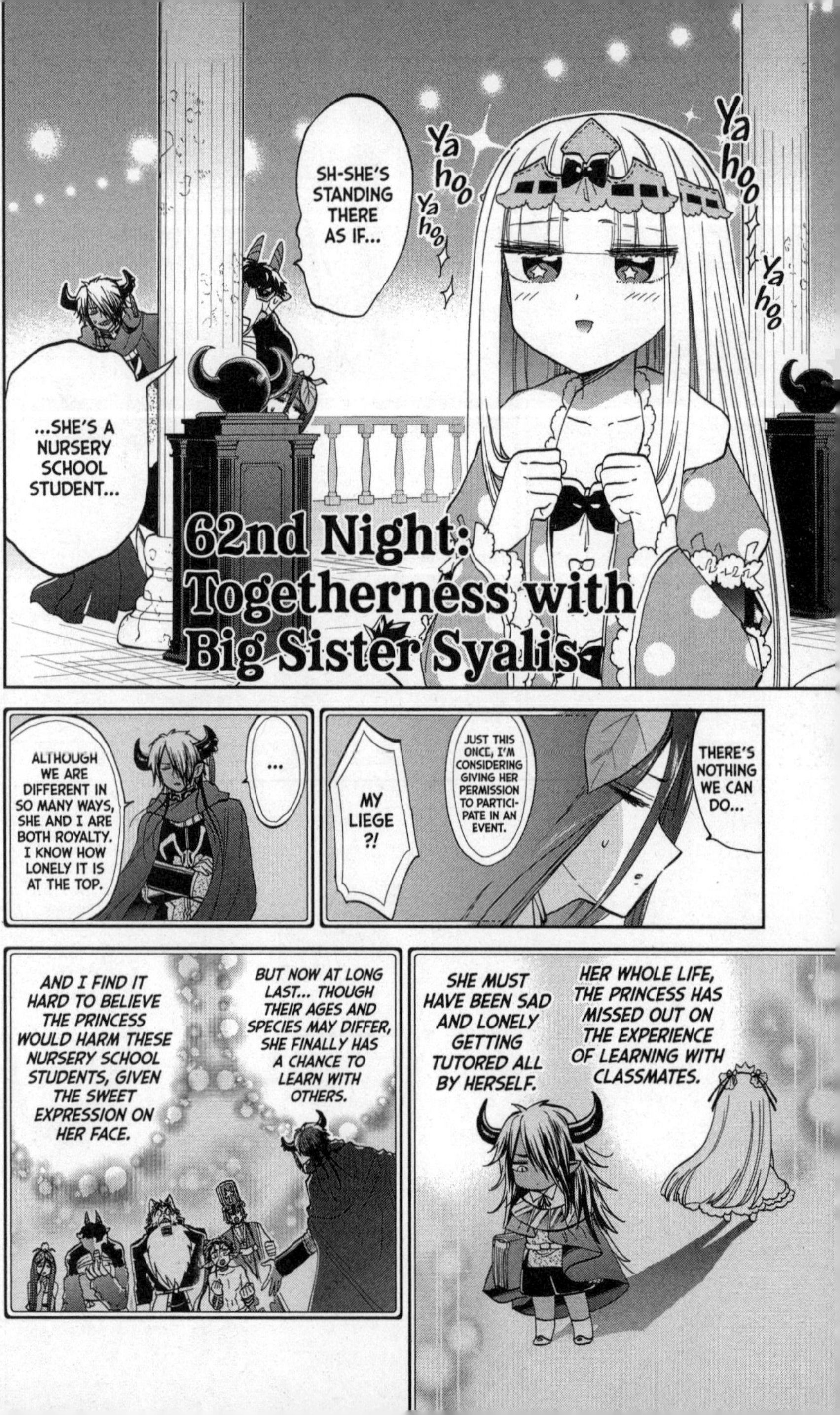
Ya hoo Ya hoo
Ya hoo Ya hoo
SH-SHE'S STANDING THERE AS IF...
...SHE'S A NURSERY SCHOOL STUDENT...
62nd Night: Togetherness with Big Sister Syalis
THERE'S NOTHING WE CAN DO...
JUST THIS ONCE, I'M CONSIDERING GIVING HER PERMISSION TO PARTICI-PATE IN AN EVENT.
MY LIEGE ?!
...
ALTHOUGH WE ARE DIFFERENT IN SO MANY WAYS, SHE AND I ARE BOTH ROYALTY. I KNOW HOW LONELY IT IS AT THE TOP.
HER WHOLE LIFE, THE PRINCESS HAS MISSED OUT ON THE EXPERIENCE OF LEARNING WITH CLASSMATES.
SHE MUST HAVE BEEN SAD AND LONELY GETTING TUTORED ALL BY HERSELF.
BUT NOW AT LONG LAST... THOUGH THEIR AGES AND SPECIES MAY DIFFER, SHE FINALLY HAS A CHANCE TO LEARN WITH OTHERS.
AND I FIND IT HARD TO BELIEVE THE PRINCESS WOULD HARM THESE NURSERY SCHOOL STUDENTS, GIVEN THE SWEET EXPRESSION ON HER FACE.

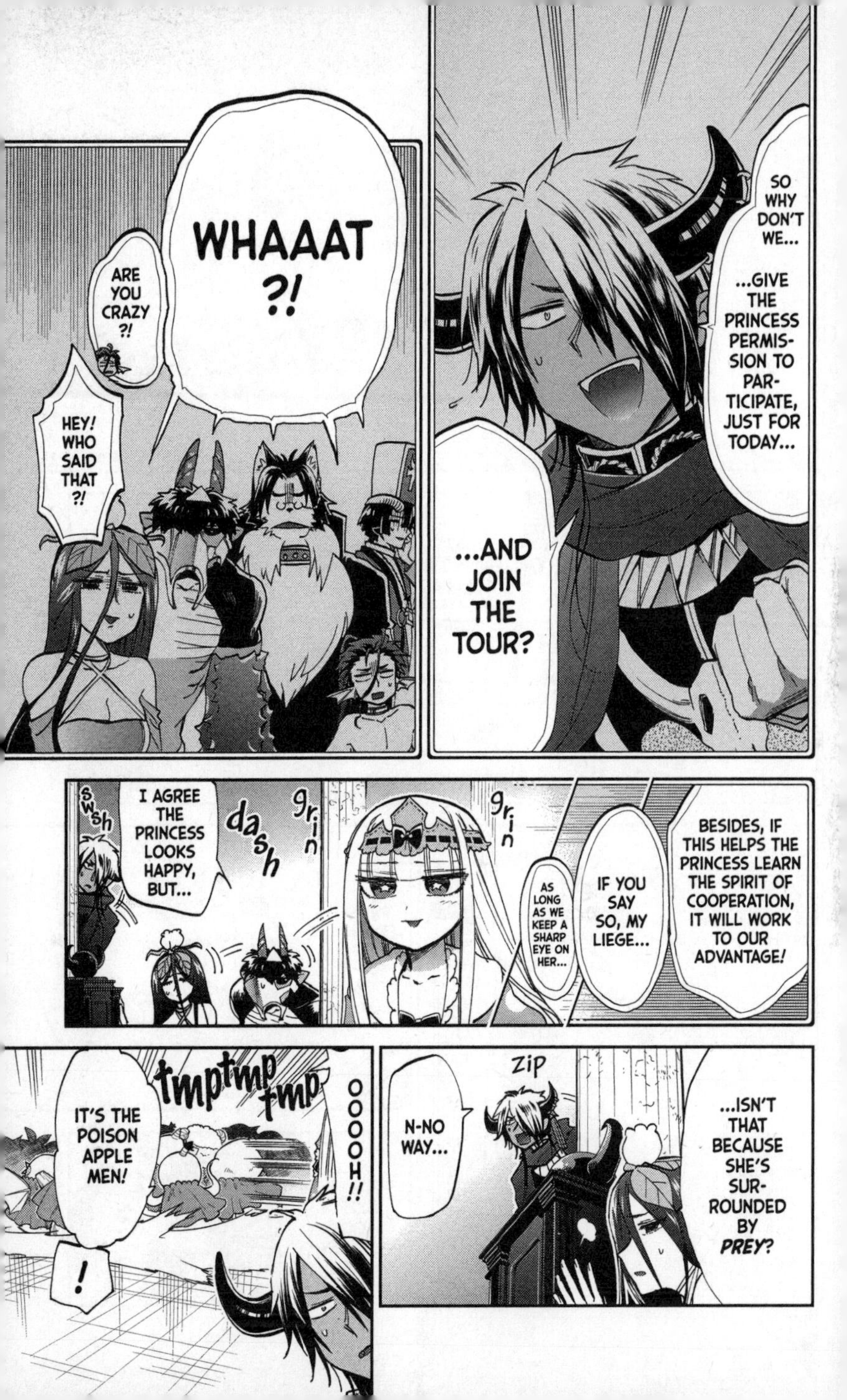
SO WHY DON'T WE...
...GIVE THE PRINCESS PERMISSION TO PARTICIPATE, JUST FOR TODAY...
...AND JOIN THE TOUR?
WHAAAT ?!
ARE YOU CRAZY ?!
HEY! WHO SAID THAT ?!
BESIDES, IF THIS HELPS THE PRINCESS LEARN THE SPIRIT OF COOPERATION, IT WILL WORK TO OUR ADVANTAGE!
IF YOU SAY SO, MY LIEGE...
AS LONG AS WE KEEP A SHARP EYE ON HER...
grin
grin
dash
I AGREE THE PRINCESS LOOKS HAPPY, BUT...
swsh
zip
...ISN'T THAT BECAUSE SHE'S SURROUNDED BY *PREY*?
N-NO WAY...
OOOOOH!!
tmptmp tmp
IT'S THE POISON APPLE MEN!
!

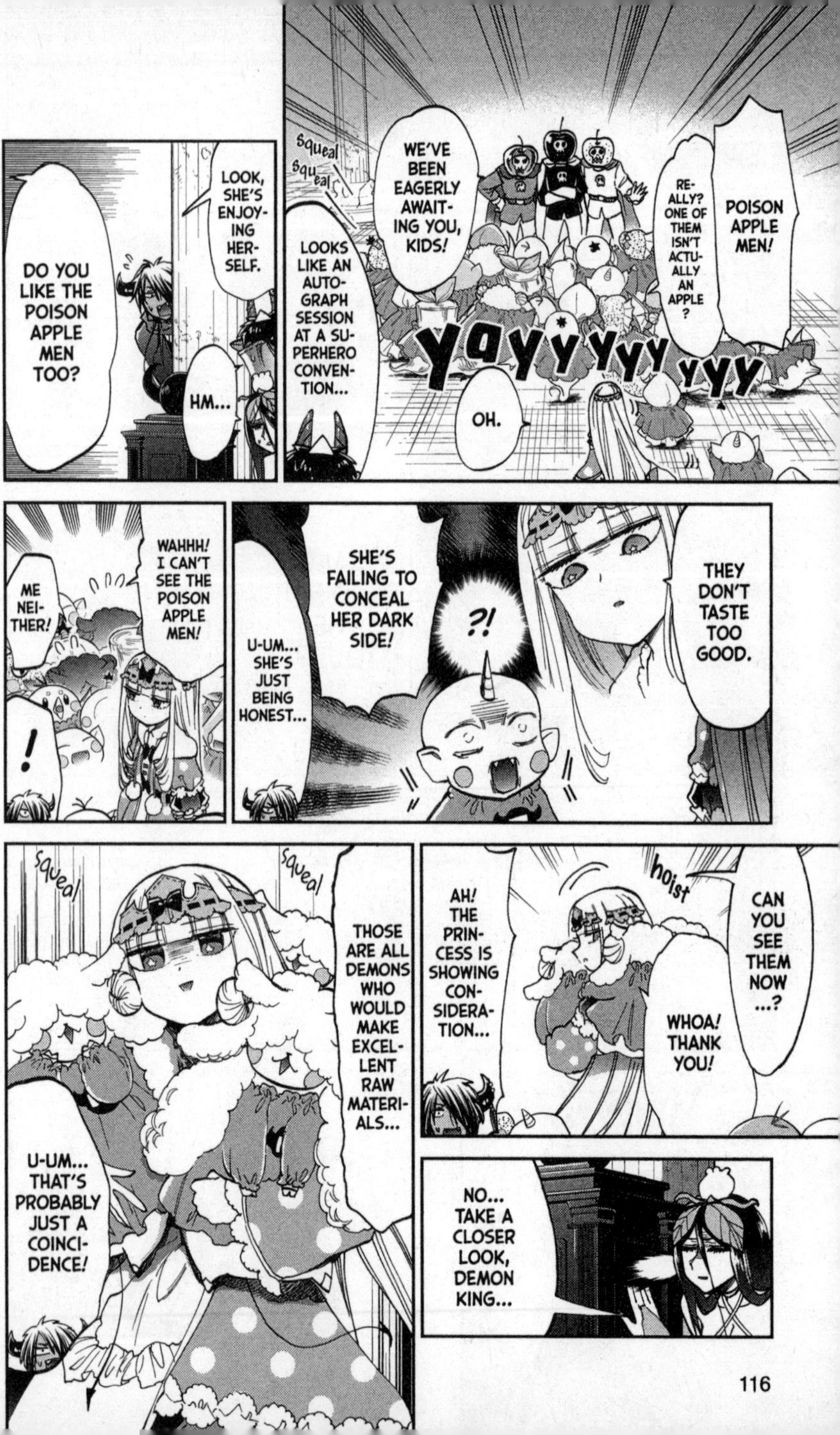
POISON APPLE MEN!
REALLY? ONE OF THEM ISN'T ACTUALLY AN APPLE?
WE'VE BEEN EAGERLY AWAITING YOU, KIDS!
squeal squeal
YAYYYYYYYY
LOOKS LIKE AN AUTOGRAPH SESSION AT A SUPERHERO CONVENTION...
OH.
LOOK, SHE'S ENJOYING HERSELF.
DO YOU LIKE THE POISON APPLE MEN TOO?
HM...
THEY DON'T TASTE TOO GOOD.
SHE'S FAILING TO CONCEAL HER DARK SIDE!
?!
U-UM... SHE'S JUST BEING HONEST...
WAHHH! I CAN'T SEE THE POISON APPLE MEN!
ME NEITHER!
!
CAN YOU SEE THEM NOW...?
hoist
WHOA! THANK YOU!
AH! THE PRINCESS IS SHOWING CONSIDERATION...
NO... TAKE A CLOSER LOOK, DEMON KING...
squeal
squeal
THOSE ARE ALL DEMONS WHO WOULD MAKE EXCELLENT RAW MATERIALS...
U-UM... THAT'S PROBABLY JUST A COINCIDENCE!

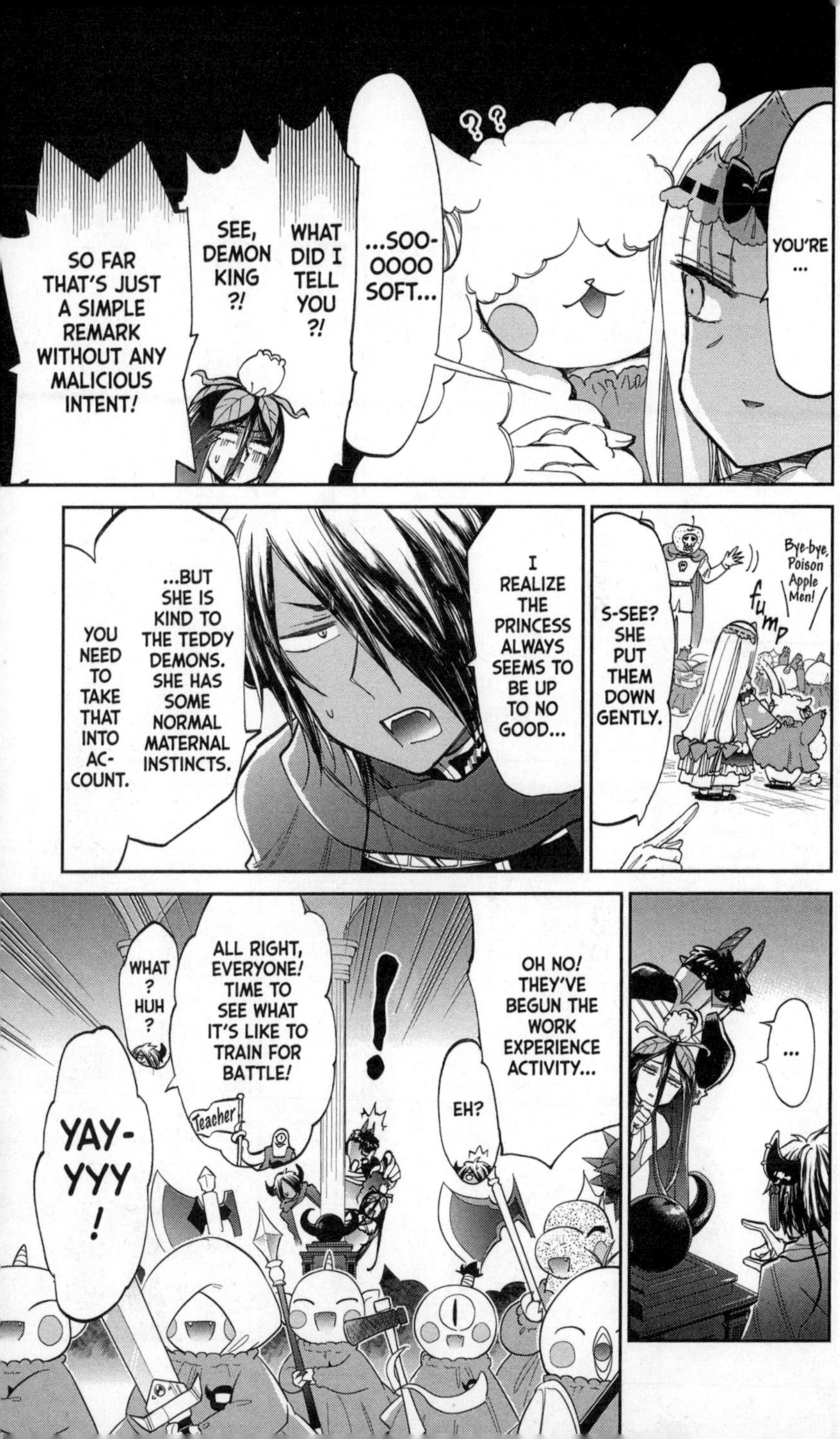
YOU'RE ...
...SOO-OOOO SOFT...
WHAT DID I TELL YOU?!
SEE, DEMON KING?!
SO FAR THAT'S JUST A SIMPLE REMARK WITHOUT ANY MALICIOUS INTENT!
Bye-bye, Poison Apple Men!
fump
S-SEE? SHE PUT THEM DOWN GENTLY.
I REALIZE THE PRINCESS ALWAYS SEEMS TO BE UP TO NO GOOD...
...BUT SHE IS KIND TO THE TEDDY DEMONS. SHE HAS SOME NORMAL MATERNAL INSTINCTS.
YOU NEED TO TAKE THAT INTO AC-COUNT.
...
OH NO! THEY'VE BEGUN THE WORK EXPERIENCE ACTIVITY...
EH?
!
ALL RIGHT, EVERYONE! TIME TO SEE WHAT IT'S LIKE TO TRAIN FOR BATTLE!
Teacher
WHAT? HUH?
YAY-YYY!

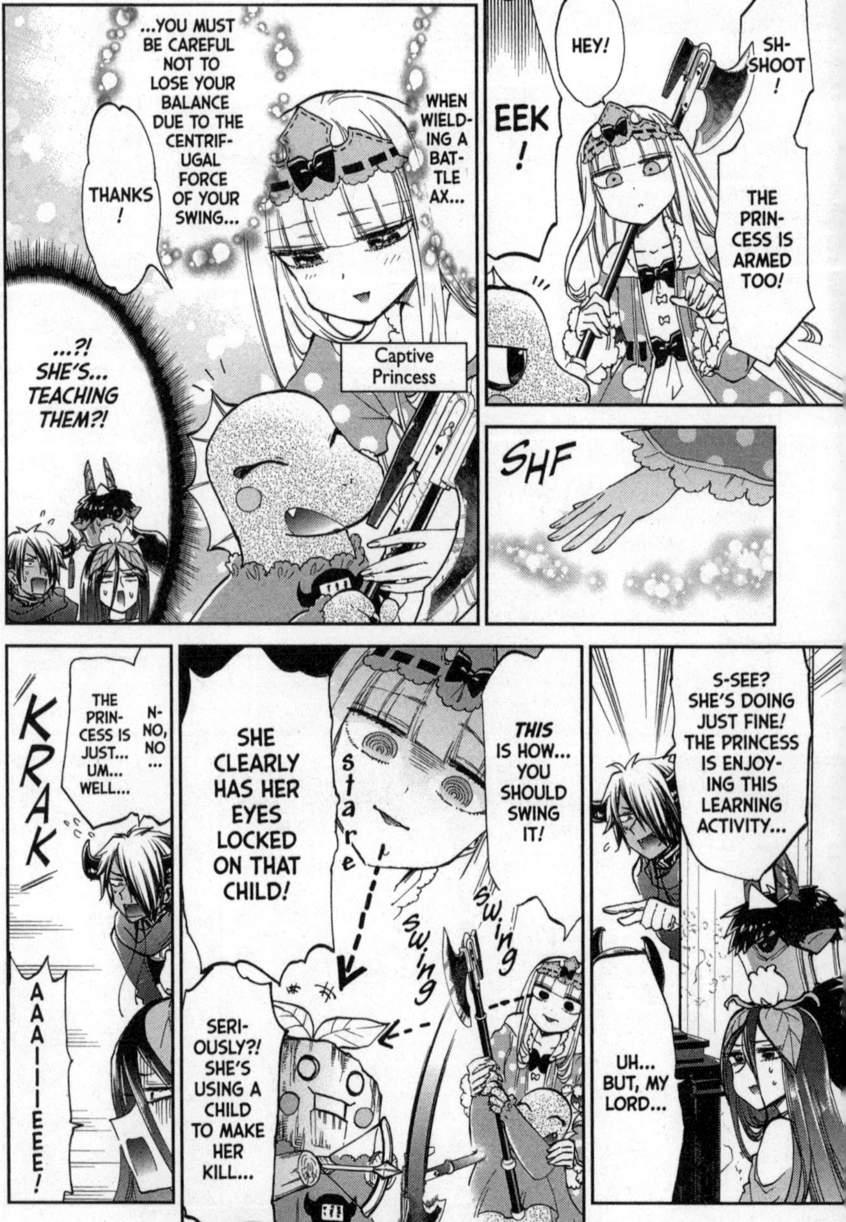
SH-SHOOT!
THE PRINCESS IS ARMED TOO!
HEY!
EEK!
SHF
WHEN WIELDING A BATTLE AX...
...YOU MUST BE CAREFUL NOT TO LOSE YOUR BALANCE DUE TO THE CENTRIFUGAL FORCE OF YOUR SWING...
THANKS!
Captive Princess
...?! SHE'S... TEACHING THEM?!
S-SEE? SHE'S DOING JUST FINE! THE PRINCESS IS ENJOYING THIS LEARNING ACTIVITY...
UH... BUT, MY LORD...
THIS IS HOW... YOU SHOULD SWING IT!
swing swing
SHE CLEARLY HAS HER EYES LOCKED ON THAT CHILD!
stare
SERIOUSLY?! SHE'S USING A CHILD TO MAKE HER KILL...
N-NO, NO...
THE PRINCESS IS JUST... UM... WELL...
KRAK
AAAIIIEEE!

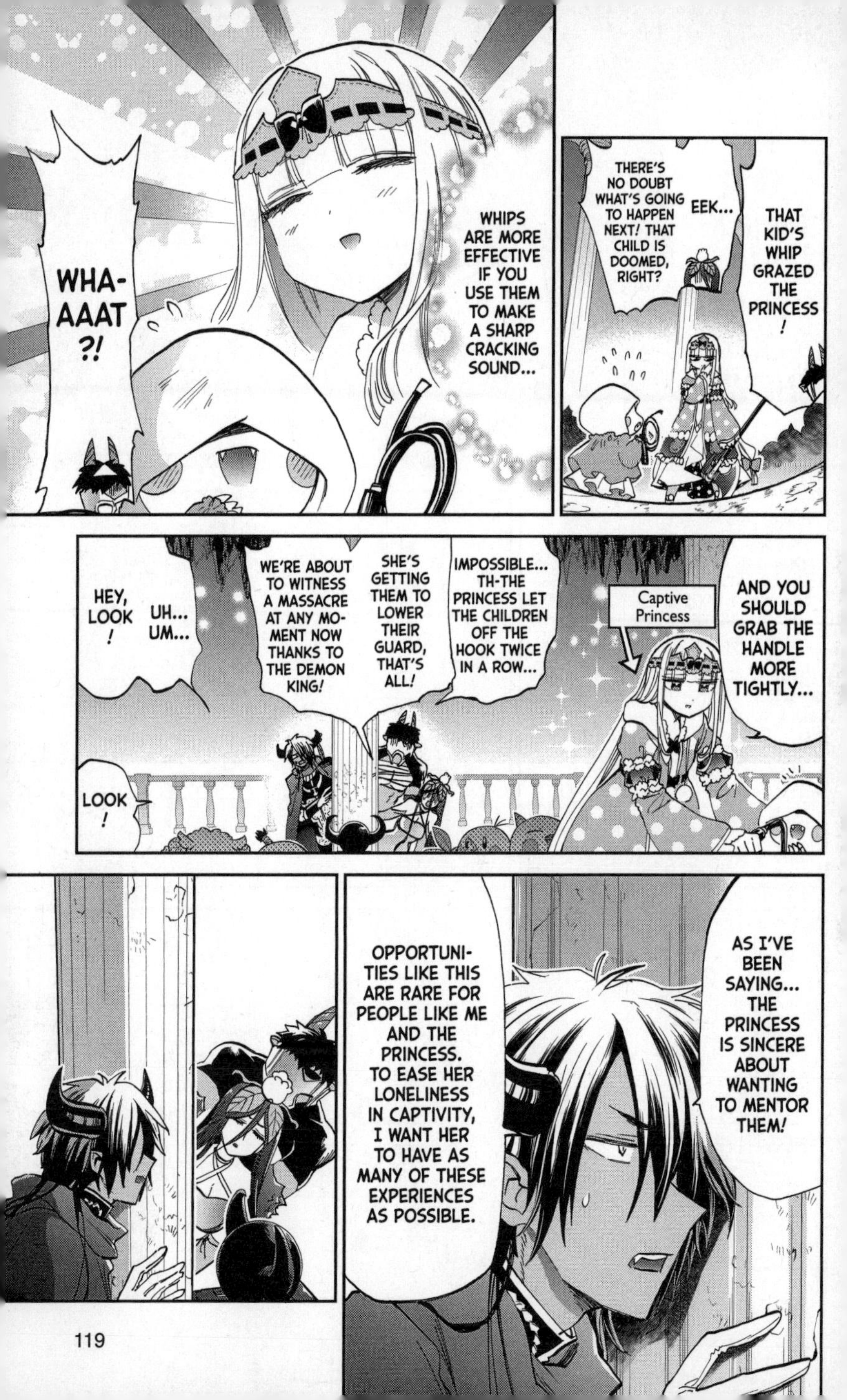

THAT KID'S WHIP GRAZED THE PRINCESS!
EEK...
THERE'S NO DOUBT WHAT'S GOING TO HAPPEN NEXT! THAT CHILD IS DOOMED, RIGHT?
WHIPS ARE MORE EFFECTIVE IF YOU USE THEM TO MAKE A SHARP CRACKING SOUND...
WHA-AAAT?!
AND YOU SHOULD GRAB THE HANDLE MORE TIGHTLY...
Captive Princess
IMPOSSIBLE... TH-THE PRINCESS LET THE CHILDREN OFF THE HOOK TWICE IN A ROW...
SHE'S GETTING THEM TO LOWER THEIR GUARD, THAT'S ALL!
WE'RE ABOUT TO WITNESS A MASSACRE AT ANY MO-MENT NOW THANKS TO THE DEMON KING!
UH... UM...
HEY, LOOK!
LOOK!
AS I'VE BEEN SAYING... THE PRINCESS IS SINCERE ABOUT WANTING TO MENTOR THEM!
OPPORTUNI-TIES LIKE THIS ARE RARE FOR PEOPLE LIKE ME AND THE PRINCESS. TO EASE HER LONELINESS IN CAPTIVITY, I WANT HER TO HAVE AS MANY OF THESE EXPERIENCES AS POSSIBLE.

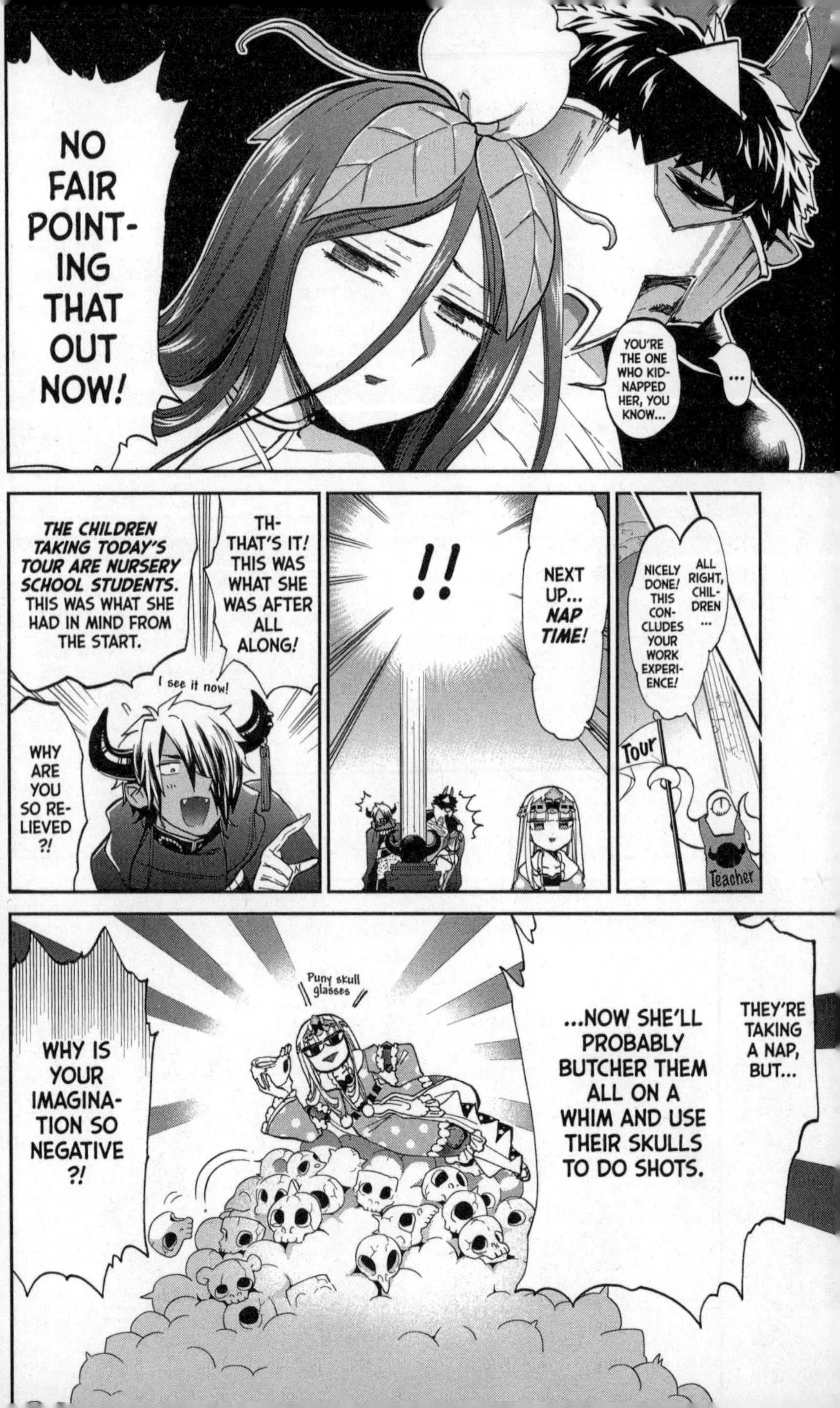
YOU'RE THE ONE WHO KIDNAPPED HER, YOU KNOW...
...
NO FAIR POINTING THAT OUT NOW!
ALL RIGHT, CHILDREN...
NICELY DONE! THIS CONCLUDES YOUR WORK EXPERIENCE!
Tour
Teacher
NEXT UP... NAP TIME!
!!
TH-THAT'S IT! THIS WAS WHAT SHE WAS AFTER ALL ALONG!
I see it now!
THE CHILDREN TAKING TODAY'S TOUR ARE NURSERY SCHOOL STUDENTS. THIS WAS WHAT SHE HAD IN MIND FROM THE START.
WHY ARE YOU SO RELIEVED?!
THEY'RE TAKING A NAP, BUT...
...NOW SHE'LL PROBABLY BUTCHER THEM ALL ON A WHIM AND USE THEIR SKULLS TO DO SHOTS.
Puny skull glasses
WHY IS YOUR IMAGINATION SO NEGATIVE?!

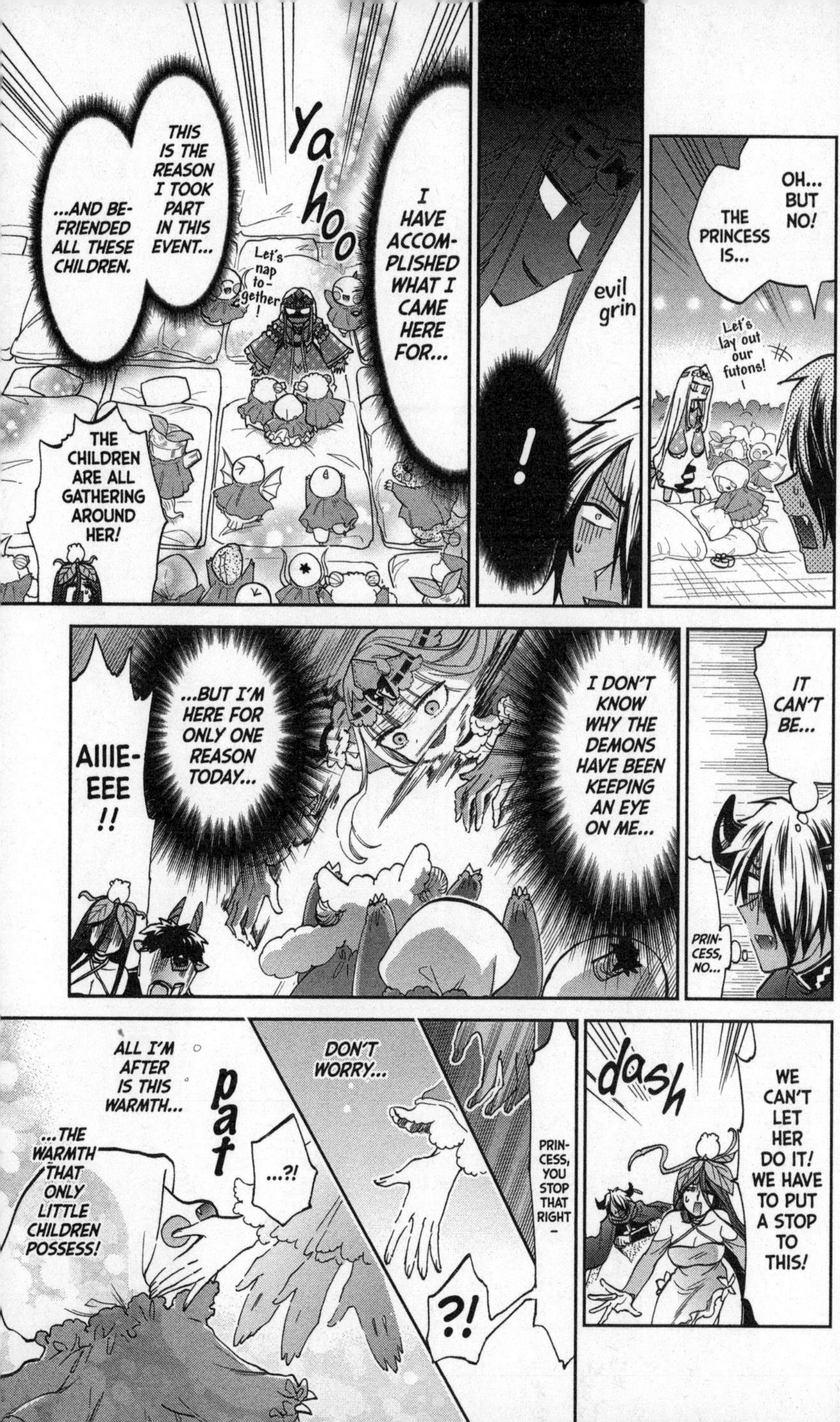
OH... BUT NO!
THE PRINCESS IS...
Let's lay out our futons!
evil grin
!
I HAVE ACCOMPLISHED WHAT I CAME HERE FOR...
Yahoo
THIS IS THE REASON I TOOK PART IN THIS EVENT...
...AND BEFRIENDED ALL THESE CHILDREN.
Let's nap together!
THE CHILDREN ARE ALL GATHERING AROUND HER!
IT CAN'T BE...
PRINCESS, NO...
I DON'T KNOW WHY THE DEMONS HAVE BEEN KEEPING AN EYE ON ME...
...BUT I'M HERE FOR ONLY ONE REASON TODAY...
AIIIE-EEE!!
dash
WE CAN'T LET HER DO IT! WE HAVE TO PUT A STOP TO THIS!
PRINCESS, YOU STOP THAT RIGHT-
DON'T WORRY...
ALL I'M AFTER IS THIS WARMTH...
...THE WARMTH THAT ONLY LITTLE CHILDREN POSSESS!
pat
...?!
?!

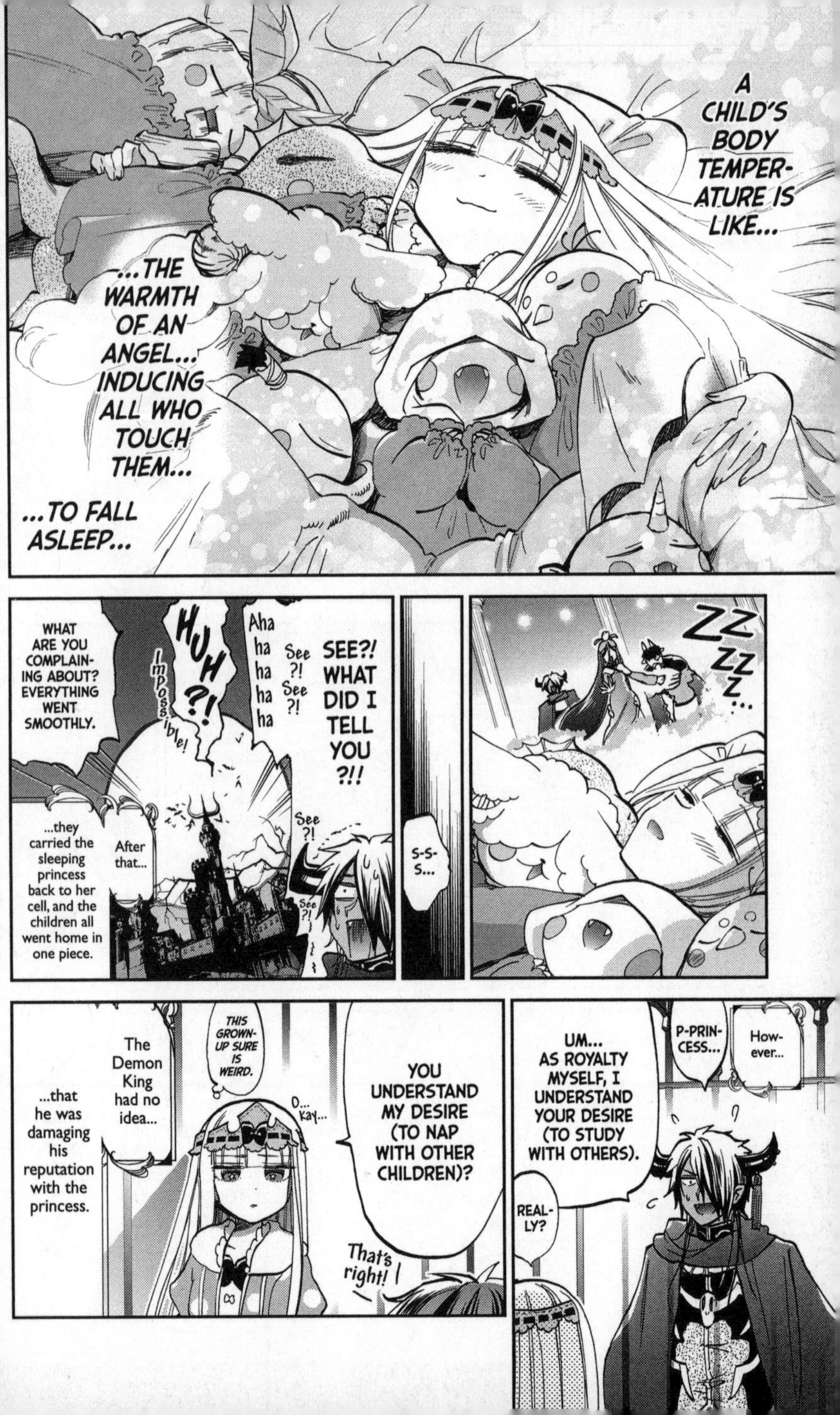
A CHILD'S BODY TEMPERATURE IS LIKE...
...THE WARMTH OF AN ANGEL... INDUCING ALL WHO TOUCH THEM...
...TO FALL ASLEEP...
ZZZZZZ...
S-S-S...
SEE?! WHAT DID I TELL YOU?!!
See?! See?!
Aha ha ha ha ha
HUH?!
Impossible!
WHAT ARE YOU COMPLAINING ABOUT? EVERYTHING WENT SMOOTHLY.
See?!
See?!
After that...
...they carried the sleeping princess back to her cell, and the children all went home in one piece.
How-ever...
P-PRIN-CESS...
UM... AS ROYALTY MYSELF, I UNDERSTAND YOUR DESIRE (TO STUDY WITH OTHERS).
REAL-LY?
YOU UNDERSTAND MY DESIRE (TO NAP WITH OTHER CHILDREN)?
That's right!
O... Kay...
THIS GROWN-UP SURE IS WEIRD.
The Demon King had no idea...
...that he was damaging his reputation with the princess.

Royal Demon Nursery School

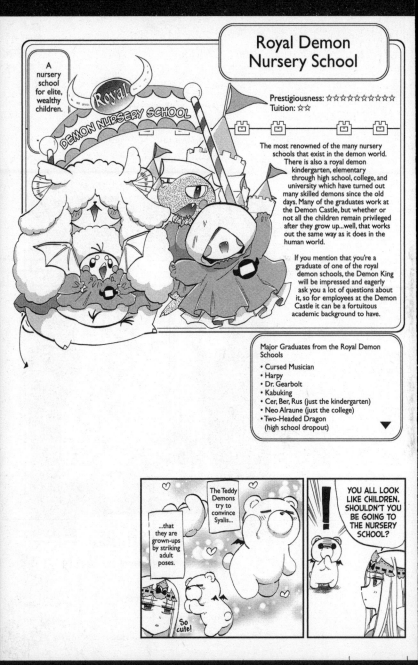

A nursery school for elite, wealthy children.

Royal
DEMON NURSERY SCHOOL

Prestigiousness: ☆☆☆☆☆☆☆☆☆☆
Tuition: ☆☆

The most renowned of the many nursery schools that exist in the demon world. There is also a royal demon kindergarten, elementary through high school, college, and university which have turned out many skilled demons since the old days. Many of the graduates work at the Demon Castle, but whether or not all the children remain privileged after they grow up...well, that works out the same way as it does in the human world.

If you mention that you're a graduate of one of the royal demon schools, the Demon King will be impressed and eagerly ask you a lot of questions about it, so for employees at the Demon Castle it can be a fortuitous academic background to have.

Major Graduates from the Royal Demon Schools

- Cursed Musician
- Harpy
- Dr. Gearbolt
- Kabuking
- Cer, Ber, Rus (just the kindergarten)
- Neo Alraune (just the college)
- Two-Headed Dragon (high school dropout)

!
YOU ALL LOOK LIKE CHILDREN. SHOULDN'T YOU BE GOING TO THE NURSERY SCHOOL?
The Teddy Demons try to convince Syalis...
...that they are grown-ups by striking adult poses.
So cute!

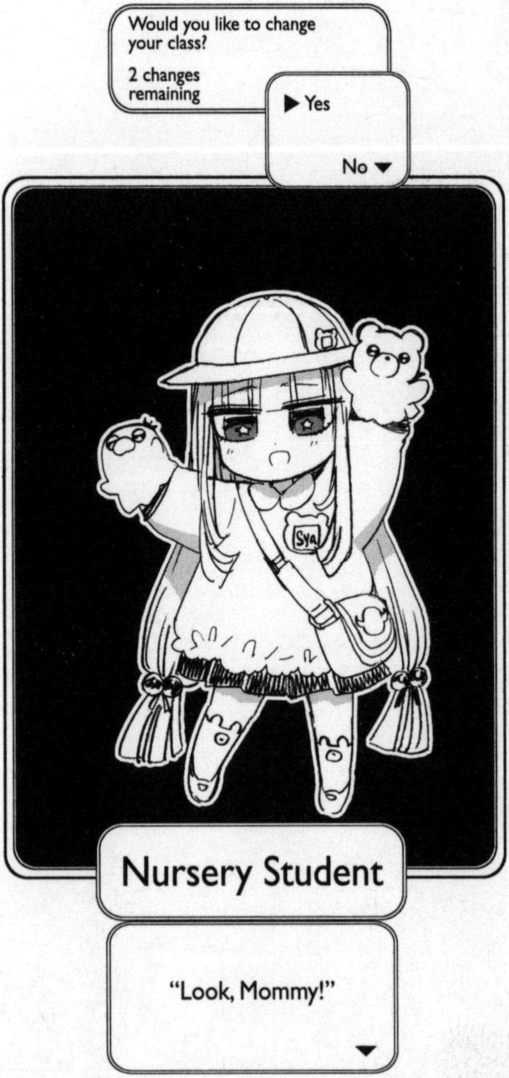
Would you like to change your class?
2 changes remaining
▶ Yes
No
Nursery Student
"Look, Mommy!"

63rd Night: Don't Look Away

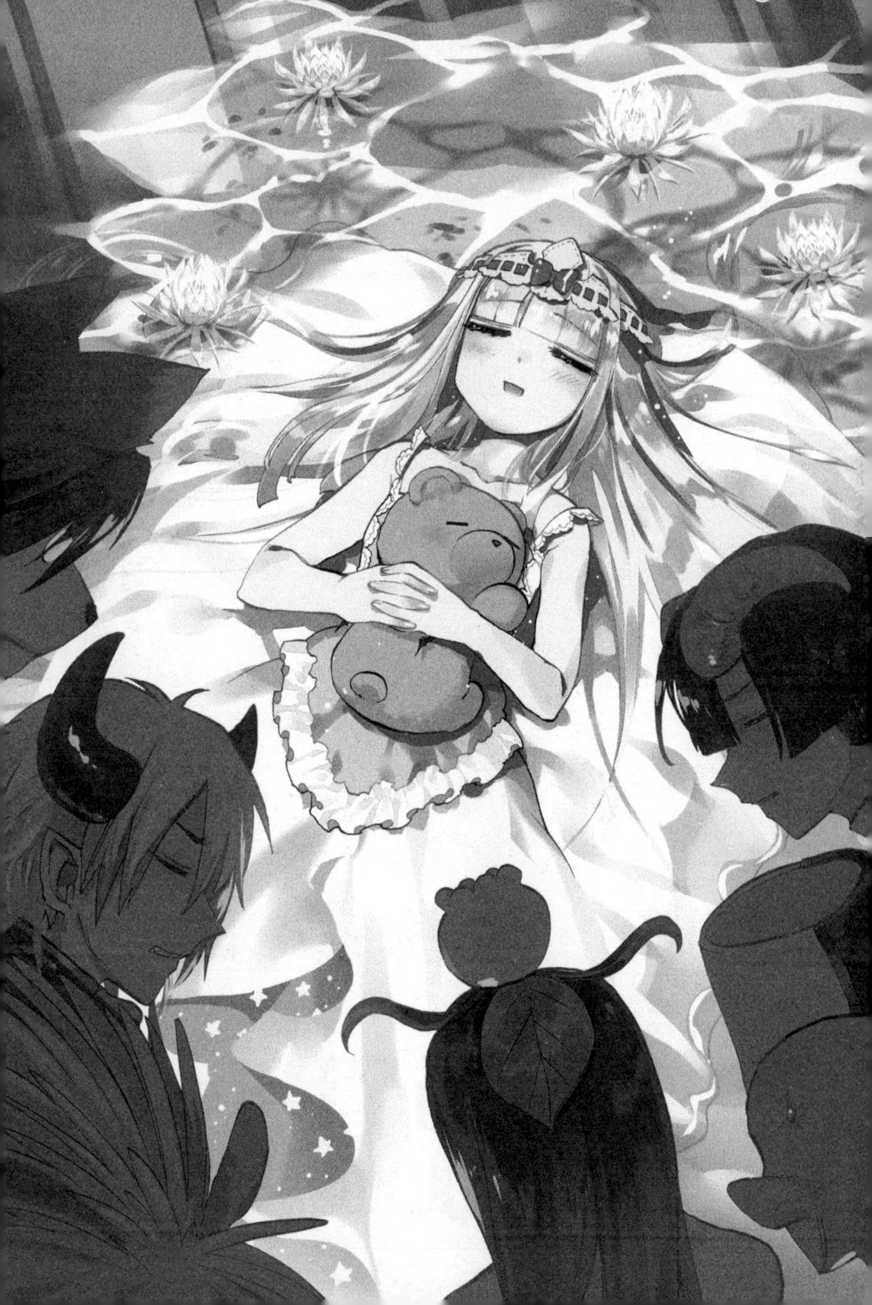

SLEEPY PRINCESS
IN THE DEMON CASTLE

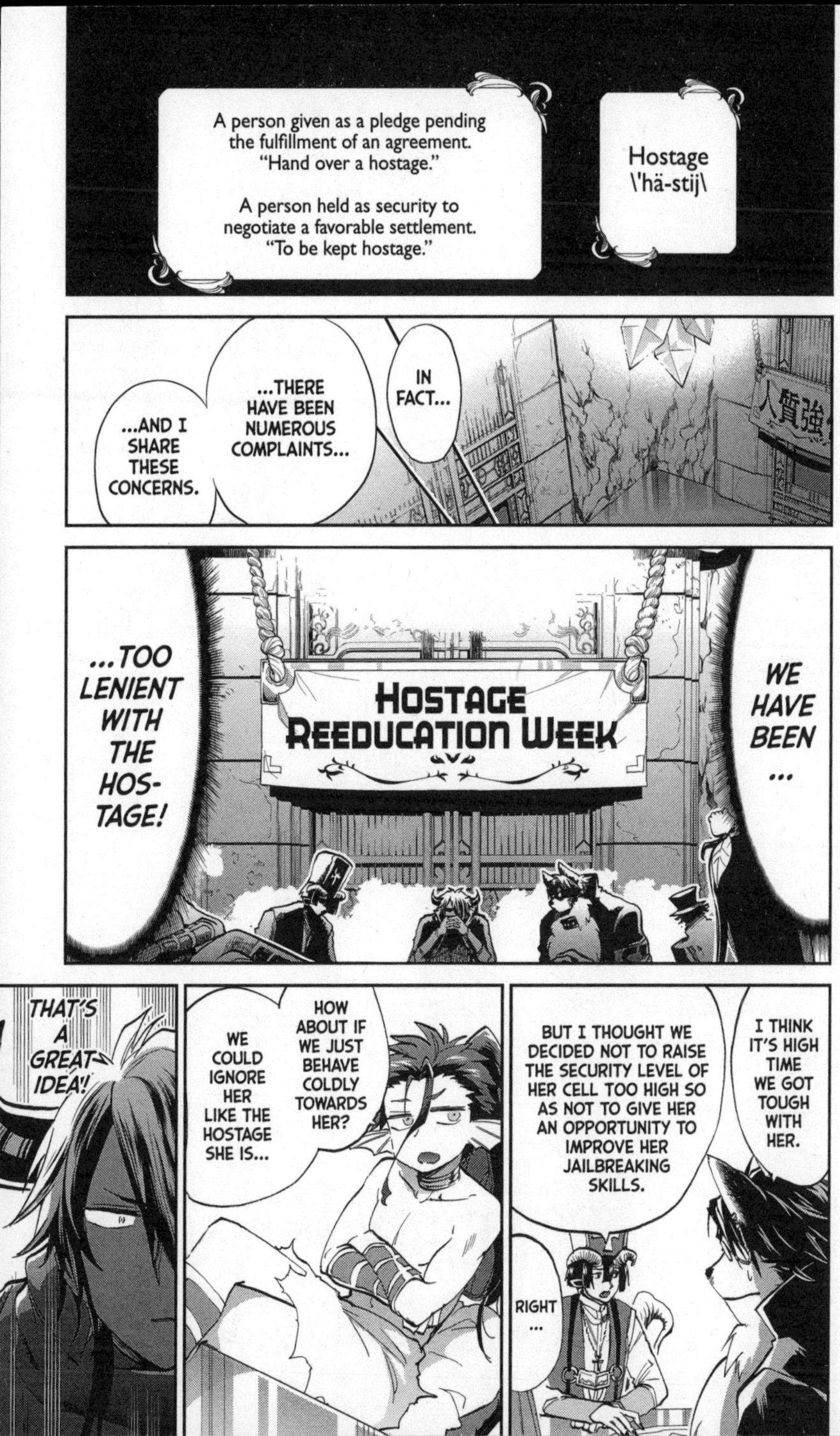
Hostage \'hä-stij\
A person given as a pledge pending the fulfillment of an agreement. "Hand over a hostage."
A person held as security to negotiate a favorable settlement. "To be kept hostage."
IN FACT...
...THERE HAVE BEEN NUMEROUS COMPLAINTS...
...AND I SHARE THESE CONCERNS.
人質強
WE HAVE BEEN...
HOSTAGE REEDUCATION WEEK
...TOO LENIENT WITH THE HOSTAGE!
I THINK IT'S HIGH TIME WE GOT TOUGH WITH HER.
BUT I THOUGHT WE DECIDED NOT TO RAISE THE SECURITY LEVEL OF HER CELL TOO HIGH SO AS NOT TO GIVE HER AN OPPORTUNITY TO IMPROVE HER JAILBREAKING SKILLS.
RIGHT...
HOW ABOUT IF WE JUST BEHAVE COLDLY TOWARDS HER?
WE COULD IGNORE HER LIKE THE HOSTAGE SHE IS...
THAT'S A GREAT IDEA!

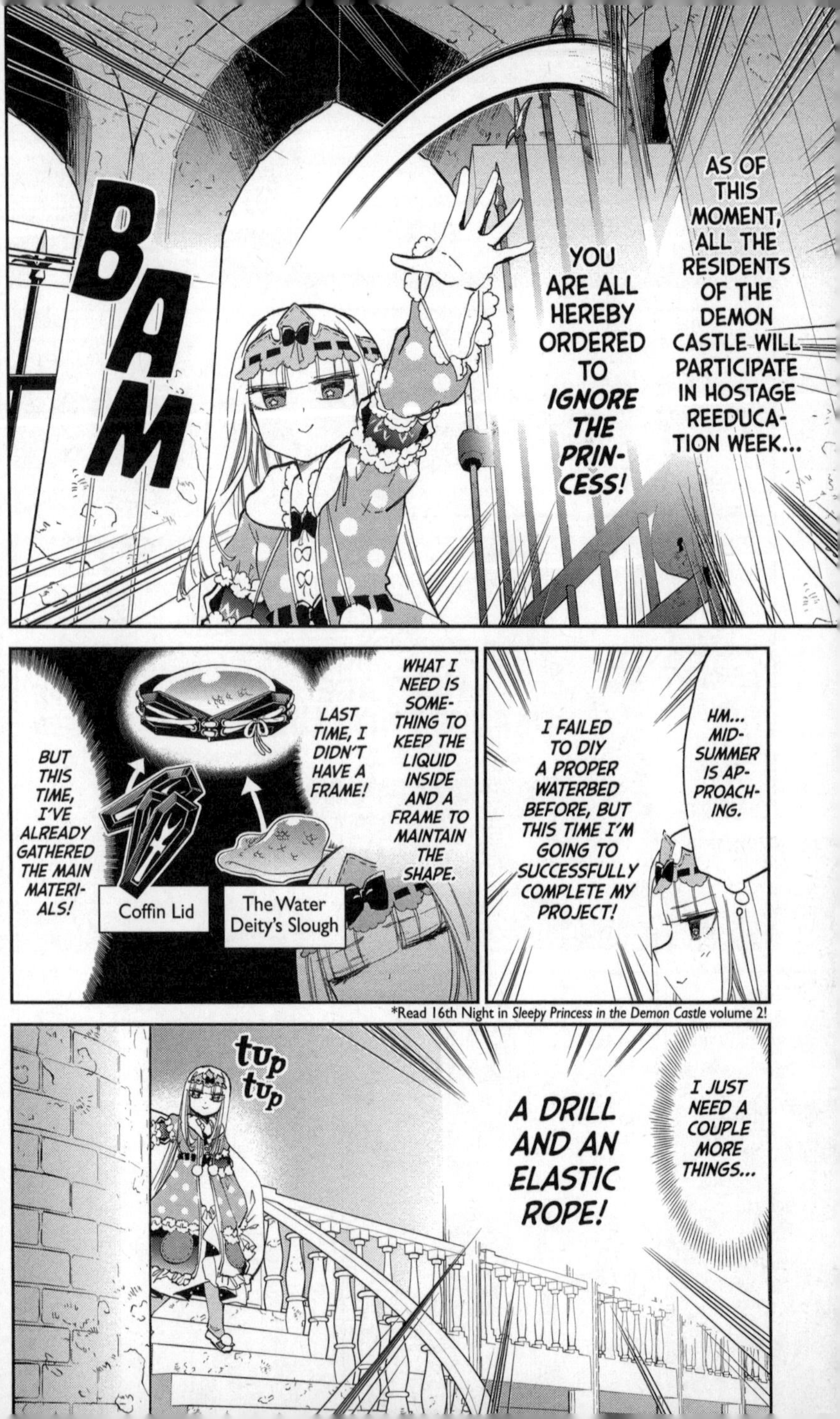
AS OF THIS MOMENT, ALL THE RESIDENTS OF THE DEMON CASTLE WILL PARTICIPATE IN HOSTAGE REEDUCATION WEEK...
YOU ARE ALL HEREBY ORDERED TO *IGNORE THE PRINCESS!*
BAM
HM... MIDSUMMER IS APPROACHING.
I FAILED TO DIY A PROPER WATERBED BEFORE, BUT THIS TIME I'M GOING TO SUCCESSFULLY COMPLETE MY PROJECT!
WHAT I NEED IS SOMETHING TO KEEP THE LIQUID INSIDE AND A FRAME TO MAINTAIN THE SHAPE.
LAST TIME, I DIDN'T HAVE A FRAME!
BUT THIS TIME, I'VE ALREADY GATHERED THE MAIN MATERIALS!
The Water Deity's Slough
Coffin Lid
I JUST NEED A COUPLE MORE THINGS...
A DRILL AND AN ELASTIC ROPE!
tup tup

*Read 16th Night in *Sleepy Princess in the Demon Castle* volume 2!

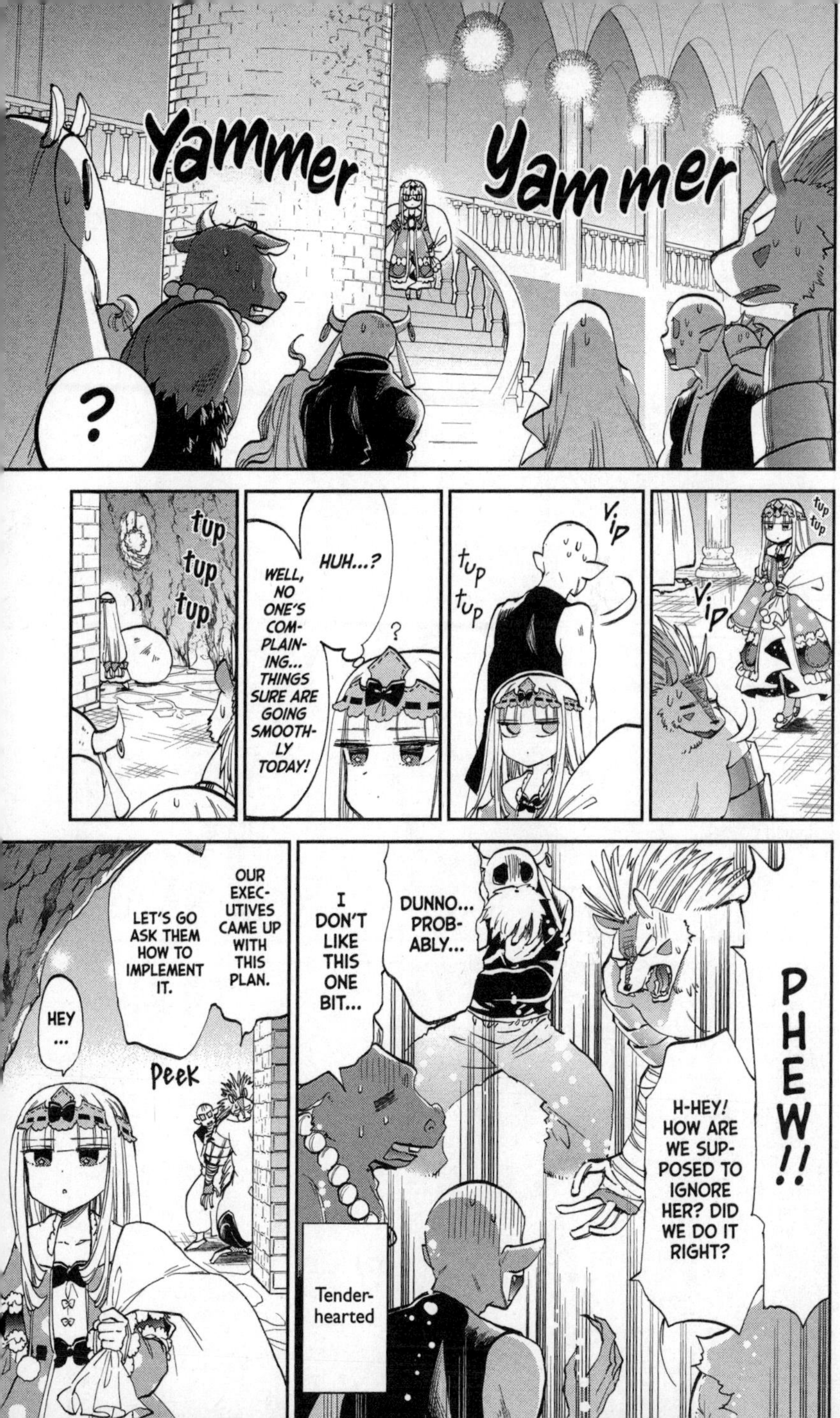
Yam mer
Yammer
?
tup tup
Vip
Vip
tup tup
HUH...?
WELL, NO ONE'S COMPLAINING... THINGS SURE ARE GOING SMOOTHLY TODAY!
?
tup tup tup
PHEW!!
H-HEY! HOW ARE WE SUPPOSED TO IGNORE HER? DID WE DO IT RIGHT?
DUNNO... PROBABLY...
I DON'T LIKE THIS ONE BIT...
Tender-hearted
OUR EXECUTIVES CAME UP WITH THIS PLAN.
LET'S GO ASK THEM HOW TO IMPLEMENT IT.
HEY...
Peek

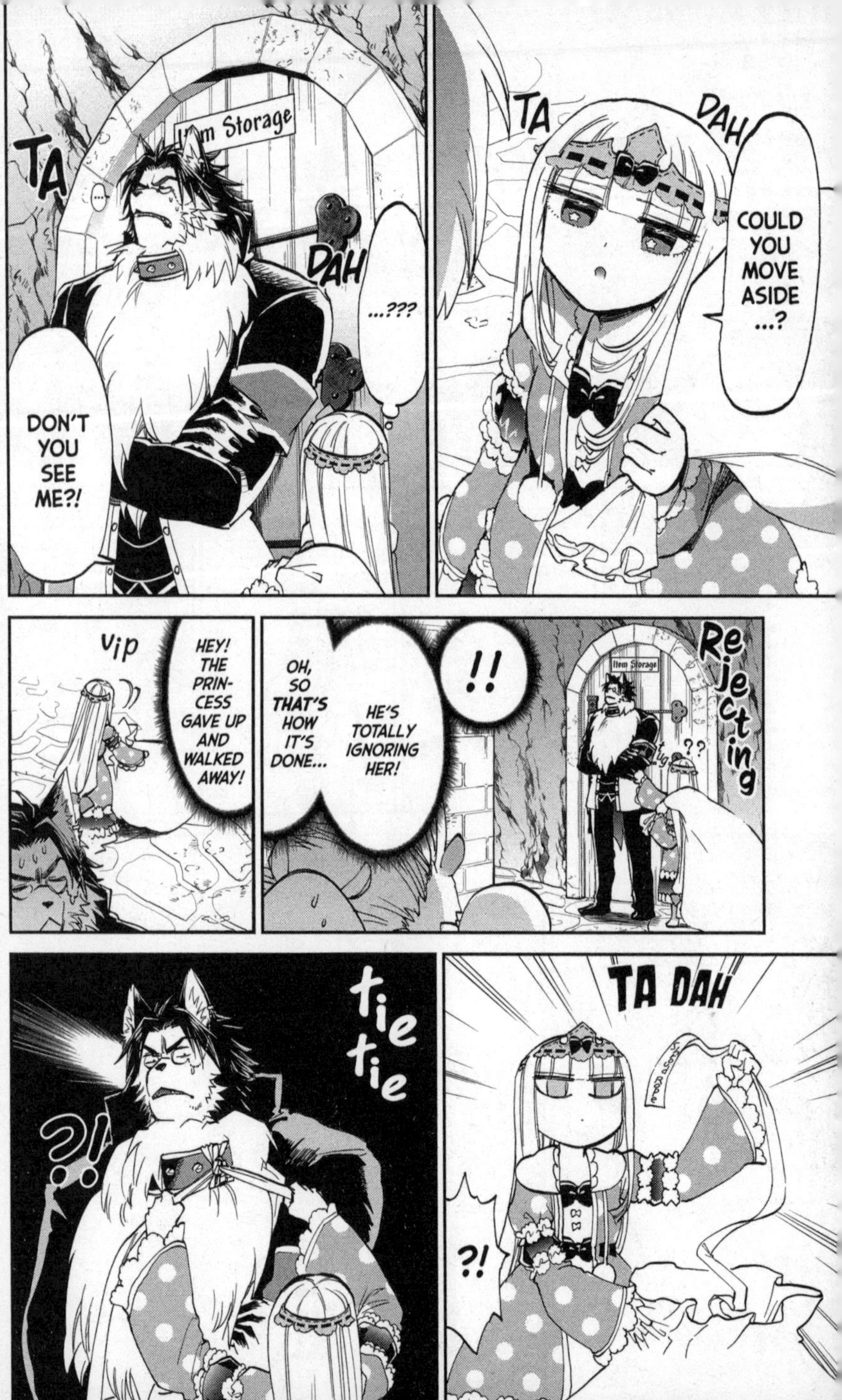
TA
DAH
COULD YOU MOVE ASIDE ...?
Item Storage
TA
...
DAH
...???
DON'T YOU SEE ME?!
Rejecting
Item Storage
tug
??
!!
HE'S TOTALLY IGNORING HER!
OH, SO THAT'S HOW IT'S DONE...
HEY! THE PRIN-CESS GAVE UP AND WALKED AWAY!
vip
TA DAH
?!
tie tie
?!

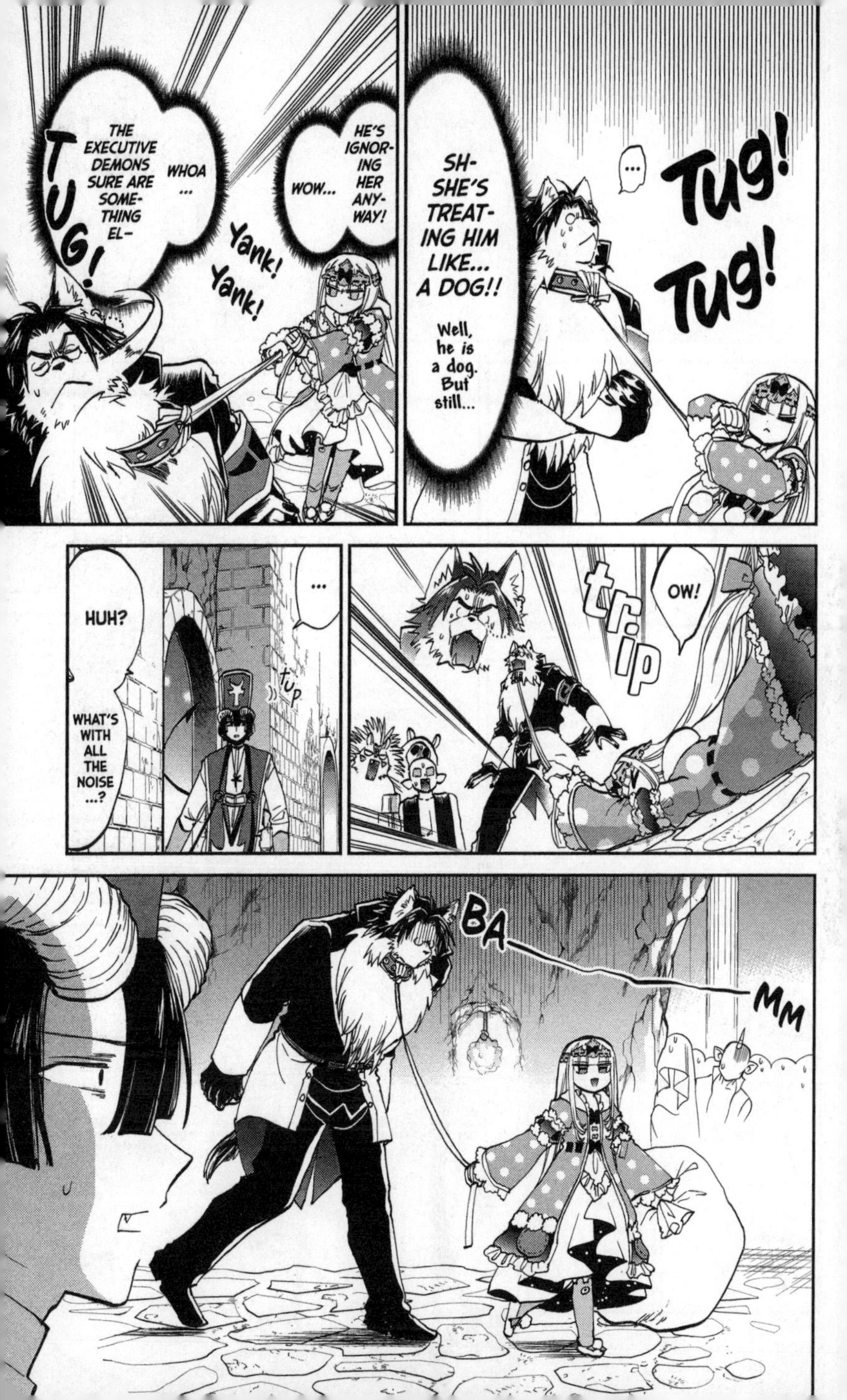
Tug! Tug!
...
SH-SHE'S TREATING HIM LIKE... A DOG!!
Well, he is a dog. But still...
HE'S IGNORING HER ANYWAY!
WOW...
Yank! Yank!
WHOA...
THE EXECUTIVE DEMONS SURE ARE SOMETHING EL–
TUG!
OW!
trip
...
tup
HUH?
WHAT'S WITH ALL THE NOISE...?
BA–MM

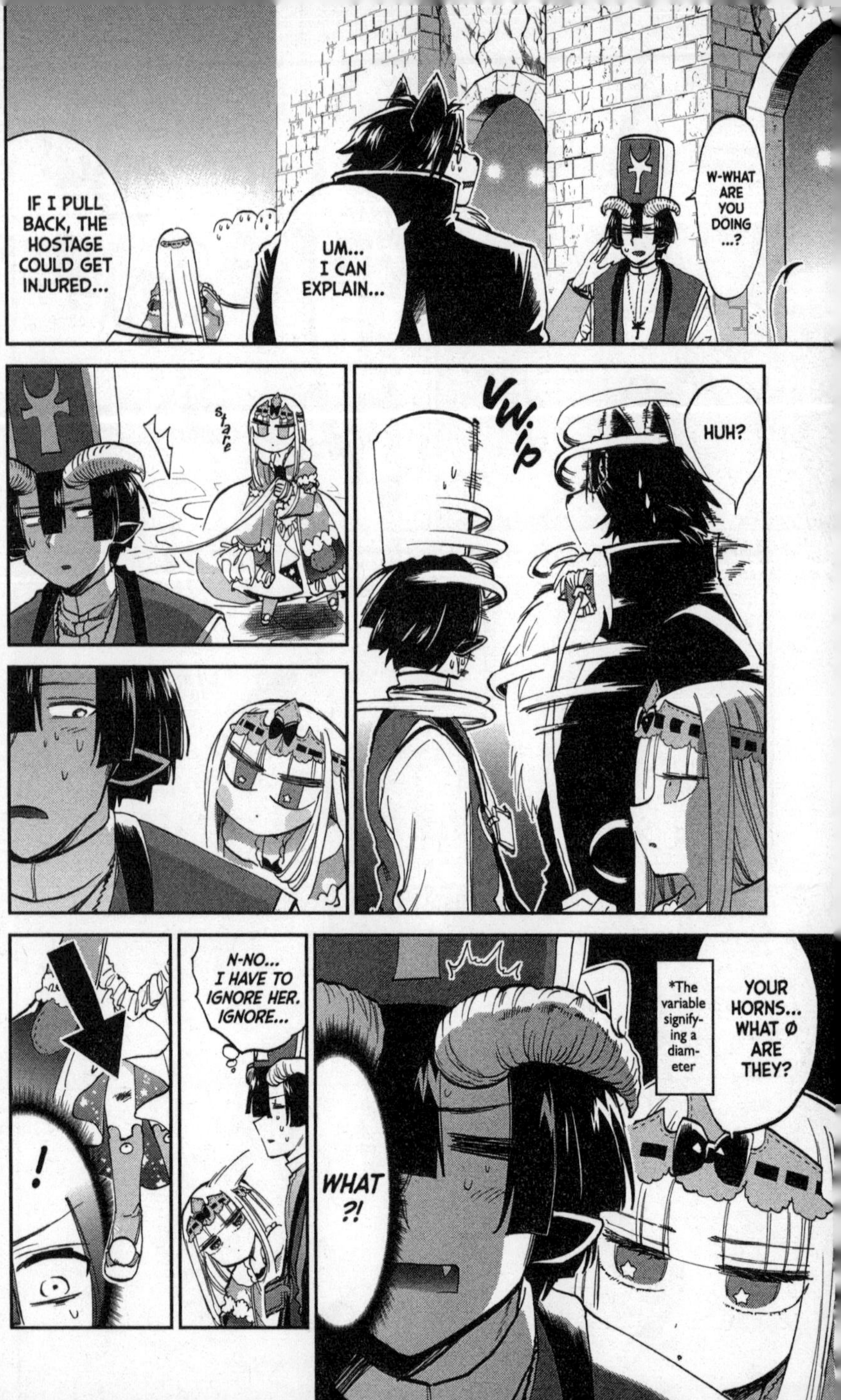
W-WHAT ARE YOU DOING ...?
UM... I CAN EXPLAIN...
IF I PULL BACK, THE HOSTAGE COULD GET INJURED...
VWIP
HUH?
stare
YOUR HORNS... WHAT Ø ARE THEY?
*The variable signifying a diameter
WHAT ?!
N-NO... I HAVE TO IGNORE HER. IGNORE...
!

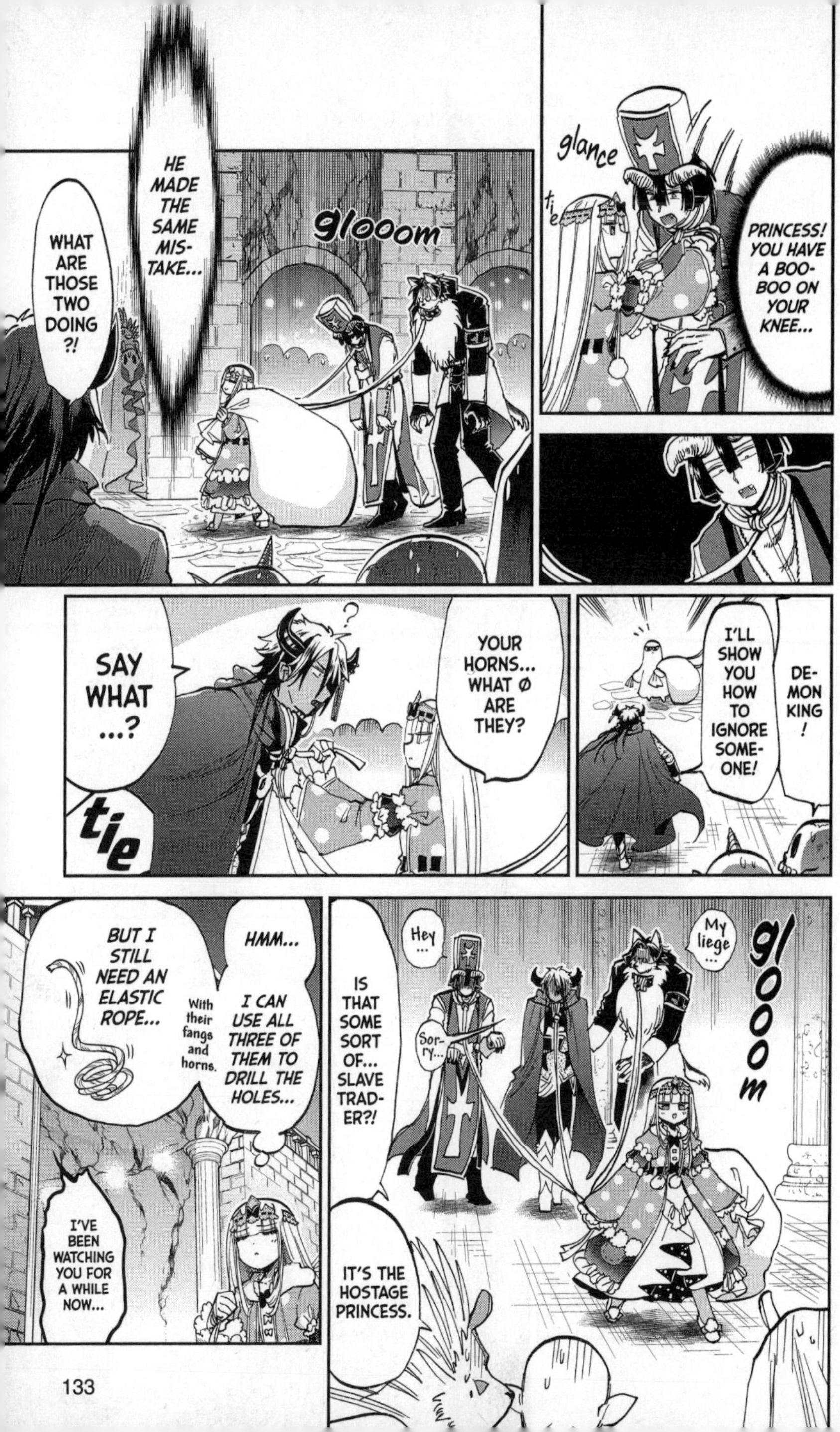
glance
tie
PRINCESS! YOU HAVE A BOO-BOO ON YOUR KNEE...
HE MADE THE SAME MIS-TAKE...
glooom
WHAT ARE THOSE TWO DOING?!
DE-MON KING!
I'LL SHOW YOU HOW TO IGNORE SOME-ONE!
YOUR HORNS... WHAT Ø ARE THEY?
SAY WHAT...?
tie
My liege...
glooooom
Hey...
Sor-ry...
IS THAT SOME SORT OF... SLAVE TRAD-ER?!
IT'S THE HOSTAGE PRINCESS.
HMM...
I CAN USE ALL THREE OF THEM TO DRILL THE HOLES...
With their fangs and horns.
BUT I STILL NEED AN ELASTIC ROPE...
I'VE BEEN WATCHING YOU FOR A WHILE NOW...

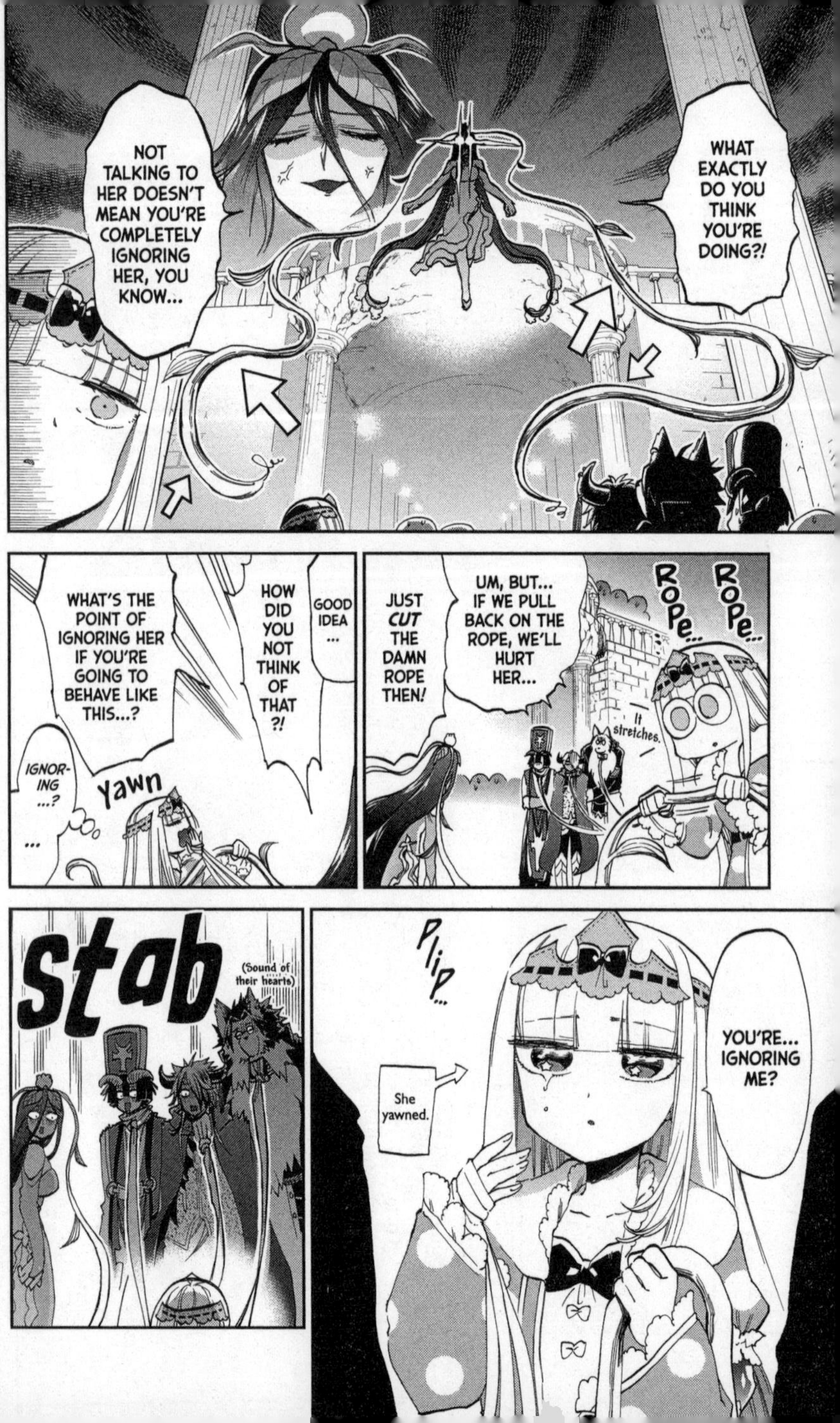
WHAT EXACTLY DO YOU THINK YOU'RE DOING?!
NOT TALKING TO HER DOESN'T MEAN YOU'RE COMPLETELY IGNORING HER, YOU KNOW...
Rope... Rope...
UM, BUT... IF WE PULL BACK ON THE ROPE, WE'LL HURT HER...
JUST CUT THE DAMN ROPE THEN!
It stretches.
GOOD IDEA...
HOW DID YOU NOT THINK OF THAT?!
WHAT'S THE POINT OF IGNORING HER IF YOU'RE GOING TO BEHAVE LIKE THIS...?
Yawn
IGNORING...?
...
Plip...
YOU'RE... IGNORING ME?
She yawned.
(Sound of their hearts)
stab

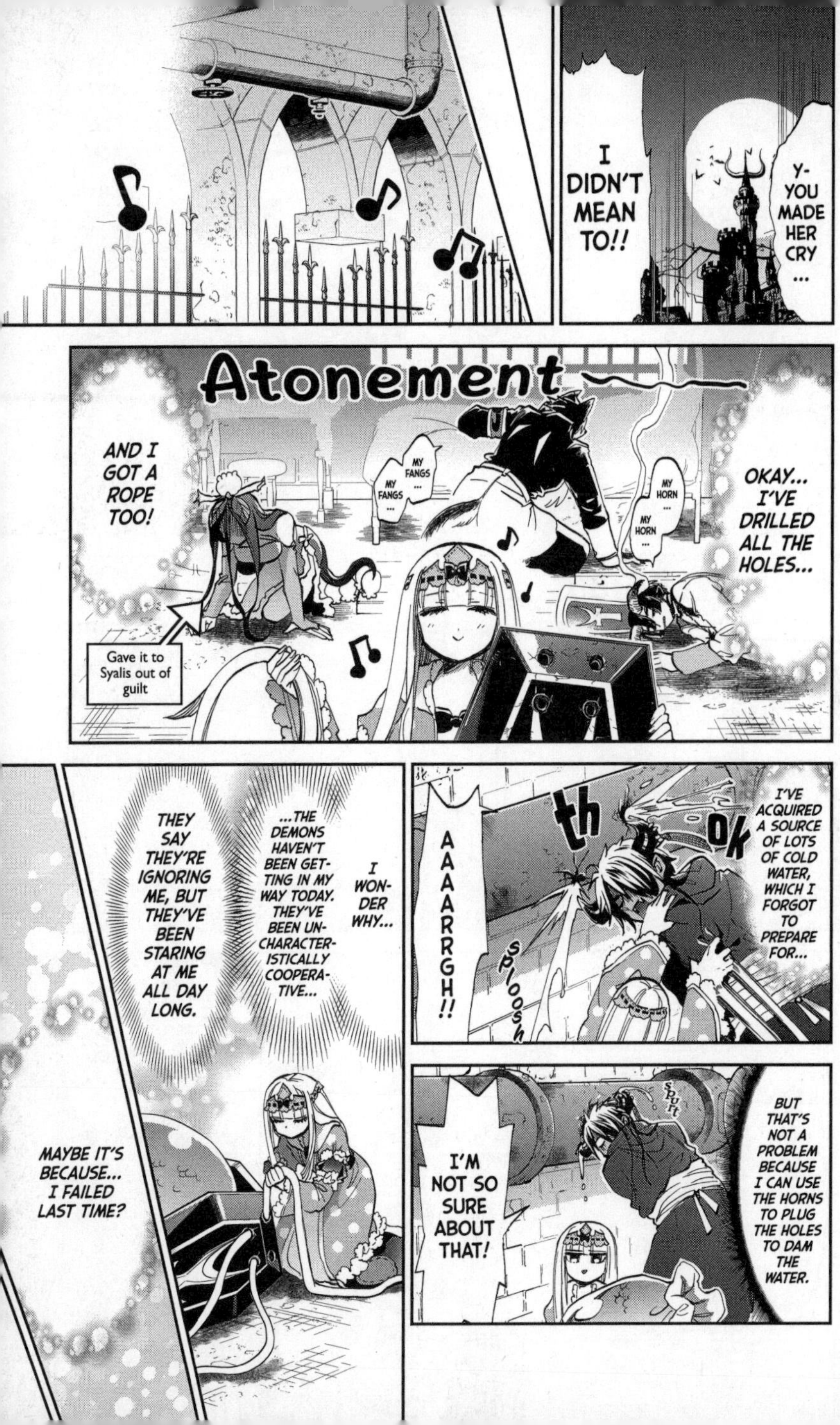
Y- YOU MADE HER CRY ...
I DIDN'T MEAN TO!!
Atonement
OKAY... I'VE DRILLED ALL THE HOLES...
MY HORN ...
MY HORN ...
MY FANGS ...
MY FANGS ...
AND I GOT A ROPE TOO!
Gave it to Syalis out of guilt
I'VE ACQUIRED A SOURCE OF LOTS OF COLD WATER, WHICH I FORGOT TO PREPARE FOR...
th ok
AAAARRGH!!
SPLOOSH
BUT THAT'S NOT A PROBLEM BECAUSE I CAN USE THE HORNS TO PLUG THE HOLES TO DAM THE WATER.
SPURT
I'M NOT SO SURE ABOUT THAT!
I WONDER WHY...
...THE DEMONS HAVEN'T BEEN GETTING IN MY WAY TODAY. THEY'VE BEEN UNCHARACTERISTICALLY COOPERATIVE...
THEY SAY THEY'RE IGNORING ME, BUT THEY'VE BEEN STARING AT ME ALL DAY LONG.
MAYBE IT'S BECAUSE... I FAILED LAST TIME?

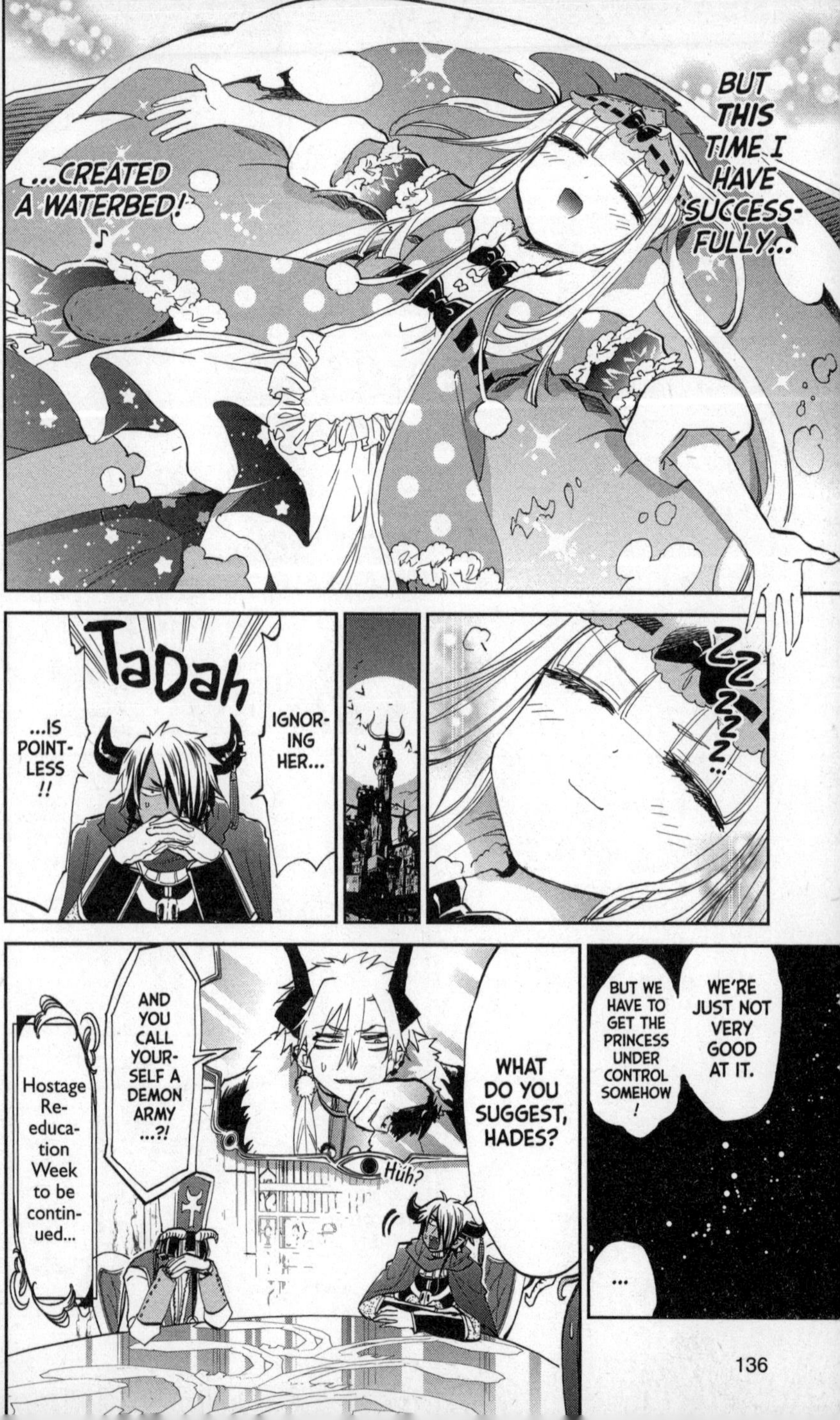
BUT THIS TIME I HAVE SUCCESSFULLY...
...CREATED A WATERBED! ♪
ZZZZZ...
IGNORING HER...
TaDah
...IS POINTLESS !!
WE'RE JUST NOT VERY GOOD AT IT.
BUT WE HAVE TO GET THE PRINCESS UNDER CONTROL SOMEHOW!
...
WHAT DO YOU SUGGEST, HADES?
Huh?
AND YOU CALL YOURSELF A DEMON ARMY ...?!
Hostage Re-education Week to be continued...

Intercastle Communication Window

Large screen and high-definition!

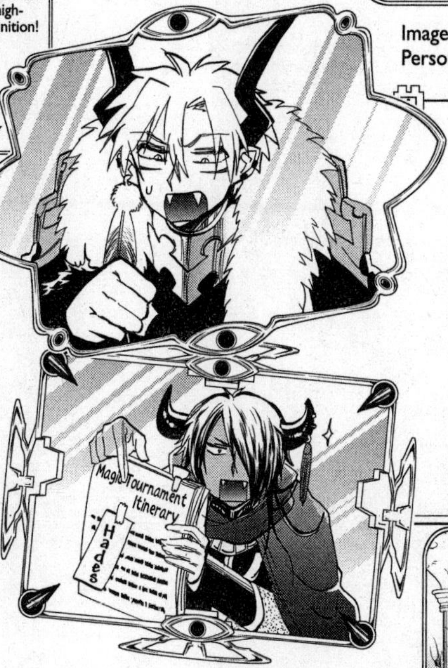

Magic Tournament Itinerary
Hades

Image Quality: ☆☆☆☆☆☆☆☆
Personal Usability: ☆☆☆☆☆☆☆

A communication window that connects the current Demon Castle and the Old Demon Castle. It's an extremely useful device that can monitor all kinds of areas through its attachment, the Eye See You. But it is often employed for personal use instead of official work. Basically, nowadays it has become the Demon King's personal videophone.

Since the Old Demon Castle summit, the window is often used for debates about which are better: big dogs or small dogs. The others have given this usage tacit approval since it always leads to a cute, peaceful conversation.

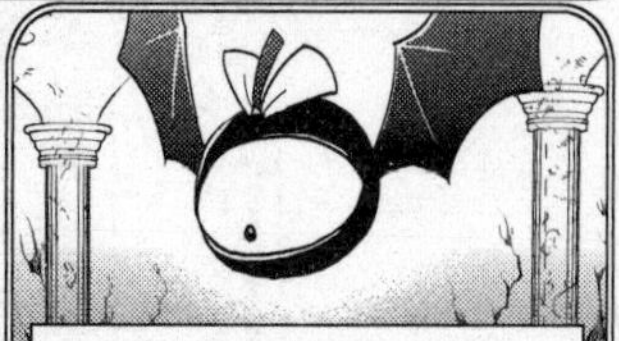

Eye See You at work

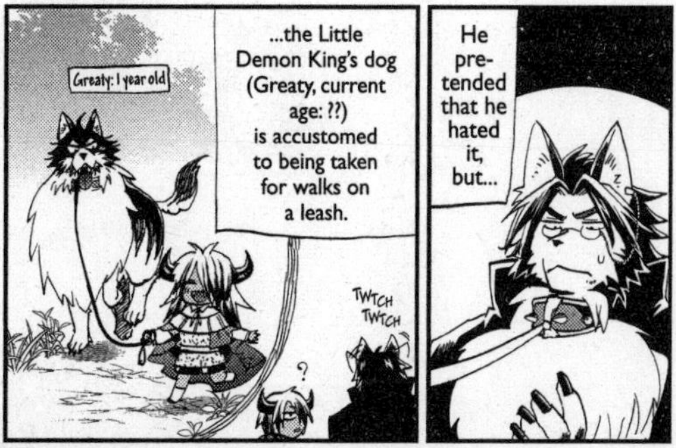

He pretended that he hated it, but...
...the Little Demon King's dog (Greaty, current age: ??) is accustomed to being taken for walks on a leash.
Greaty: 1 year old
TWTCH TWTCH
?

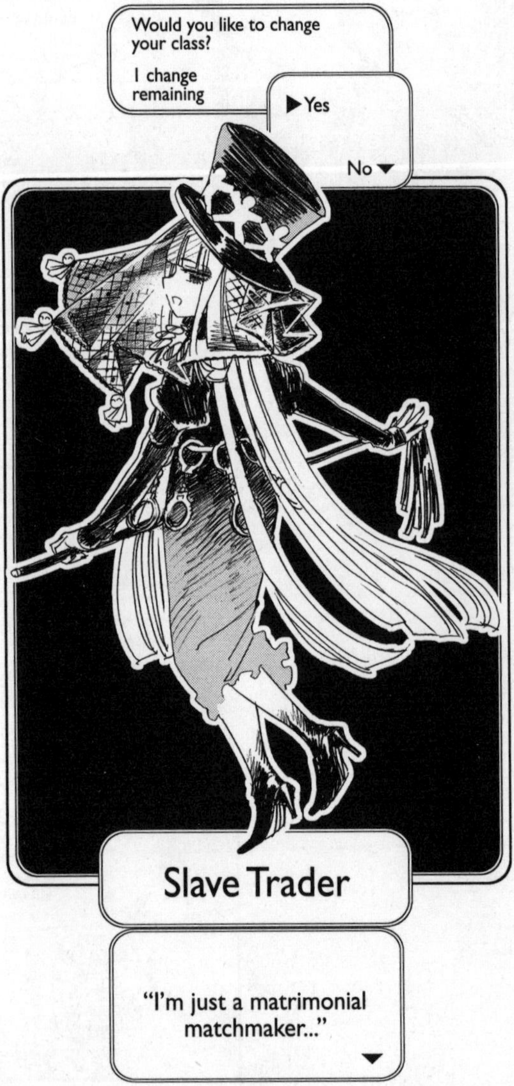
Would you like to change your class?
I change remaining
▶Yes
No
Slave Trader
"I'm just a matrimonial matchmaker..."

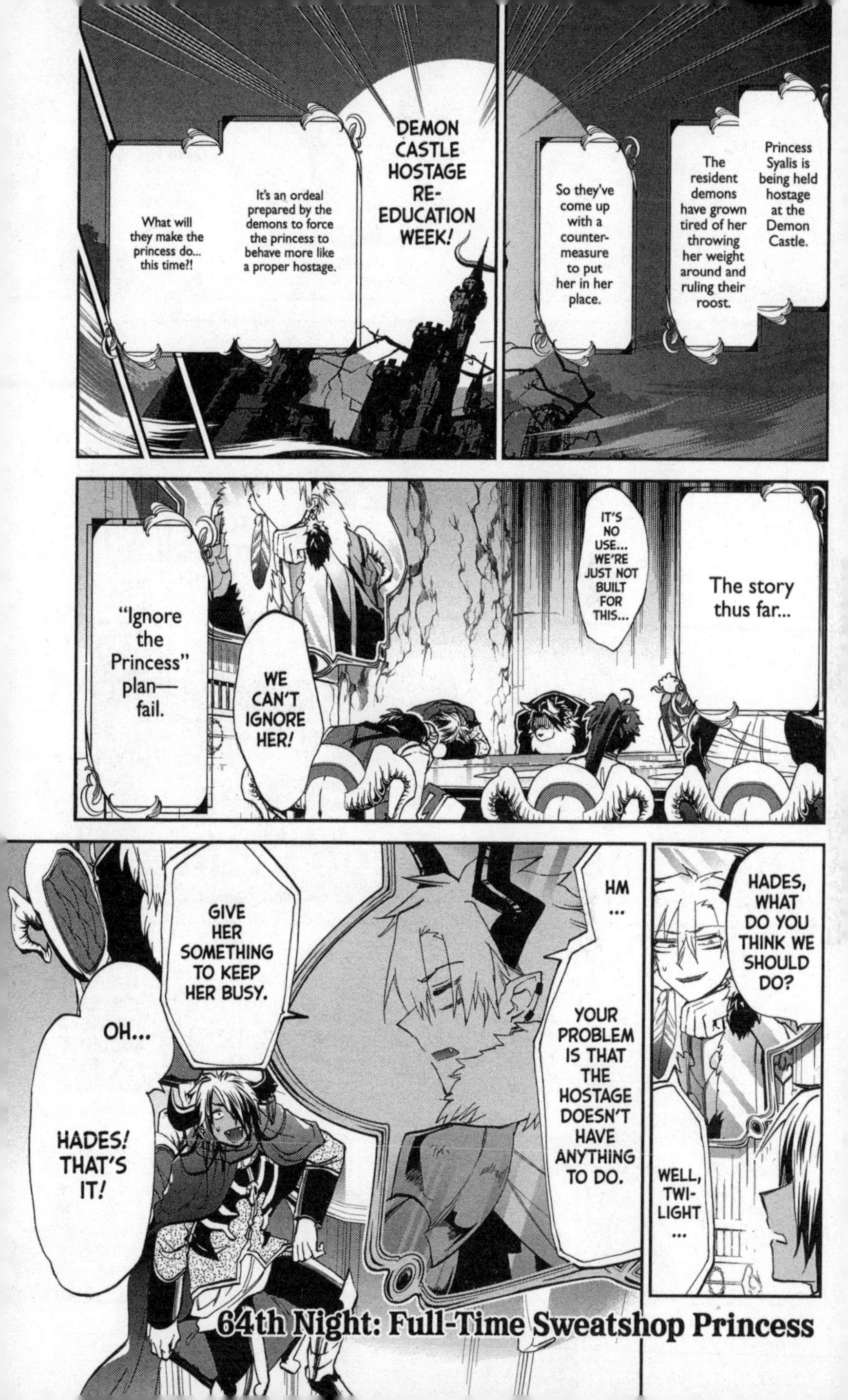
Princess Syalis is being held hostage at the Demon Castle.
The resident demons have grown tired of her throwing her weight around and ruling their roost.
So they've come up with a counter-measure to put her in her place.
DEMON CASTLE HOSTAGE RE-EDUCATION WEEK!
It's an ordeal prepared by the demons to force the princess to behave more like a proper hostage.
What will they make the princess do... this time?!
The story thus far...
IT'S NO USE... WE'RE JUST NOT BUILT FOR THIS...
WE CAN'T IGNORE HER!
"Ignore the Princess" plan—fail.
HADES, WHAT DO YOU THINK WE SHOULD DO?
WELL, TWI-LIGHT ...
HM ...
YOUR PROBLEM IS THAT THE HOSTAGE DOESN'T HAVE ANYTHING TO DO.
GIVE HER SOMETHING TO KEEP HER BUSY.
OH...
HADES! THAT'S IT!

64th Night: Full-Time Sweatshop Princess

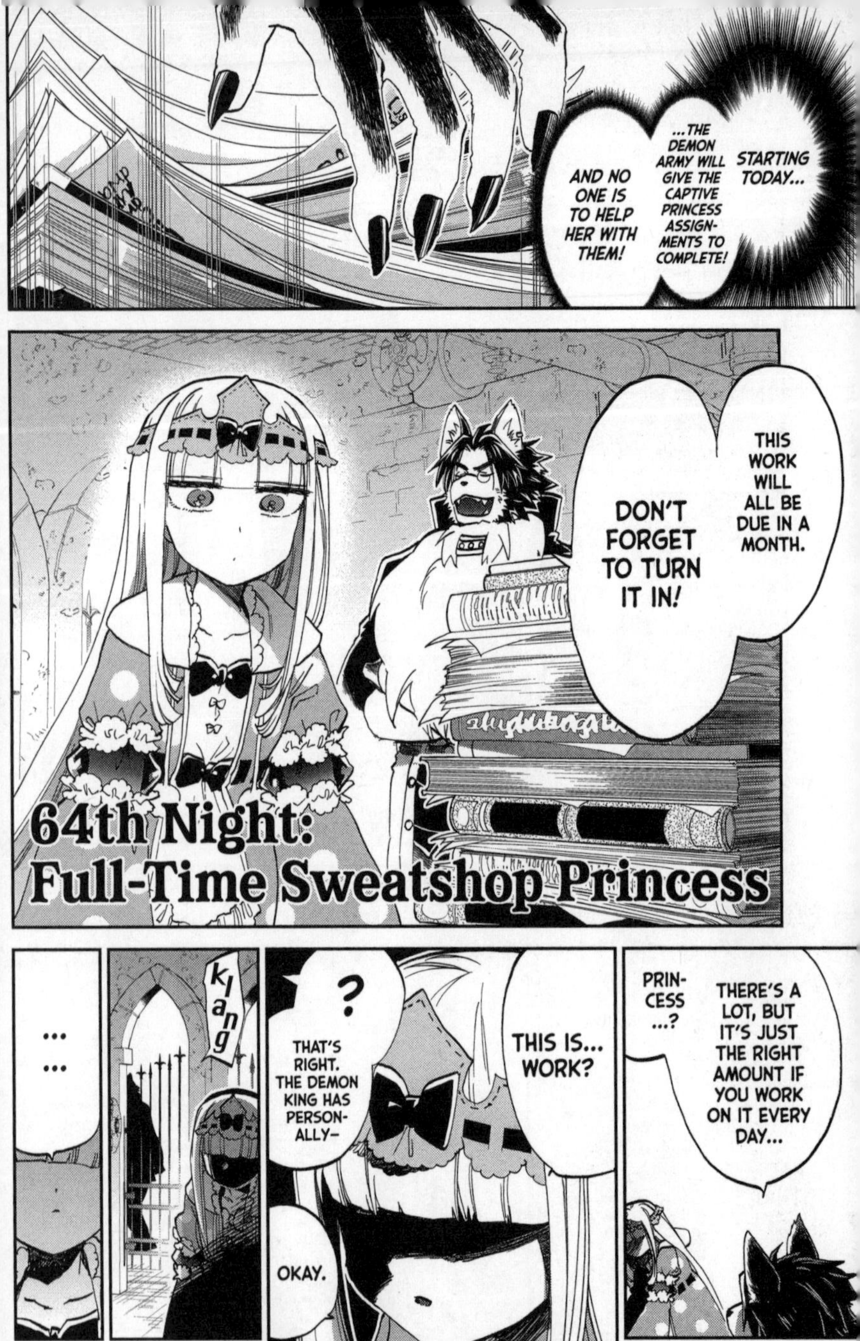
STARTING TODAY...
...THE DEMON ARMY WILL GIVE THE CAPTIVE PRINCESS ASSIGNMENTS TO COMPLETE!
AND NO ONE IS TO HELP HER WITH THEM!
THIS WORK WILL ALL BE DUE IN A MONTH.
DON'T FORGET TO TURN IT IN!
64th Night: Full-Time Sweatshop Princess
THERE'S A LOT, BUT IT'S JUST THE RIGHT AMOUNT IF YOU WORK ON IT EVERY DAY...
PRIN-CESS ...?
THIS IS... WORK?
?
THAT'S RIGHT. THE DEMON KING HAS PERSON-ALLY–
OKAY.
klang
... ...

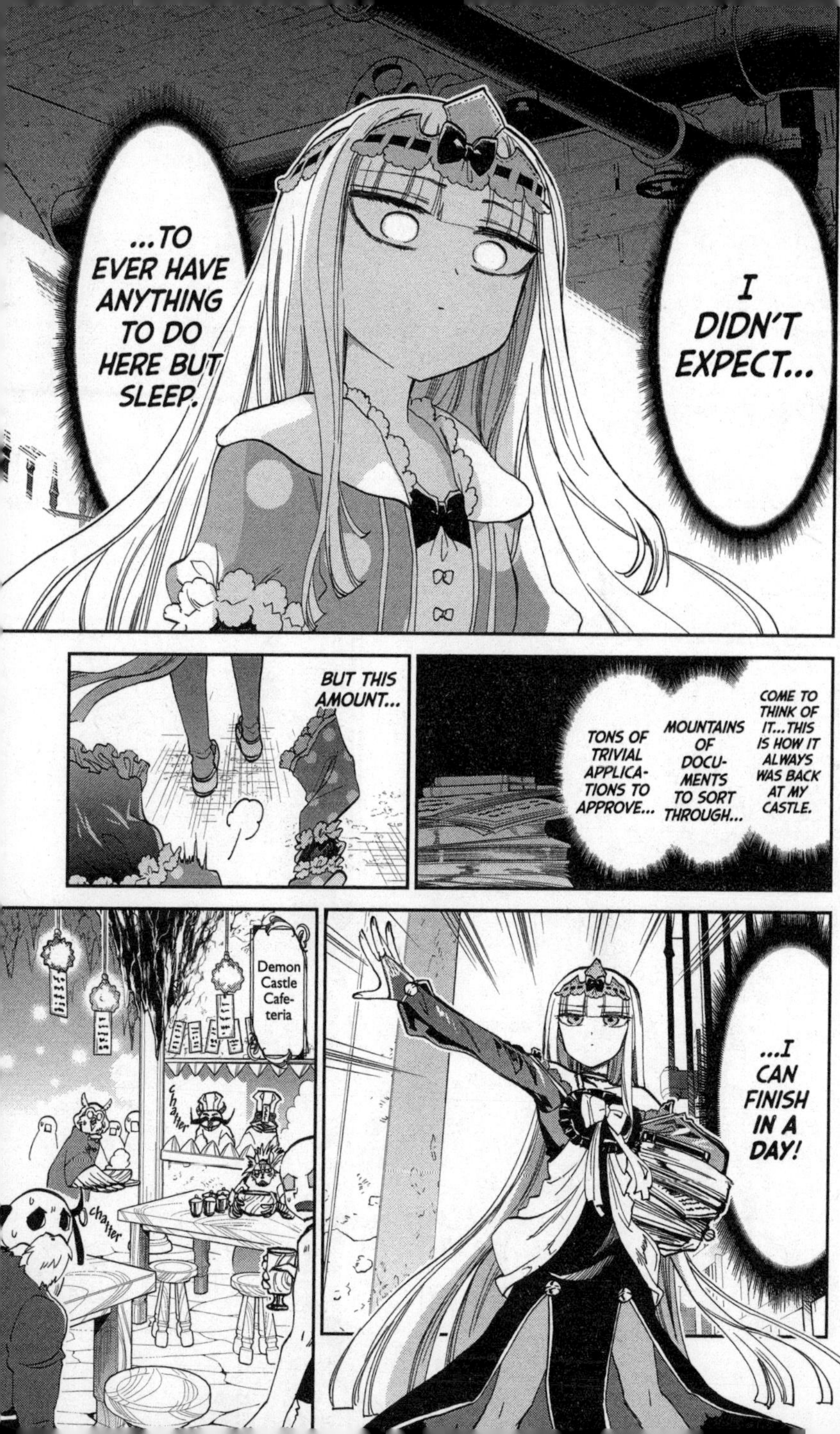
I DIDN'T EXPECT...
...TO EVER HAVE ANYTHING TO DO HERE BUT SLEEP.
COME TO THINK OF IT...THIS IS HOW IT ALWAYS WAS BACK AT MY CASTLE.
MOUNTAINS OF DOCUMENTS TO SORT THROUGH...
TONS OF TRIVIAL APPLICATIONS TO APPROVE...
BUT THIS AMOUNT...
...I CAN FINISH IN A DAY!
Demon Castle Cafeteria
chatter
chatter

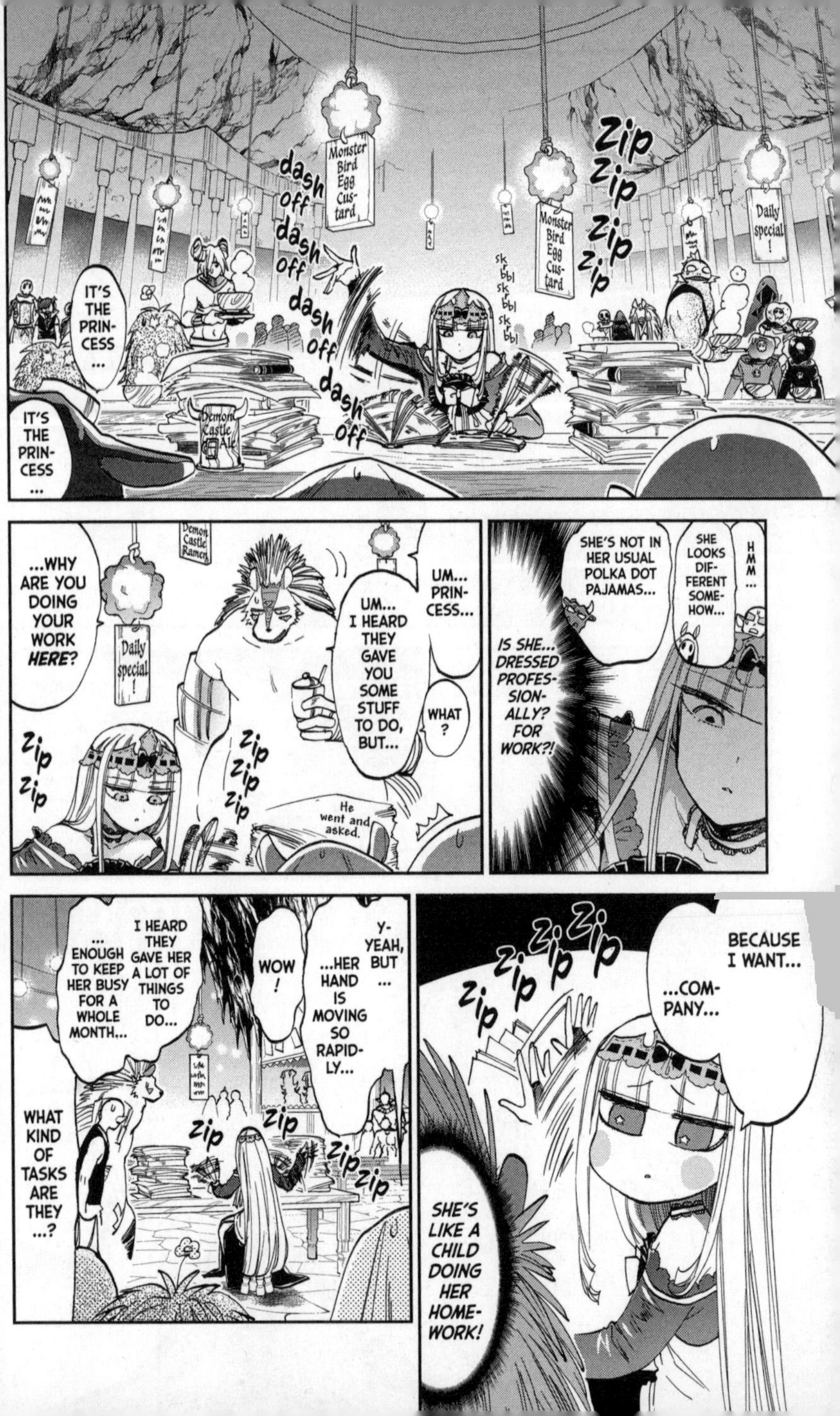
Daily special!
Monster Bird Egg Custard
Zip zip zip zip
sk rbbl sk rbbl sk bbl
Monster Bird Egg Custard
dash off dash off dash off dash off
IT'S THE PRINCESS...
Demon Castle Ale
IT'S THE PRINCESS...
HMM...
SHE LOOKS DIFFERENT SOMEHOW...
SHE'S NOT IN HER USUAL POLKA DOT PAJAMAS...
IS SHE... DRESSED PROFESSIONALLY? FOR WORK?!
UM... PRINCESS...
UM... I HEARD THEY GAVE YOU SOME STUFF TO DO, BUT...
WHAT?
Demon Castle Ramen
...WHY ARE YOU DOING YOUR WORK *HERE*?
Daily special!
zip zip zip
zip zip
He went and asked.
BECAUSE I WANT...
...COMPANY...
zip zip zip zip
SHE'S LIKE A CHILD DOING HER HOMEWORK!
Y-YEAH, BUT...
...HER HAND IS MOVING SO RAPIDLY...
WOW!
I HEARD THEY GAVE HER A LOT OF THINGS TO DO...
...ENOUGH TO KEEP HER BUSY FOR A WHOLE MONTH...
WHAT KIND OF TASKS ARE THEY...?
zip zip zip zip

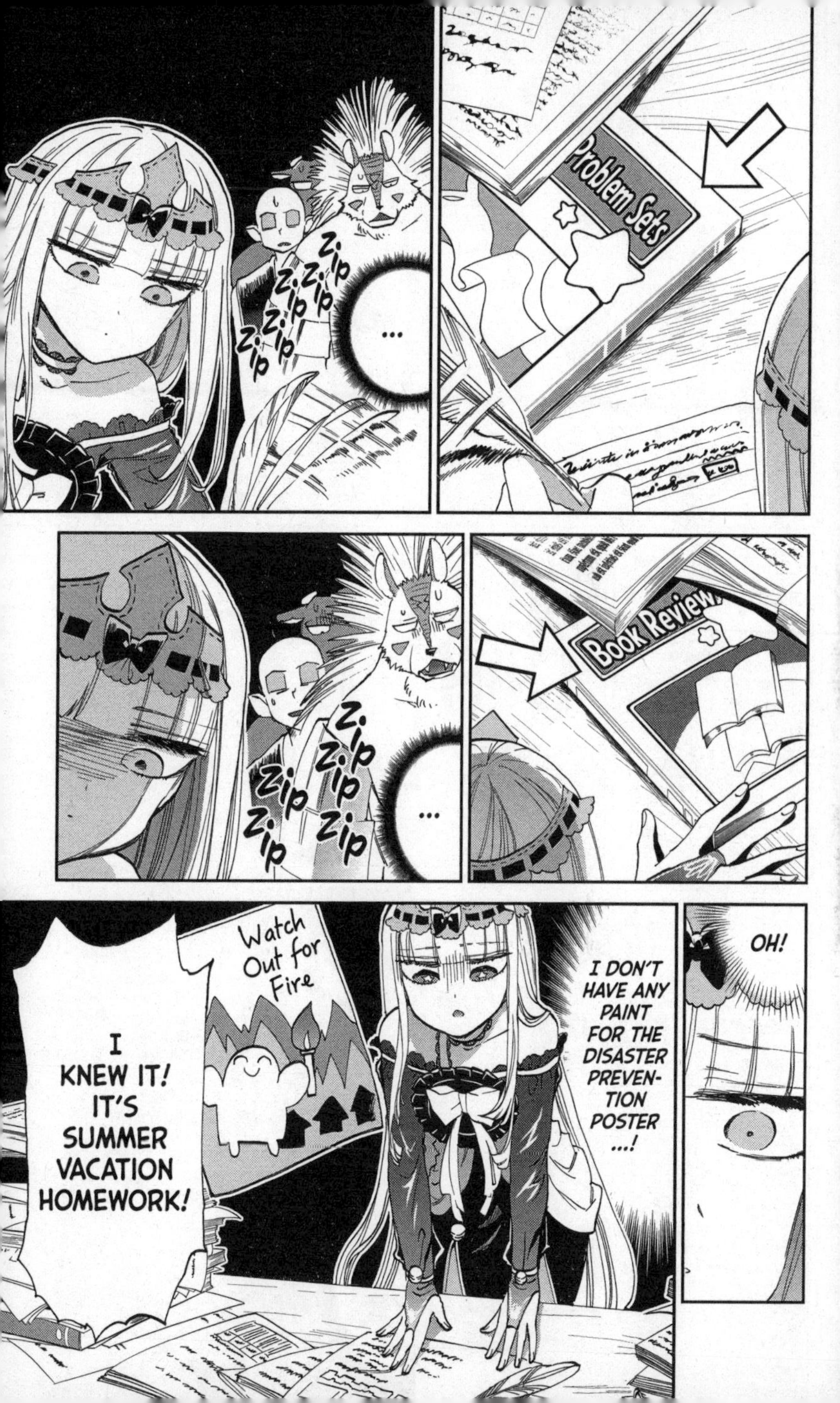
Problem Sets
Zip Zip Zip Zip Zip
...
Book Review
Zip Zip Zip Zip Zip Zip
...
OH!
I DON'T HAVE ANY PAINT FOR THE DISASTER PREVENTION POSTER ...!
Watch Out for Fire
I KNEW IT! IT'S SUMMER VACATION HOMEWORK!

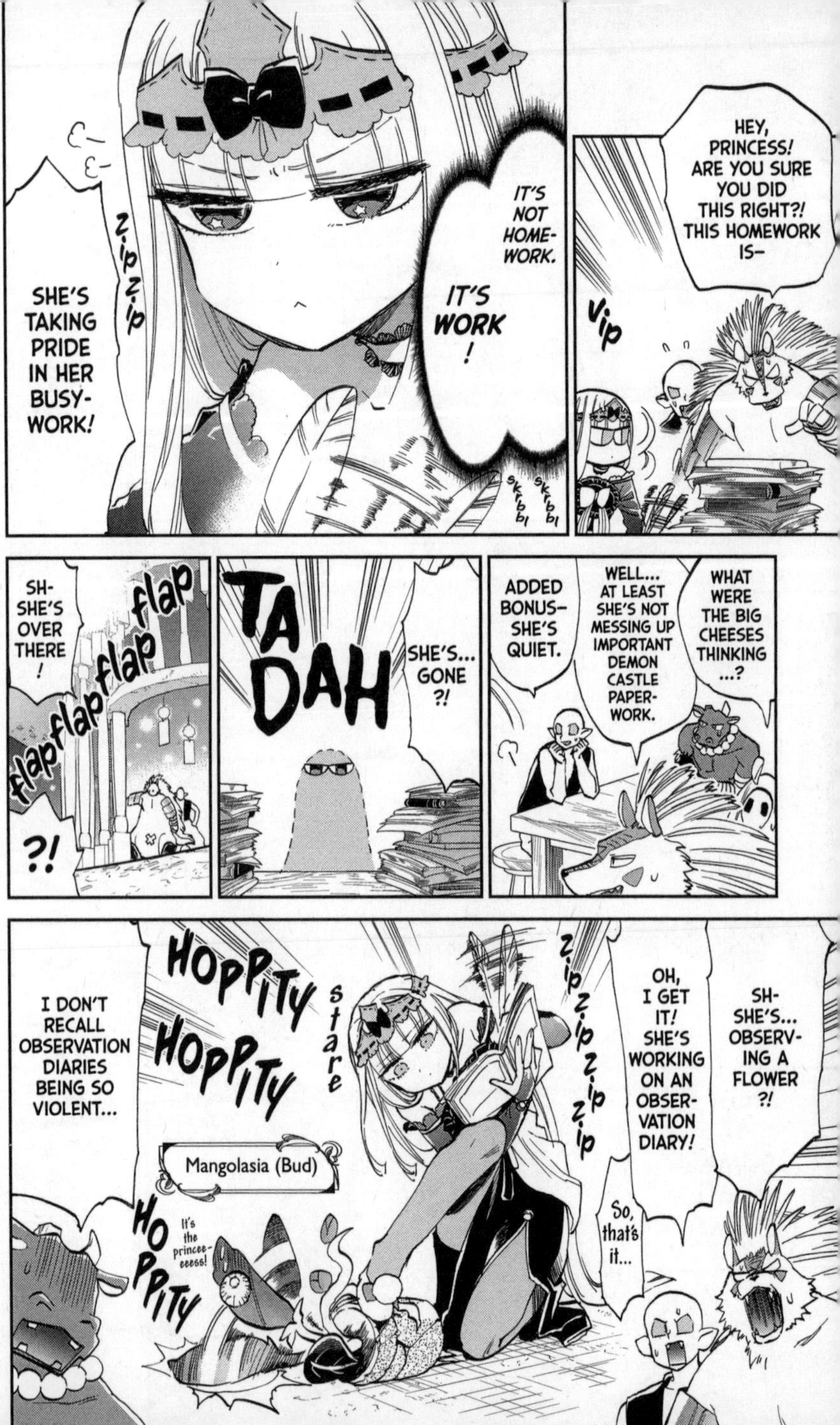
HEY, PRINCESS! ARE YOU SURE YOU DID THIS RIGHT?! THIS HOMEWORK IS—
Vip
IT'S NOT HOMEWORK.
IT'S WORK!
skrbbl skrbbl
zip zip
SHE'S TAKING PRIDE IN HER BUSYWORK!
WHAT WERE THE BIG CHEESES THINKING...?
WELL... AT LEAST SHE'S NOT MESSING UP IMPORTANT DEMON CASTLE PAPERWORK.
ADDED BONUS—SHE'S QUIET.
SHE'S... GONE?!
TA DAH
flap flap flap flap
SH-SHE'S OVER THERE!
?!
SH-SHE'S... OBSERVING A FLOWER?!
OH, I GET IT! SHE'S WORKING ON AN OBSERVATION DIARY!
So, that's it...
zip zip zip zip
stare
HOPPITY HOPPITY
Mangolasia (Bud)
It's the princeeeeess!
HOPPITY
I DON'T RECALL OBSERVATION DIARIES BEING SO VIOLENT...

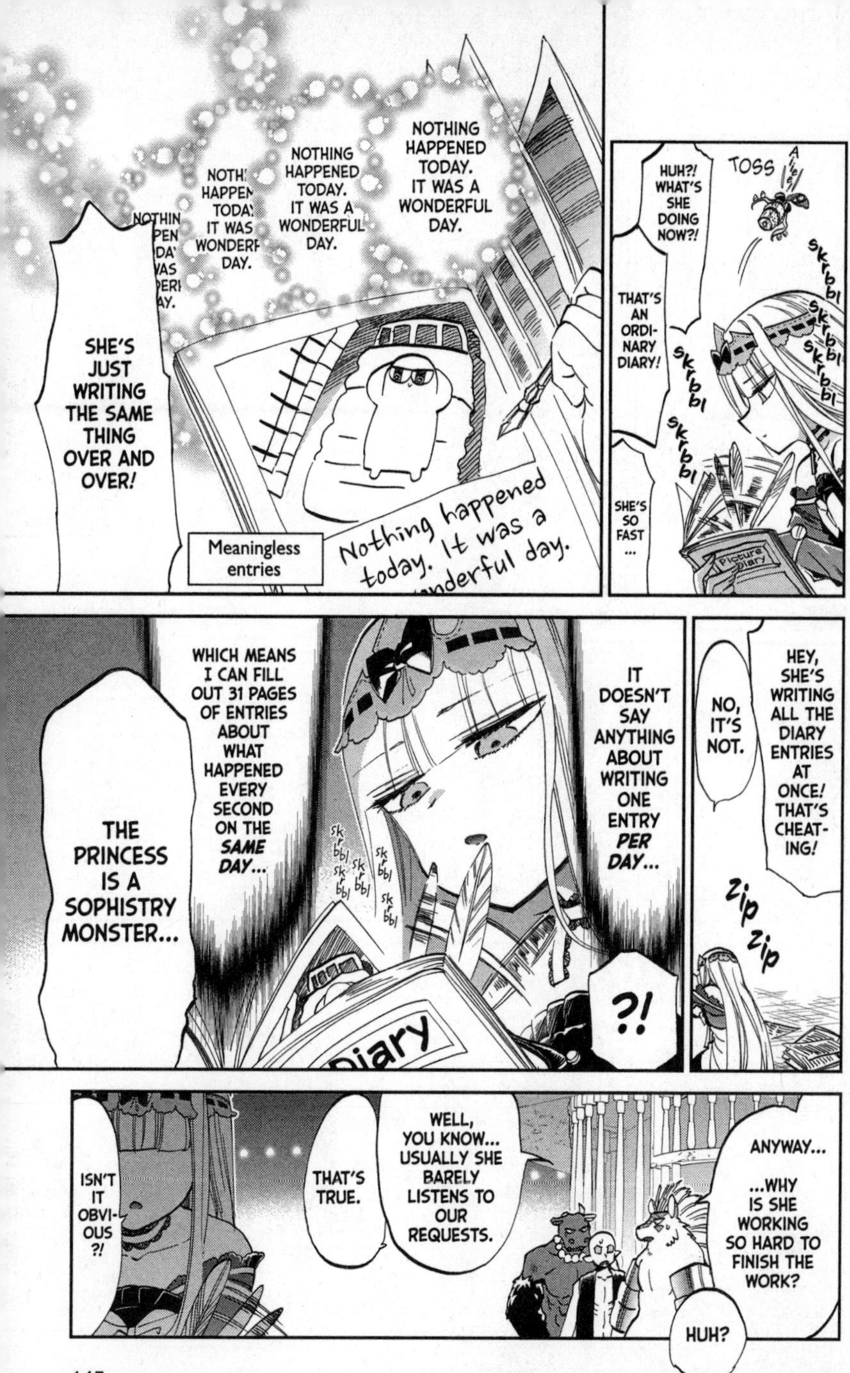
TOSS
HUH?! WHAT'S SHE DOING NOW?!
skrbbl
skrbbl
skrbbl
THAT'S AN ORDINARY DIARY!
skrbbl
skrbbl
SHE'S SO FAST...
Picture Diary
NOTHING HAPPENED TODAY. IT WAS A WONDERFUL DAY.
NOTHING HAPPENED TODAY. IT WAS A WONDERFUL DAY.
SHE'S JUST WRITING THE SAME THING OVER AND OVER!
Nothing happened today. It was a wonderful day.
Meaningless entries
HEY, SHE'S WRITING ALL THE DIARY ENTRIES AT ONCE! THAT'S CHEATING!
NO, IT'S NOT.
zip zip
IT DOESN'T SAY ANYTHING ABOUT WRITING ONE ENTRY *PER DAY*...
?!
WHICH MEANS I CAN FILL OUT 31 PAGES OF ENTRIES ABOUT WHAT HAPPENED EVERY SECOND ON THE *SAME DAY*...
skrbbl skrbbl skrbbl skrbbl skrbbl
THE PRINCESS IS A SOPHISTRY MONSTER...
Diary
ANYWAY...
...WHY IS SHE WORKING SO HARD TO FINISH THE WORK?
HUH?
WELL, YOU KNOW... USUALLY SHE BARELY LISTENS TO OUR REQUESTS.
THAT'S TRUE.
ISN'T IT OBVIOUS?!

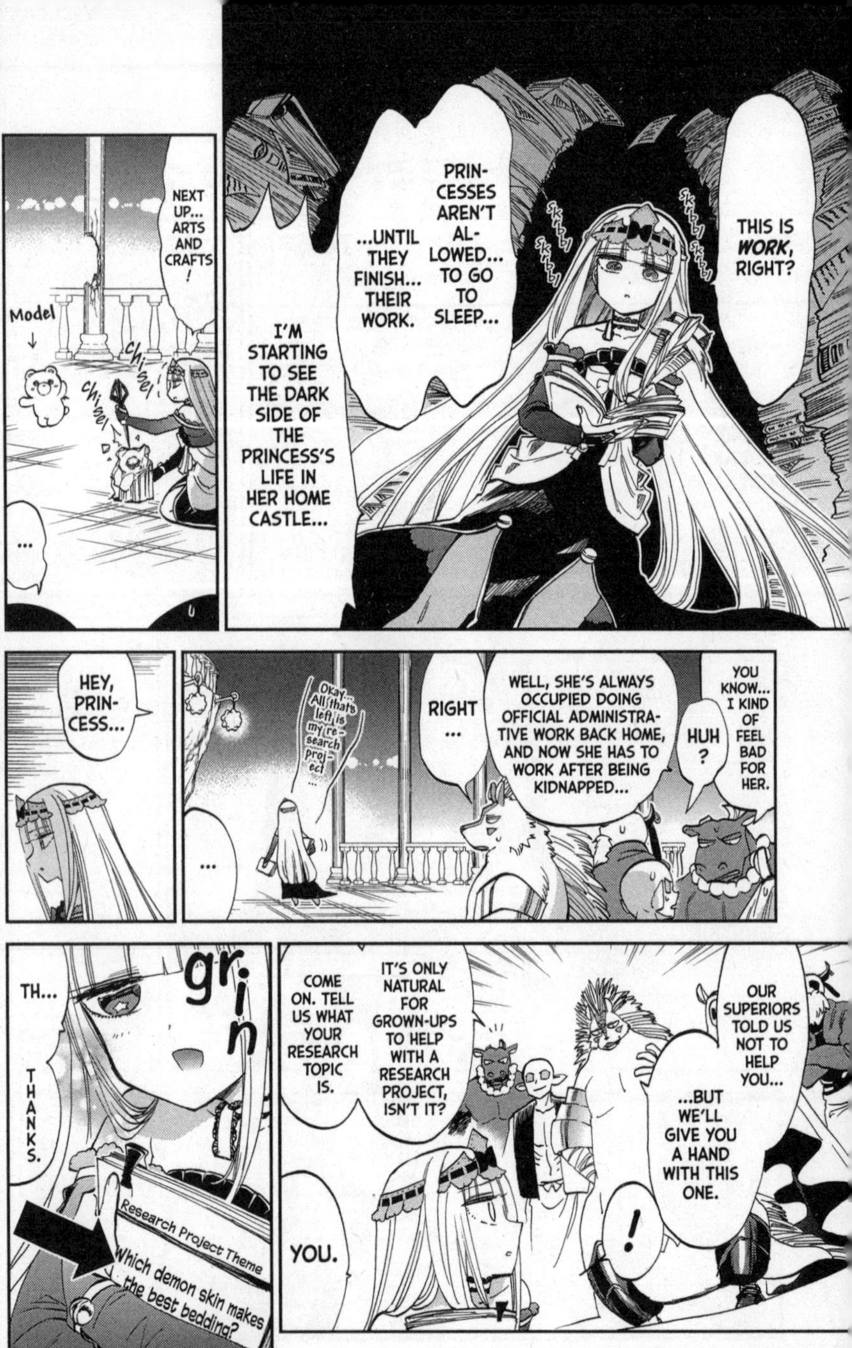
THIS IS *WORK*, RIGHT?
skribbl skribbl
skribbl skribbl
PRINCESSES AREN'T ALLOWED... TO GO TO SLEEP...
...UNTIL THEY FINISH... THEIR WORK.
I'M STARTING TO SEE THE DARK SIDE OF THE PRINCESS'S LIFE IN HER HOME CASTLE...
NEXT UP... ARTS AND CRAFTS!
Model ↓
chisel
chisel
...
YOU KNOW... I KIND OF FEEL BAD FOR HER.
HUH?
WELL, SHE'S ALWAYS OCCUPIED DOING OFFICIAL ADMINISTRATIVE WORK BACK HOME, AND NOW SHE HAS TO WORK AFTER BEING KIDNAPPED...
RIGHT...
Okay... All that's left is my research project...
...
HEY, PRINCESS...
OUR SUPERIORS TOLD US NOT TO HELP YOU...
...BUT WE'LL GIVE YOU A HAND WITH THIS ONE.
!
IT'S ONLY NATURAL FOR GROWN-UPS TO HELP WITH A RESEARCH PROJECT, ISN'T IT?
COME ON. TELL US WHAT YOUR RESEARCH TOPIC IS.
YOU.
TH...
grin
THANKS.
Research Project Theme
Which demon skin makes the best bedding?

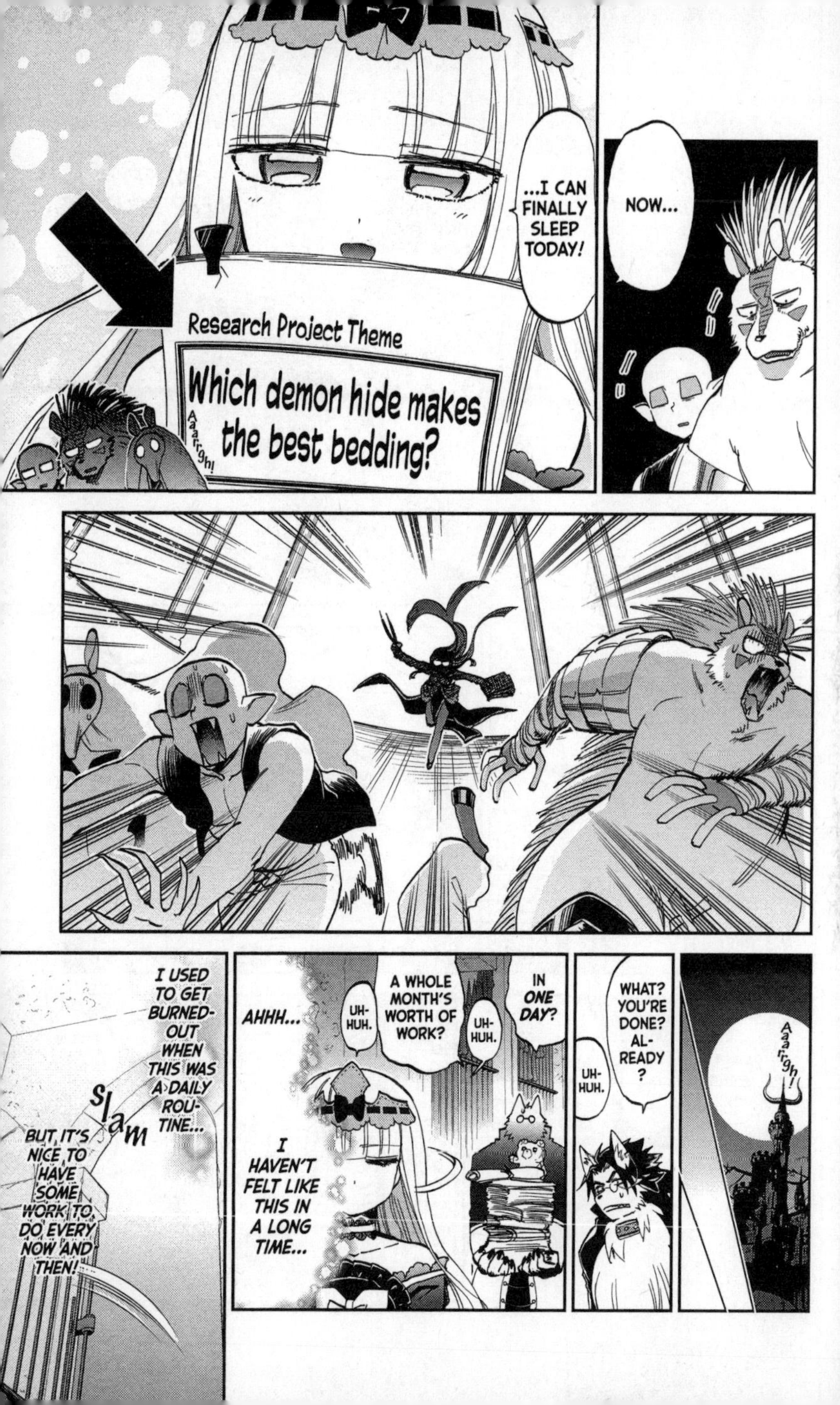
NOW...
...I CAN FINALLY SLEEP TODAY!
Research Project Theme
Which demon hide makes the best bedding?
Aaarrgh!
Aaarrgh!
WHAT? YOU'RE DONE? AL-READY?
UH-HUH.
IN ONE DAY?
UH-HUH.
A WHOLE MONTH'S WORTH OF WORK?
UH-HUH.
AHHH...
I HAVEN'T FELT LIKE THIS IN A LONG TIME...
I USED TO GET BURNED-OUT WHEN THIS WAS A DAILY ROUTINE...
slam
BUT IT'S NICE TO HAVE SOME WORK TO DO EVERY NOW AND THEN!

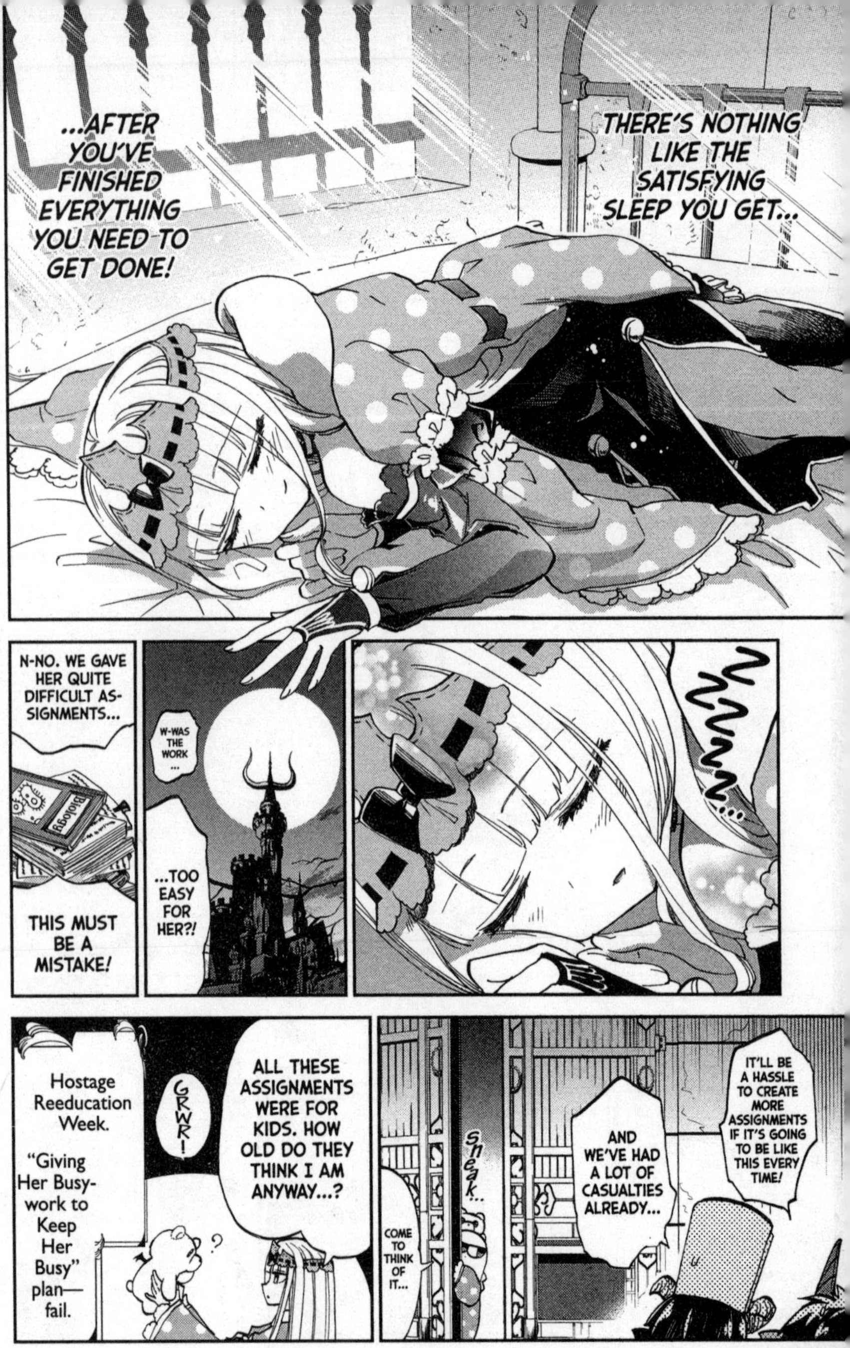
THERE'S NOTHING LIKE THE SATISFYING SLEEP YOU GET...
...AFTER YOU'VE FINISHED EVERYTHING YOU NEED TO GET DONE!
ZZZZZ...
W-WAS THE WORK...
...TOO EASY FOR HER?!
N-NO. WE GAVE HER QUITE DIFFICULT AS-SIGNMENTS...
Biology
THIS MUST BE A MISTAKE!
IT'LL BE A HASSLE TO CREATE MORE ASSIGNMENTS IF IT'S GOING TO BE LIKE THIS EVERY TIME!
AND WE'VE HAD A LOT OF CASUALTIES ALREADY...
SNEAK...
COME TO THINK OF IT...
ALL THESE ASSIGNMENTS WERE FOR KIDS. HOW OLD DO THEY THINK I AM ANYWAY...?
GRWR!
Hostage Reeducation Week.
"Giving Her Busy-work to Keep Her Busy" plan—fail.

Demon Castle Cafeteria

Popular with even the highest-ranking demons.

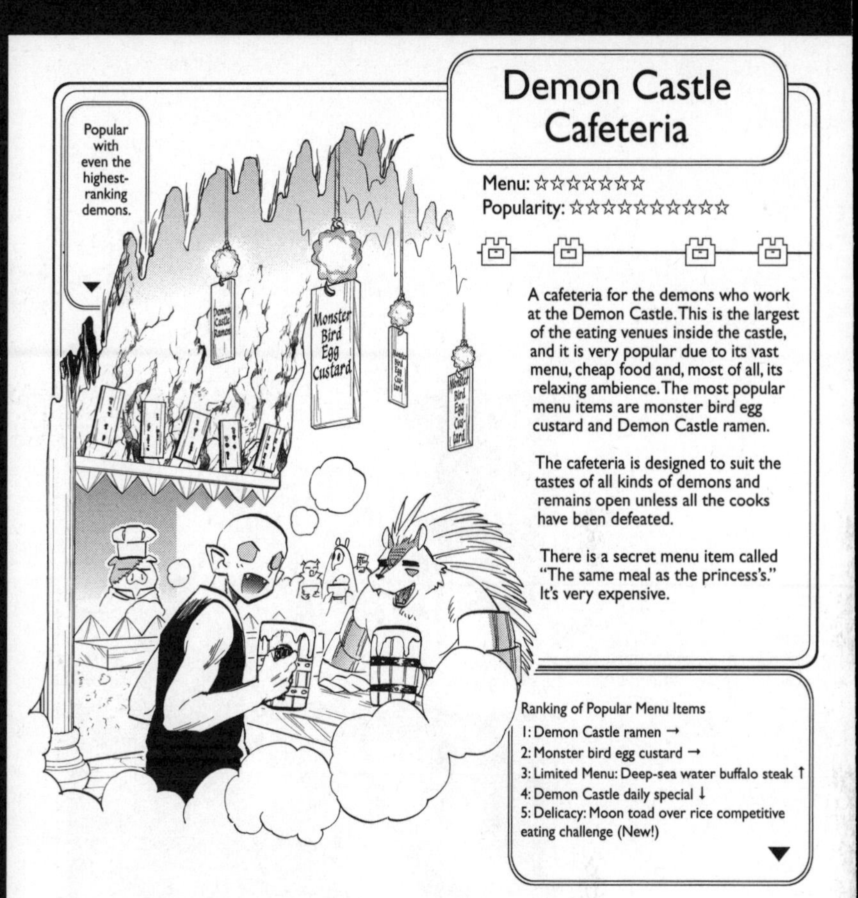
Demon Castle Ramen
Monster Bird Egg Custard
Monster Bird Egg Custard
Monster Bird Egg Custard

Menu: ☆☆☆☆☆☆☆
Popularity: ☆☆☆☆☆☆☆☆☆☆

A cafeteria for the demons who work at the Demon Castle. This is the largest of the eating venues inside the castle, and it is very popular due to its vast menu, cheap food and, most of all, its relaxing ambience. The most popular menu items are monster bird egg custard and Demon Castle ramen.

The cafeteria is designed to suit the tastes of all kinds of demons and remains open unless all the cooks have been defeated.

There is a secret menu item called "The same meal as the princess's." It's very expensive.

Ranking of Popular Menu Items

1: Demon Castle ramen →
2: Monster bird egg custard →
3: Limited Menu: Deep-sea water buffalo steak ↑
4: Demon Castle daily special ↓
5: Delicacy: Moon toad over rice competitive eating challenge (New!)

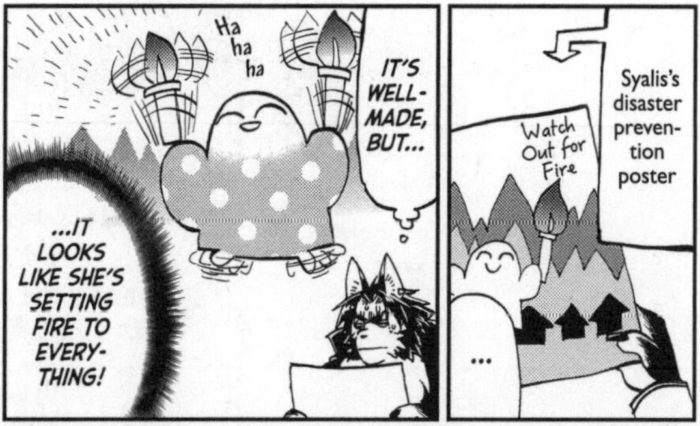
Syalis's disaster prevention poster
Watch Out for Fire
...
Ha ha ha
IT'S WELL-MADE, BUT...
...IT LOOKS LIKE SHE'S SETTING FIRE TO EVERYTHING!

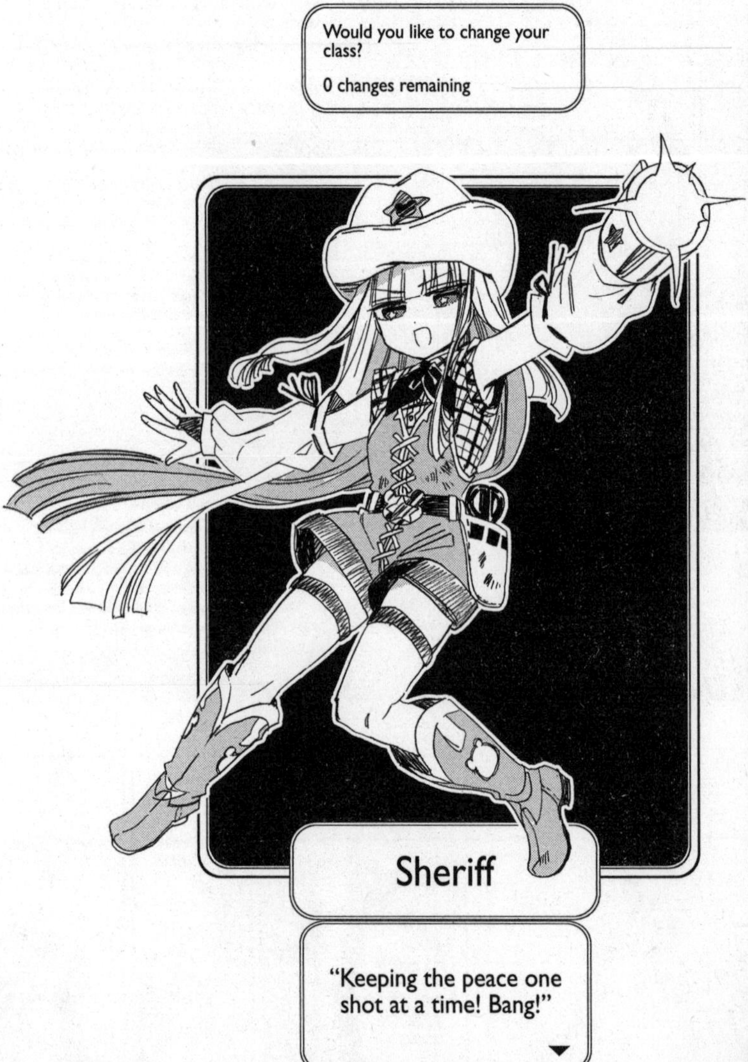
Would you like to change your class?
0 changes remaining
Sheriff
"Keeping the peace one shot at a time! Bang!"

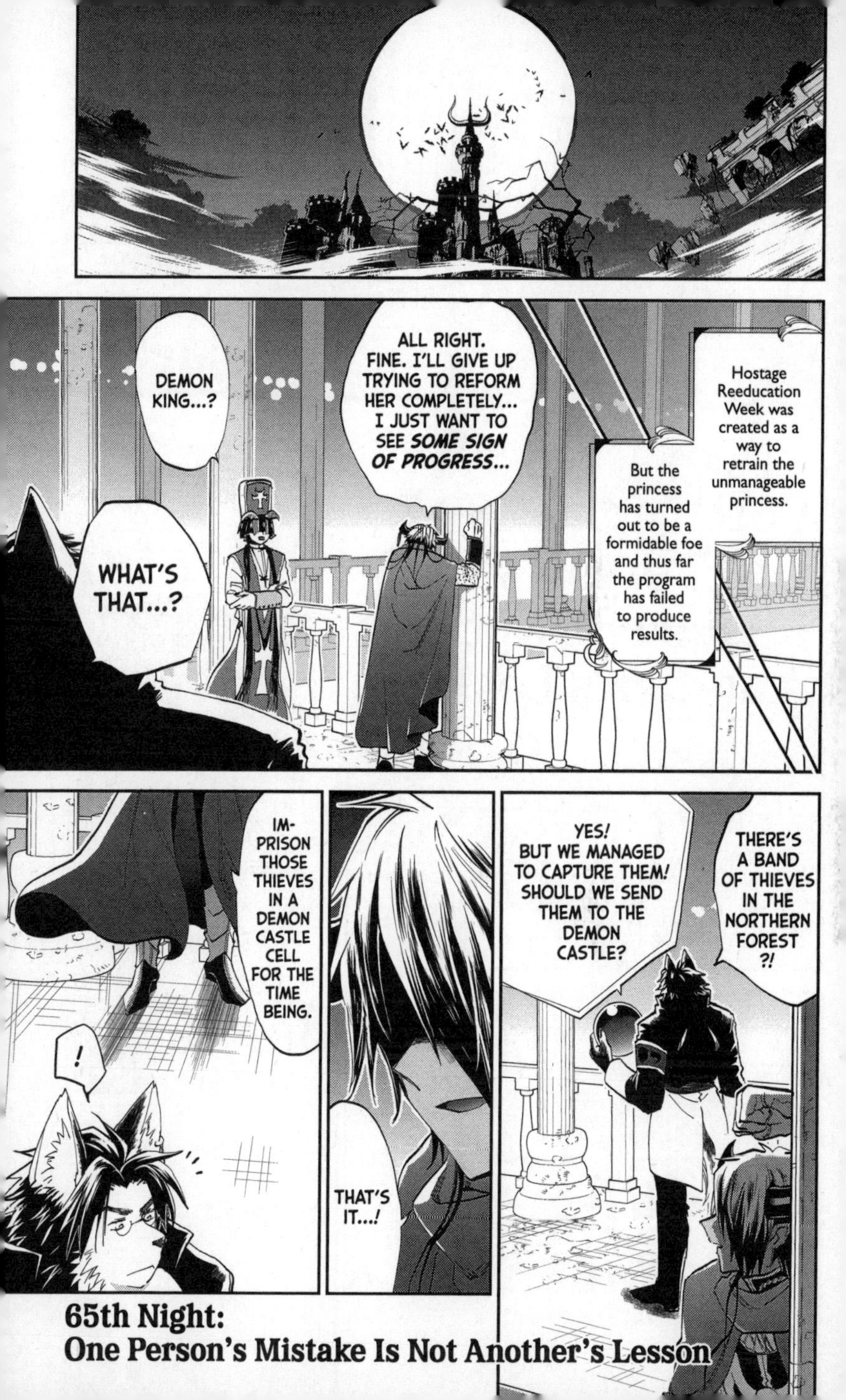
Hostage Reeducation Week was created as a way to retrain the unmanageable princess.
But the princess has turned out to be a formidable foe and thus far the program has failed to produce results.
ALL RIGHT. FINE. I'LL GIVE UP TRYING TO REFORM HER COMPLETELY... I JUST WANT TO SEE *SOME SIGN OF PROGRESS*...
DEMON KING...?
WHAT'S THAT...?
THERE'S A BAND OF THIEVES IN THE NORTHERN FOREST ?!
YES! BUT WE MANAGED TO CAPTURE THEM! SHOULD WE SEND THEM TO THE DEMON CASTLE?
THAT'S IT...!
IM-PRISON THOSE THIEVES IN A DEMON CASTLE CELL FOR THE TIME BEING.
!

65th Night: One Person's Mistake Is Not Another's Lesson

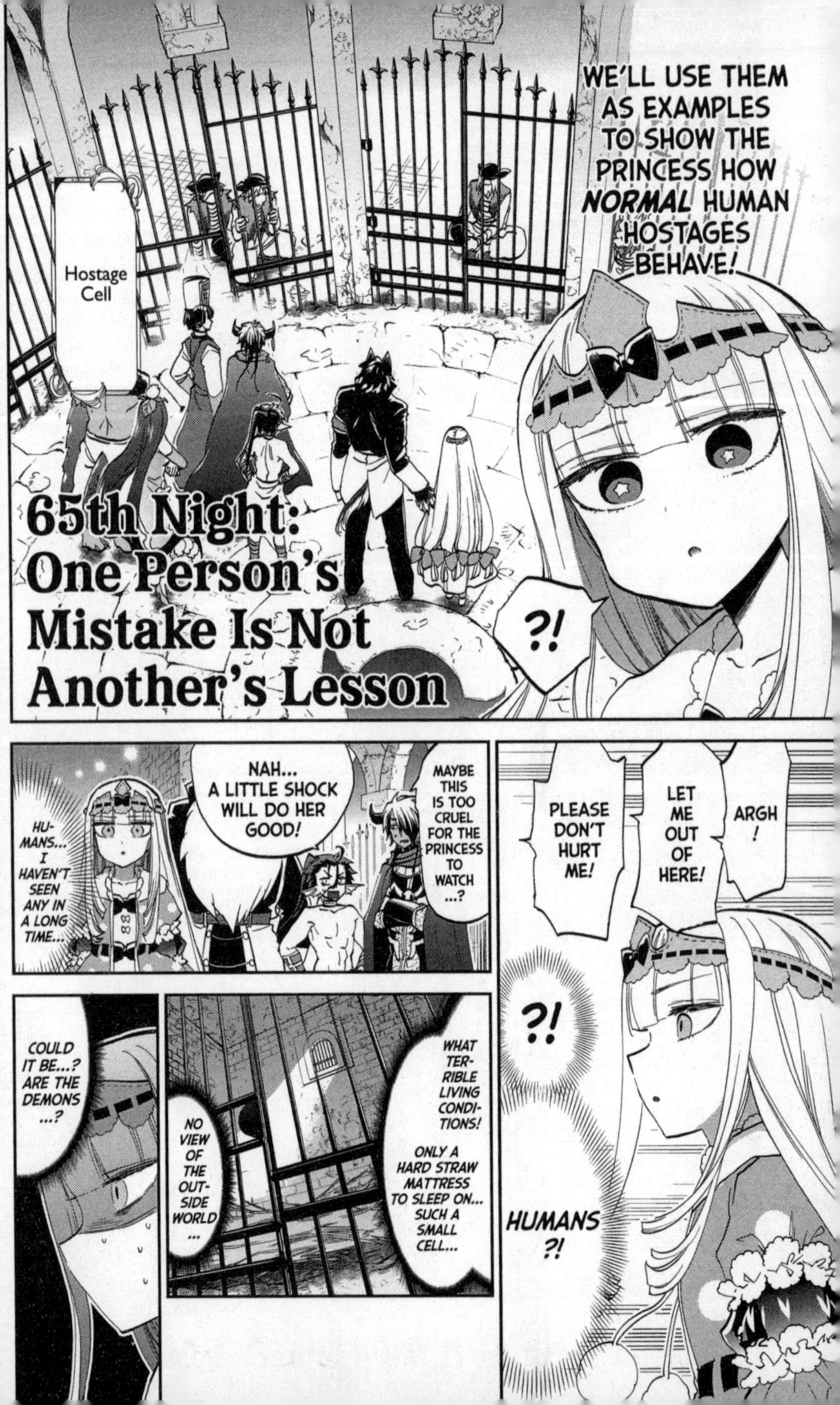
WE'LL USE THEM AS EXAMPLES TO SHOW THE PRINCESS HOW NORMAL HUMAN HOSTAGES BEHAVE!
?!
65th Night: One Person's Mistake Is Not Another's Lesson
Hostage Cell
ARGH!
LET ME OUT OF HERE!
PLEASE DON'T HURT ME!
?!
HUMANS?!
MAYBE THIS IS TOO CRUEL FOR THE PRINCESS TO WATCH...?
NAH... A LITTLE SHOCK WILL DO HER GOOD!
HU-MANS... I HAVEN'T SEEN ANY IN A LONG TIME...
WHAT TER-RIBLE LIVING CONDI-TIONS!
ONLY A HARD STRAW MATTRESS TO SLEEP ON... SUCH A SMALL CELL...
NO VIEW OF THE OUT-SIDE WORLD...
COULD IT BE...? ARE THE DEMONS...?

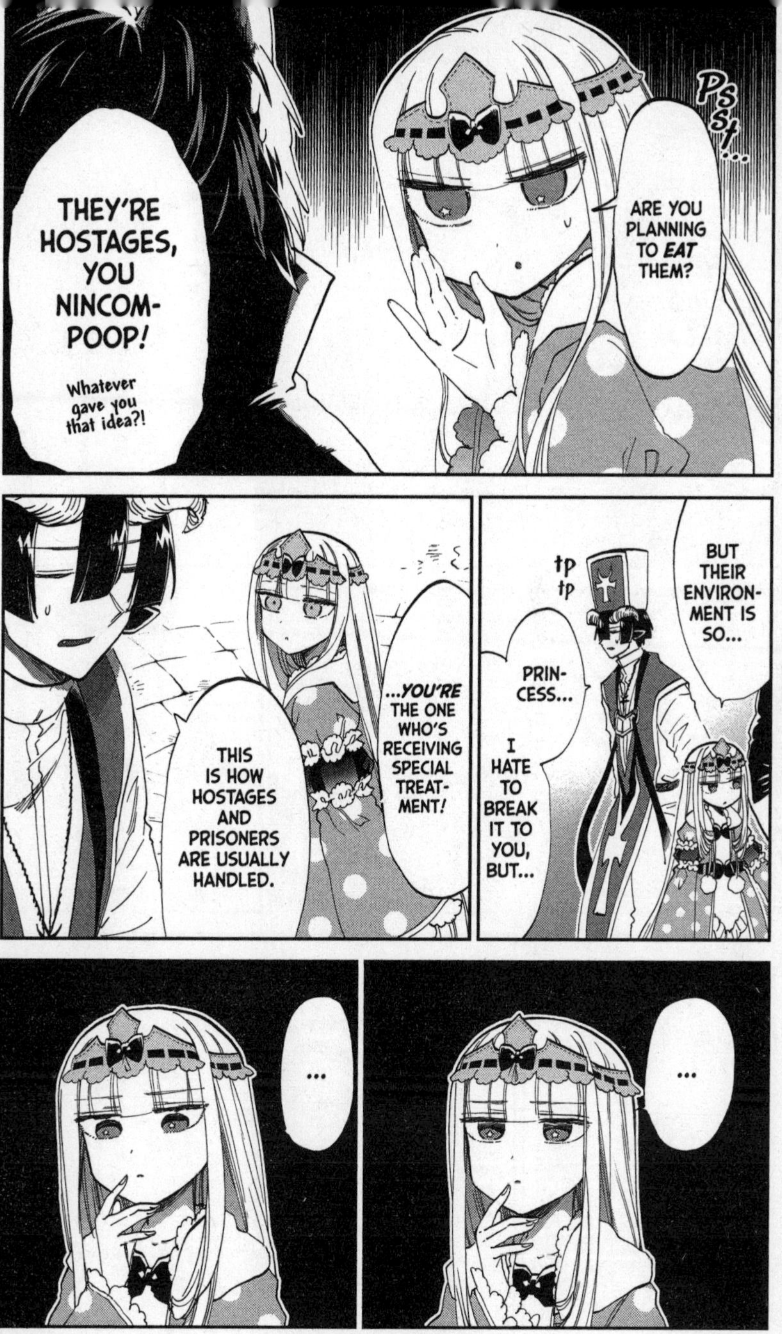
Psst...
ARE YOU PLANNING TO EAT THEM?
THEY'RE HOSTAGES, YOU NINCOMPOOP!
Whatever gave you that idea?!
BUT THEIR ENVIRONMENT IS SO...
tp tp
PRINCESS...
I HATE TO BREAK IT TO YOU, BUT...
...YOU'RE THE ONE WHO'S RECEIVING SPECIAL TREATMENT!
THIS IS HOW HOSTAGES AND PRISONERS ARE USUALLY HANDLED.
...
...

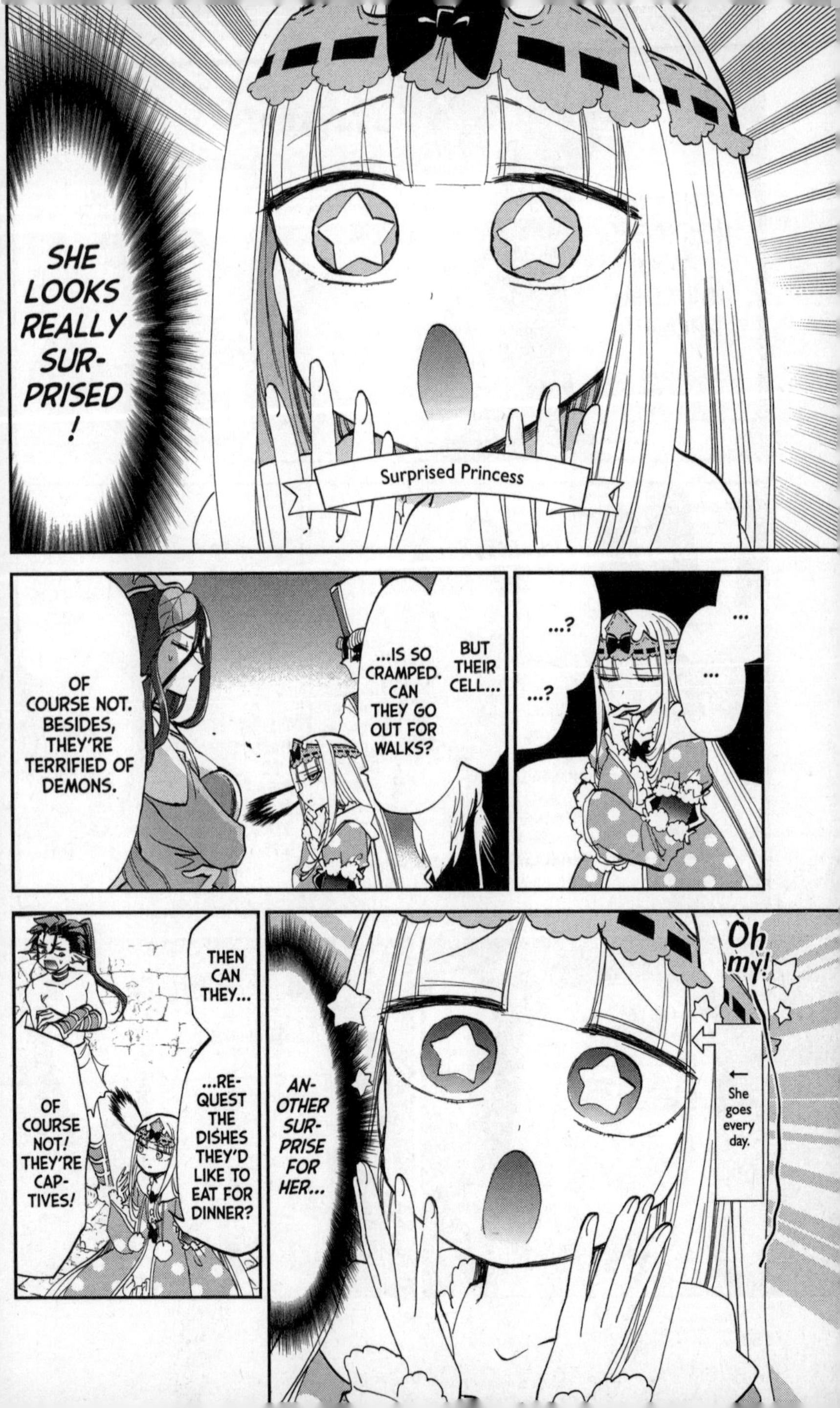
SHE LOOKS REALLY SUR-PRISED!
Surprised Princess
...
...
...?
...?
BUT THEIR CELL...
...IS SO CRAMPED. CAN THEY GO OUT FOR WALKS?
OF COURSE NOT. BESIDES, THEY'RE TERRIFIED OF DEMONS.
Oh my!
← She goes every day.
AN-OTHER SUR-PRISE FOR HER...
THEN CAN THEY...
...RE-QUEST THE DISHES THEY'D LIKE TO EAT FOR DINNER?
OF COURSE NOT! THEY'RE CAP-TIVES!

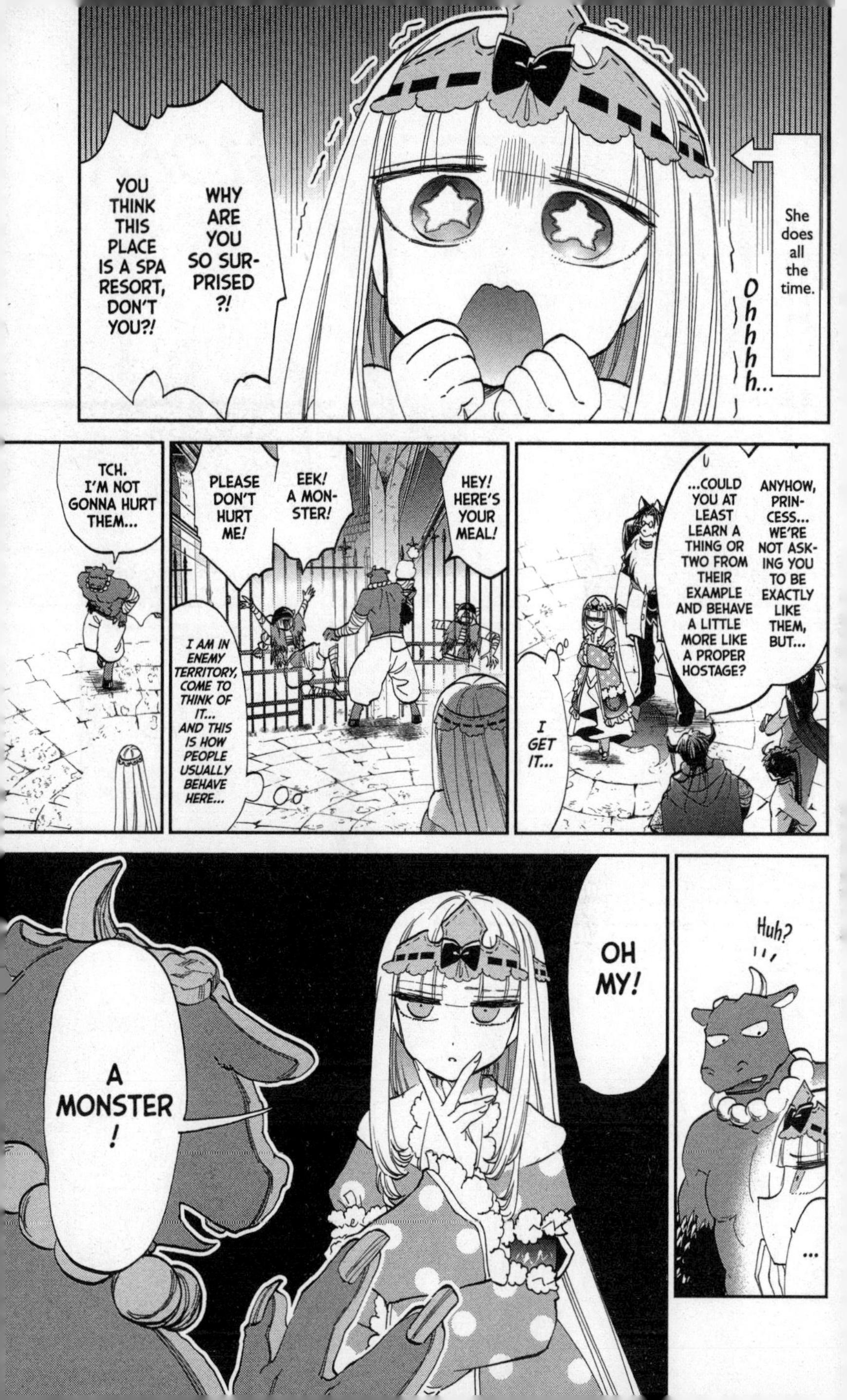
She does all the time.
Ohhhh...
WHY ARE YOU SO SURPRISED?!
YOU THINK THIS PLACE IS A SPA RESORT, DON'T YOU?!
ANYHOW, PRINCESS... WE'RE NOT ASKING YOU TO BE EXACTLY LIKE THEM, BUT...
...COULD YOU AT LEAST LEARN A THING OR TWO FROM THEIR EXAMPLE AND BEHAVE A LITTLE MORE LIKE A PROPER HOSTAGE?
I GET IT...
HEY! HERE'S YOUR MEAL!
EEK! A MONSTER!
PLEASE DON'T HURT ME!
I AM IN ENEMY TERRITORY, COME TO THINK OF IT... AND THIS IS HOW PEOPLE USUALLY BEHAVE HERE...
TCH. I'M NOT GONNA HURT THEM...
Huh?
...
OH MY!
A MONSTER!

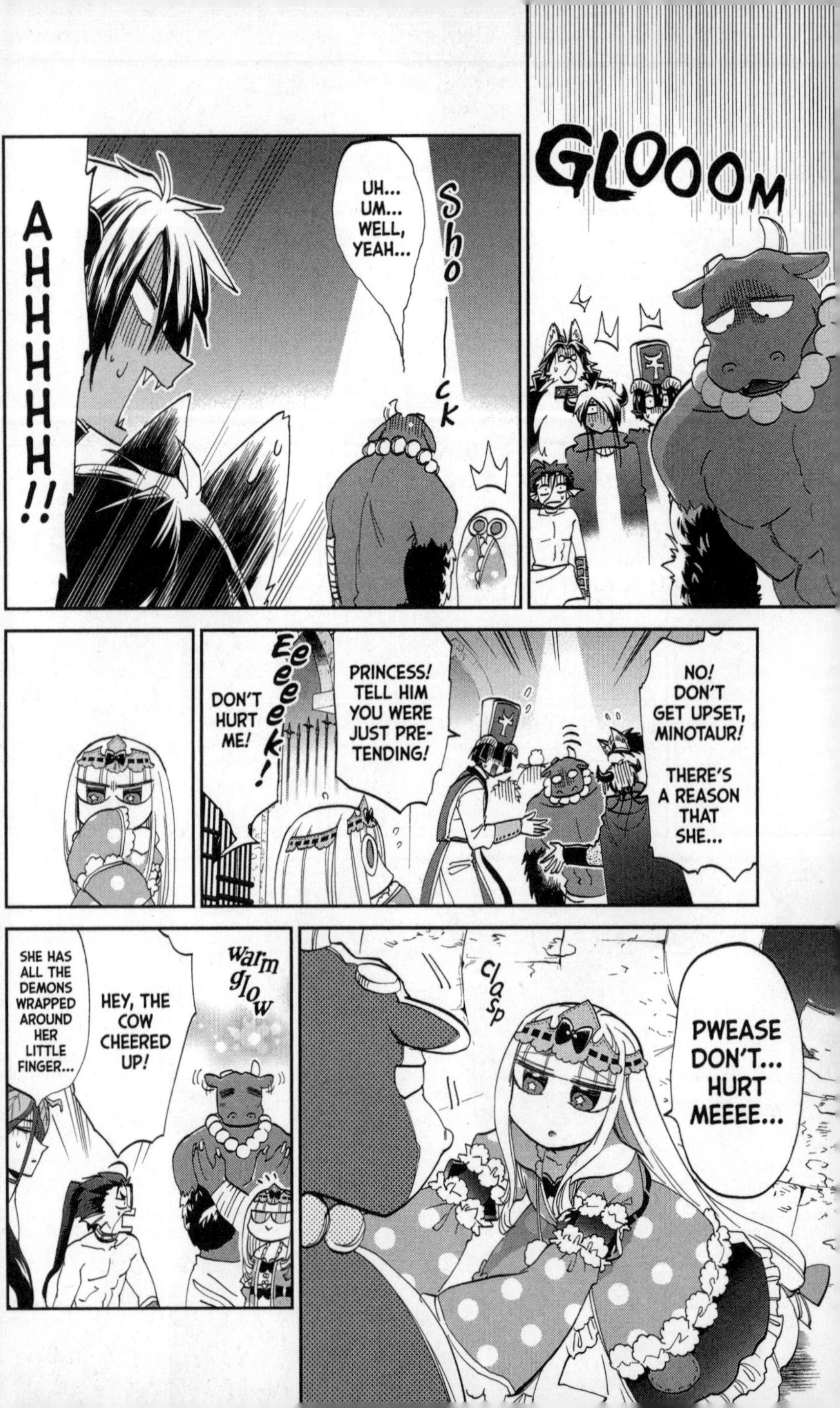
GLOOOM
UH... UM... WELL, YEAH...
Shock
AHHHHHH!!
NO! DON'T GET UPSET, MINOTAUR!
THERE'S A REASON THAT SHE...
PRINCESS! TELL HIM YOU WERE JUST PRE-TENDING!
Eeeeeek!
DON'T HURT ME!
clasp
PWEASE DON'T... HURT MEEEE...
warm glow
HEY, THE COW CHEERED UP!
SHE HAS ALL THE DEMONS WRAPPED AROUND HER LITTLE FINGER...

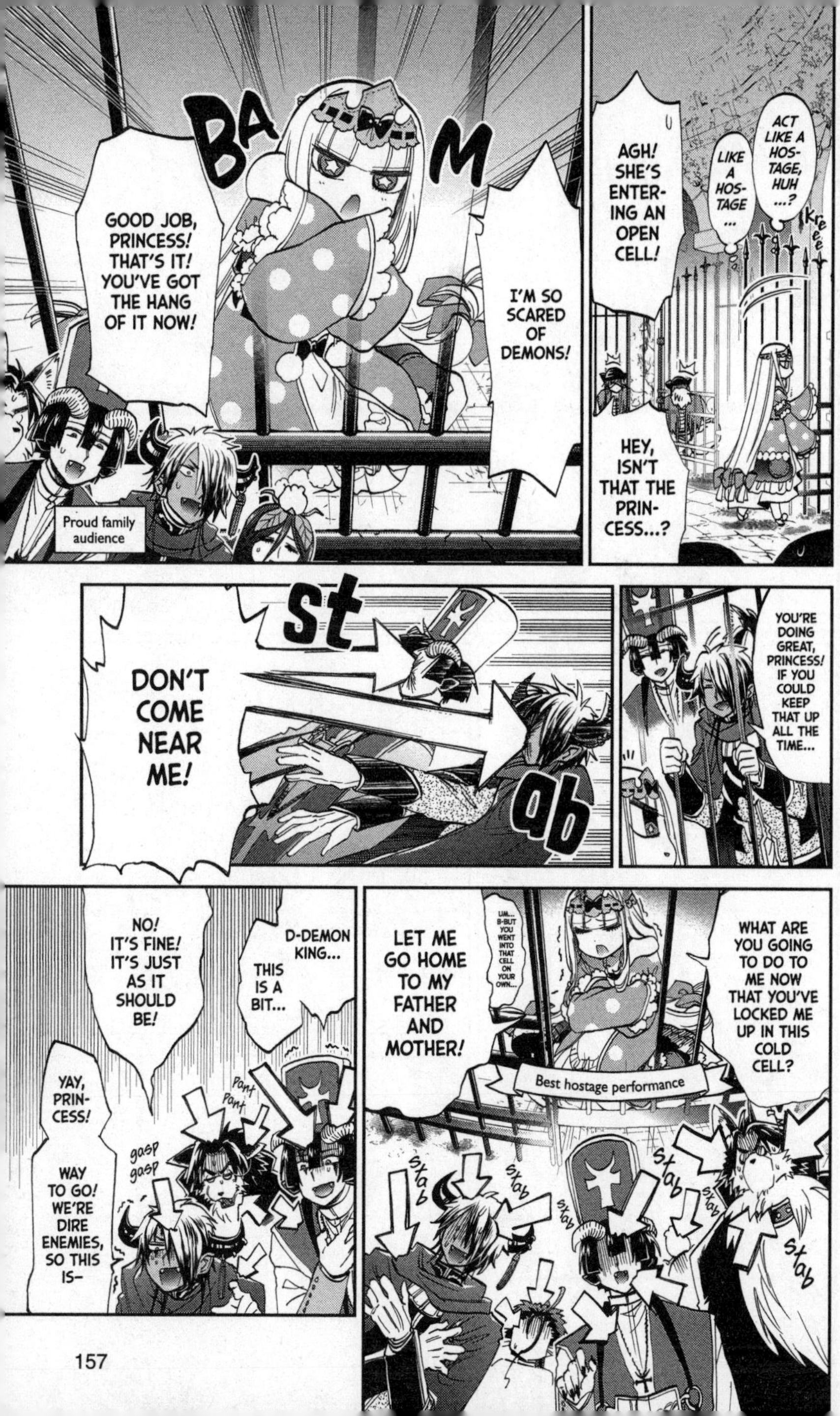
ACT LIKE A HOSTAGE, HUH ...?
LIKE A HOSTAGE ...
Kreee
AGH! SHE'S ENTERING AN OPEN CELL!
HEY, ISN'T THAT THE PRINCESS...?
BAM
I'M SO SCARED OF DEMONS!
GOOD JOB, PRINCESS! THAT'S IT! YOU'VE GOT THE HANG OF IT NOW!
Proud family audience
YOU'RE DOING GREAT, PRINCESS! IF YOU COULD KEEP THAT UP ALL THE TIME...
stab
DON'T COME NEAR ME!
WHAT ARE YOU GOING TO DO TO ME NOW THAT YOU'VE LOCKED ME UP IN THIS COLD CELL?
UM... B-BUT YOU WENT INTO THAT CELL ON YOUR OWN...
LET ME GO HOME TO MY FATHER AND MOTHER!
Best hostage performance
stab stab stab stab stab stab
D-DEMON KING... THIS IS A BIT...
NO! IT'S FINE! IT'S JUST AS IT SHOULD BE!
Pant Pant
YAY, PRINCESS!
gasp gasp
WAY TO GO! WE'RE DIRE ENEMIES, SO THIS IS–

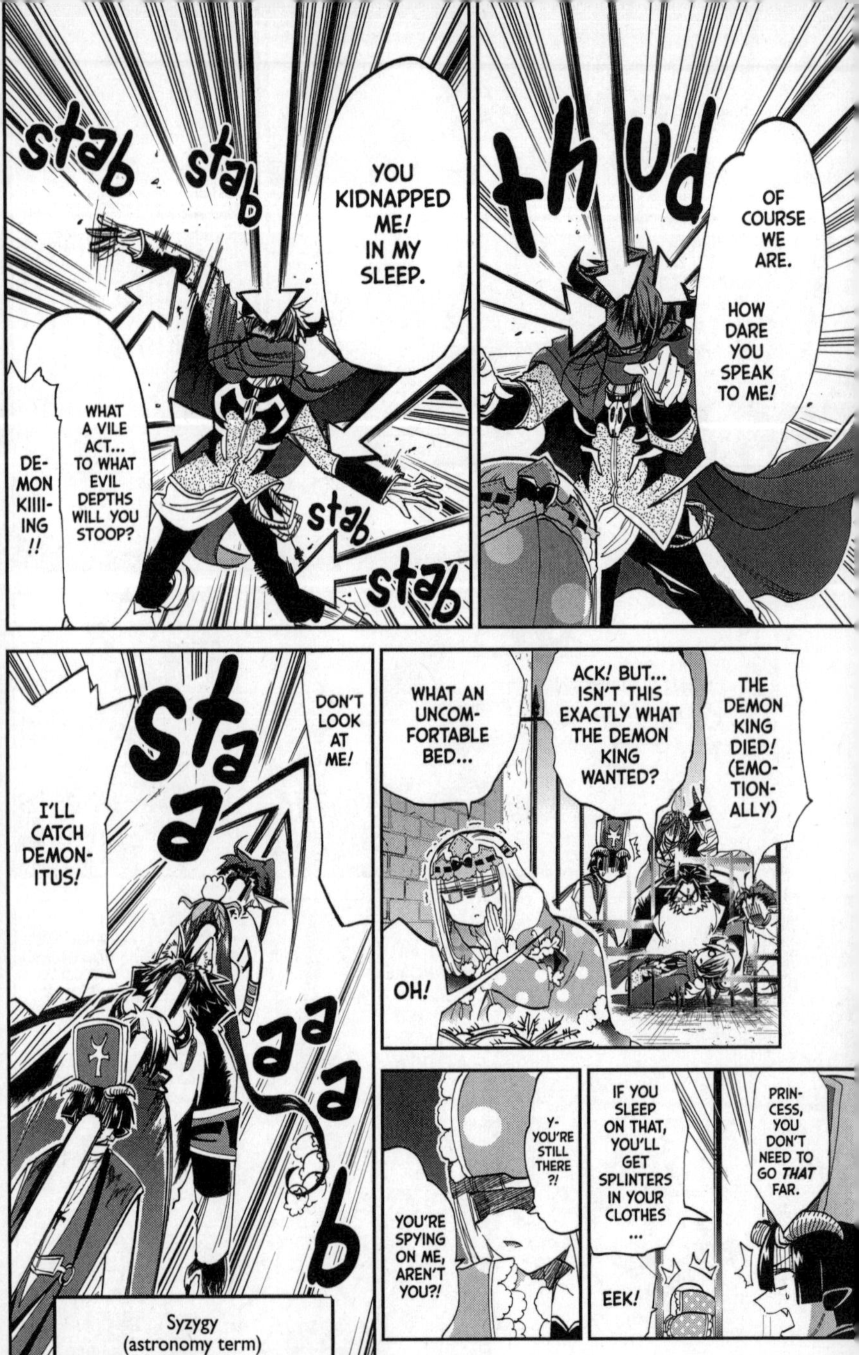
thud
OF COURSE WE ARE.
HOW DARE YOU SPEAK TO ME!
stab stab
YOU KIDNAPPED ME! IN MY SLEEP.
WHAT A VILE ACT... TO WHAT EVIL DEPTHS WILL YOU STOOP?
DE-MON KIIII-ING!!
stab stab
THE DEMON KING DIED! (EMO-TION-ALLY)
ACK! BUT... ISN'T THIS EXACTLY WHAT THE DEMON KING WANTED?
WHAT AN UNCOM-FORTABLE BED...
OH!
PRIN-CESS, YOU DON'T NEED TO GO THAT FAR.
IF YOU SLEEP ON THAT, YOU'LL GET SPLINTERS IN YOUR CLOTHES ...
EEK!
Y-YOU'RE STILL THERE?!
YOU'RE SPYING ON ME, AREN'T YOU?!
DON'T LOOK AT ME!
Staaaaab
I'LL CATCH DEMON-ITUS!
Syzygy (astronomy term)

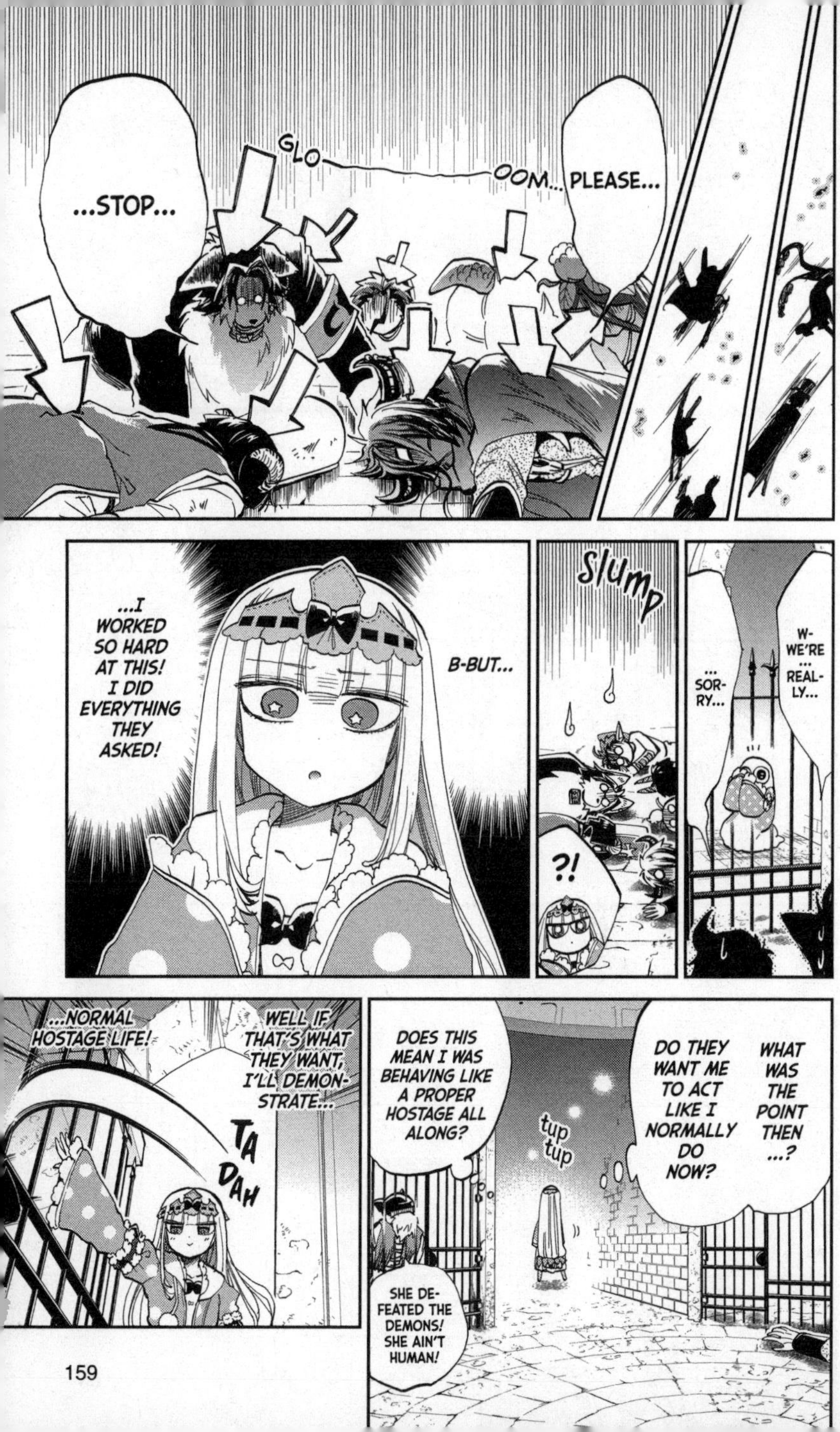
PLEASE...
GLO—OOM...
...STOP...
W- WE'RE ... REAL- LY...
... SOR- RY...
SLUMP
?!
B-BUT...
...I WORKED SO HARD AT THIS! I DID EVERYTHING THEY ASKED!
WHAT WAS THE POINT THEN ...?
DO THEY WANT ME TO ACT LIKE I NORMALLY DO NOW?
DOES THIS MEAN I WAS BEHAVING LIKE A PROPER HOSTAGE ALL ALONG?
tup tup
SHE DE- FEATED THE DEMONS! SHE AIN'T HUMAN!
WELL IF THAT'S WHAT THEY WANT, I'LL DEMON- STRATE...
...NORMAL HOSTAGE LIFE!
TA DAH

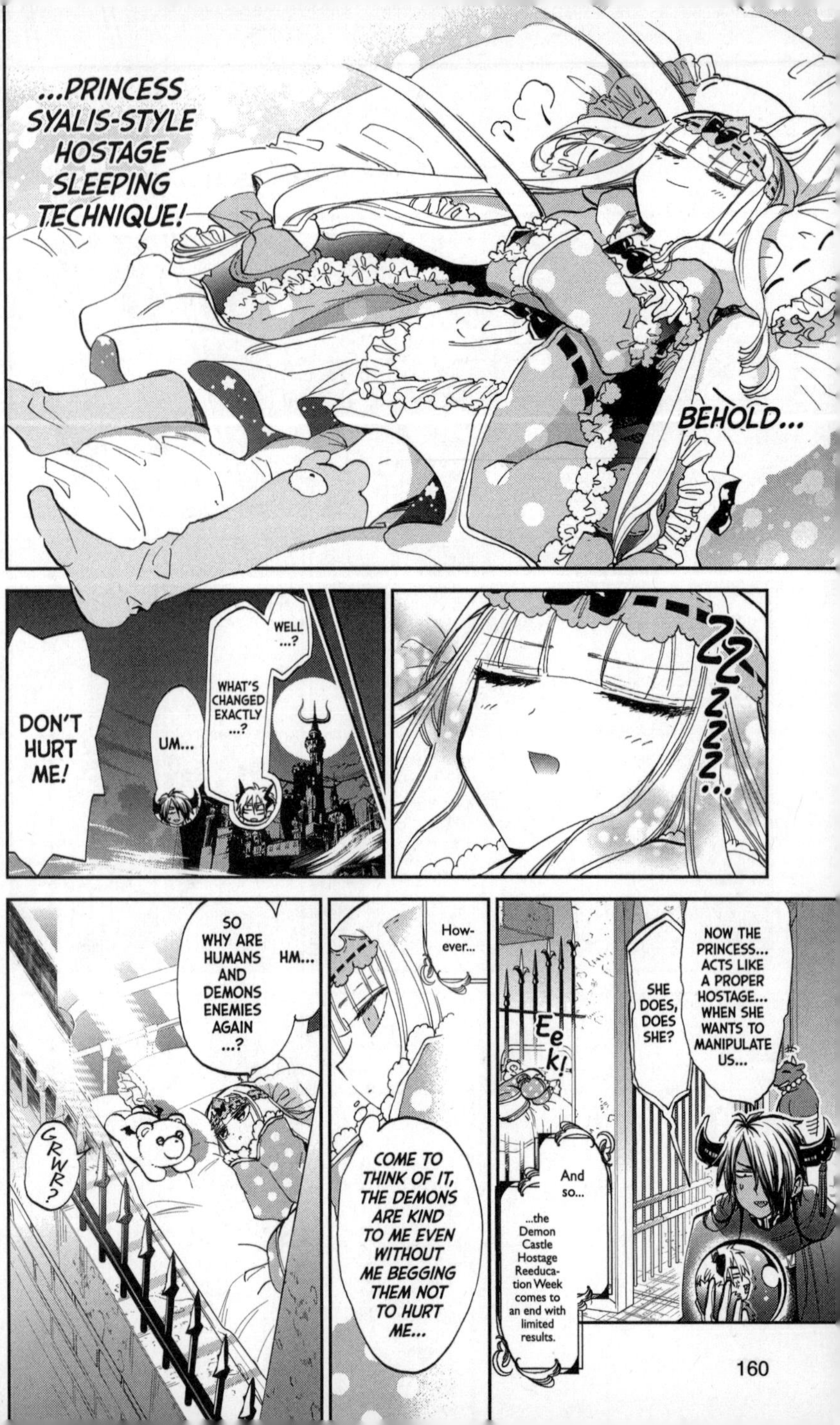
BEHOLD...
...PRINCESS SYALIS-STYLE HOSTAGE SLEEPING TECHNIQUE!
ZZZZZ...
WELL ...?
WHAT'S CHANGED EXACTLY ...?
UM...
DON'T HURT ME!
NOW THE PRINCESS... ACTS LIKE A PROPER HOSTAGE... WHEN SHE WANTS TO MANIPULATE US...
SHE DOES, DOES SHE?
Eeek!
And so...
...the Demon Castle Hostage Reeduca-tion Week comes to an end with limited results.
How-ever...
COME TO THINK OF IT, THE DEMONS ARE KIND TO ME EVEN WITHOUT ME BEGGING THEM NOT TO HURT ME...
HM...
SO WHY ARE HUMANS AND DEMONS ENEMIES AGAIN ...?
GRWR?

Demon Castle Homework Re-completed!

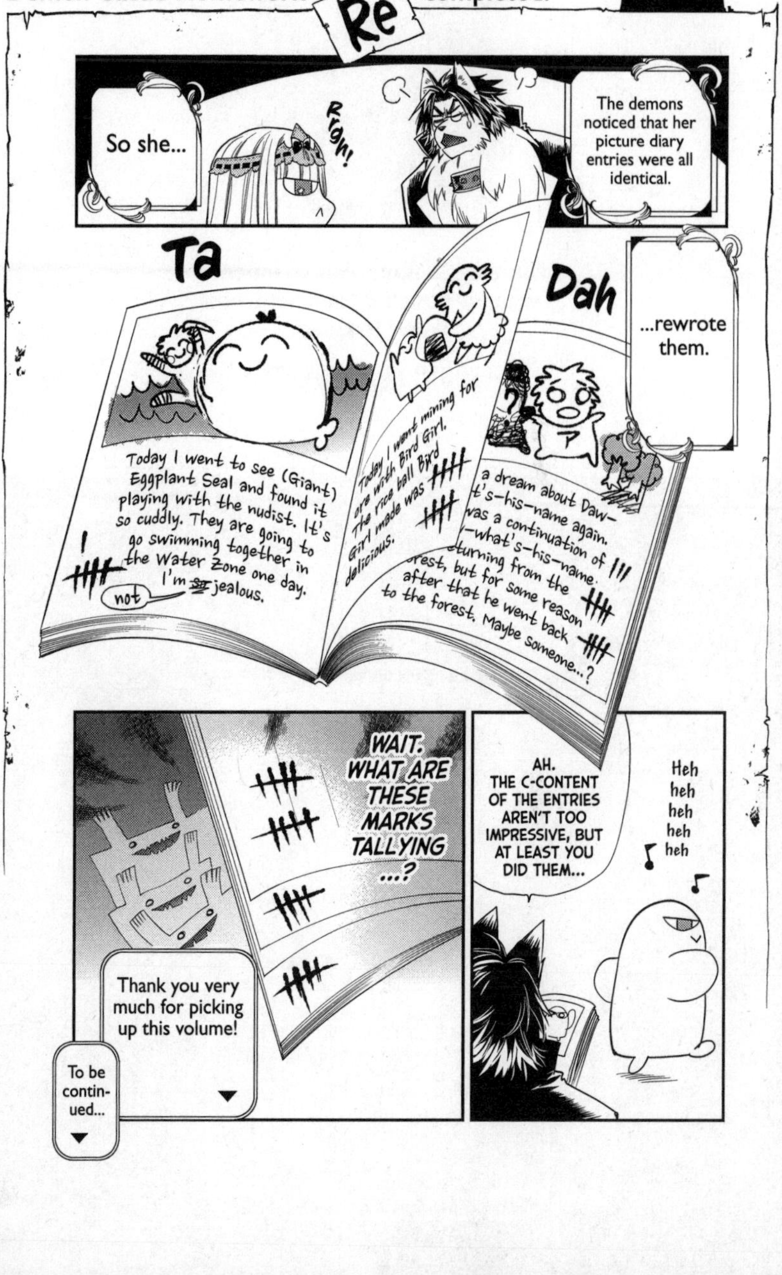

The demons noticed that her picture diary entries were all identical.
Rrgh!
So she...
...rewrote them.
Ta
Dah
Today I went to see (Giant) Eggplant Seal and found it playing with the nudist. It's so cuddly. They are going to go swimming together in the Water Zone one day. I'm so not jealous.
!
Today I went mining for ore with Bird Girl. The rice ball Bird Girl made was delicious.
a dream about Daw- t's-his-name again. vas a continuation of -what's-his-name. eturning from the orest, but for some reason after that he went back to the forest. Maybe someone...?
!!!
AH. THE C-CONTENT OF THE ENTRIES AREN'T TOO IMPRESSIVE, BUT AT LEAST YOU DID THEM...
Heh heh heh heh heh
WAIT. WHAT ARE THESE MARKS TALLYING ...?
Thank you very much for picking up this volume!
To be contin-ued...

**Volume 5! Thank you so much!
I wonder how long the princess
is going to sleep!**

— KAGIJI KUMANOMATA

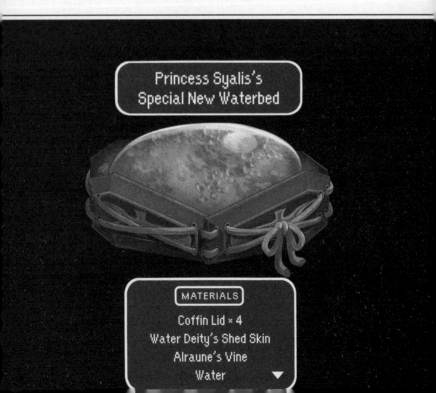

Princess Syalis's
Special New Waterbed

MATERIALS

Coffin Lid × 4
Water Deity's Shed Skin
Alraune's Vine
Water

Those who lurk beneath the cover...

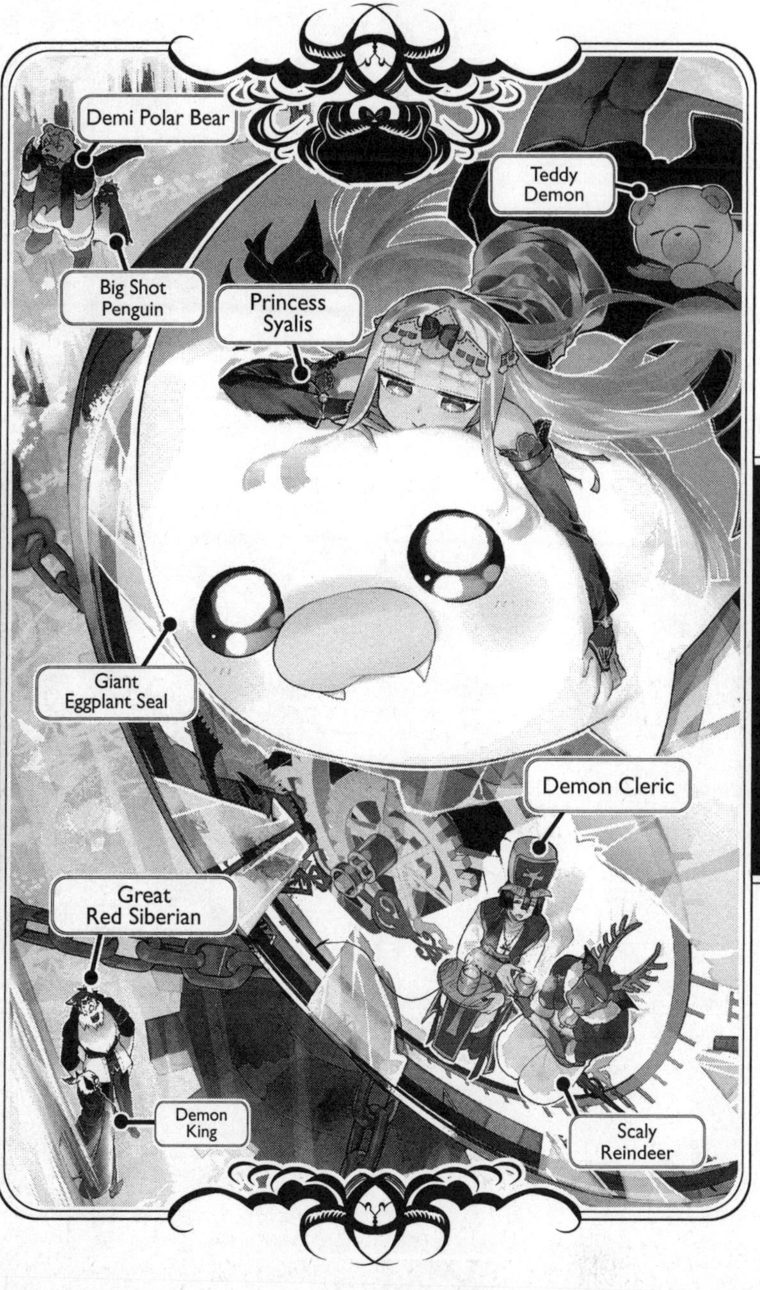
Demi Polar Bear
Teddy Demon
Big Shot Penguin
Princess Syalis
Giant Eggplant Seal
Demon Cleric
Great Red Siberian
Demon King
Scaly Reindeer

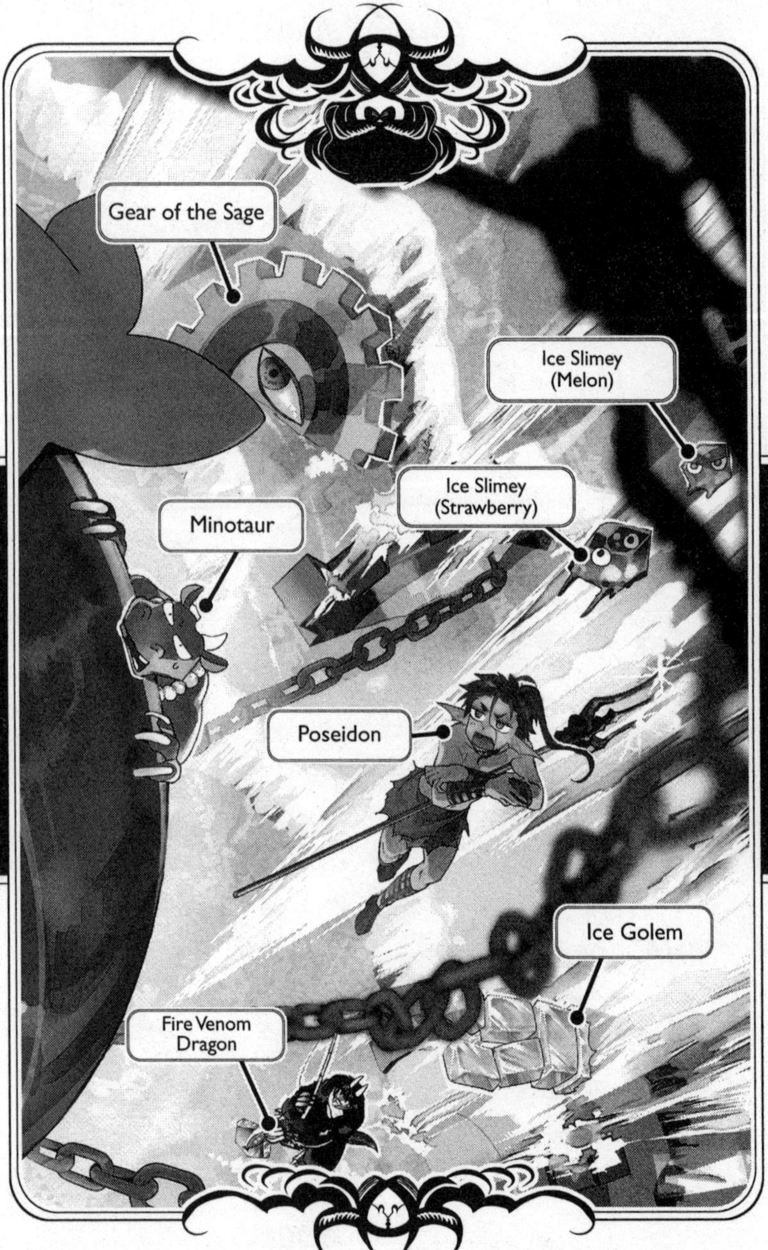
Gear of the Sage
Ice Slimey (Melon)
Ice Slimey (Strawberry)
Minotaur
Poseidon
Ice Golem
Fire Venom Dragon

SLEEPY PRINCESS IN THE DEMON CASTLE

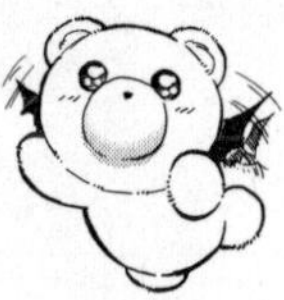

5

Shonen Sunday Edition

STORY AND ART BY

KAGIJI KUMANOMATA

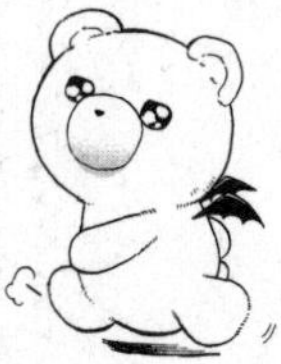

TRANSLATION **TETSUICHIRO MIYAKI**
ENGLISH ADAPTATION **ANNETTE ROMAN**
TOUCH-UP ART & LETTERING **SUSAN DAIGLE-LEACH**
COVER & INTERIOR DESIGN **ALICE LEWIS**
EDITOR **ANNETTE ROMAN**

Printed in the U.S.A.

Published by VIZ Media, LLC
P.O. Box 77010
San Francisco, CA 94107

10 9 8 7 6 5 4 3 2 1
First printing, February 2019

ratings.viz.com RATED T TEEN

PARENTAL ADVISORY
SLEEPY PRINCESS IN THE DEMON CASTLE is rated T for Teen and is recommended for ages 13 and up. This volume contains fantasy violence.

VIZ MEDIA
viz.com

SHONEN SUNDAY
shonensunday.com

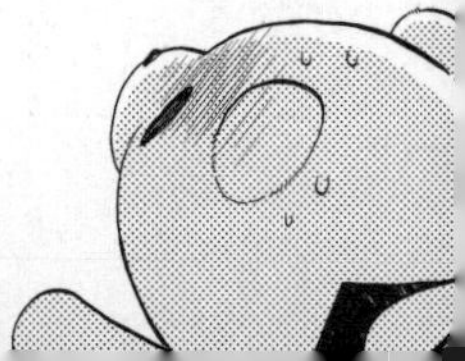

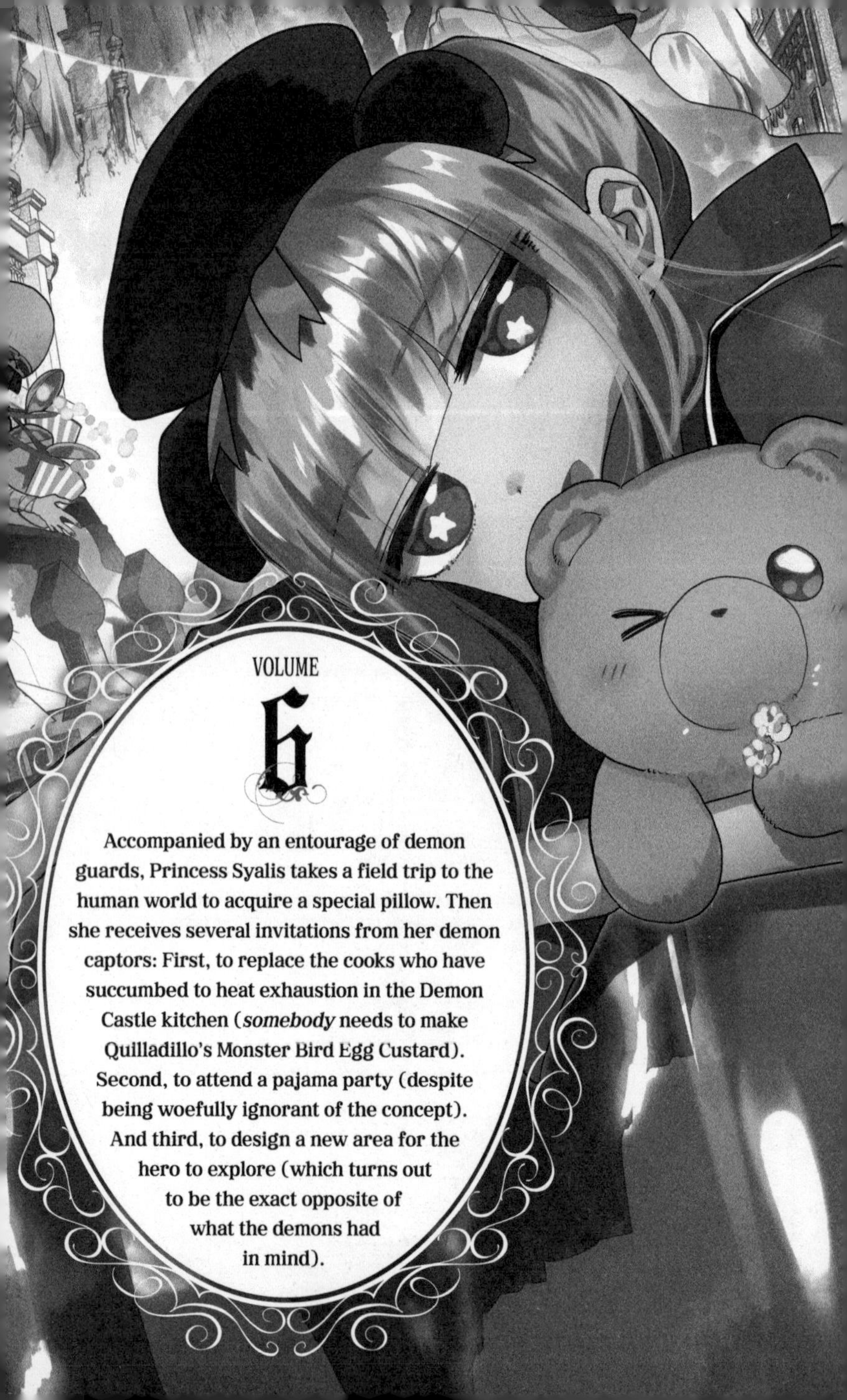
VOLUME
6
Accompanied by an entourage of demon guards, Princess Syalis takes a field trip to the human world to acquire a special pillow. Then she receives several invitations from her demon captors: First, to replace the cooks who have succumbed to heat exhaustion in the Demon Castle kitchen (*somebody* needs to make Quilladillo's Monster Bird Egg Custard). Second, to attend a pajama party (despite being woefully ignorant of the concept). And third, to design a new area for the hero to explore (which turns out to be the exact opposite of what the demons had in mind).

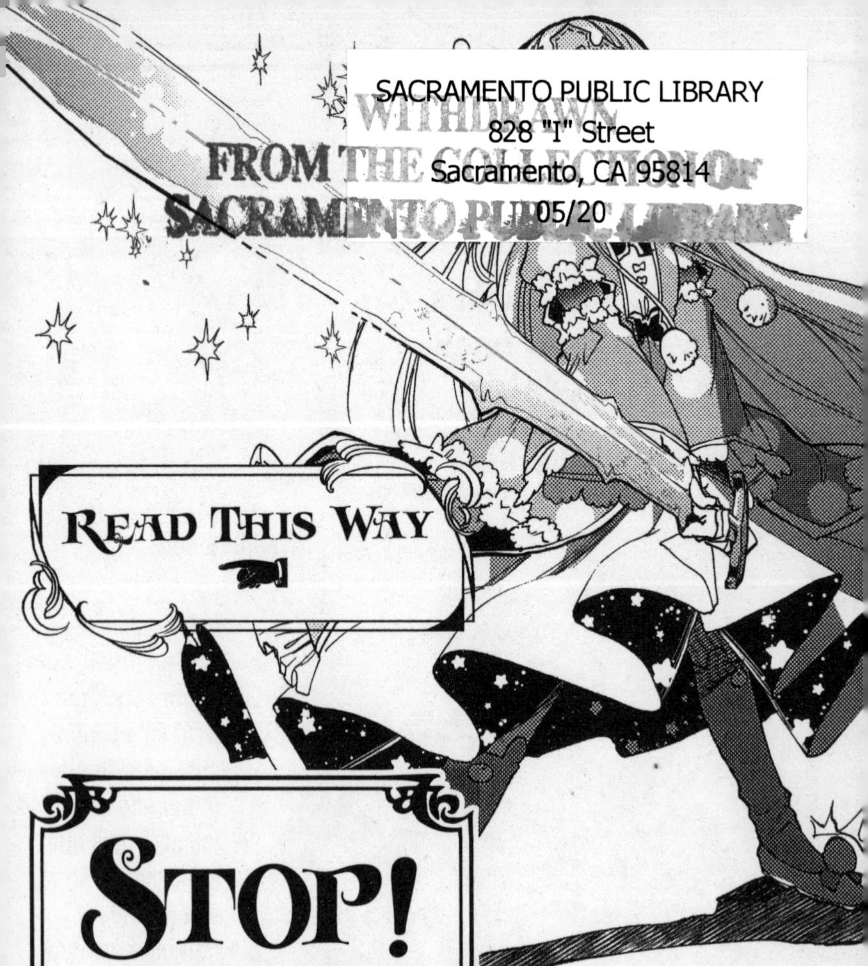
READ THIS WAY

STOP!

You may be reading the wrong way!

In keeping with the original Japanese comic format, this book reads from right to left—so action, sound effects and word balloons are completely reversed to preserve the orientation of the original artwork.

Check out the diagram shown here to get the hang of things, and then turn to the other side of the book to get started!

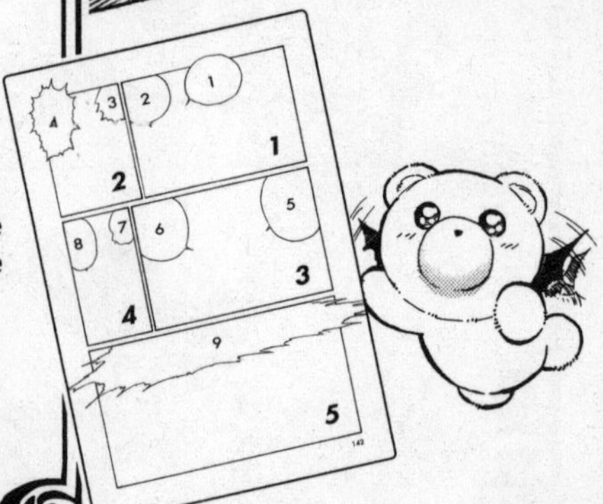